PRAISE FOR *A SECRET LIFE*

"*A Secret Life* is a real-life spy thriller that reveals the passions and tensions faced by Polish leaders under the thumb of Moscow during the 1970s and '80s. Weiser has produced a fascinating portrayal of Kuklinski, who decided that the best way to serve Polish nationalism was to become a spy for the West... Weiser's lively narrative describes Kuklinski's nine years working for U.S. intelligence, converting interviews and a mountain of documentation into a page-turner... But the human dimension is what sets the story apart."—*Washington Post Book World*

"Books about espionage, fiction or not, can be cliché flypaper—encrusted with tired plot twists and morbid atmosphere. Exceptions, like John le Carré's novels and Thomas Powers's histories, are rare. But Weiser's tale... is in that elevated company. *A Secret Life* is thrilling not only in its chronicle of an honorable betrayal during the Cold War's endgame but also in its portrait of the strangely loving epistolary relationship between the spy and his American handlers."—*The New Yorker*

"At a time when most people are focused on stories of CIA bungling, Weiser's book... provides a blueprint of what an agency success ought to look like."—Anne Applebaum, *Newsweek International*

"*A Secret Life* is a story of danger and stolen documents, of dual identities and hair-raising risk."—*The Wall Street Journal*

"This meticulously documented real-life spy story is alive with the tension of secret meetings, clandestine handoffs, near-fatal slipups and—at last—a very narrow escape to the West."—*Forbes FYI*

"Under what conditions can betrayal become an act of patriotic heroism? This moral hypothetical is cast into firm detail by Benjamin Weiser's extraordinary account of Col. Ryszard Kuklinski."—*The Philadelphia Inquirer*

"A compelling and... suspenseful narrative... Weiser's multilayered approach enables him to brighten and humanize the furtive world of espionage... Indeed, the longer Weiser lingers over the subtleties and quirks of Kuklinski's personality, the more intriguing an individual emerges."
—*Times Literary Supplement*

A SECRET LIFE

The Polish Officer,

His Covert Mission, and the Price He Paid

to Save His Country

BENJAMIN WEISER

PublicAffairs *New York*

Selected lines [14] from "Report from the Besieged City" from *Report from the Besieged City and Other
Poems* by Zbigniew Herbert. Translated with an Introduction and Notes by John Carpenter and Bog-
dana Carpenter. Copyright © 1985 by Zbigniew Herbert. Reprinted by permission of HarperCollins
Publishers Inc.

   Ryszard Kuklinski speech on page 333: Polish Radio 1, Warsaw, in Polish 1034 gmt 29 Apr 98 / BBC
Monitoring.

   All photographs courtesy of Ryszard Kuklinski except: *David Forden, the longtime CIA case officer,*
courtesy of David Forden; *Forden and his two roommates, Peter Falk and Alan Goldfarb,* courtesy of Alan
Goldfarb; *Kuklinski receives a blessing from Pope John Paul II,* courtesy of the Vatican (Photo "L'Osserva-
tore Romano")

Book design by Mark McGarry
Set in Dante

Library of Congress Cataloging-in-Publication data
Weiser, Benjamin.
A secret life : the Polish officer, his covert mission, and the price he paid to save his country /
Benjamin Weiser.—1st ed.
p. cm.
Includes bibliographical references and index.
ISBN 978-1-58648-305-0 (pbk)
1. Kuklinski, Ryszard Jerzy, 1930– 2. Spies—United States—Biography. 3. Poland—Armed Forces—
Officers—Biography. 4. Espionage, American—Poland. 5. United States. Central Intelligence Agency.
6. Cold War. I. Title.
UB271.U52K858   2004   327.1273'0438'092—dc22
[B]
2003065930

10 9 8 7 6 5 4 3 2

For Dorothy

Dear Daniel,

...I would also like to assure you that I am deeply aware of the enormous need for pulling out of the shadows of darkness of the tightly closed communist system everything which does not serve peace of the world and freedom of nations.

In this conviction, I once more want to confirm my readiness to serve our common cause to the limits of my strength and capability....

Sincerely,
P.V.

Letter from Colonel Ryszard J. Kuklinski to the CIA
Sept. 22, 1980

CONTENTS

Introduction
ix

Prologue
I

1

Crossing the Line
5

2

"The Soil of Nobody"
29

3

A Double Life
56

4

"Stabbing Back"
87

5

Near Miss
I2I

CONTENTS

6
——————
"Standing on Ice"
140

7
——————
Tremors of Change
166

8
——————
"Out of the Shadows of Darkness"
186

9
——————
Preparing to Crush Solidarity
229

10
——————
"Everything Is Pointing to the End of My Mission"
266

11
——————
Patriot or Traitor?
292

12
——————
Return
315

Author's Notes
343

Acknowledgments
367

Index
371

INTRODUCTION

I first met Colonel Ryszard Kuklinski in 1992 in a hotel suite in Reston, Virginia. As I entered the room, he was standing in the corner by the window, a cigarette dangling from his mouth. He turned and greeted me with a broad smile. I didn't know much about him. I had read that he had been a key officer under Communist Polish Defense Minister Wojciech Jaruzelski, and that he was a crucial source for the CIA on the events in Poland in 1980–1981, leading up to the imposition of martial law and the crushing of the independent trade union Solidarity. But that day I learned something that no one had ever disclosed outside the CIA: For nine years Kuklinski had cooperated with the West against the Soviet Union and the Warsaw Pact in a clandestine operation of breathtaking scope and danger. Kuklinski told me that he had provided the CIA with tens of thousands of pages of classified Soviet and Warsaw Pact documents. They included the Soviet war plans for Europe, information on new weapons systems, hidden Soviet wartime bunkers, and Soviet preparations to invade Poland. As one CIA official later put it, his material "was the touchstone, the basic standard."

I had first decided to get in touch with Kuklinski after reading in *Veil*, a book about the CIA by Bob Woodward, a brief description of his role in providing the martial law documents to the United States. Not knowing how to reach him, I sent him a letter through the CIA's public affairs office. The agency had been protecting Kuklinski under high security, and for good reason: He had been convicted, in absentia, of treason by a Communist-era military court and sentenced to death (the sentence was later reduced to twenty-five years). There was an outstanding warrant for his arrest in Poland.

"I think I have to unveil what I have done," Kuklinski told me early in our first interview. "My motivation. My goals. And the consequences of it. And let's judge based on what I have done—what my 'treason' was all about."

It was clear from the outset that Kuklinski, whose job on the Polish General Staff was to prepare for war with the West, was motivated by ideology. He was a proud Pole who harbored a deep rage toward the Soviet Union, which had taken control of Poland at the end of World War II, imposed a Communist regime, and effectively turned the Polish military into a subsection of the Soviet armed forces. By 1972, at the age of forty-two, Kuklinski had received a steady series of promotions, and seemed destined to become a general. But instead, he decided to take an extraordinary step that endangered his own life and placed his family's security in jeopardy. I wanted to know why.

Thus began a series of unusual interviews, held in anonymous hotel rooms and a private home in the Washington suburbs. I did not know, as each session began, where Kuklinski had arrived from, or where he went afterward to return home, and I was not told the name that he used outside our meetings. The sessions were arranged by the CIA, which initially had a representative attend the interviews, although the CIA officer did not attempt to control what Kuklinski told me. (After I decided to write this book, I continued to interview Kuklinski over the years, by phone and in person, without the agency's presence.)

In 1992, I published two articles, in the *Washington Post* and the *Post Magazine*, describing Kuklinski's activities against the Soviet Union and the Warsaw Pact. In Poland, the articles contributed to a furious debate about the meaning of patriotism. Having betrayed the Communist regime, was Kuklinski a patriot or a traitor? "Newspapers devote entire pages to the issue, panel shows on television speak of little else, and people argue about it on street cars," my *Post* colleague, Blaine Harden, wrote from Warsaw at the time.

In preparing for the book, I asked the CIA for access to its internal files on the operation. These included cables and reports prepared by CIA officers, the transcripts of their meetings with Kuklinski, and the letters he wrote to the agency. They would offer a contemporaneous account of Kuklinski's lengthy clandestine activity, and allow me to write a chronological narrative based on more than just the memories of those involved. I particularly wanted to focus on the human side of the operation—the interaction between Kuklinski and the Americans he worked with. I had been told, for example, about a collection of personal letters that were exchanged during the operation between Kuklinski and "Daniel," the CIA case officer in whom he confided in a way that he could with no one else, including his family.

My request led to lengthy discussions with the CIA over terms of the access to the documents. Thanks to a new policy of openness initiated by the former director Robert M. Gates, and continued by his successors, the CIA has occasionally granted outsiders access to its files, but only under special conditions. An author must obtain a security clearance, for example, and agree to submit a manuscript before publication to a special review board that can seek deletions of material that could harm national security or reveal the agency's sources and methods.

I understood the reasons for such procedures, and there was particular concern in Kuklinski's case because it was relatively recent, but I did not want to have the CIA review and possibly censor my manuscript before publication. I made a proposal: to hire someone who already had a security clearance, who would research the files for me. His notes and whatever material he copied would be put through the review process, with the necessary deletions made before they were released to me. I could then use the material unfettered. In essence, I wanted the CIA to be a source for my book which, like any other source, could seek to control what information it provided to me, but could not determine how the material would finally be used.

The person I would hire to research the archive was Peter Earnest, a retired CIA case officer who had worked for thirty-six years in the agency, including more than two decades in clandestine operations. He had also been the agency's director of media affairs and its spokesman; he knew how the press worked, and was respected by reporters for his straightforward approach. Peter would work on my behalf, although he was of course bound by the agency's rules.

I made my case to agency officials through the public affairs office, and after lengthy consideration, the agency finally gave its approval. In a process that ultimately took more than a year, Peter worked at a desk in the Soviet/East European Division at the CIA's Langley headquarters, delving into dozens of boxes, and ultimately producing some 750 pages of raw notes and files. These included often lengthy excerpts of cables, memos, transcripts, letters, and his own descriptions of various aspects of the operation. There were about seventy files, each in an orange folder marked with the case name and file number and dates covered. Many documents were on the original flimsy paper, and the files also included photographs, operational site surveys, maps, and sketches of locations where dead drops and other clandestine acts would take place. "There was a little bit of an archeological thrill to this," Peter recalled. "I knew that no one had touched them for a long time." But the material was not from a different era entirely. As he immersed himself in the project, he was often visited by people in the Division who had in some way been involved in the case.

When the material was ultimately processed for my use, it offered a rare look at a single human intelligence operation, including Kuklinski's statements and letters to the CIA over the nine years he cooperated with the Americans. This material largely confirmed his earlier oral accounts to me, and offered leads for further questioning.

The publications review board made modest deletions before the material was released to me, which I do not believe affected the larger story. Not every document I received placed the agency in a positive light, suggesting that the review was even-handed. I also believe that through extensive interviews with Kuklinski and others, I have been able to fill in many of the holes. Of course, there were some important areas that I could not fully explore, which can be generally categorized under the "sources and methods" of the agency. Peter Earnest, having reviewed the complete file, said that he believes nothing in it contradicts the central theme—that Kuklinski was motivated by his political convictions, acted in a way that he believed would help his country, and did great damage to the Soviet Union and the Warsaw Pact. This book, then, is a bit of an experiment, and joins several others by authors who have sought ways to avoid prepublication review in the interest of writing substantive and independent works based in part on CIA records.

There may be no more controversial an institution in America than the Central Intelligence Agency, which has endured justified criticism over the years for assassination plots against foreign leaders, civil rights abuses, bungled operations, intelligence failures, and an inability to root out spies working against the United States. More recently, there has been renewed debate about the effectiveness of the CIA's human intelligence capabilities, particularly since the September 11 terror attacks, and the Bush administration's war in Iraq.

The Kuklinski case tells a different story, showing how human intelligence operations can succeed when they are handled with scrupulous care and imagination. The operation reveals a side of the CIA that is not often seen—of case officers who joined the agency because they were attracted by the excitement and intrigue of undercover work and by the idea of public service. The CIA is the face America first offers people who, like Kuklinski, are inspired by Western ideals. To the extent the CIA fails to carry out such operations, the United States loses a powerful means of understanding nations, regimes, and groups that are hostile to the West.

At a time when the dangers of the Cold War era have receded, and when Russia is struggling to reconcile its Communist past with its halting moves toward a more democratic system, it is sometimes hard to recall what it meant to have Soviet and Warsaw Pact forces poised at Europe's border. As Kuklinski pointed out, if the Soviets had moved to invade Europe, the United States would likely have responded with nuclear weapons targeting Soviet forces as they passed through Poland. His intelligence offered a critical early-warning system for the West, and, he believed, for Poland, which was doomed to destruction in any Soviet attack. "Even if we win, what do we gain?" he said in one interview.

Although Kuklinski had risen to a high and sensitive post on the Polish General Staff, he was in many ways a typical Pole in a country whose heritage includes powerful symbols—of heroic soldiers, the Catholic Church, and a vast empire that once stretched across Central and Eastern Europe. But that heritage remained mostly a myth as Poland's borders kept changing along with its masters. From the end of the 1700s until 1918, Poland was partitioned out of existence by Russia, Prussia, and Austria. It then re-emerged as an independent country, only to be taken over again in 1939 when Nazi Germany invaded; later the Soviets assumed control. The historian Simon Schama once told me that Poles have a spectral notion of themselves, like a political hologram. "They're visible; they're invisible. And they constantly have the sense that their national identity is contingent really on sustaining some inner belief against those who say, 'We'll allow you to be a nation, provided you act as our satellite.'" Even during the Communist era, the Poles never fully accepted this subservient role. They attended church. Many kept their private farms, resisting pressure to join the collective farms set up by the state. They listened to Radio Free Europe, and assiduously maintained whatever contacts they could with friends or family in the West. They knew that someday their country would be freed, although they realized that would not be achieved without struggle from within. That was Kuklinski's conviction, and helps to explain why he acted as he did. His case is a poignant reminder of how hard it was for Communist-era officers who were inspired by Western values to live patriotic lives.

That day in the hotel room in Virginia, Kuklinski emphasized that he did not see himself as an American spy or mole; he always felt that he had acted on behalf of his own country, and that he had in effect "recruited" the United States to work against Poland's Communist leadership and the Soviet Union.

"In the beginning I asked myself if I had the moral right to do this," he said. "I was a Pole. I understood that Poles should be free and that the United States was the only country that might support the fight for freedom for Poland. On the other hand, I was providing so much important information, and there always will be this question of whether a human being has this right, based on his own individual decision, particularly if the interests of the whole country and maybe the lives of millions are involved. It was a dilemma, my moral dilemma, but I became convinced that I not only had the right, I had the moral obligation."

Benjamin Weiser
November 11, 2003

The New York Times

Benjamin Weiser has been a metropolitan reporter on the *New York Times* since 1997, where he has covered legal issues and terrorism. Before joining the *Times* he spent eighteen years as a reporter for the *Washington Post*, where he served on the investigative staff. His journalism has received the George Polk and Livingston awards.

PROLOGUE

Thursday, December 4, 1980, 10:00 p.m.

Snow had been falling heavily on Warsaw for hours, and Colonel
Ryszard J. Kuklinski drove cautiously, squinting to see beyond the pelt-
ing flakes in the reflected glare of his headlights as he struggled to
keep his car from veering out of control. Warsaw dimmed its streetlights in winter to conserve energy, but he had committed this route to
memory and did not need maps or signs. Still, he had to pay close
attention to his driving, because the wipers barely cleared the snow
from the windshield before it was covered again.

He wore a thick woolen cap and a heavy overcoat, which concealed
his closely cropped blond hair and his army uniform. As he drove, he
encountered few cars or pedestrians, but the snowy calm was decep-
tive. Poland was in the midst of a revolution. Just five months earlier,
factory workers in Polish cities had begun organizing wildcat strikes,
which spread quickly to hundreds of factories across the country. In
August, Lech Walesa, a thirty-six-year-old electrician with a handlebar
mustache and a fierce, charismatic personality, climbed over an iron
fence at the Lenin shipyard in Gdansk, and led thousands of workers in
a historic strike that inspired the creation of Solidarity, Poland's first
independent trade union.

The Communist leadership of Poland, under intense pressure from Moscow, had been trying to crush the workers movement. The Polish Interior and Defense Ministries had developed plans to impose martial law, to arrest activists across Poland, and to restore order. The secret police, Sluzba Bezpieczenstwa, known as the SB, would carry out the assault with support from the army. With tanks and hundreds of thousands of soldiers, the crackdown would be swift and brutal.

The heart of the army's planning for martial law was being conducted in the Polish General Staff, where a small cell of officers worked under tight secrecy in an imposing four-level sandstone building in central Warsaw. They had been entrusted with coordinating the Army's role in crushing Solidarity. Only two sets of the full plans existed, and each was locked in a General Staff safe.

One copy was held by Colonel Kuklinski, a highly respected officer on the General Staff who was part of the select group working on the army's role in martial law. Kuklinski had more than thirty years of experience in army operations, war planning, and military exercises. He had become a valued staff officer for General Wojciech Jaruzelski, the defense minister, and he worked closely with senior members of the Warsaw Pact Supreme Command in Moscow.

Kuklinski appeared to be the embodiment of the loyal officer, but he was privately repulsed by the planned crackdown and the army's involvement. As a Pole, he resented the subservience of Poland's military leaders to Moscow. He admired Walesa's determination and courage and knew that many Solidarity members had served in the Army, along with their sons and brothers. But a confrontation seemed inevitable. For days, Soviet troops had been massing on the Polish border. The only question was whether the suppression of Solidarity would be carried out by the Poles themselves or come from the outside.

Kuklinski gripped the wheel of his blue Opel Rekord and concentrated on the circuitous series of back roads he was following to reach his destination, which was just a few hundreds yards from his house. He had been driving for more than an hour, and wanted to be certain that he was not being followed by the SB.

He turned down the Wislostrada, the broad boulevard that ran parallel to the Vistula, the largest river in Poland, and one of the few thoroughfares where the streetlights stayed on in the winter. Kuklinski began to count the lampposts that lined the street. He gradually slowed and then hit the brake forcefully, causing the car to skid into the curb. He switched off the engine and picked up a tightly wrapped cellophane package from the seat beside him. The package contained two sheets of paper on which Kuklinski had outlined, in carefully hand-printed lettering, Moscow's plans to have eighteen Soviet, Czech, and East German divisions ready to cross the border into Poland in four days. These were the deepest secrets of the Warsaw Pact countries, and Kuklinski, one of only a few men with access to them, was prepared to give them away. Kuklinski trudged to the front of his car and with one hand began brushing snow from his windshield. With the other, he dropped the small package on the ground beneath the streetlamp.

He drove home, parked, and walked behind his house to a wooded area in Traugutt's Park. He hid behind a clump of trees. In the distance, he could see the Wislostrada and the spot where he had left the cellophane package. He knew his footprints would soon disappear in the falling snow, but he prayed that his friends would arrive before the package was completely buried. He waited for some time, shivering as an occasional car drove by.

1

CROSSING THE LINE

ONE AUGUST DAY in 1972, a German employee of the U.S. Embassy in Bonn was sorting through the morning mail when an airmail letter caught his eye. It was postmarked August 11, three days earlier, from Wilhelmshaven, a port on Germany's North Sea coast. The front of the envelope was addressed in large letters, written in blue felt-tip pen:

U.S.A. AMBASSY BONN
EXPRESS

The clerk opened the envelope and found another inside, this one addressed to the U.S. military attaché. He carried both envelopes to the office of the defense attaché and handed them to a warrant officer. The warrant officer opened the inner envelope, found a letter, and turned everything over to the army attaché, who at the time was the embassy's senior military officer. The officer, a pipe-smoking colonel, read the letter and walked to the front of the embassy compound, where the CIA station chief was based.

The seven-story American Embassy in Bonn, which was located just south of the city, overlooked the Rhine and had been built on stilts, to protect against floods. To one CIA officer there, the 1950s-era structure looked like a hulking prefab barracks. Several hundred

Americans worked in the embassy, of whom about one-third were from the Central Intelligence Agency. The CIA's Bonn Station was a critical hub, overseeing smaller bases in Hamburg, Frankfurt, Munich, and, of course, Berlin, where East and West were in the closest physical proximity, and where CIA officers could meet their sources, debrief and polygraph them, and look them in the eye.

Bonn Station was led by John P. Dimmer Jr., a red-haired, slightly built Down-Easter from Portland, Maine. Dimmer was the son of a deep-sea fisherman from Newfoundland who, as Dimmer liked to say, fished in the days of iron men and wooden ships. Dimmer, who was fifty-two, had the same strong constitution as his father but had no interest in following his father's line of work. Self-confident and bookish, he became the Maine state spelling champion at age twelve. In 1942 he earned a degree in civil engineering from the University of Maine and went on to serve in the Army. After World War II, he ran a POW camp for 10,000 German war criminals and security suspects. His posting in Bonn was the culmination of a CIA career of more than two decades, most of which he had served overseas.

That August, while most Europeans were on holiday, Dimmer and his staff were preparing for the Munich Olympics, which were just a few weeks away. Hundreds of Soviet and East bloc athletes were expected to attend, and among them, the CIA knew, would be KGB spies.

That morning, Dimmer was in his office, reviewing the usual stack of incoming cables and reports at his wooden L-shaped desk, when his secretary appeared to announce a visitor. The army attaché entered and handed Dimmer the envelopes. Dimmer thanked him and began to read the letter, which was handwritten in garbled English.

Dear Ser,

    I'm sorry for my English.

    I am an foregen MAF from Communistische Kantry. I want to meet (secretly) with U.S. Army Officer (Lt Colonel, Colonel) 17 or 18, 19.08 in Amsterdam or 21, 22 in Ostenda.

    It have no many time. I am with my camrade end they kan't know.

The writer said he would telephone the U.S. Embassy military attaché upon his arrival in Amsterdam. Whoever answered "must speak Russian or Polish," the writer added.

The letter was signed "P.V."

Dimmer had no idea what P.V. stood for, but he sent a cable to CIA headquarters in Langley, Virginia, recommending that Bonn Station try to make contact with P.V. The cryptic initials "MAF" might stand for "man," he wrote, and the postmark suggested that the writer might be a seaman. His itinerary—Amsterdam followed by the port of Ostend in Belgium—suggested the writer was headed west. But why? Dimmer had guessed there might be a sporting event, perhaps related to the Olympics, in one of those cities, but a cursory check turned up nothing.

At headquarters in Langley, the cable arrived on the desk of David Blee, the chief of the Soviet Division.*

Fifty-five years old, balding, and austere, Blee was the quintessential gray man. He could have passed for a professor of electrical engineering at any university in the United States. To his subordinates, he appeared aloof at times, but he had a sardonic wit and was known as a free thinker who was not afraid to challenge the common wisdom.

The CIA director, Richard Helms, had asked Blee to take over the Soviet Division a year earlier. He was an unconventional choice, never having served in Moscow or, for that matter, anywhere in Eastern Europe. But Helms had been determined to make some changes. A decade earlier, one of the CIA's most prized agents, Oleg Penkovsky, the GRU (Soviet military intelligence) colonel who had turned over thousands of pages of highly classified Soviet documents that helped the Kennedy administration decipher the capabilities of Russian weaponry during the Cuban missile crisis, had been arrested and executed by Moscow. Since then, the CIA's operations in Moscow had

---

* In the mid-1960s, the CIA merged the Soviet Russia (SR) and East Europe (EE) Divisions into the Soviet Bloc (SB) Division, and in the 1970s, into the SE (Soviet–Eastern Europe) Division. In this book I refer simply to the Soviet Division, as it was commonly called by officers.

been virtually moribund. In Blee's view, this was because the CIA hadn't yet recovered from the influence of James J. Angleton, the notorious director of counterintelligence in the 1960s who became convinced that Moscow had penetrated the CIA, and that any Russian volunteer had to be a Moscow-controlled plant.

Under Angleton, old sources were cut off, and walk-ins, as volunteers were known, were rejected. At least one was betrayed by the CIA and sent back to the Soviet Union, where it is believed he was executed. Robert M. Gates, a former director of the CIA, has written that "thanks to the excessive zeal of Angleton and his counterintelligence staff, during this period we had very few Soviet agents inside the USSR worthy of the name."

Blee had had a distinguished career in the CIA as an expert on the Middle East. A native of San Francisco and a graduate of Stanford University and Harvard Law School, he had operated in the agency's predecessor organization, the Office of Strategic Services (OSS). During World War II, he served behind enemy lines, dropped secretly by submarine on an island off Thailand to monitor the Japanese fleet. Blee joined the CIA at its founding in 1947 and served as station chief in South Africa, Pakistan, and India, where in the mid-1960s his officers whisked Svetlana Stalin out of the country after she walked into the embassy seeking political asylum. In 1968 he took over the CIA's Near East Division.

Blee was astonished when Helms assigned him to head the Soviet Division in 1971. He told Helms he knew nothing about the Soviet Union and didn't want the job.

Helms replied: "'Don't argue with me. I've made up my mind.... Besides, I've tried everything else. I want to put somebody in that job who doesn't know anything about it.'...Helms wasn't getting the product he wanted out of Soviet operations," Blee recalled.

Blee began by traveling to Moscow on a tourist passport, the first time a CIA officer of his rank had visited the Soviet capital. It was a useful journey. He had expected, for example, to find few automatic elevators in Moscow buildings, but they were practically everywhere, and he discovered that many of the control panels were covered by a piece of plywood. Blee decided that the space behind the wood would make a perfect "dead drop" in which the CIA and its agents could hide messages for one another.

At Langley, Blee surrounded himself with officers from outside the Soviet Division, including some who had been involved in running operations in Eastern Europe, an area where Angleton had not meddled. Blee believed that the ideal place to recruit Russians was not in Moscow, Berlin, or even Warsaw, but in places like Africa, Europe, South America, or wherever Moscow sent its diplomats and spies before they returned home. Blee's staff quietly got in touch with several former sources who had been cut off during the Angleton years, and some renewed their ties with the agency. "He told us, 'Recruit 'em, and run 'em,'" said Clair George, one of the officers brought in by Blee.

Blee's approach caused some tension in the division, including at least one heated exchange in a conference room when he berated a senior officer who had suggested that a particular plan wouldn't work. Blee felt the trouble with the old guard was that "they thought they knew everything—and they were wrong. I'm convinced that if we are reasonably skeptical we can figure out whether somebody is giving us a line. People say they want to work for you; let's find out what they can do."

When the cable about P.V. arrived at headquarters, Katharine Hart, chief of the Division's Reports and Requirements Staff, expressed skepticism that an Eastern European seaman, as Dimmer had suggested P.V. might be, was likely to emerge as a valuable source on the Soviet Union. "There's nothing he can tell us that I don't have covered already," she told Blee.

But Blee ordered Bonn Station to move expeditiously to set up a meeting with P.V. After approving the operation, he left the details to his staff at Langley and in Bonn. Blee liked to say that the problem with Allen Dulles, a veteran of the OSS, a founding father of the CIA, and its director under Eisenhower, was that he knew too much and became overly involved in operations. Blee laughed as he once imitated the gifted Dulles wading into the minutiae of setting up a secret meeting with an agent.

"Why don't you tell him to meet under an apple tree instead of a pear tree?" Dulles would say. "The apple trees have all their leaves at that time of year."

In Bonn, Dimmer summoned Walter Lang,* a forty-five-year-old officer serving under U.S. Army cover who specialized in Soviet operations. Lang had grown up in Springfield, Illinois, where he once planned to sell Monroe calculating machines, as his father had. But after working in army intelligence in the Korean War, he changed his mind. He had served with the CIA in Munich, Berlin, and Bonn. Lang, whose business card read "US Army Program Evaluations Group," had an office in the rear of the embassy where, as he liked to point out, his view of the Rhine was better than that of the big shots out front.

Dimmer described the assignment to Lang and the need for secrecy. "I want 'zero' on this," he cautioned. He said that they would also need a CIA operative fluent in Russian. Lang suggested an Estonian officer based in Hamburg. He was known as Wally† and had worked with Lang before. Dimmer approved.

Wally came to Bonn. He and Lang were close, and when he was in town, he usually stayed with Lang in Plittersdorf, about a mile and a half up the Rhine. A robust fifty-three years old, Wally was six feet, two inches tall and weighed 225 pounds. He had a full head of wavy silver hair and wore gold-rimmed glasses over a bronzed face. Wally would never become a chief of station—he was inept at administration and a poor manager—but his reputation as a street officer was unri-

* Pseudonym.
† Nickname of an officer whose true name is not used here.

valed. He projected serenity and self-assurance and knew how to make a source feel comfortable. When Stalin had captured the Baltic nations, Wally was an officer in the Estonian Navy. His unit was lined up, and each soldier was offered two choices: Join the Red Army, or be shot. Wally chose to survive, but he was consumed with hatred for the Soviets and vowed to work against them.

When Hitler invaded Russia, Wally deserted the Russian Army and joined the German forces. He was commissioned as a captain in Hitler's army, but as soon as an opportunity presented itself, he deserted again and fought the Nazis as part of the Danish underground. After the war, Wally joined the newly created CIA and became involved in Soviet operations in Eastern Europe.

For the P.V. operation, Wally was given a cover name: Lt. Col. Henry P. Morton, U.S. Army Management and Planning Unit, Frankfurt, Germany. He became known as Colonel Henry.

The newly named Colonel Henry Morton and his partner, Walter Lang, took the train to The Hague. They carried suitcases and were dressed like tourists. They didn't know where P.V. would surface. He had said he would call the U.S. Embassy in Amsterdam, but the United States had only a consulate there. Because P.V. might not have known that, Henry rented a car and drove to the consulate, where he waited in case P.V. called there. Lang, meanwhile, remained at the embassy in The Hague, waiting for a call in the defense attaché's office.

On Thursday, August 17, neither man heard from P.V. Friday began uneventfully as well. Then, at 4:30 P.M. in The Hague, the switchboard operator passed a call to Lang, telling him that a Russian-sounding man had asked about a letter to Bonn.

Is this P.V.? Lang asked in English.

The caller hung up.

Five minutes later, the phone rang again.

Speaking in broken English, P.V. asked for a meeting. He said he would be leaving the next morning for Rotterdam.

"No uniforms," he said.

His voice sounded distant and formal.

Lang said that he and his partner, an army colonel, would meet P.V. at the central railroad station in The Hague that night between nine and ten o'clock. Lang said his partner would have a copy of *Time* magazine under his arm.

Can he speak Polish? P.V. asked.

That was not a problem, Lang said.

P.V. said that he would be wearing a tan suit and would make the first signal. Then he hung up.

Henry returned from Amsterdam and drove with Lang to the railroad station, arriving at about 9:00 P.M. Another CIA officer based in The Hague joined them. He discreetly performed countersurveillance, to ensure that they were not being watched. Even at that late hour, the station was bustling with commuters and tourists, and the three officers blended easily into the crowd. Lang stood at a tram stop about 100 meters away from the station; Henry took up a position at the entrance, flipping through his magazine.

More than an hour passed, and they saw no one who fit P.V.'s description. Then at about 10:10 P.M., Henry saw a man he thought might be their target. He began to follow him, but the man made no attempt to signal back and soon disappeared. At about the same moment, Henry saw another man, wearing a light suit, briefly make eye contact and then turn away. His eyes darted around the station, as if he were checking to see that he was not being observed. Then he looked back.

Henry nodded purposefully and began to walk out of the station. The man followed without hesitation. Lang walked in front of them both, leading them about 200 meters around the corner to their car. Without hesitation, the man got into the backseat and was joined by Henry.

Lang got behind the wheel, then turned and introduced himself. In the dark, he could barely see the man's face, but he never forgot the handshake: P.V.'s grip was firm, but his palm was icy cold.

★

Lang pulled up at the nearby Central Hotel and dropped Henry and P.V. at the front entrance. After parking, he entered the lobby and found the CIA support officer who had performed countersurveillance in the railroad station and had followed them in another car. Lang said the trip was "worth it"—a prearranged signal that meant everything had gone as planned. Lang said he would soon return with more details.

Soon they were all in a hotel room, where P.V. introduced himself.

"My name," he said, "is Ryszard Kuklinski." He had been born in Warsaw, on June 13, 1930, and was a lieutenant colonel on the Polish General Staff.

Henry displayed his military ID and introduced himself as "Pulkownik Henryk," or "Colonel Henry." He offered P.V. some coffee or cognac.

Kuklinski shook his head. Speaking in broken English, he said that he had had enough of both drinks for the evening.

Kuklinski and Henry sat in two armchairs; Lang perched on the end of the bed. Henry asked Kuklinski for some identification, and he immediately handed Henry his military identification card and passport.

Switching to Russian, Kuklinski identified himself as the captain of the *Legia*, a fifty-foot yacht owned by the Polish General Staff, and commander of its nine-member crew, which was made up of army, navy, and air force officers. They had left Poland two weeks earlier, were visiting German, Dutch, and Belgian ports, and would leave for home in late August. Kuklinski described himself as an experienced yachtsman and said he had organized the voyage with the approval of his superiors. They were sailing as tourists, dressing casually, and spending their time sightseeing and shopping. Kuklinski had even brought along his seventeen-year-old son, Boguslaw, also known as Bogdan, who loved to sail with his father. But as Kuklinski had explained to his bosses, the trip would actually serve as cover for a Polish Army surveillance mission, to spy on Western ports and naval installations. They would scout the coastline, rivers, ports, bridges, channels, and canals that they knew only from their military maps.

Of course, Kuklinski said, he did not tell his superiors his other ulterior motive for the trip: It was an elaborate scheme to enable him to make contact with the West.

Kuklinski seemed agitated and excited, but he also appeared to be driven by a strong will. He had told his crew to return to the *Legia* by midnight, which meant that he had only about ninety minutes. A Polish counterintelligence officer on their boat had directed that they go out in groups of two or more, a rule he had broken by leaving alone. There was plenty of time for a crew member to notice his absence and ask questions. Because Kuklinski assumed that he would have only one meeting, one opportunity to make his case, he made an emotional plea for Henry to understand his reasons for making contact with the American military. He smoked constantly as he talked, stabbing the air with his cigarette.

Poland had not chosen its place in this divided world, Kuklinski said. And the Polish Army had not chosen to be part of a Soviet war machine. He felt Poland's interests were much more aligned with the West's than with Moscow's, and he wanted Poland to be free of Soviet domination. He did not see America as an adversary and believed that for mutual security, the Polish and American armies should open a line of communication. Kuklinski said he had reached this conclusion while serving as an officer on the General Staff, where he had access to the military secrets of his country and the Warsaw Pact. For almost nine years, his assignment had been to prepare for a "hot war" with the West. But everything he had seen confirmed his belief that his country was on the wrong side.

Henry asked him what materials he might have access to. Kuklinski replied that he had in-depth knowledge of, and access to, the Soviet war plans for Western Europe. They included Soviet orders directed to Polish and Warsaw Pact forces in the event of war, and important elements of the order of battle for East German and Czech forces and for Soviet troops in East Germany. He knew of the latest military exercises—he had written many of them. They were based on collected data concerning the strengths and mobilization speeds of Warsaw Pact troops. He could provide testing reports for Soviet rockets, bombs, and tanks, the information on which the battle-readiness plans were based. He had access to all major calculations for the mobilization, deployment, and regrouping of Warsaw Pact troops. He could provide copies of the top-secret Soviet journal *Voyennaya Mysl* (Military Thought). It was too risky to have carried anything on the boat, but he could provide copies as soon as he returned to Poland.

Kuklinski said he had concluded that NATO had a significant blind spot in its knowledge of Soviet war strategies, and he wanted to help close that gap, to strengthen the Western forces, which was the best way to keep the peace.

He said he would do anything to demonstrate his sincerity, even take a "truth test," as he put it. He knew a little English, he said, but had always been lazy about mastering the language. He would do that as soon as possible.

Kuklinski said he frequently withdrew large numbers of files from the classified vaults of the Ministry of Defense. He had considerable rapport with the officers who maintained the files and could get virtually any document from them. He identified other officers who shared his concern about Poland's survival in the event of war, listing their names, ranks, and positions. He proposed to form a conspiracy to provide an early warning to the West in the event of an unprovoked and surprise attack. Any such attack would depend on the Soviet Union's ability to move a huge ground force known as the Second Strategic Echelon across Poland as it moved into Western Europe. Kuklinski's plan was to paralyze the communications and command systems of the Warsaw Pact and try to thwart the movement of this force.

He had not yet broached the idea with other officers, but he was convinced that if asked, they would agree to help him. Kuklinski and his co-conspirators would issue their own directives, ordering soldiers to stand down and not join an offensive unless the West attacked first. Kuklinski said he had committed to memory the location of every strategic highway, bridge, canal, railroad, radio tower, and refueling stop that the Second Strategic Echelon would have to use in crossing Poland.

Kuklinski was correct. The Pentagon's most deep-seated fear was that Moscow and the Warsaw Pact, with its advantage in conventional forces, would attack Western Europe without a big buildup, "a bolt out of the blue," as one American officer put it.

Kuklinski said that Soviet war planners believed the only way the Pentagon could counter such an attack was to retaliate with nuclear weapons. But America was unlikely to use them on Soviet territory, because to do so would dangerously escalate a conflict. Instead, the West would take an intermediate step: Use nuclear weapons to hit the Second Strategic Echelon, after it had left Soviet territory but before it arrived in Western Europe.

There was only one place where that could occur: Poland.

Almost 95 percent of the thousands of tanks and other vehicles that made up the Second Strategic Echelon would have to pass through Poland before reaching West Germany, France, Holland, and Belgium. That meant Poland would be targeted by NATO for 400 to 600 direct nuclear hits. Even if the Soviet Union and the rest of the Warsaw Pact succeeded in such an attack, Kuklinski said, Poland would be destroyed.

Henry listened attentively and interpreted for Lang. He told Kuklinski that he sympathized with his antipathy toward Moscow, but a peacetime conspiracy of Polish officers was doomed to fail. Kuklinski and his co-conspirators would lose their lives.

Henry said that the best way for Kuklinski to achieve his goals was by operating alone and keeping the United States informed about their mutual enemy.

As the two men spoke, Lang scrutinized Kuklinski and later wrote: "He is a small man with tousled blond hair, penetrating blue eyes and the gestures and mannerisms of a man within whom an unbounded supply of energy is tightly bottled up. He smiles briefly from time to time, but humor seems to play only a small part of his general behavioral pattern."

Kuklinski spoke with assurance, even a slight air of superiority. "He wanted us to know exactly what he wanted to do, and exactly what he could provide," Lang noted.

"I will tell you all I know . . . " Kuklinski said. "You can copy all of my documents. . . . When I help you, I am helping my own country."

As the conversation progressed, Lang excused himself. He took Kuklinski's identification card and passport into the bathroom, removed a notebook from his hip pocket, and copied the information, adding brief details of the conversation Henry had interpreted for him. Returning to the room, Lang again excused himself and said he would return soon. He then went to the lobby of the hotel, found the CIA support officer, and turned over his notes.

When Lang returned, Kuklinski and Henry were deep in conversation, and although Lang did not speak Russian, he could see the men were discussing their mutual revulsion for the Soviet system and taking turns damning communism. Kuklinski volunteered only fragments of information about his life: His father had been murdered in a German concentration camp. He had joined the Polish Army after the war, in 1947, when he was seventeen years old. In 1952 he married Joanna, whom he affectionately called Hanka. They had two sons. In 1967 he was promoted to lieutenant colonel.

This was not the first time he had thought about contacting the West. From November 1967 to May 1968, he had served in Vietnam with the Polish delegation to the International Control Commission (ICC), which included Poland, Canada, and India and which monitored the Geneva accords. As Kuklinski observed the American soldiers in Saigon, he debated finding a U.S. officer of Polish descent in whom to confide. In the end, he decided the moment was not right, but he left Saigon with the feeling that the West was not as decadent as Polish and Soviet officials always portrayed it. He acknowledged that he had prospered in the Communist system; he expected to be promoted to a full colonel that fall and might be made chief of staff for a division. But two events had compelled him to act: the 1968 invasion of Czechoslovakia, in which Polish troops assisted the Soviets, and the Polish Army's shooting of workers on the Baltic Coast two years later.

Henry checked the time. Kuklinski needed to get back to his boat. They agreed to meet again, and Kuklinski suggested they wait a few days, until the *Legia* reached Ostend. But Henry pressed for a meeting the next day in Rotterdam. Lang suggested they find each other at the Euromast, a well-known tourist attraction, which was easy to find and convenient to the harbor. Kuklinski could go there without drawing attention, Lang said, although he should take care, as it was a popular tourist site and might attract others from his crew. Henry said they would watch for him at 5:00 P.M. at a TV tower in the park, and if he was not there, they would return at seven o'clock, and again, if necessary, at ten.

They discussed how to create a cover for Kuklinski's trips away from the *Legia*. Kuklinski said that a plausible excuse would be that he had gone shopping for a carburetor or other parts for his 1968 Opel.

At 11:40 P.M., both Henry and Lang embraced Kuklinski, with genuine admiration. As they prepared to leave, Lang asked Kuklinski about the mysterious signature he had used in the letter to Bonn.

"What does P.V. mean?" Lang asked.

Kuklinski thrust his right index finger toward the ceiling and smiled. "I am the Polish Viking," he said.

After dropping Kuklinski near the railroad station, which was about a five-minute walk from where his boat was moored, the two officers returned to the embassy in The Hague. At midnight they prepared two cables for headquarters, recounting their first meeting and their plans for later sessions. In the first cable, they concluded with an assessment of his motivation: "Apparently strictly ideological, based on strong patriotic and anti-Soviet feelings."

In the second, they offered more detailed observations. In Henry's view, Kuklinski had seemed "utterly security conscious. . . . Very concerned about quality of our security practices, concerned over his own security and particularly for his family."

Henry quoted Kuklinski as saying, "'Don't relay my reports by electronic means. I have heard a rumor in the General Staff that they can read your codes.'" Henry noted that when they had driven him back, Kuklinski "wanted to be left off in [a] dark corner to avoid all possibility colleagues would see him."

"As patriotic Pole with no love left for Soviets, he felt he should contribute to the West," Henry wrote. "He impressed me as courageous: ... 'Give me tape recorder and any topic you choose, and I'll tell you all I know.'... He's like a waterfall."

Henry pointed out that Kuklinski was a "military type," and not an "intel officer." He added: "He's either very sincere or a hell of a good actor." Kuklinski reminded him of his own experiences in World War II. "In short, he's a Pole."

In Lang's portion of the cable, he offered a series of words to describe Kuklinski: "Earnest." "Convinced." "Pride." "Intelligent." "Wiry." "It seems we are indeed dealing with a man of far above [average] intelligence and talents," he wrote. He estimated that Kuklinski was about five feet, nine inches tall, and 150 pounds "of solid bone and muscle." Lang added: "Although I am his size and have at least a 10-pound advantage on him, I have the feeling I would not like to box, wrestle, or go at him in any way physically. He is one tough hombre."

Lang added, "I had the feeling he was scarcely nervous at all. Nervous or not, he certainly knows what his association with us means in real terms and it takes a brave man, knowing this, to take the step he took.... He was there for business and was all business. I'm glad he's on our side."

The cable ended with the team's observation that "father's death, Saigon experiences and long pent-up feelings suggest next few contacts should be oriented toward man who [is] having catharsis yet torn with conflicts between his success in his world and Western idealism."

Henry and Lang added a request for "intelligence requirements"—questions that Langley wanted them to pose to Kuklinski and what documents they should ask him to provide.

The cable was sent at 2:04 A.M. Headquarters responded almost immediately with a five-line message confirming the existence of a file on Kuklinski that included biographical details and his role on the ICC in Vietnam. The names Kuklinski had offered in the first meeting were generally accurate, the cable said, and Lang and Henry were asked to focus in the second meeting on how the CIA should communicate with him after he returned to Poland. It said that should Kuklinski and his family need emergency assistance to escape from Poland, it would be provided. Henry and Lang were to continue to leave the impression that they were from the army, not the CIA.

Early Saturday morning, Lang and Henry made the short drive to Rotterdam, where they reserved another hotel room. To maintain their businessmen pretense, they filled an empty suitcase with shoes to give it some weight. They were joined by a technical officer from Bonn Station, a handyman who could fix a broken camera, tape recorder, or just about anything else. He was asked to go shopping for a carburetor.

Late that afternoon, Lang and Henry headed for the RV park to wait for Kuklinski. At about five o'clock, they saw him, accompanied by a teenage boy with wispy blond hair. Kuklinski and the boy passed Henry, who was snapping photographs as if he were a tourist.

"Sir, my son," Kuklinski said softly.

He and the boy walked on, taking pictures and mingling with a tour group.

Several minutes later, Lang and Henry saw Kuklinski say something to his son, and the boy strolled away. Kuklinski approached Lang, who led him across a pedestrian bridge, and with Henry, they drove to the hotel.

Once in the room, Kuklinski beamed as he spoke about his son, Bogdan. The boy did not understand English, Kuklinski said, and would have assumed that his father's greeting was merely a friendly gesture to a fellow tourist. Kuklinski said he had told his son that he was going shopping for Hanka, and had given him ten guilders for sodas and candy. Bogdan would be fine for several hours. They had agreed to meet later in the park, but if Kuklinski was not there, Bogdan was to return to the boat without him. Kuklinski would arrive later.

Kuklinski, who was still chain-smoking and coughing occasionally, seemed more relaxed than he had been the previous evening. Lang placed on the table a Philips cassette tape recorder, which had a small detachable microphone.

"I live in Warsaw," Kuklinski began, "on Jana Olbrachta Street, Number 19A, Apt. 55." It was a block inhabited only by military people and their families. His building was nine stories tall; the surrounding complexes had only four. Kuklinski lived on the sixth floor, which was served by two elevators. He said his immediate neighbor was an Olympic fencing star, Egon Franke, who now worked as a coach at a sports club. Franke's apartment was the only one with a wall that directly abutted his. Kuklinski said he was unaware of the names of his other neighbors on his floor.

"I occupy three rooms with a kitchen," Kuklinski said. "There is only one entrance to my apartment. There are three windows with a big balcony which look out on a residential quarter."

The street was guarded by uniformed militiamen on motorcycles or in radio-equipped cars, especially after dark. "Generally speaking, I work after hours," he said. He often arrived home as late as eleven o'clock and sometimes later.

"Sometimes, when my car is not operating or I want to save money on gasoline, I use my boss's official car, a Fiat, which he often leaves after working hours," Kuklinski said. "If I am alone, the driver takes me on my own route home. If there are several of us, we decide who will be dropped off first."

Kuklinski said that he liked to socialize with other officers in the General Staff's yacht club, called Atol, on Wisniowa Street. He was vice president of the club. He enjoyed sailing with his family and tried to set aside weekends for his wife Hanka, Bogdan, and his other son, Waldemar, who was nineteen.

Kuklinski said Hanka worked as a bookkeeper in a lathe factory, and together they earned enough "for a modest living." He had borrowed to buy a garage for their car and was paying for car repairs after two accidents. The boys needed clothes and school supplies. Waldemar was constantly buying books and had an extensive collection.

Lang was impressed at Kuklinski's mastery of detail. At times during the meeting, and in a third session held a few days later in Ostend, Kuklinski grabbed the microphone of the recorder and paced around the room. At one point, he delivered a forty-five-minute exposition on his military education, his past and current assignments, and his access to secret documents, gesticulating as if he were addressing a staff meeting. Kuklinski had "apparent total command of subject," Lang and Henry later wrote, and an "outstanding ability [to] organize and articulate material."

Kuklinski said he had joined the General Staff in 1963 and now worked in the operations directorate, which was a kind of nerve center for the Defense Ministry. He described his six-month stint in Vietnam, where he had gotten a close look at American troops. In 1969 he was the chief author of a signals exercise for Polish, East German, Czech, and Soviet troops. To prepare for this exercise, he had traveled to Moscow, where he worked closely with Warsaw Pact commanders. He was well-regarded and was assigned to write all of Poland's military training exercises. He was the chief author of exercises called "Summer 70," "Summer 71," and "Spring 69," each of which required collaborating with twenty to forty Warsaw Pact officers.

Kuklinski had written the annual operational training directives for Defense Minister Wojciech Jaruzelski, in which he had analyzed the state of training throughout the Polish Armed Forces, and developed new plans for each year. He had been sent to Romania to study its military training and planning. In the fall, he would accompany Jaruzelski to the Soviet Union to watch Polish Army exercises, which would include the launching of Scud missiles and Polish air-defense missiles.

Kuklinski had no family or friends abroad. But he kept in regular touch with officers in other Warsaw Pact militaries and had developed a network of experts who supplied him with the latest information he needed for his job. He often visited military units around Poland and met directly with the field commanders, who treated him with respect.

As Kuklinski talked, he puffed on his cigarette, which he held between his thumb and middle finger, European style.

Henry and Lang told Kuklinski that he would be given a miniature camera to photograph secret documents. They also spent part of the meeting explaining an initial system of communications inside Poland. Kuklinski was asked for details of his daily life, from where he parked at work (often on a public street) to the streets he took back and forth. He was told that whenever possible, he should drive his own car—rather than take the bus or his official car—and to adhere to the same route each way. Henry explained that the information would allow the Americans to keep track of him and leave him signals, and if he deviated from his routine, they could begin to worry.

Simplicity was the key, Henry said. The United States would make initial contact with him in Warsaw by dropping a letter into his car window. The letter would contain innocuous writing and a hidden message, visible only when pressed with an iron (the CIA calls this scorch technique "SW," or secret writing). The message would confirm the time and place of their first meeting in Warsaw. Henry told Kuklinski to use the pseudonym "Jack Strong" when signing letters to the Americans.

The Americans also assured Kuklinski that if the worst case happened, that if he believed he was about to be arrested and had to flee Poland, the U.S. government would take care of him and his family. They said the Americans would begin to put aside funds for this purpose. Kuklinski, who understood the risks he was taking, was surprised at the statement. He had assumed he was dealing with the U.S. Army as officer to officer, and he had made clear that his motivation was ideological, not financial. He wanted to remain in Poland and work against the Soviet Union, and what he wanted was America's support.

As the second meeting drew to a close, Kuklinski addressed Henry and Lang directly. He said he had no desire to talk about areas in which he lacked expertise. "I do not propose to dwell on my political views." After all, he said, he was a military person. "Nonetheless, as every Pole, I understand that we find ourselves in a forced situation, and were harnessed into the Communist yoke."

Having been in the army for twenty-five years, he said, "observing life and happenings in the world, starting with the Korean War and followed by the situation in Indochina, events in Czechoslovakia, the dramas in our own country—have convinced me that the Communist [side] is, unfortunately, the aggressive side."

In his view, the Polish Armed Forces, in case of a war, could never be "harnessed to the Soviet war machine." For centuries, he said, Poland had a tradition of freedom, and the Polish Army was "where freedom was fought for."

But even though Poland was deep inside the Communist bloc, he continued, "the place of our armed forces, the place of our army, although inside the defense system of the Soviet Union, is on the side of freedom. It is where your army is, the army of the United States."

At 9:05 P.M., the three men embraced again. The technical officer arrived with a carburetor for Kuklinski. They agreed to meet again in Ostend.

That weekend in Warsaw, a CIA officer named Ed Schooley* got into his battered British Singer and went for a drive known as a surveillance detection run, or SDR. Warsaw Station had received a "flash" cable from headquarters describing a potentially significant military official who was volunteering information elsewhere in Europe. Schooley was given Kuklinski's name and address and asked to visit his apartment building, and then to scout for a location where the first meeting could be held. Headquarters wanted a site that had not previously been used. "We want it new, fresh; we want it up in his area," Schooley was told.

It was not unusual for Schooley to go driving on weekends, and he

_____
* Pseudonym.

had built regular trips into his routine. For example, on Fridays, he regularly borrowed 16-mm movies from the defense attaché's office, which gave him an excuse to return them to the embassy on Sundays. That day, Schooley made his meandering SDR around Warsaw in an effort to establish whether he was being followed by the SB, the Polish secret police. CIA officers were trained to carry out their missions even when there was surveillance, but it was important to know whether it was there. As he drove, Schooley glanced frequently into his rearview mirror and eventually concluded that he was "clean." He headed toward Kuklinski's neighborhood, a place an American driver with diplomatic plates would ordinarily not go, and parked several blocks away. He then began to case the area on foot, but as he reached Kuklinski's street a woman called to him from a window above, asking what he was doing.

Schooley had become convinced that a favorite pastime of elderly women in Warsaw was to lean out of apartment windows and watch people on the street. Schooley, who was dressed informally and wearing a light jacket, said he was trying to find an address. He called out a nearby street and number. The woman pointed. Schooley thanked her and began to walk away, but then he slipped behind a building and returned, trying to avoid being noticed. Finally he found Kuklinski's building, set back from the street. In the lobby, he scanned the mailboxes and found Kuklinski's name. He examined the box to see if it could be opened without a key, which would make it a good dead drop, or place to leave messages for Kuklinski, but it was locked. Schooley considered trying to find Kuklinski's apartment, but decided it was more important to locate a site for their first meeting.

As he walked around Kuklinski's neighborhood, Schooley came upon the Powstancow Warszawskich cemetery. He entered and started to look for the correct configuration—a double right turn and an escape route. He soon found an area that seemed promising. It had a row of bushes and a path that crossed the road through the cemetery. There was only one flaw: The road looped back to the entrance. That violated a cardinal rule about the layout of operational sites: For security reasons, a CIA officer was supposed to enter and leave by different routes. If the officer was being followed, he could leave directly, drawing any trailing cars with him, while the source could scurry away on foot.

But it was late and Schooley needed a site. With enough of a gap, the looping road would still work. He counted the number of steps from the entrance to where the exchange would occur, which he would include in his written description. He then prepared a cable for Langley. The information would be routed to Henry and Lang for discussion with Kuklinski.

The next two meetings, in Ostend and Brussels, went smoothly. When the Powstancow Warszawskich cemetery was suggested to Kuklinski as the site for their first exchange, he was elated. It was an historic location, the hallowed burial ground for victims of the 1944 Warsaw Uprising. He had walked there many times and knew of a wooded area where he could enter without being seen. Kuklinski was given further instructions on how to communicate with the Americans in Warsaw, including how to leave messages in dead drops, which in some cases were out in the open. Often the darkest place, Kuklinski came to learn, was under the lantern. He was given several souvenir key rings and postcards, evidence for his crewmates and son that he had been shopping.

In Belgium, the officers posed thirteen questions from headquarters. The first was: "Describe in detail war plans of the armed forces of Poland, Russia, and other members of the Warsaw Pact during a state of emergency, and first-strike plans as well as for a limited war conception."

Kuklinski answered adeptly, talking for some twenty minutes without interruption, using a map of Europe to orient himself as he sketched out invasion routes. Finally, he stopped and said that it would take him "at least a week of solid taping" to answer that and the other questions.

The final meeting was held in Kiel, Germany, on August 25, one day before Kuklinski was to sail back to Poland. During the session, Kuklinski said matter-of-factly that he was considered to be a member of what Jaruzelski called the Army's "gold fund" (or "golden boys"), who were frequently rotated to new assignments to ensure that they gained well-rounded experience in preparation for promotion to the highest levels of the Polish Armed Forces.

As the three-hour meeting came to a conclusion, Lang and Henry handed Kuklinski some more souvenirs that he could have plausibly bought in Kiel tourist shops, including a large piece of coral for Kuklinski's home aquarium, shampoo for Hanka, and a pocket chess set with a metallic board.

Kuklinski then grew emotional. "Please forgive me," he began, "if my last statement is somewhat chaotic, but my nerves play a certain role here. I would like to express my deep joy that the thoughts which got hold of me no less than 20 years ago have now, during my stay in the West, materialized. I am very happy about it."

Citing his willingness to work secretly against the Soviet Union, he added:

I do not consider this a hazardous game, playing some risky game, because I know that my country's place is in the free world.

I would like to extend, above all on my own behalf, to the defense leadership of the United States, my assurance that just as I think, think almost 30 million Poles. It is our deep yearning to find ourselves with you in the free world. My country's situation is not an easy one. We are placed in the middle of our brothers who we have not chosen but who were given to us by fate, that is, the Soviet Union, which has armies in front of us, and behind, and the situation is hard. But I think that in moments of trial, Polish Armed Forces will stand shoulder to shoulder with the American Army.

He felt certain that Polish soldiers would abdicate their role in an attack on the West and leave an opening for NATO forces. "Our forces might be added to—and counted with—the forces of the free world," Kuklinski declared.

Kuklinski returned to his boat, and Lang and Henry spent the night in the hotel. The next morning, they walked to the harbor and sat on a large rock by the water. They could see Kuklinski's yacht in the distance and watched for a while as the *Legia* disappeared over the horizon. "I don't think we said a word," Lang recalled. "We just hoped for the best for him."

2

"The Soil of Nobody"

KUKLINSKI HAD ALWAYS loved the sea, which he imagined as a way to link people, nations, and ideas. Now, leaning over the wheel of the *Legia*, he felt liberated. As a young officer stationed on the Polish Baltic coast, he had often stood on the beach scanning the horizon. Even on the clearest days he was unable to see the free world, the Scandinavian coastline, just 100 miles to the north, but he could sense it. Now, as he returned from his first meetings with the Americans, he was convinced that his voyage would be his bridge to the West, and even though the Americans had not agreed to his organizing a conspiracy, it was a first step. One night the wind puffed gently in the *Legia*'s sails. Suddenly his crew began shouting for him. A freighter was heading straight for them. Kuklinski grabbed the wheel, started the engine, and turned quickly to the right, the law of the sea. The freighter also should have turned right, allowing each boat to pass safely, but instead it turned left, and the vessels almost collided. With the freighter a dozen feet away, Kuklinski spun the wheel and swerved the *Legia* out of danger.

Although Kuklinski joined in his crew's cheers and nervous relief, the incident seemed like an omen; he knew his life had irreversibly changed and that it would be far more dangerous. But he was convinced he had made the right decision: Emotionally, he had crossed the line years before.

At forty-two, Kuklinski was already a decorated officer and could expect further promotions in the years ahead. Hardy and compactly built, he had competed as a runner in school and in the military. He was bright, serious, modest, and a tireless worker. He had won the confidence of his superiors for his intellect and calm competence and had earned the loyalty of his staff for his courteousness. But as he rose in the army and joined the inner circle of the Polish military leadership, he said later, "I started to enter this world of secrets, and I gradually discovered the most tragic plans for humanity."

For as long as Kuklinski could remember, Poland had existed under the control of outside powers. He had only the sketchiest memory of a different time. He had lived with his parents in a modest one-bedroom apartment on the fourth floor of a five-story brick building at 13 Tlomackie Street in the center of Warsaw, next to the Great Synagogue, a majestic center of Jewish life that dated to 1878. A short distance away were the national theater and the city hall. Kuklinski's father, Stanislaw, held a series of jobs. He worked in a machine factory that produced tanks and tools and as a waiter at one of Warsaw's finest restaurants at the time, U Lija. Kuklinski remembers him as a gentle man who loved to row on weekends on the Vistula River and instilled in his son a love for the sea. Kuklinski's mother, Anna, was confident and strong-willed and had also worked at U Lija before she and Stanislaw married. Roman Barszcz, Kuklinski's closest childhood friend, remembers Anna as "beautiful, very intelligent, and also very tolerant" and said there was never a shortage of bread, jam, or herring in the family household. Kuklinski's parents guided him toward an understanding of his heritage and a sense of pride and obligation. "They breathed the air of patriotism," Barszcz recalled.

In the summertime Kuklinski's parents took him to a village called Niedabyl, about seventy kilometers south of Warsaw, where Kuklinski's uncle had a farm. Kuklinski and his cousins rode horses and played in the forest with their friends. Here Kuklinski and Barszcz became known for their practical jokes. Local farmers would haul in hay from the fields and at times fell asleep on top of their carts. Kuklinski and Barszcz once crept up behind a cart and, with the farmer still napping, rolled it into a pond. The enraged farmer waded out of the water, shouting at the boys as they ran away. Another time, they took apart a cart and rebuilt it on top of a barn, where it sat for days.

At the time, young Polish boys aspired to be military officers, priests, or engineers. For Kuklinski, there was never any question that he wanted to be an officer. But on September 1, 1939, as he was walking to school on Elektoralna Street, he was startled by the wail of a siren. The skies began to darken as German bombers made lightning strikes on the city, launching the Nazi invasion of Poland and World War II.

Kuklinski, who was just nine, raced to school with his friends and arrived to find the corridors filled with screaming classmates. Their principal, a large man who terrified them all, motioned for silence. He was a member of the army reserve and said he was going to fight the Germans. Kuklinski was reassured. "If he is in the war," Kuklinski felt, "we will win."

Kuklinski's parents, both Catholic, sought to shield their son, but it became impossible as the bombs fell. An artillery shell crashed into the courtyard behind their home, killing several horses that Polish soldiers had tied up there. Kuklinski never forgot the Nazis' brutality. One day, he saw the Germans install barbed wire along the street and force elderly Jews to shovel dirt along the makeshift fence. He also heard that the Nazis would use lighters to burn the beards of Jewish men who did not cut them off quickly enough when ordered to do so. A classmate who lived in his building broke down in tears one day, saying her mother had been hurt, and Kuklinski later overheard his parents discussing the incident: The girl's mother had been raped by German soldiers.

Kuklinski's father, who had become a caretaker for a building inside the Jewish ghetto, was able to move in and out freely, although some nights he remained behind the ghetto wall, while Kuklinski and his mother stayed alone in their apartment. On those days, Kuklinski would deliver his father's dinner in a small can to the ghetto gate. He later learned from his father that the food was passed around to people inside who were starving. The Germans built a large barbed-wire fence around the Great Synagogue, turning it into a transit camp for prisoners, and Kuklinski remembered approaching it with his friends and being asked by people behind the wire to buy food or cigarettes for them or to mail letters.

During the occupation, Kuklinski's parents decided to move him to a different school. In the public school, the Germans had eliminated many subjects, including the Polish language program. In the small monastery school located behind a church in Old Town, the teachers had more freedom, and Kuklinski's parents hoped that he would receive a better education. The school was overcrowded but admitted Kuklinski after his father agreed to build him a desk, a small table that was placed in the corner of a classroom.

One cold day in March, Kuklinski and several of his friends skipped school, took two kayaks, and went paddling on the Vistula. They were moving through whitewater, with ice chunks floating around them, when a large piece of ice knocked Kuklinski's kayak into a stone bridge support. The current held the boat against the bridge, terrifying Kuklinski and another boy in his boat. Kuklinski's friend stopped paddling and began to pray. Kuklinski took his paddle and poked his friend on the head, threatening to kill him if he did not start paddling immediately. They finally reached the shore.

In school, Kuklinski felt isolated and spent much of his time reading during the priests' dull lectures. One day, as he lost himself in a Polish translation of *Uncle Tom's Cabin*, he felt a priest grab his ear and admonish him. Kuklinski was expelled. As he later recalled, God seemed to be saying, *Be careful, Ryszard. Be careful with America.*

As the occupation continued, Kuklinski could not avoid witnessing what was happening behind the ghetto wall. From a fourth-story window in his building, he peered down at a high brick wall topped by barbed wire and broken glass that divided Leszno and Przejazd Streets and marked the border of the ghetto, and he watched with uncomprehending horror as his neighbors were slaughtered in the street. One day, he witnessed the mass execution of dozens of Poles on Leszno Street outside the ghetto wall. Then Nazi storm troopers ordered two Poles whose lives had been spared to load the bodies on a flatbed truck and to sprinkle sand on the bloodstained sidewalk. Kuklinski had a small prayer book, which he took to the street afterward and pressed it on the spot where the massacre had been carried out.

Kuklinski's father often took him to the homes of friends and asked him to bring his toy accordion. When they arrived at such gatherings, Kuklinski found other children with instruments—harmonicas, drums, even a violin. The children played noisily, with the music drowning out their parents' hushed voices. It was Kuklinski's introduction to the underground, the Polish resistance.

When the Nazis began to liquidate the ghetto in 1943, Kuklinski watched as soldiers burned apartment buildings, forcing the screaming residents into the streets. From his window, Kuklinski saw one hysterical woman trapped inside her third-floor apartment at 5 Leszno Street. As the smoke and flames filled her room, she went to the window several times for air. Finally, she climbed out onto the ledge and stood silently and unmoving as flames began to billow out the window. Then she stepped off. Kuklinski prayed as she tumbled to her death below. In spring 1943, the SS blew up the Great Synagogue next to Kuklinski's building. Later, he walked through the ruins.

As the months passed, he watched as Jews and other Poles were forced from their homes, lined up and shot, or sent to concentration camps. Kuklinski's parents took him more frequently to the country, afraid that the devastation in the ghetto would spread to the rest of Warsaw. One day, Kuklinski and some friends were at an amusement park near Krasinski Square, which bordered the ghetto near the Old Town. As he whirled around on a carousel, Kuklinski could hear gunfire; people in an apartment building were shooting at German soldiers on the street below. Kuklinski and his friends inched closer, and from a slightly elevated spot, they could see people running and fighting behind the ghetto wall. In the chaos Kuklinski saw several German soldiers grab a man and a woman in the entranceway to a large building. The two people appeared to be frantically trying to comply with the soldiers' shouted orders. As Kuklinski watched in terror, the man and woman stood face to face, clutching in an awkward embrace, and began to rub up against each other, simulating intercourse, as the soldiers laughed and jeered. Then one soldier raised his pistol and executed them both.

When Kuklinski was thirteen, he and a group of older friends went to a local fire station and asked to join the Home Army, the country's largest underground organization, which was under the command of the Polish government in exile in London. Kuklinski's friends were accepted, but he was told he was too young and was sent home. One group, Sword and Plow, finally allowed him to put up posters.

On May 13, 1943, Kuklinski was heading home when he saw that the Germans had surrounded his block. Afraid to enter the apartment building, he slept that night in a nearby potato patch located on the front lawn of a historic arsenal building on Dluga Street. The next day, he entered his apartment and found it a shambles; his mother was sitting alone and weeping. She said the Gestapo had stormed the apartment, dragging along a bloodied informant. In a blatant setup, one of the storm troopers had stuffed a handful of ammunition under his father's pillow and demanded, "What's this?" His father, Stanislaw, who did not own a weapon, had no idea. The soldier upended a heavy oak table in the dining room, broke off one leg, and used it to beat Stanislaw. As Anna was forced into another apartment, she could hear her husband's screams, accompanied by the music of Kuklinski's accordion, which another storm trooper was playing to mask the sounds of torture.

After the Gestapo officers had left, Anna said, she returned and found the apartment walls splattered with blood and her husband gone. His mother said she would seek refuge with close friends near Niedabyl and asked her son to go with her. But Kuklinski decided to go into hiding. He found shelter in the homes of friends and then in the forests outside Warsaw near Radzymin, where teenagers and young men he knew were roaming in small bands, forming an organized resistance. Kuklinski joined a group of about a half dozen boys, the oldest a Jewish teenager of about eighteen. They had heard that the Nazis were advertising for Polish citizens to work in the occupied zones. Kuklinski and his friends devised a plan, which in retrospect seemed naive: They would volunteer to work in France, where they hoped to steal a fishing boat and make their way to Britain. They had learned that Polish airmen were with the British, and they wanted to join them. As a gesture of solidarity, they tattooed their left arms with a picture of a boat and the word "Atlantyk."

The boys showed up at a recruiting office and said they wanted to go to France. They were put on a train, but were unloaded instead in German Silesia, in southwestern Poland. Nearby were several prison camps, in which the Germans were detaining POWs of all nationalities, including Soviets, Italians, Americans, and British. Kuklinski spent the next eighteen months at forced labor in German wartime factories, which were producing propellers and other airplane parts.

In the winter of 1945, Kuklinski was ordered to join hundreds of prisoners, mostly women, who were being evacuated from a concentration camp. As they walked through the freezing rain and snow in tattered prison garb, Kuklinski and two older boys, one of them the Jewish teenager he knew from Warsaw, escaped through an open field. They spent the next few months hiding in small villages, scrounging for clothing and food, and sleeping in barracks that housed laborers who were being forced to work on the large German farms. They traveled only after dark. One night, as they walked along a rural road, they encountered an SS soldier guarding a machine gun in a defensive position.

"Hands up!" he ordered, asking who they were.

"We are Polish workers," Kuklinski and his friends replied, explaining that they were trying to find the next village, Neudorf, where they wanted to obtain food. The soldier cursed but pointed the way to the village.

Kuklinski and his two friends walked several more kilometers through a snowy field, shivering in their tattered clothes. They came upon a brick house, which was dark inside. They approached it cautiously, aware that retreating German soldiers often took refuge in such houses as they foraged for food. They broke a window in the basement and climbed in. Finding jars of food, they had a quick meal. Then the three friends crept up the stairs to the kitchen. Suddenly, they heard a voice speaking in German and saw a man in uniform in the hallway. He picked up a hunting rifle and called out. The boys tried to defend themselves, and in the struggle, one of the older teenagers grabbed the man and pushed him down the basement stairs, where the other beat him with the man's own rifle, killing him. Both older boys and Kuklinski ran from the house to the next village, where they were given shelter by a Pole who hid them in his basement for months. One day in the spring, they noticed tanks rolling into the village, led by soldiers in fur caps and the traditional khaki uniforms of the Soviet Army. Kuklinski had never seen Russians before. As he and his friends watched, the Germans tried to put up a fight, but they were vastly outnumbered, and the shooting ended within hours. As Kuklinski and his friends ran to welcome the Soviet forces, they witnessed the savagery of the Soviet troops, who casually finished off hundreds of German soldiers who were lying wounded in a large field.

Kuklinski joined a column of refugees returning east in carriages and carts, drawn by bedraggled horses. At one point, he left the caravan and rode a train that was carrying Poles back into Warsaw. He found the city leveled, and his apartment building reduced to rubble. There was no sign of his parents. Kuklinski hiked for two days to Niedabyl, where his uncle's farm was located. He found his aunt in the front yard. She looked up and began to scream, "Ryszard! Ryszard! Ryszard!" and then his mother's name, "Anna! Anna! Anna!"

Anna came running and embraced her son for the first time in two years. But in their tearful reunion, she told him that his father had not returned. She showed him three postcards from his father, who had been held in the Pawiak Prison in Warsaw and later sent to the Oranienburg-Sachsenhausen concentration camps near Berlin.

After the German surrender on May 7, 1945, Kuklinski took a

Soviet military transport train to Berlin and hitched a ride to the camps, which were almost empty. Kuklinski found a prisoner who led him into Block 4A, where his father had been held and where sick prisoners still lay. Kuklinski walked from one bed to the next, talking to each survivor, but none of them knew his father. They reported that dozens of infirm prisoners had been hanged before the war ended, and thousands of others had been taken on a death march to the north.

Kuklinski walked for several days along a country road that led north. He saw bodies of former prisoners scattered along the path. He slept in barns or in the homes of friendly farmers. But there was no trace of his father, and he finally turned back.

Kuklinski felt no special claim as a victim; his father was one of 6 million Poles—including virtually all of the country's 3 million Jews—exterminated by the Nazis. But he concluded that his country had to become strong again, in order to defend itself against outside aggression. Poles could never let an invading power cross their borders again.

In the first years after the war's end, Kuklinski moved to Wroclaw in the southwestern part of Poland and took a job as a night watchman in a soap factory, attending school in the daytime. He loved to draw and dreamed of becoming an architect. On September 25, 1947, at the age of seventeen, he decided to enlist in the army. But he soon discovered Poland had a new oppressor, the Soviet Union. During his three years in officers school in Wroclaw, Kuklinski's commanding officer and the school's commandant, both of whom had served in the prewar Polish Army, were replaced by Soviets who could not even speak Polish. The deputy commandant for political matters—a Polish Jew—was replaced with a Soviet who quickly imposed the new order. In 1949, Moscow installed a new Polish defense minister: Polish-born Konstanty Rokossowski, Marshal of the Soviet Union and a career Soviet officer. Members of the Home Army were tried on trumped-up espionage charges.

When Kuklinski joined the army, he did not believe that it would necessarily end up being Communist. The new army was made up not only of Polish officers from the eastern front, who had served under command of the Soviet Army and helped it liberate Poland, but also of other officers who had served with the western forces and returned home. The result was a struggle between officers who were indoctrinated by the Soviets and gradually accepted communism, and those who wanted Poland to be independent and believed that the army should serve the national interest, not the party interest.

Kuklinski hoped that in spite of the Soviet dominance and the purging of dissent, young officer candidates like him might someday replace their Soviet commanders. He threw himself into his studies and quickly became the top-ranked student in his class. He excelled in shooting drills and in track, regularly winning races of 3, 5, and 10 kilometers. He also completed 15-kilometer marches while carrying a heavy backpack and other equipment.

But Kuklinski quickly saw that the army was being remade along Soviet lines: their teachers, their drills—how to stand, how to turn, how to use a rifle—even their uniforms and caps. The round Soviet cap, with its red band, replaced the four-cornered cap of the Polish Army. Strict loyalty to the Soviet system was enforced. In class, Polish heroes were no longer discussed, only Soviet figures. In the field, training exercises were run only in a westerly direction—as in an offensive action against Europe—and soldiers were forbidden to attack toward the east. "It was a parody, absurd," Kuklinski felt. "We didn't feel as if we were in Poland anymore." The soldiers had once sung patriotic songs and said prayers before bedtime. Now they felt only fear as the Communists carried out purges of the army ranks.

Under pressure, Kuklinski joined the Communist Party. At night, as he studied in bed, his roommate, Konstanty Staniszewski, a devout Catholic who ranked second in the class, prayed quietly beneath a blanket. Kuklinski, knowing that prayer was forbidden, won his roommate's loyalty by saying nothing. They remained close.

In 1950, a few months from graduation, Kuklinski was made sergeant. "He was liked by everybody," recalled Stanislaw Radaj, a classmate and friend who described Kuklinski as kind and generous. But it was around that time that Kuklinski also got his first taste of party discipline. He had repeated a joke to a classmate about Soviet attempts to force collectivization on Poland and was expelled from the party and later from the officers school. During a shooting exercise, his name was called out. Several sergeants pointed their rifles at him and escorted him off the field. One of his closest friends saw what was happening and turned away. Kuklinski was devastated.

Kuklinski was told to get his belongings and was given a document transferring him to the Eleventh Mechanized Regiment in Biedrusko, near Poznan, where he was to spend two years as a simple soldier.

"I'm a sergeant," he protested.

"Not anymore," one sergeant replied, telling Kuklinski he had been stripped of his rank.

As he prepared to leave, he was almost overcome with emotion when another classmate, a sergeant from a prominent Communist family, approached and expressed anger at what happened. He said he had passed a hat around and taken up a collection. "We know you are in trouble," the soldier said. "This is from us."

From his new post in Biedrusko, Kuklinski filed an appeal and was told to appear before a special Communist Party commission in Warclaw. He was told to bring letters from people who knew him as a child, guaranteeing that he had not been a member of an organization that opposed Communists. As he waited outside the commission office, the door opened and a gray-haired colonel walked out sobbing. When it was Kuklinski's turn, he was ordered to sit at a large table before a dozen people. He acknowledged that he had once tried to join the underground, to fight the Nazis, but had been rejected. He had done nothing more than put up posters. He was a teenager, he said, and not part of any formal organization that sought to undermine the Communist Party. The commission reprimanded Kuklinski and warned him, as he later put it, that he was "stupid, but not an enemy of the people." He was told to return to school for his exams, and he finished at the top of his class. Still, he was promoted only to warrant officer, just below the rank of full officer.

In the fall of 1951, after a year-long stint with the Ninth Mechanized Regiment in Pila, Kuklinski began higher military studies in Rembertow, just outside Warsaw, where the Communists had converted Poland's most famous war college into an infantry officers school with a Soviet commander.

In July 1952, at the age of twenty-two, Kuklinski married his long-time girlfriend Hanka, then nineteen. A month or so later, after graduating from Rembertow, he was promoted to first lieutenant, and was sent back to the Ninth Mechanized Regiment in Pila, where he was made a company commander. Upon his arrival, he ran into Konstanty Staniszewski, the roommate from officers school who had prayed at bedtime beneath the covers. Staniszewski, who had become a counterintelligence officer, had heard of Kuklinski's troubles with the party. "Your file is thick with lies," Staniszewski said. He led Kuklinski into his office in the Prussian-style barracks and said that he had gone to his superiors, described Kuklinski's mistreatment, and vouched for him. Staniszewski had received permission to destroy his file. As Kuklinski watched, Staniszewski lit a coal stove, picked up the file, and threw it in.

In 1953, Kuklinski was promoted to captain and made chief of staff of the Fifteenth Anti-Landing Battalion, which had 300 soldiers, 100 horses, and 18 cannon. Based in Kolobrzeg, the battalion was part of Moscow's new effort to bolster Poland's coastal defense, undertaken after Gen. Douglas MacArthur's daring fall 1950 amphibious landing at Inchon that changed the direction of the Korean War. Moscow, realizing that superior offensive operations could be undermined by failure to defend the rear, had created nine battalions along the length of the 500-kilometer Polish coast.

While Kuklinski was in Kolobrzeg, Hanka remained in Pila, working as a bookkeeper. In September 1953 their first child, Waldemar, nicknamed Waldek, was born. Hanka and Waldek joined Kuklinski in Kolobrzeg, and they moved into an apartment building that had been German barracks before the war. Hanka took a job as a bookkeeper with a government fishing enterprise. In 1954, Kuklinski was made commander of the Eighteenth Anti-Landing Battalion, one of the three battalions that composed the brigade in Kolobrzeg. In March 1955, Bogdan, their second son, was born.

Kuklinski doted on his children, and in his spare time, he loved to sail. He and a group of friends—an architect, a judge, a doctor, several artists, and the local harbormaster in Kolobrzeg—organized the Joseph Conrad Yacht Club, which Kuklinski named after his favorite author. The harbormaster was named president, and Kuklinski was made vice president. The club created a marina in an old Napoleonic fort situated on the Parsenta River, where it enters the Kolobrzeg harbor.

In the face of friendly skepticism from his colleagues, Kuklinski also began to rebuild a wrecked twenty-eight-foot German sailboat that had been sunk in the war. Working on the rusty cast-iron keel in his basement, he reattached the planks in the oak hull with copper nails that he formed out of snips of telephone wire.

In September 1956, Kuklinski began a regimental commander's course in Wesola, near Warsaw, just months after a workers uprising in Poznan had been violently crushed by the Polish Army, leaving dozens dead and hundreds of others injured. In October a government shakeup led to the naming of Wladyslaw Gomulka, a previously purged official, as party secretary. Tensions between the Soviet Union and Poland escalated, with Russian troops even marching on Warsaw. Gomulka, who had tried to respond to the Poles' demands for more freedom, ordered Soviet Marshal Konstanty Rokossowski and other Russians holding senior Army posts to leave the country.

In his first few months in Wesola, Kuklinski was thrilled by the prospect of change, and what it might mean for the Polish Army. "Maybe the Army was not the best institution for democracy," he said, "but we were part of the society, and we wanted to serve the nation, not the party." He asked a local newsstand owner to save him copies of *Po Prostu*, the weekly reformist newspaper, and other periodicals. Many of his military colleagues were also upset at Poland's unequal relationship with the Soviet Union, the presence of Soviet generals in the Polish Army, and the lack of freedom of expression. Kuklinski attended meetings where resolutions were passed calling for change.

But Moscow's suppression of the Hungarian uprising in November 1956 changed everything. Hearing that Poles were being asked to donate blood for the Hungarians, Kuklinski asked for permission to go to Warsaw to give blood, but was told he could not leave the barracks. And Gomulka quickly turned back what seemed to Kuklinski to be a burgeoning revolution in Poland. Although the Russians were largely out of the picture in the Polish Army, Gomulka shut down *Po Prostu* and imposed a hard-line Socialist agenda on the country. It all led Kuklinski to conclude that true liberalization in Poland was doomed.

In September 1957, Kuklinski was made a battalion commander in the Fifth Mechanized Regiment in a division based in Szczecin. Several weeks after his arrival, he was told that the division was getting a new commander, Wojciech Jaruzelski.

One night in the forest, while Kuklinski and several other officers were sitting on tree stumps around a fire, Jaruzelski appeared. Seven years older than Kuklinski, he was one of the youngest generals in the Polish Army. An older officer rose and offered Jaruzelski his seat, but Jaruzelski waved him off, saying, "Please sit, General." Kuklinski was impressed with Jaruzelski's gesture, which he believed showed character.

But Kuklinski had mixed views of Jaruzelski. He knew that Jaruzelski had long argued that the Russians should be allowed to continue to stay in Poland and run the Polish Army, and that Jaruzelski was extremely pro-Soviet. Kuklinski found this surprising, given Jaruzelski's harsh wartime experiences. Jaruzelski, his sister, and his mother had all been imprisoned in a Siberian labor camp, where he had suffered permanent injuries to his back and eyes, which forced him to hold himself stiffly and to wear dark glasses.

At Szczecin, Jaruzelski had ordered a complete cleanup of the barracks, which were decrepit and dirty. He had the walls painted white, and the driveways and sidewalks cleared. Jaruzelski clearly was attentive to aesthetics and detail, but Kuklinski wondered whether the shine was only on the surface.

Kuklinski performed well in his assignment in Szczecin, but was unhappy about the continued suppression of democracy in Poland. For a while, he considered leaving the military and looking for a civilian job or going to school to study architecture. In the end, he stayed at his post, but after four months, he obtained a transfer back to Kolobrzeg, where his family remained. He remained there until the end of the decade. Even with the move, he continued to question his career choice. His ambivalence stemmed in part from events in Poland that seemed to herald change, yet never deliver it.

In 1959, Kuklinski finished rebuilding the German sailboat, which he and Hanka christened *Legend*. They launched it into the Baltic from the marina used by the Joseph Conrad Yacht Club.

He also continued to read voraciously. He found inspiration in the works of Conrad, the son of a Polish rebel from an earlier age who had also despised the Russians. (Conrad's father had been jailed and then exiled with his mother to Vologda in Russia.) Conrad, a seaman for twenty years, was passionate about the sea, and Kuklinski identified with his use of ships and seamen as moral symbols. Kuklinski was entranced by Conrad's 1917 novel *The Shadow Line*, in which a young sea captain attains emotional maturity and a sense of his own identity. Kuklinski was much taken with Conrad's existential message and his depiction of that moment in life when "one perceives ahead a shadow-line warning one that the region of early youth, too, must be left behind."

Conrad had written:

Only the young have such moments. I don't mean the very young. No. The very young have, properly speaking, no moments. It is the privilege of early youth to live in advance of its days in all the beautiful continuity of hope which knows no pauses and no introspection.

One closes behind one the little gate of mere boyishness—and enters an enchanted garden. Its very shades glow with promise. Every turn of the path has its seduction. And it isn't because it is an undiscovered country. One knows well enough that all mankind had streamed that way. It is the charm of universal experience

from which one expects an uncommon or personal sensation—a
bit of one's own.

Kuklinski read and reread the book, and he pondered the question:
In a police state, how does one reach the enchanted garden?

In 1960, Kuklinski was accepted into the General Staff Academy in
Warsaw, where he was introduced to Boleslaw Chocha, a Polish general who specialized in territorial defense issues. Chocha's philosophy,
which he shared with Kuklinski, was that the war of the future would
be different, with no clear front lines and with armies suffering major
casualties because of the effectiveness of long-range missiles. In such a
scenario, he felt, Poland would be particularly vulnerable. Kuklinski
was fascinated by Chocha's views and appreciated his candor.

Kuklinski graduated in 1963. Cited for superior performance, particularly in writing and mapping, he was offered a position on the General Staff, the central command-and-control organ of the Polish armed
forces. Kuklinski, by then a major, was given an office at the General
Staff headquarters in Warsaw and assigned to work on major military
exercises concerning strategic operations. Thus he began his ascent in
the Polish Army.

That winter he got his first important assignment—to devise an
exercise to show how Moscow would deliver nuclear warheads to Polish armed forces in wartime. A Polish colonel who had served as a
rocket brigade commander had been given the assignment, but his
work was found unsatisfactory, and Kuklinski was asked to take over.

The exercise was jointly managed by the Soviet and Polish defense
ministers, and it would be observed by a select group of Polish generals. It was the height of the Cold War, in the aftermath of the Cuban
missile crisis and the Kennedy assassination—and at one point, Kuklinski went deep into a Polish forest and put his hand on an actual warhead, an object that officially did not exist on Polish soil.

Despite a severe blizzard, the exercise went flawlessly, and Kuklinski was recognized as an imaginative officer who could get a job done. Over the next nine years, he became the leading author of the military exercises conducted by Poland with the Warsaw Pact. He also worked closely with Jaruzelski, who was elevated to chief of staff. Fluent in Russian, Kuklinski regularly visited his Warsaw Pact counterparts in Moscow, Eastern Europe, and the western part of the Soviet Union. He became an expert in troop movements, combat readiness, air defense, communications, and chemical and electronic warfare. His mission, he was told, was to prepare for war with the West.

As his responsibilities grew, he won the respect of the Operations Directorate, which was staffed by 80 to 100 officers, and coordinated the work of other directorates, such as intelligence, armament planning, and mobilization. As Kuklinski's access to Soviet and Warsaw Pact secrets increased, he began to discern flaws in his country's military relationship with the Soviet Union.

The Soviet and Warsaw Pact military strategy was exclusively offensive. Every military exercise began with the pretense that it was a response to a NATO attack. But Kuklinski, who was writing the exercises, knew the plans called for a massive first strike by Soviet and Warsaw Pact forces. More than 600,000 Polish troops would participate in a first wave that would sweep west and north to attack West Germany, Holland, Belgium, and Denmark. A few days later, the second wave, the Second Strategic Echelon, would follow. This huge force, consisting of 50 divisions, 2 million soldiers, and more than 1 million armored vehicles and rockets, was stationed in the western Soviet Union, including Ukraine, Byelorussia, and the Baltic republics. It was in many ways, Moscow believed, the key to a victory in Europe.

On the General Staff, Kuklinski worked near Jaruzelski's office and did assignments for him, although they did not have daily contact. He worked more closely with General Chocha, who had risen to become deputy chief of staff for operations. General Chocha, who had a deep voice and firm manner, was an astute and demanding boss and was well liked and respected. Born in Grodno, he had come from a family of Polish intellectuals and had been attending college in 1940 when the

Soviets expelled him and his family to Kazakhstan, where he was put to work in a wood-processing combine. He was drafted in 1943 into the First Mechanized Division of the Soviet-backed Polish First Army and eventually worked his way up the ranks, becoming Jaruzelski's deputy on the General Staff.

One day in 1967, Kuklinski and Chocha took a train to Berlin for a meeting with the leadership of the German and Soviet troops in Germany. After some drinks, Chocha began to open up, and he complained to Kuklinski about Poland's vulnerability in the Soviet war scheme. Why was it an offensive strategy? Chocha asked. Why were Polish troops attacking NATO? Shouldn't they only defend Poland?

Chocha said he had raised the issue with Jaruzelski and other top generals, but had gotten nowhere. Kuklinski decided he had an important intellectual ally on the General Staff.

In the summer of 1967, Kuklinski was considered for the post of military attaché to Washington, but instead was sent in October to Vietnam for about six months as a member of Poland's delegation to the ICC, the body created to ensure compliance with the Geneva accords. The experience served to reinforce Kuklinski's views of the superpowers. He admired the American soldiers in Vietnam, and he knew growing up that the Americans had bombed the Germans and helped to destroy the Nazi war machine. He also worried that antiwar sentiment in the United States might cause it to reassess its commitment to fighting the Soviets around the world, or worse yet, to withdraw its troops from Europe.

In Saigon, Kuklinski found himself in close proximity to Americans. One evening during the January 1968 Tet offensive (the major surprise attack by the Communists in towns and cities throughout South Vietnam), as he was watching the fighting from a hotel roof with several other Polish officers detailed to the ICC, an American who was known to be of Polish descent appeared before them. He was in civilian clothes, and greeted Kuklinski in Polish. Kuklinski, who was in his uniform, suspected that the American was a CIA officer. Kuklinski's delegation had been warned not to speak to Americans, but Kuklinski started to make small talk. He definitely wanted to meet this man, and as a pretext, asked if he would buy an item for him in the American Post Exchange (PX). The man said he would be delighted to, and he invited Kuklinski to visit him anytime at his hotel. Kuklinski was never able to make the visit and felt he had missed an important opportunity.

In 1968, Kuklinski's career received a boost when Jaruzelski was named defense minister and Chocha was appointed chief of the General Staff.

In August 1968, a few months after he returned from Vietnam, Kuklinski's suspicions about Soviet intentions were reinforced dramatically after he got an order to go to Legnica, a city in southwestern Poland, to assist in planning the Polish role in military exercises, codenamed "Danube," being conducted by Marshal Ivan Yakubovsky, commander of the Warsaw Pact forces. When Kuklinski arrived, he found representatives from each Warsaw Pact country except Czechoslovakia and Romania. He knew Czech forces were marked on their military maps in blue, the color usually reserved for the enemy. Kuklinski was confused at first, then realized he was seeing plans for an impending invasion of Czechoslovakia to put down "Prague Spring."

Around the command post, no one spoke of armed intervention—those words were reserved for describing the Western imperialist forces. These were "training exercises." Kuklinski was astonished and angry about the participation of Polish troops in the plans. He had been monitoring foreign radio reports and had heard nothing to suggest that the West was aware of how close an invasion really was. At one point, he drafted a short, anonymous letter to Radio Free Europe and had a driver take him along a highway outside Legnica, hoping to find a car being driven by a Western diplomat. He would make up some story to his driver and try to pass along the note. But he had no luck. He then feigned a family illness and succeeded in getting recalled to Warsaw, where he hoped to try again. But he ended up working around the clock in a special operations center in the General Staff as a member of the small group of officers who were to monitor the activity of Polish forces in Czechoslovakia. It was impossible to get away and approach a Western diplomat.

On the night of August 20, 1968, Soviet paratroopers landed at the Prague airport, and Polish troops crossed the border, along with other Warsaw Pact armies. In the command center, Kuklinski served as the communications link between Major General Florian Siwicki, the commander of Polish forces in Czechoslovakia, and Jaruzelski and party chief Gomulka. From his unique vantage point, Kuklinski learned that Jaruzelski had told Siwicki, one of his closest friends, "Florian, be gentle. Don't harm anybody."

Later, Siwicki radioed Kuklinski, telling him to convey to Jaruzelski that Polish troops had arrived in designated areas in northern Czechoslovakia, and that he had driven to Prague to report to the Czech president, Ludvik Svoboda. "Our troops are at his disposal," Siwicki said.

Kuklinski ultimately did not regret the assignment because it allowed him to see raw reporting from Siwicki and other commanders, which Kuklinski summarized in reports for Jaruzelski and Gomulka. As Kuklinski wrote later, "I had a unique opportunity for gaining insight into our contribution to this disgraceful postwar history." But his inability to send out an alert led him to conclude that "some kind of communication with the West should be established—*must* be established," particularly if his own country was ever at risk.

Jaruzelski organized a symposium in Warsaw to review Poland's role in the "exercise." In attendance were senior military officials and representatives from the Warsaw Pact command in Moscow. Kuklinski later described the "gala occasion":

> The symposium participants competed in complimenting the activity of the Polish units. It is true that they did not encircle the Czech garrisons as quickly as did "the world's best—Soviet—" units, but they compensated for it later through their exceptionally successful persuasion of Czech commanders to back changes at the highest levels of their party and government.

Recognized for exceptional achievement was the fact that, despite the hostile attitude of the Czech population, which formed live barricades in front of the tanks and armored cars, we had actually managed to avoid any greater human and material losses; that under the Polish tanks perished only a single child and that only because of an accident.

In general, the symposium acknowledged that Operation Danube had been a great military and political success of the community of Socialist countries to which the Polish Peoples' Armed Forces made a significant contribution.

But Kuklinski added that in informal conversations, people had reached different conclusions.

Participation of the Polish Armed Forces in the invasion of Czechoslovakia was estimated almost generally to have been an inexcusable blunder of the then political and military leadership of the Polish People's Republic, for which we will pay dearly once Poland matures and claims its inalienable right to live in dignity and to make democratic-social changes unacceptable to the USSR. My own views were very much along this line and that probably affected my future orientation.

Kuklinski was enraged at his superiors' enthusiasm for the invasion. Although there were no formal legal agreements requiring Poland to participate in such a venture, Jaruzelski said he was proud to send Polish troops across his ally's border. He, too, spoke in euphemisms. Of course, he did not want to do it in the brutal Soviet way, as Kuklinski put it, but with white gloves.

Early the following year, Moscow decided to mount a large military exercise, "Spring 69," to demonstrate how a war would be conducted in central Europe, known as the "Western Theater of Military Operations."

The Poles were assigned to manage the exercise under the supervi-

sion of the Warsaw Pact command in Moscow. Chocha assigned Kuklinski to prepare the offensive scenarios for the Soviets and each Warsaw Pact army. At the time, Kuklinski knew little of the Soviet
wartime mission and troop structure in Germany, so he and two communications officers went for consultations to Wunsdorf, East Germany, where Soviet troops were based.

Kuklinski received a warm welcome there from the Russian commander. While the two Polish communications officers went to meet
their Russian counterparts, Kuklinski was granted access to senior
Soviet operational officers and was soon reviewing some of the Soviet
Union's most sensitive war-planning documents for Europe.

He immersed himself in the material and consulted with Soviet
officers. "They shared the basic concepts of running the war with me,"
he recalled. He took careful notes and drew his own map.

After returning to Warsaw, Kuklinski worked three more weeks on
the plans, re-creating the operational scenario for a Soviet-run war in
central Europe. When he was done, the Polish General Staff's intelligence division, which had sophisticated printing equipment, produced
several high-quality copies of the map for a presentation to Soviet officials. One map was ordered destroyed because the color was slightly
off. Kuklinski took it and placed it in his safe. At the time, he could justify doing so, for war planning was within his area of assignment.

Kuklinski and a general in charge of Polish communications troops
were sent by train to Moscow for a formal presentation to the Warsaw
Pact commander, Marshal Yakubovsky. They were received by his
chief of staff, General S. M. Shtemenko, the legendary former head of
operations on the Soviet General Staff under Stalin.

Kuklinski had studied history's great war-planners, from Clause-
witz to Moltke, but he would never forget meeting Shtemenko, a hero
to him, the man who had planned the Soviet strikes against Hitler. As
they shook hands, Kuklinski noticed that one of Shtemenko's fingers
was disfigured or slightly broken, perhaps an old war injury.

Kuklinski displayed his map and documents before Shtemenko and
explained the operational scenario for Spring 69. He left a second copy

of the map at the Soviet General Staff, where he made a second presentation. Soon the original copy, signed and approved by Marshal Yakubovsky, was returned to him. Later, in his presence, a Polish general named Sliwinski, who served as representative to the Warsaw Pact command, called General Chocha in Warsaw, saying the plan for Spring 69 had been approved. "The colonel is on his way back, waiting for his next promotion," Sliwinski said.

Some time later, hundreds of Warsaw Pact officers met in a town in western Poland to carry out the exercise, which also included the use of coded radio communications. At one point, Chocha, who was managing the exercise, summoned Kuklinski to his office.

He made clear that there had been a complaint from Moscow. Chocha said he was pleased with Kuklinski's work, but Soviet officials were upset that Kuklinski's plans for the exercise included too many similarities to the Soviet war plans. "There is a cable from the Soviet General Staff," Chocha said. "Get all documents back from people who participated. Destroy everything."

Chocha then said in Russian, "Molodets!" (which translates roughly as "attaboy"). Chocha seemed proud that the Russians were unnerved and said sarcastically that perhaps Moscow would now realize that the Poles were not as stupid as the Soviets thought.

In the summer of 1970, Kuklinski was working at the General Staff on an exercise approved by Jaruzelski that was based on a surprise NATO nuclear attack on Warsaw Pact troops in their barracks. Kuklinski had been preparing the exercise for six months. Late one night, as he and several other officers were putting the final touches on the maps, the red phone on his desk rang. It was Chocha.

"Are you still working?" Chocha asked.

"Yes," Kuklinski said.

"But how long are you going to work?" Chocha asked.

"Maybe an hour or more," Kuklinski responded.

"Fine, let's work together," Chocha said. He asked Kuklinski to bring his work with him.

Kuklinski was unsettled, fearing that Chocha, who was known for calling people at night after he had been drinking, would order drastic changes. Nevertheless, he went to Chocha's office.

"Please display your map," said Chocha, who seemed clear-headed that night.

But as Kuklinski complied, Chocha reached over and turned up his radio to prevent their conversation from being overheard.

"Colonel," Chocha began, "why are we always concerned about our external front?"

"That is the topic of our exercise," Kuklinski said.

"The external front should be a Soviet concern," Chocha insisted. *Why weren't Polish troops defending Poland?*

"General, we've discussed this," Kuklinski said, referring to their conversation on the train to Berlin three years earlier.

Chocha was not deterred. He continued to ask searching questions about Poland's military doctrine. Where would NATO have to use its nuclear weapons?

Kuklinski replied that in a war between the superpowers, NATO would target a nuclear response on the Second Strategic Echelon. But such an attack would not occur while the forces were on Soviet territory, nor once they reached Germany. They would be attacked in between.

Where? Chocha asked.

"On the soil of nobody—in Poland."

Kuklinski could see that his boss was worried, and he pushed further. "It's not a question of the exercise. It's the doctrine. We must change our policy. The whole doctrine," Kuklinski said.

It was, for Kuklinski, the troubling question faced by every patriotic Pole: Whom did one serve? He and his fellow officers were caught up in the aggressive war-making agenda of the Soviet Union, and not the interests of Poland, and in doing so they were ensuring their country's destruction in a time of war.

Chocha said he had continued to press the issue with top officials. "I have been talking and talking, but they don't listen to me," Chocha said as music from the radio continued to play loudly.

"General," Kuklinski replied, if there could be no common under-standing among the Poles and their allies in the Warsaw Pact, "per-haps it would be in our interest to reach a mutual understanding with our enemy."

"Colonel!" Chocha said, waving his arms over his head. "We have reached the abstract. We are talking about what is impossible, what is not real." Chocha paused. "I think it's time to finish the work."

Kuklinski asked whether he had to make any changes in his exercise. "Nothing," Chocha said. "Let's go home."

But Kuklinski felt he was being sent a message: Chocha had not dismissed him or rejected his suggestion. He hadn't even disagreed.

Another event that compelled Kuklinski to cross the line occurred in December 1970, when Polish troops in Gdansk, Gdynia, and Szczecin were ordered to shoot into demonstrations of shipyard workers, who were protesting the raising of food prices before Christmas. Some forty-seven "wreckers of order in the people's state" were killed. Among them were seven trade-school students. More than 1,000 vic-tims were hospitalized.

Kuklinski knew one regimental commander whose men had been ordered to fire at workers in Gdynia. "We were shooting and crying," he told Kuklinski. "I had no choice. I got orders." He said that he had ordered his soldiers to fire at the ground, but the bullets ricocheted up, hitting the marchers.

The orders to fire were given by the Polish leadership. Kuklinski felt the officers had no such right. He was outraged at the casualness with which the orders were given, and that no one had refused to carry them out. Kuklinski started to think in concrete terms, and he devised his plan to reach out to the West. He began reading books on American military doctrine. He worked late at night, confronted by moments of self-doubt and uncertainty. But as he analyzed his choices, he became convinced he was right, and he concluded that his plan, if well thought out, might succeed. Some kind of cooperation must work.

Ultimately, he wanted the U.S. Army to know that he believed other Polish Army officers, in the event of war, would be willing to help eliminate the command-and-control systems of the Warsaw Pact and sabotage the Second Strategic Echelon as it crossed Poland.

The consummate sailor, he got approval from an unwitting General Chocha to lead the surveillance trip on the *Legia* through western Europe with a crew of eight or nine officers. Their mission would be to "complete a study of the western theater of military operations." Kuklinski also took along his teenage son, Bogdan. He offered the captain's berth to a crewmate, preferring to share a berth with his son and several others.

Chocha had authorized Kuklinski to carry the necessary food and money on the fifty-foot yacht, which had a hull and superstructure made of mahogany and teak. The General Staff would cover all expenses, as they were on an official mission. Kuklinski, who knew no English, spent weeks practicing with a Polish-English dictionary. He imagined the text of the letter he would send from the boat.

On August 2, 1972, Kuklinski, Bogdan, and the rest of the crew loaded up at Gdansk. They would sail through the Baltic Sea and into the Kiel Canal, along the Elbe River to Hamburg, to the North Sea and to Cuxhaven, and on to Wilhelmshaven, their final stop in Germany. From there, they would travel to four Dutch ports, including Den Helder, Amsterdam, The Hague, and Rotterdam. Their final stop would be Ostend, a port in Belgium, before returning to Poland. Kuklinski, the commander of the surveillance group and captain of the vessel, offered his crew as much freedom as possible, in order to win their confidence. "Do you know who the captain is?" he shouted at one point. "You are!" the crew shouted back. "You're right!" Kuklinski declared, "From this moment on, everybody does what he wants."

The crew fell into a daily routine, leaving the boat to explore ports, shop, and visit museums.

On August 11 the *Legia* arrived in Wilhelmshaven. Kuklinski had waited to send his letter from this port, a former German naval headquarters, because of its rich history. On May 6, 1945, the Polish First

Armored Division, which participated in the invasion of Normandy and helped to liberate France and Holland, accepted the surrender of much of the German fleet at Wilhelmshaven. Germany made its formal surrender the next day to a British admiral who was accompanied by a Polish officer. Kuklinski reveled in this history and had always considered the Polish troops at Wilhelmshaven to be heroes. But with Poland under Soviet domination, Kuklinski felt that the town symbolized unfinished business.

Kuklinski waited until his crew had left the ship. With Bogdan busy elsewhere on the boat, Kuklinski shut his cabin door. Sitting at a small table, Kuklinski removed two sheets of onionskin paper, the kind commonly used for airmail letters in Europe. He began to print carefully, slanting each letter to the left, unlike his usual writing style. He decided to address his note to the American military attaché, seeking to meet with an officer of similar rank.

He placed the letter in an envelope, which he addressed to the military attaché, and then sealed it in a second envelope. He had bought the envelopes at their last stop in Germany. Kuklinski then tossed his pen into the water and left the *Legia*. After a short walk, he hailed a taxi and rode to a post office, where he addressed and mailed his letter. Then he returned to the *Legia*, where he sat on the deck, waiting for his crew to return. Seagulls coasted above the boat, interrupting his thoughts with their loud cries. This was *his* Polish resistance.

3

A DOUBLE LIFE

AFTER LANG RETURNED to Bonn Station he got a visit from a senior officer. "You really hit one over the fence," the officer said. "It's a shame that nobody is going to know what you did."

The officer had a cable from CIA headquarters, which commended Lang and Henry for their success. The cable said that Kuklinski, apart from his considerable potential for delivering intelligence, "seems, because of his current and projected assignment, well situated to provide a unique and meaningful early-warning capability within the Warsaw Pact forces superior to that we have previously had."

Lang was told to shred his files on the P.V. operation, which meant headquarters had decided the project was worth pursuing and would run it through Warsaw Station. At Langley, additional measures were taken to restrict information on the case. Knowledge of the operation would be limited to a small group of officers under Soviet Division chief David Blee, and Kuklinski would need a code name. Blee, aware of Kuklinski's fondness for the sea, chose "Gull."

On August 31, 1972, about a week after Kuklinski returned to Poland, Blee sent a cable to Warsaw Station soliciting ideas for an internal "commo" (communications) plan once Gull was back in

Poland. His motivation appeared to be "ideological, nationalistic, and anti-Soviet," Blee wrote. He cited Kuklinski's experience in Vietnam and his belief that the West was "not as decadent as portrayed by his government."

"Soviet invasion [of] Czechoslovakia completed his disenchantment with Sovs and convinced him Sovs have no real concern for Gull's country," Blee wrote. As a Polish patriot and nationalist, Gull believed he was in a position to assist "in effort which may in time free [Poland] from Soviet domination."

Blee said Gull had been told that "we will do all possible to exfiltrate [him] and provide safe haven in West should he feel security required it or his life [was] in danger." Blee also cited Gull's claims of broad access to secret documents, including war plans, training exercises, and classified Soviet military journals. The CIA had said its highest-priority requirements were for all Soviet Warsaw Pact directives, articles from Soviet military journals, war-planning documents, and "any Soviet or Warsaw Pact preparations for major hostile actions or political ventures requiring military preparations." Addressing Gull's credibility, Blee wrote, "Nothing in the recent contacts with Gull suggests that he [is] other than sincere and dealing with us in good faith."

It was several months before Kuklinski was contacted by Warsaw Station. At the time, the station consisted of just three people—Carl E. Gebhardt, the newly arrived chief of station, his deputy, and an administrative assistant, who opened the diplomatic pouch, maintained the site files, and performed other duties.

Gebhardt, a slightly built thirty-nine-year-old with blond hair and distinctive light-blue eyes, worked out of an expansive office near the ambassador's suite in the white-marble embassy building on Aleje Ujazdowskie. There was also a vaulted room with a darkroom, sink, shelves, a refrigerator for film, and cabinets that held concealment devices for use in dead drops. Gebhardt was posted under State Department cover and listed as second secretary in the political section. As a diplomat, he was expected to act the role, attending the political counselor's meetings and carrying out other official tasks.

Warsaw Station made several attempts to contact Kuklinski. The CIA prepared a letter, written in invisible ink, to confirm the time and place for their first meeting in the Powstancow Warszawskich cemetery. The station spray-painted the envelope black to absorb light in case Kuklinski's car was parked under a streetlight. One evening, Gebhardt took his blond Afghan hound, Ladybug, out for a walk. Gebhardt believed no CIA officer should be without a dog when serving in "denied areas"—places where officers' movements were highly restricted, and where they were subject to constant and unfriendly surveillance, such as in the Soviet Union and the East bloc. Dogs had to be walked every day and offered a plausible cover for carrying out operational acts. Gebhardt approached Kuklinski's Opel, which was parked on a side street near the General Staff, and slipped the envelope through a crack in the window on the driver's side, flipping his wrist to be sure it landed on the seat. But Kuklinski did not appear at the cemetery at the scheduled time. The CIA prepared another letter, proposing a new date before Christmas, and dropped it into his car once again.

Kuklinski had been just as impatient to make contact. He had returned to Poland on August 24 and had tried to go about his daily routine as he waited for a signal from the Americans. But as the weeks passed, he found himself preoccupied, nervous, and moody. Hanka could tell he was distracted. She did not press for an explanation, but he found it hard to keep the truth from her. They were extremely close, and he relied on her companionship, good instincts, and sense of humor. They had met in 1946, when Kuklinski was sixteen. He had been working in the town hall of Wroclaw, a town in Silesia in southwest Poland that had been taken back from the Germans after World War II. Kuklinski worked for Hanka's father, who managed security for the town's buildings. One day, Kuklinski heard the faint sound of a piano being played in the town hall, and he peeked into a room to find a slight, blond, thirteen-year-old girl practicing. Kuklinski introduced himself and asked her if she would teach him to play the song.

Hanka smiled shyly and began to show him the proper keys. She burst out laughing as he took over and deftly played the entire piece.

They began dating three years later, when she was sixteen and Kuklinski was in officers school. On July 16, 1952, they were married. Over the years, as Kuklinski's career progressed, Hanka worked as a factory bookkeeper and took care of their sons. She did not gossip with neighbors and had only a few close friends. Kuklinski knew she was uninterested in politics, but he appreciated her independent streak and her spirited outlook on life. After he was punished in officers school for making the joke about communism, and feared he had jeopardized his career, Hanka dismissed his concerns. There would be other opportunities, she told him.

In the fall of 1972, as Kuklinski's dark moods continued, she grew concerned and asked what was wrong. Finally, he told her that when he had been in Vietnam, he had become friendly with some American soldiers. While sailing in Germany that summer, he said, he had been surprised to run into them again. He had been sympathetic to the American effort in Vietnam and was pleased to know they survived the war, and he decided to pursue the friendship. But there were enormous risks in talking to the Americans, and the relationship had to stay secret.

The story was not entirely true, of course. Kuklinski had not linked up with Americans in Saigon, although he had tried to. But for Hanka's protection, he decided not to tell her any more about what he was doing, and he said nothing to his sons.

Even though he had not heard from the Americans, Kuklinski began photographing secret documents that he planned to give the Americans in his first delivery. He used a Russian camera he owned called a Zorka, which the commander of the Warsaw Pact forces had presented him for his work on a military exercise. Kuklinski enjoyed the irony: The gift would be used against the Soviets.

He built a darkroom in a bathroom. He told his family and friends that he was taking up photography again, a hobby he had dropped years earlier. He bought an enlarger, trays, chemicals, and other supplies. And because a Polish lieutenant colonel and his Russian wife lived above them, Kuklinski took other precautions. He suspected the KGB used such couples to spy on Polish citizens, and he worried they could hear his camera clicks as he photographed documents in his bedroom. In what he called a "home remodeling project," Kuklinski installed wooden paneling on his concrete ceiling to deaden the sound.

He took photographs at home, around the city, and on sailing trips. He shot nature scenes on long weekend walks with his family and their energetic sheepdog, Zula, a Hungarian puli. Her black fur was so long that it was sometimes hard to tell her front from her back.

At work, Kuklinski took classified documents out of the General Staff in a briefcase. The rules were strict: Documents removed from the General Staff vaults for delivery to another institution had to be carried in sealed envelopes and opened only by the official designated to receive the papers. Papers stamped "Secret—of Special Importance" could be removed only with the authorization of a commanding officer and under armed escort. Even tighter restrictions existed for "Series K" documents. But the rules were not always observed, and Kuklinski could find plausible reasons to remove documents, to make visits to other offices, or to take quick trips home during the day.

Zula sometimes posed a problem. She would bound to the door whenever Kuklinski arrived at home, barking loudly and scraping the floor. Kuklinski tried to train her to be quieter, so that his arrivals would not be noticed by his neighbors. Once, when one of his sons returned home with Zula after a walk, Kuklinski got down on his hands and knees and started barking and asking, "Is it nice if I welcome you this way?"

One day after Zula was taken out for a walk, the doorbell rang, and Kuklinski got down and began to bark. But as he reached up and opened the door, a repairman greeted him. "I was supposed to fix the refrigerator," the startled visitor said. Kuklinski hastily tried to explain. "I wasn't barking at you—I was barking at my dog." A day or so later, a secretary teased him at work: "Ryszard, I heard you wanted to bite my brother."

In October, Kuklinski was promoted to full colonel and told he was in line to become chief of staff for a mechanized division outside War-saw. The two-year assignment would be valuable training for a higher position when he returned to the General Staff. But he demurred. His position in the General Staff gave him extraordinary access to Warsaw Pact secrets, and he had no desire to leave. He had not heard from the Americans and could not seek their advice. He thanked his superiors, but asked that the posting be delayed.

For some reason, Kuklinski did not find the first letter dropped into his car. But when he found the second, he returned to his apartment and tried to follow Henry's instructions. He took an iron and pressed on the blank side of the sheet, waiting for the secret writing to appear. No message emerged. He ironed the page more firmly, again without success. Hanka entered the room. Kuklinski said he was trying to iron something, but that it wasn't working. Hanka suggested he turn up the heat. He did and immediately he saw the words appear on the sheet: the time and place of the meeting.

Late on the night of December 17, as a mist settled over Warsaw, Sta-tion Chief Carl Gebhardt and his wife Nancy began a surveillance detection run to see if they were being followed by the SB. Like all CIA spouses being posted to denied areas, Nancy, who was not an officer, had been trained to assist in clandestine operations. Satisfied that that they were free of surveillance, they drove to the Powstancow Warsza-wskich cemetery and headed up the road to where Kuklinski was to be standing. As they approached him, they were shocked to see that he was in his full army uniform. He was waving energetically at them.

Gebhardt didn't know whether to brake or speed away. He pulled up so that Gull was by Nancy on the passenger's side of the car. They passed him a package, and he handed back a container that looked like a cigar box.

Gebhardt leaned over and made eye contact with Gull. He wrote later: "Gull looked like a first-rate person, honest and sincere, and a man we'd like to know under different circumstances. This is very subjective, but it is what comes through of the man's character and is reflected in his face, and we think it is accurate."

Gull's package contained a letter and eighteen rolls of film—so many that Gebhardt had trouble finding enough lead-shielded containers to protect the film from airport X-ray machines when it was carried in the diplomatic pouch to the United States. At Langley the CIA discovered the film contained 300 pages of classified documents, including Soviet and Warsaw Pact war-planning materials. Kuklinski signed his letter "Jack Strong"—the pseudonym the Americans had given him.

The Americans also had prepared a letter for Kuklinski:

On behalf of our representatives who met you in the summer and at the special request of very senior officials of our government and senior officials in our military command, we wish to express our appreciation for your making contact with us and to welcome your cooperation in mutually beneficial undertaking in the cause of freedom. The worthy purposes and principles of our cooperation will endure and survive the yoke which now binds your nation, its government, and its military forces.

We understand and appreciate your concerns and your personal situation and are confident that your contributions to the cause of right and justice will benefit both our nations and the larger cause of world peace. We also wish to re-affirm to you the commitments we have made to you and our pledge and promise to assist you in any way which we can manage securely....

We look forward to a long and valuable association with you and send you our best wishes for the future.

The letter was signed "Eagle."

The agency provided Kuklinski with supplies that he would need for the operation, including water-soluble paper for messages, and two cameras. The first, an Olympus, resembled a camera that could be purchased in any shop, although it used special film canisters that held twice as many pictures as the commercial model. The second, a Tubka, was an example of the CIA's advances in miniaturization. It could be configured into a dozen forms and was small enough to conceal inside the head of a ballpoint pen or the fob of a key chain. One case officer, aware of Kuklinski's love of the sea, proposed inserting his Tubka in a sextant. Ultimately, because of Kuklinski's smoking habit, he received one inside a lighter. There was also detailed information on how Kuklinski should communicate with his American friends through chalk signals, dead drops, and exchanges through car windows.

Within the Soviet Division of the CIA, excitement about the operation was growing. On January 8, 1973, a senior member of the Reports and Requirements Staff, which disseminated Gull's material to the rest of the intelligence community, said in an analysis of the first documents he had delivered: "This source has made excellent choices of documents to copy. This sense of what is important information . . . promises to make him one of the two or three best sources we have had in Eastern Europe."

On January 15, the Soviet Division sent a memorandum to the CIA's Deputy Director for Plans* on the status of the operation, which said that so far Gull had provided "a large quantity of very valuable, highly classified, documentary intelligence directly responsive to priority national intelligence requirements."

Yet another briefing paper for top CIA officials called Gull "the best-placed source now available to [the U.S. government] in the Bloc,

* Later, this position became known as Deputy Director for Operations, or DDO.

in terms of the collection of priority information." It continued: "He has already reported on a Soviet air defense system on which there was no information other than interpretation of technical collection projects. His access affords [the U.S. government] excellent insight into the plans, actions and capabilities of the Warsaw Pact, including our best existing potential for early warning of Pact hostile action."

A senior official in the Soviet Division also cabled Lang, Henry, and other officers involved in the initial stages of the operation commending them on their performance: "Although full impact of his intelligence info to date is not yet apparent to the community, it is already clear to me that if you can keep Gull alive and producing the case will be of historic significance."

Blee was concerned that the sudden flood of Warsaw Pact materials from Kuklinski could tip off astute analysts in the intelligence community that the CIA had a new and highly placed source in the Warsaw Pact. He consulted with Katharine Colvin Hart, chief of his Reports and Requirements Staff, whose members were adept at masking the identity of sources before disseminating their contributions to the intelligence community.

With Hart's assistance, Blee made it appear that Kuklinski's intelligence was emanating from two longtime sources, who had recently become more active. Kuklinski's classified Polish Warsaw Pact materials would be credited to a longtime Polish military agent, code-named QT-LUX, who lacked Kuklinski's access to sensitive operational material but would be a plausible source of the information. Meanwhile, Kuklinski's Russian materials would be attributed to a longtime Soviet source.

As Blee later described the masking of Kuklinski's identity: "I cut him into two halves. Both halves already existed. Nobody ever doubted that these were the same sources that they had been reading for some time."

There were also tight restrictions on access to Gull's intelligence. Only a single photographic print was made from each negative. The print was sent to the Reports and Requirements Staff to be translated. The reports that resulted were disseminated in what was known as the "blue border" series (each page had a blue border down the right side). That meant they were issued as Top Secret, with full security controls. They could not be sent overseas or shown to a foreign national or a contract employee. The reports had to be stored in their own special walk-in vaults, which in turn were inside room-sized vaults that housed some of the most sensitive technical intelligence. Only a limited number of people were given access to the Gull material; each had to sign in to review it, and the review had to be done inside the inner vault. Any notes they took had to remain in the vault. Any reports they produced had to be sent back to Reports and Requirements for approval. In limited cases, the material could be hand-carried to a select group of senior government officials on the so-called bigot list. After being reviewed, the material had to be returned.

Even the Polish and Russian translators in the Reports and Requirements Staff, who worked out of different vaulted rooms as they translated the thousands of pages of documents Kuklinski provided, assumed they were translating materials from different sources.

One Soviet Division translator was aware of Kuklinski's identity—Stanislaw Longin Patkowski, who was known to all as Stan. He was a Polish-born CIA officer who was assigned to translate the personal letters Kuklinski wrote to the CIA and those the agency sent back.

A slight man in his fifties, Stan had unruly eyebrows, wore his hair combed straight back, and almost always had a cigarette dangling from his mouth. He often sat hunched over his desk, his reading glasses perched precariously on his nose, and his head cocked over a pile of messages that he would read slowly, scratching out words and scribbling in new ones. He would ruminate over how to translate a particular intelligence request, or "requirement," before it was transmitted to a source. At times, he admonished case officers for the way they communicated with sources. "You can't say that to this man," he would say. "You have to put it in these words." Stan immersed himself in the Gull case, trying to know him as any translator would—through his words.

★

Throughout the winter of 1972–1973, Kuklinski continued to live his hazardous double life. He remained attentive to any sign, however circumstantial, that he might be under suspicion. One day, he learned that Poland's Interior Minister, who oversaw the SB and counterintelligence, had claimed that the United States was collecting large quantities of intelligence on Poland. Kuklinski wondered whether that was a reference to his own activities.

At the General Staff, he photographed whatever he could lay his hands on. One day, he obtained thirteen past issues of the Soviet journal *Voyennaya Mysl* (Military Thought), a highly restricted classified publication. Kuklinski began photographing the journal in his office, but the job was too big, and he took several issues home. He worked late into the night but could not finish. Known for his early arrival at work, he was back in his office before dawn, where he completed the job.

In his apartment, Kuklinski was careful to hide all traces of his secret work, but he once made a critical error. The Americans had provided an emergency escape plan for him and his family, which included a key to the American Embassy compound in Warsaw and a detailed map and instructions. If he felt he was about to be arrested, he was to use the key to enter the compound on a side street, through the locked door of an apartment building that housed embassy employees. He was to leave through a rear exit and follow a path by a tennis court that led to a side entrance to the embassy. There, he was to identify himself as "Jack Strong." The U.S. Marine guards had been briefed.

Kuklinski kept one copy of the plan, which he had not yet memorized, on a piece of microfilm and another on a sheet of water-soluble paper. He kept it taped to the underside of a kitchen cabinet and studied it each night.

One evening when he arrived at home, he found the paper on the kitchen counter. His nineteen-year-old son, Waldek, said it had fallen off the cabinet. Waldek said he assumed the document was his father's and seemed to have no interest in it. Kuklinski was unnerved by his own sloppiness and asked Waldek not to discuss the paper with anyone. Waldek never brought it up again.

Still on edge, Kuklinski delivered a message to the Americans in January, saying he had a special request. He was convinced that if he were arrested, he would be tortured and executed. Even the strongest men confessed in such situations, he knew, and it was inevitable that the Poles would use his case as propaganda against the West, ruining his family's name. He wanted to be sure he was not taken alive and asked for "a pill, which would help me to resolve the matter in a critical moment."

"After this black paragraph, a bit of optimism," he added, saying there was nothing to indicate that anyone suspected him of cooperating with the West.

Later, Kuklinski received a reassuring letter from the Americans about the Polish Interior Minister's comments that U.S. intelligence was focusing on Poland. After investigating the matter, the Americans wrote, they had concluded that the comments had no connection to their activities, were general in nature, and were typical of what "the Soviet KGB provides to its counterparts within the Warsaw Pact.

"We are convinced that the Minister's remarks had no significance for our relationship," the letter said.

In March 1973, Kuklinski sent a reply to the Americans, thanking them for the "Eagle" letter of welcome. His message, like others that followed, was rendered in clear block print, with almost sixty lines to a page.

That spring, Kuklinski also told the Americans that the surveillance voyage the previous summer had been so popular that the General Staff would do it again, and that two yachts—*Legia* and *Opal*—would sail through West German ports in late June.

At CIA headquarters, Blee considered Gull's request for a suicide pill. The issue had arisen in previous cases, and Blee tended to oppose such steps, mostly for practical reasons. In a moment of uncertainty or fear, even the most experienced agent might panic and ingest a pill unnecessarily. There was also a risk the pills would be discovered and held against the CIA, with the KGB denouncing the agency for trying to kill its citizens. In one earlier case, Blee had ordered his staff to prepare a phony pill for an agent.

As Blee explained, "Every time an agent asks for suicide material, headquarters is of two minds. They always used to say, 'If this is what this man wants he ought to have it.' And other people say, 'No, it won't help us in the long run.' That's where I often said, 'Give it to him, but make sure it doesn't work.'"

Blee added with characteristic bluntness: "He'll go on working for us, confident that all he's got to do is bite this thing and he'll die. Meanwhile, I'll get my production."

Blee's senior deputy for operations, Bill Donnelly, shared Blee's reluctance about providing Kuklinski with "termination measures," but he suspected Blee's opposition was not as cold-blooded as Blee led others to believe. Donnelly believed that Blee, who was deacon of his church in suburban Maryland, had religious objections. No decision was reached immediately.

Meanwhile, Blee decided that if Kuklinski was going to remain in place, the agency would need a case officer who spoke fluent Polish to meet him on his annual voyages through Europe. Several officers were considered, and the search eventually narrowed to David W. Forden, an officer based in Mexico City. Donnelly, who knew Forden well, was sent to tell him.

"How is your Polish?" Donnelly asked when he arrived in Mexico City.

"A little rusty," Forden replied.

"Well, find a tutor," Donnelly said.

Forden was advised to prepare to fly to Washington in June, where he would review the files, and then to Europe to meet Kuklinski. He would keep his involvement secret, even from his colleagues in Mexico City, suggesting only that he was being recalled to Langley for training and consultations on his next assignment.

Forden found a tutor at the University of Mexico and began brushing up on his Polish. He was tutored at home, rather than at the embassy, in order not to arouse the curiosity of his colleagues.

Forden was an improbable spy. At forty-three, three months younger than Kuklinski, he had always wanted to enter public service, imagining that he might someday go into state or federal government. He often wondered how he had ended up working for the CIA.

Born in Buffalo, New York, he had joined the agency after the first generation of mostly Ivy League graduates who had served in the OSS and signed up at the CIA's creation after World War II. Forden's mother, Amy, had grown up on a farm, and his father, William "Ted" Forden, worked as a clerk in a boiler factory. After losing his job in the Depression, Ted worked in a succession of WPA jobs that included digging ditches, operating lift bridges, and working in a homeless shelter. As children, Forden and his older sister, Mary, never forgot their parents' struggle to survive. On many nights, they lay in bed in their flat on Virgil Avenue, listening to their parents discussing how to pay the $15 monthly rent. In 1939 the family moved about seventeen miles south to the town of East Aurora, and in September, as the war began in Europe, Forden was entering fourth grade at East Aurora Elementary School. His father got his job back at the foundry, where he retired after twenty more years, only to be told that he had just missed qualifying for the company's new pension plan. Outraged at his father's treatment, Forden realized that the family would never have pulled through without the help of the federal government.

Forden was an industrious child. He would collect wood scraps at a nearby toy factory and drag his wagon around, selling them door-to-door to be used as kindling for furnaces. He later became an Eagle Scout, was elected president of his high school class, and was accepted on scholarship to Wesleyan University. He majored in government and was in the glee club and president of his fraternity. One day during a joint concert with Vassar College, Forden met a student named Sally

Carson, who was in the Vassar glee club, and they began dating. After graduation, Forden, an unabashed Stevenson Democrat, was awarded a fellowship at the Maxwell School of Citizenship and Public Affairs at Syracuse University, where he obtained a master's degree in public administration.

At Maxwell, he shared an off-campus flat with two students, one of them Peter Falk. The fiery Falk, a graduate of the New School for Social Research in Manhattan, and the soft-spoken Forden, who was known as Chip, reinforced each other's enthusiasm for political change. Falk, three years older than Forden, had quit college after four months and been turned down by the U.S. Marines because he was blind in one eye. He eventually joined the Merchant Marine and later traveled to Yugoslavia with his girlfriend and dog after Tito invited left-leaning youth to help build railroads. In Falk's opinion, Forden was smart, reserved, and well grounded. "There was something special about Chip," Falk recalled. "He was connected to himself. He knew who he was." They debated politics, particularly the case against Julius and Ethel Rosenberg, and listened to Billie Holiday records. Falk, who acted in university productions, even persuaded Forden to audition for a play, but Forden didn't get the part.

In April 1953, Forden, Falk, and a group of other Maxwell students went to Washington, D.C., in search of work. The trips were a Maxwell tradition: The students met with prominent alumni in the State Department, Pentagon, and other agencies. It was the first few months of the Eisenhower years, the first Republican administration in two decades, and the students quickly learned that there were no jobs. One day, Forden heard that the CIA was seeking recruits. He and Falk decided to go for interviews. Falk recalled, "I thought, why not be a spy?"

Forden's interview at the agency, then at 2430 E Street NW, went well, and he was invited back the next day. Falk was not. The CIA interviewer who met with him noticed the New School on his résumé and said, "That school is considered a little pink." While Forden waited for clearance to be hired, he and Falk got jobs in the office of Governor Abraham Ribicoff in Hartford, Connecticut. In September, Forden was offered a job at the CIA. Falk stayed in Hartford, joined a theater group in New Haven, and eventually went on to a successful career as an actor, most notably as the gruff TV detective Columbo.

Forden sometimes wondered what qualified him for a life of der-ring-do, and he felt nervous taking the job. His other roommate at Maxwell, Alan Goldfarb, a strapping college football player who wrote poetry, recalled being surprised at Forden's decision to join the agency. "I had this idea people like this were bold and adventurous types, and I never felt that that was his nature. Obviously, I was wrong."

Like all new hires who lacked military service, Forden was placed in the junior officer training program; he underwent ten weeks of ori-entation, then was told to enlist in the army. After sixteen weeks of basic training at Fort Knox, Kentucky, he was accepted into Infantry Officer Candidate School at Fort Benning, Georgia. His yearbook pho-tograph shows him in a white T-shirt with a military buzz cut and dark-rimmed glasses. The entry depicts him as a twenty-two-year-old straight arrow, who was nicknamed "the professor" and was known for "his sociability."

"Dave woke up in time to save many a command conference with his spontaneous orations," the entry says. It jokingly describes him as "author of that popular new book, 'An Unbiased Account of the 1952 Election,' written from a Democratic viewpoint." Forden "corrected many a Republican junior candidate's 'misguided' political views with an appropriate number of pushups," the entry says. It concludes: "Basically not a drinking man."

Forden graduated in October 1954, and was soon commissioned a second lieutenant. In the spring of 1955, after six months in the Air-borne at Fort Campbell, Kentucky, he was ordered to report to the CIA in Washington and told to maintain his cover. He was sent to Camp Peary, the CIA's training center known as "the farm" near Williamsburg, Virginia. There, in groups of three or four, the junior trainees, known as JOTS, learned the work of espionage, including recruitment operations, conducting and detecting surveillance, and mastering clandestine tradecraft. That summer, Forden also married his girlfriend, Sally Carson, who had graduated from Vassar and had become a journalist, working for the *Reporter Dispatch* in White Plains, New York.

Forden's first CIA assignment was on the Czech desk where, as a JOT, he helped support worldwide operations against Czech targets. In September 1956, Forden was sent to Frankfurt, Germany, as a junior case officer. While there, Sally studied German and worked as a translator, and their first daughter, Sara, was born. In January 1961, Forden was reassigned to the German desk at Langley.

He volunteered next for a Latin American assignment after he heard there were some State Department cover slots available. He was accepted—and only then was told that he would have to serve in "non-official" capacity, a riskier status than diplomatic cover. The CIA had persuaded American companies to allow officers to work secretly as employees overseas, but the officers first had to "resign" from the CIA to take such private jobs and had no diplomatic immunity if they were arrested.

Forden "resigned" and went to work for a New York consulting firm that had reopened an office in Buenos Aires after the CIA agreed to subsidize its cost and the hiring of Forden as its single employee. He spent two years in Argentina, assisting in CIA operations. He and Sally also had their second child, a son named Daniel. But the work was slower paced than he expected, and in 1964, when asked if he would replace Bill Donnelly as Chief of Station Warsaw, Forden accepted.

Forden returned to Washington, where he was "rehired" by the CIA. Over the next ten months, he immersed himself in intensive Polish-language study at the Foreign Service Institute in the basement of a Rosslyn, Virginia, apartment building. There he met Ron Estes, an officer who was learning Czech before becoming Prague Station Chief.

In the spring of 1965, Forden and Estes began three weeks of training at CIA headquarters to prepare for assignment in a denied area. It was a propitious time in CIA history, with some creative officers developing new methods to communicate securely with agents.

Until that time, the preferred method of communicating in denied areas was through a "dead drop," typically a small place, such as a crevice in a stone wall, a crack behind a mailbox, or a spot on the ground where a message could be left. The "sticks and bricks" staff was adept at hollowing out stones or even fashioning a rock of epoxy, which could be weighted down and used to conceal a message. Such techniques carried great risks, as Forden and Estes learned. A package might be found by someone else or sit unattended for days. Dead drops were also one-way transactions—messages were left or received—and they involved a complicated series of signals that could place a source in jeopardy.

A CIA officer who was to "fill" or "load" a dead drop would, for example, make a chalk mark, raise a window shade, or move a flowerpot on a porch, to signal that a package would be left for an agent. Then, after the agent retrieved the package, he would leave an "unload" signal. These actions created a thread that tied the officer and the agent, and if at any stage the process was observed, the agent's cover could be blown.

A second method of communication was the clandestine mailing, in which CIA officers sent ordinary letters to agents under their actual name. Such letters contained innocuous text as well as additional writing in invisible ink. But there were closely held horror stories at the CIA about officers being observed as they mailed letters. In one case, a CIA officer serving under State Department cover in an Eastern bloc capital dropped a letter to an agent in a mailbox across the street from the Soviet Embassy. The letter was intercepted, and the agency's source was arrested and executed.

Another time, an officer in a denied area left the American Embassy and walked around for about an hour to be sure that he was not being followed. He then returned to the vicinity of the embassy. On his way back, he dropped a letter into a mailbox as he passed through a park near the embassy. Once again, the agent to whom the letter was addressed was arrested and executed. Later, after the CIA mapped the officer's route, it discovered that he had been free of surveillance until the last minute. Had he mailed the letter anywhere else, there would have been no problem. But the park near the embassy was a surveillance-gathering point, and he tripped the wire.

Learning from each tragic mistake, CIA officers preparing to serve in denied areas began to innovate. One major advance in tradecraft was the development of the "brush contact," which is credited largely to Haviland Smith, who served as the station chief in Prague from 1958 to 1960. Smith, who was about thirty, was followed constantly in Prague by the MV, the Czech secret police. Smith, who had played for the Dartmouth College ice hockey team in the era before face masks, had a goalie's power of concentration and began to study the surveillance like a science. He noted that MV agents who trailed him tended to conduct their surveillance in random patterns. He would be driving around Prague in his 1958 Chevy, clearly identifiable with his American diplomatic plates and feeling quite alone, and the MV would suddenly appear on his tail. Smith concluded that the MV used random patterns to keep him from anticipating their moves. His first instinct was to try to elude them as he drove through Prague, whose serpentine streets, unlike Warsaw's, had survived the war intact. But Smith soon discovered that the minute he lost the MV agents, they descended on him "like a house on fire." However counterintuitive it might seem, the lesson he took from this experience was that rather than try to elude opposition surveillance, officers should develop rigid patterns of activity—driving, walking, shopping—and become as predictable as possible. The goal was to lull the surveillance agents into a mistaken sense of security. "What you don't want to do," he explained to colleagues, "is establish random patterns, because random patterns have them on edge all the time."

Smith wanted the MV to believe that when he left the American Embassy at 10:30 P.M., to take his Czech babysitter to her home, he could be expected to go and return by the same route. After a few months, the tails of the MV agents became less frequent. Eventually, he found he could be as much as five minutes late on his return. If he ran later, though, the MV would be on him again the next time he went out. He began to build other patterns into his routine, such as getting a haircut on Thursday morning at ten o'clock once a month.

Smith also noticed that when he was in Prague, the MV often had four agents follow him—two behind him and two across the street. Smith began leaving the embassy at lunchtime to go shopping. He found that if he walked along a street and turned right, he created a gap in which the agents trailing him would lose sight of him for a few seconds, and those across the street for even longer. Smith promoted his concept within the CIA—do not elude surveillance; accept it as a way of life. One of his absolutes, he liked to say, was that "when you think you're probably not under surveillance, you are probably in more danger than at any other time."

Smith moved to Germany for the CIA in 1960. He found that when he entered East Berlin, he could not identify the surveillance as he could in Prague. He tried to create predictable patterns, but was unable to determine whether he was being trailed. Either the agents were too elusive, or they were not following him at all. But he still acted as if he were always being watched and operated "in the gaps." He found mailboxes that were located near street intersections, which could be approached after a right turn. When he had to make a clandestine mailing, he would go for a walk, string out potential surveillance behind him, and post his letter in the seconds in which he created a gap. "Almost everything I did in Berlin I tried to do in the gap," he said later. He also started a training program for officers being sent into denied areas, expounding on his theories about the gap and using Berlin as a training ground.

In early 1965, Forden and Estes were the first students in a denied-area training course that Smith helped set up near Washington. The doctrine was simple: Be natural. Don't be sneaky. Go everywhere. Be interested in everything. Shop, sightsee, and love castles, and take your family to the country on picnics. But be predictable. Before you know it, you will have a dozen different routes you can walk anytime you want without alarming opposing surveillance officers. Ideas flowed in from veteran officers who had served throughout Eastern Europe.

Smith had another inspiration. One of his students was a Czech intel-

ligence official who had volunteered to work for the United States and
was receiving tradecraft lessons in New York before he was sent back to
Prague. One evening at rush hour, they were at Grand Central Terminal
in midtown Manhattan. Smith was training the agent in the use of signals and dead drops, but it was clear that the agent was reluctant to leave
a package unattended for any length of time. "Anything I put down for
you is going to incriminate me, and anything you put down for me is
going to have stuff that will incriminate me," the agent said.

Smith replied, "Your concern is that it's sitting out there with
nobody in charge?" The agent nodded. Improvising, Smith escorted
the agent to a subway entrance near Grand Central, which also led
into the old Biltmore Hotel. A pedestrian could walk straight into the
hotel or turn right and descend a flight of steps into the subway. "Let's
try this," Smith said. He asked the agent to stand inside the crowded
doorway at the top of the stairs leading down to the subway, where he
could not be seen from the street. "I'll walk through the door, and
hand you a newspaper," Smith said. "When you get that newspaper,
turn around and go down the stairs, and I'll go straight into the hotel."

Smith then carried out the exercise: He made two successive right
turns, first at the corner and then into the subway entrance. In his
mind, he was losing one set of imaginary Czech security agents who
were conducting surveillance from across the street, and a second set
of trailing agents who were following as he turned into the hotel.
Smith had only a few seconds to hand off the newspaper to his agent
before the imaginary surveillance would catch up. The agent took the
newspaper and turned down the stairs, while Smith continued his
walk into the hotel. They repeated the exercise again and again and
had other CIA officers play the role of hostile surveillance agents. Each
time Smith and the agent made a "brush pass," as it was called, the
CIA officers watching them did not detect the hand-off. By the time
the role-playing surveillance agents caught up with Smith a few seconds later, it appeared he was merely continuing his walk into the Biltmore. When the exercise was complete, the Czech agent turned to
Smith and said, "That was terrific. I'll do that in Prague."

The escape route, which in this case was the stairway into the subway, was essential. Prague, built around sharp corners and full of gated courtyards, offered countless possibilities for successive right turns and escape routes.

Smith took the concept of the brush pass to his superiors and won their approval. Together with Bronson Tweedy, then chief of the East Europe Division, they went to see Richard Helms, then deputy director for plans. Smith and Tweedy asked for approval of the brush pass for the Czech agent when he returned to Prague, but Helms refused. The arrest and execution of Oleg Penkovsky was still on his mind, and he felt it was foolhardy to carry out personal exchanges inside the Soviet bloc. "He looked at me," Smith recalled, "and said, 'I have saddle-sores all over my ass from the Penkovsky case, and I'm not going to approve this kind of operation.'"

Smith continued to press to have the concept approved for Prague. In the spring of 1965, he organized a personal demonstration for Helms. Smith had refined the technique, even consulting with a magician for tips on the art of misdirection, engaging in one action to distract attention from another. The goal was to use an orthogonal approach—at right angles—so that an agent would not walk directly into the face of opposing surveillance. Smith also drew Estes and Forden into the conversations.

Helms sent his deputy, Thomas H. Karamessines, to the demonstration, which was held in the lobby of the Mayflower Hotel in Washington. Like the subway entrance in New York, the Mayflower was an ideal place to practice the brush pass. The CIA officer could walk along the sidewalk, turn right, enter the hotel's front door, and proceed into a lobby where there was a bank of telephones.

With Karamessines and Tweedy watching from a bench in the lobby, about ten feet from the telephones, Smith had Ron Estes, the officer being assigned to Prague, act as if he were an officer in a denied area. Smith played the role of an agent and stood by the phones, pretending to make a call. Estes entered through the hotel door, with his raincoat draped over his right arm, covering the small package he was holding in his hand. In the few seconds that it took to enter the lobby and approach Smith, Estes shifted the raincoat into his left hand, shaking it slightly, and letting it flop over his left arm. The idea was to divert attention to Estes's left, while he handed the package in his right hand to Smith. After receiving it, Smith disappeared into the hallway.

Karamessines turned to Tweedy and asked impatiently, "When are they going to do it, anyway?"

"Tom, they've already done it," Tweedy replied.

That day, the concept was approved for use in Prague, though deferred for Warsaw. The Polish capital had been destroyed in the war and rebuilt on a grid with broad open intersections. As a result, Warsaw lacked the twists and turns that an officer or agent would need to find the necessary angles and escape routes for a brush pass. For now, Forden would have to rely on more traditional methods like dead drops, car tosses, and clandestine mailings.

In June 1965, David Forden flew to Vienna to meet with Bill Donnelly, whom Forden would succeed as Warsaw Station Chief. Forden wanted to debrief Donnelly, who knew Poland thoroughly and who, like Hav Smith in Prague, had been experimenting with techniques to defeat surveillance.

Forden described in detail the brush-pass concept being developed for use in Prague. "You try that here," Donnelly warned, "and you'll be caught and PNG'd."*

They talked for several days as they strolled through parks. "I picked his brain from morning to night," Forden recalled. "About Poles. About surveillance. I had a million questions, and he had a million answers."

Forden knew there would be no margin for error in Poland; you had to think like a clandestine operator all the time, or sources would

---

* Declared persona non grata and expelled.

lose their lives, and officers would be always burdened with those losses.

Donnelly shared this view, driven by the belief that the greatest danger in his profession lay not in betrayal by a Soviet mole, as Angleton would have it, but by simple mistakes in tradecraft and a failure to maintain proper compartmentalization of information. After studying the classified histories, Donnelly had reached the conclusion—not universally shared in the CIA—that the Soviet Russia Division had not been prepared to handle agents in Moscow such as Penkovsky.

Donnelly was a quiet Ohioan who could discuss the intricacies of Polish politics as easily as he could miniaturization techniques for cameras. A Korean War veteran who had joined the CIA in 1954, he had risen in the agency through East bloc assignments, culminating in Warsaw from 1959 to 1965, including the past three years as chief. At that point in the agency's history, Donnelly had probably spent more time in Eastern Europe than any other CIA officer.

In his six years in Poland, Donnelly, like Hav Smith in Prague, experienced opposing surveillance for so long that he perversely came to enjoy manipulating it. On long drives through the countryside, he found that he could pull just far enough ahead of the SB so that when he turned a curve at fifty to sixty miles per hour or disappeared over a small hill, he was able to create ten- to twenty-second gaps during which he could throw a soda can or bottle out the window and into a ditch by the road. In such "car tosses," beepers might be placed inside the object along with a message, so that an agent with a small radio could find it easily.

In his conversations with Forden, Donnelly tried to convey his passion for Poland. From the day Donnelly arrived under cover as an agricultural attaché, he had tried to understand Poland, its people and its history. More than any other country under Communist control, he felt, Poland was rich in one asset the CIA should constantly try to exploit: the rage of its people toward the Soviet Union.

It was clear to Donnelly that Poles were passionate about two great institutions—the church and the army. Donnelly remembered how he would take drives outside Warsaw and see daughters of Communist officials receiving church weddings. In June and July, wedding parties would be lined up on the roads outside the rural churches.

Religion influenced even the most sophisticated and educated urban Poles. Once, Donnelly and his wife, Margery, were invited by one such Pole to visit a church near the edge of where the ghetto had once stood. When they arrived, Donnelly and his wife found the churchyard crowded with people, almost all of them kneeling. "Do you see it?" Donnelly's friend whispered, asserting that there was a halo around the top of the church's spire. To Donnelly, it seemed like a mass psychosis. But out of politeness, he and Margery also dropped to their knees.

Another time, as he and a colleague were driving a white Ford toward Poznan, several hours west of Warsaw, they could see two Mercedes cars following about a mile away. Donnelly and the other officer were certain that they were being followed by the SB. They turned quickly onto a side road and parked behind a barn. Moments later, the two cars screeched to a stop. From behind the barn, they could see SB officers leaping out of their cars and yelling at two peasants, "Which way did the white Ford go?"

One peasant replied, "What white Ford?"

The police shoved the man into a ditch, jumped into their cars, and sped off. As the peasant got up and dusted himself off, the CIA officers drove out from behind the barn, saluted the peasants, and drove in the opposite direction.

In August 1965, Forden arrived in Warsaw. He, Sally, and their two children moved into a small duplex on Zawrat Street, not far from the Vistula River. Forden worked as a second secretary in the embassy's political section, while Sally took care of the children and studied Polish. They went out frequently at night, attending diplomatic functions and other events.

As he expected, he came under frequent surveillance by the SB as he moved around Warsaw. At one point, he compared notes with Ron Estes, who had used the brush pass with great success in Prague. (By Estes's count, he "clicked off" thirty-two brush passes in seventeen months in Prague.)

Forden pondered the possibilities for Warsaw, where the CIA had used dead drops and clandestine mailings to communicate with agents. As Forden drove, walked, and biked around the city, he found only one area with street configurations similar to those of Prague. It was the Old Town, a small crowded section that was full of tourists and heavily patrolled by the SB and the police. That was the last place he would want to carry out a risky operational act. Elsewhere the city lacked the twists and turns necessary for a brush pass and an agent's quick escape. But Forden had an idea that might work: a car pass.

Forden had noticed as he drove around Warsaw that the SB tended to stay sufficiently behind him that if he made a right turn, there was a short gap before he saw the SB car make the same turn. Within that gap, he felt, there was enough time to make a quick handoff to a source through the car window. As a precaution, he would monitor the SB through his rearview mirror. If the trailing car was too close, he would continue driving, aborting the exchange while the agent disappeared into a courtyard or alley. Forden called the technique a "moving car delivery," or MCD. He found two sites in Warsaw that seemed suitable. His favorite, which he code-named Morze (sea in Polish) was down the hill from the Polish Sejm, or parliament, toward the Vistula River. The site had an escape route and was in an area that was virtually deserted at night. Forden submitted both sites to the agency in early 1967. But his MCD plan was rejected by headquarters as "too risky, dangerous, wouldn't work." Forden left detailed notes about the sites in the files of Warsaw Station, in the hope they might be used someday.

Forden completed his tour as Warsaw Station Chief that year and was reassigned to the Polish desk at Langley. One year later, he was named chief of the branch responsible for Poland, Czechoslovakia, and Hungary. In 1968 he and Sally had their third child, a daughter, Caty.

In August 1970, Forden was sent to Mexico City to run Soviet and East European operations there. His boss, Chief of Station John Horton, found him to be serious and organized. On his office wall, Forden hung the passport photographs of Soviet intelligence officers stationed in Mexico—his own rogues' gallery. On May 3, 1973, Forden got a message from Donnelly that he was needed for a temporary assignment in Europe.

In June, Forden flew to Washington for briefings on the Gull case. He was pleased to learn that Warsaw Station had dusted off his moving-car delivery proposal, which had finally been approved, and made its first exchange with Kuklinski at Morze, the site Forden had found near the Polish parliament. In reviewing the files, though, Forden concluded that Gull, in his dedication to his cause, was moving too fast and turning over too much information. Fatigue could cause mistakes.

Forden also had to select an alias for himself. He chose the name of his son: Daniel.

On June 22, 1973, Colonel Henry walked around the harbor area of Kiel, looking for Kuklinski, whose yacht was supposed to arrive that morning. Henry had arrived at 8:00 A.M., and he combed the area until about noon. He saw three other Polish vessels but not the *Legia*. At 12:10 P.M., he went to a prearranged meeting place a few blocks away and waited twenty minutes, but did not see Kuklinski. At 2:10 P.M., he returned, but again did not see the colonel. Finally, at 3:00 P.M., he saw the *Legia* moored by the harbor police station and soon was able to make eye contact with Kuklinski, who was still aboard. Kuklinski froze when he saw Henry. Then he gathered himself, disembarked, and strolled along a water-level catwalk below the pier, following Henry for forty or fifty yards, until he was out of sight of the yacht.

They talked for thirty seconds, barely able to hear each other over the din of a helicopter landing at the nearby police station. Speaking in Russian, Kuklinski told Henry that he was pleased their conversation was being drowned out by the helicopter's background music, and that he hoped to make their meeting that evening.

At 6:15 P.M., Henry went to the block where he had arranged to meet Kuklinski, but did not see him. Kuklinski did not appear two hours later or at 10:15 P.M., the third backup time. About half an hour later, Henry returned and saw Kuklinski having a party with some people on his boat. After an hour passed, it became clear that Kuklinski would not be able to get away, and Henry left for his apartment.

Kuklinski had seen Henry, but he decided not to risk leaving the boat that evening. There had been a series of unusual incidents, and he did not want to raise suspicions. The problems began when the *Legia*, trailed by the *Opal*, left Gdansk and sailed for two days to Swinoujscie, the westernmost town on the Polish coast. At the border, the passports of all the crew members were taken and not immediately returned. Six hours passed. Finally, crew member Stanislaw Radaj, an old friend of Kuklinski's who was acting as the counterintelligence officer for the trip, was summoned to a harbor office to talk by phone with Warsaw. Radaj disappeared for an hour. Kuklinski wondered why he, as commander of the voyage, had not been called. When Radaj returned, he told Kuklinski that the boat had been held up because of concerns about another crew member, a naval officer who was suspected of having contacts with foreigners. Feigning alarm, Kuklinski said that they should keep an eye on him. Radaj seemed reassured, and they were soon allowed to sail. But Kuklinski knew that if the boat was being closely monitored, it would be hard to carry out his clandestine activities.

At the docks in Kiel, Kuklinski and his crew were surprised to hear a German man call out Kuklinski's name. Kuklinski told his crew that he had no idea why someone was shouting his name; perhaps someone had seen it on the crew list, which had been sent ahead. The explanation seemed to satisfy his crew, but the incident left Kuklinski unsettled.

That night, Kuklinski had decided to have a party for the crew to celebrate their arrival in Kiel. As the crew drank through the night, Kuklinski listened carefully, hoping that loose tongues might reveal whether his crew was in any way suspicious of him. He learned nothing, however, and, dropped into bed, exhausted, at 3:00 A.M.

On Saturday, June 23, at about 8:00 A.M., Henry returned to the harbor area and waited on a bench about 200 yards from the *Legia*. Almost two hours later, he saw Kuklinski, who left the boat and met Henry at his car. Henry handed Kuklinski a hat and a pair of sunglasses.

At the safe-house apartment, Kuklinski apologized for missing the meeting the night before, describing the incidents on board and explaining that he had instigated the crew's drinking spree "to find out whether there are any suspicions." Kuklinski admitted that he was feeling very nervous.

Kuklinski said that their meetings had been "well conceived" and that his crew usually dispersed for several hours to shop. "I can break away from my colleagues most often in big department stores," Kuklinski said. After discussion about their communications in Poland, Kuklinski moved to more substantive areas.

He said he had flown the previous fall to a Soviet base in Kazakhstan north of Astrakhan to observe a missile-launching exercise. He had been struck by the contrast between the Soviet Union's high-tech weaponry and the poverty of its soldiers, who were crowded into squalid shacks with four to five men sharing a single straw bed. Kuklinski and his colleagues had been put up in a hotel that lacked toilet paper. The toilets were broken, and water leaked onto the floor. Rather than fix the toilets, the Soviets had placed concrete blocks on the floor so their guests could keep their shoes dry.

During the return flight, Kuklinski had spoken to General Jozef Urbanowicz, Poland's first deputy defense minister. "Urbanowicz left the other generals, came to me, offered me a glass of cognac," Kuklinski said. At one point, Kuklinski had made a comment about the abject conditions of the Soviet soldiers—"these people who are building communism," as he put it.

Urbanowicz said that he and the others had noticed it as well, commenting, "It pains us." But the Soviets had to pay large sums for weapons, he added, noting that Moscow apportioned 30 percent of its national revenues for the arms race.

"I realized that I had no idea," Kuklinski said.

Kuklinski and his colleagues had visited Volgograd and a museum commemorating the Battle of Stalingrad. They had stopped in Kiev, where they were received by the leadership of the Ukrainian Military District. Throughout the trip, the Soviets made the Poles feel welcome. Kuklinski said that Urbanowicz was greeted particularly warmly because he was considered a 'Soviet man.'"

But Kuklinski had been shocked by an incident in Kiev in which a military official, the air defense commander of the Kiev Military District, had made a racist toast. "He said, 'To the health of the whites. Let not those black bastards interfere with our problems,'" Kuklinski recalled. Urbanowicz had then joined in, saying, "'and also the yellow bastards.'"

Kuklinski believed the remarks were directed at the Arabs and Chinese. At the airport in Kiev, as the Poles were about to depart, the Kiev official lavishly kissed Urbanowicz and made more racist comments.

Before their meeting ended, Henry told Kuklinski that in two days, when they next met in Hamburg, he would meet an American fluent in Polish, whose rank was comparable to a two- or three-star general. Kuklinski seemed surprised at the introduction of a new person into the operation, although pleased that he would be able to speak in his own language. He asked whether Henry was leaving. Henry reassured him that he would "be good for a few more years."

They discussed Kuklinski's concerns about the future, his security, and his request for a suicide pill. Kuklinski said that he wanted to stay in Poland "for as long as I can continue my personal battle" against the

Soviets. But if caught, he would rather die the death of "a silent hero" and not confess any details to Polish authorities in return for a lesser punishment.

Henry said, "I think you are a very brave and dedicated man, and it is a great honor to be your friend."

Kuklinski checked his watch and asked to be dropped off at a shopping area near the *Legia*, so that he could make some purchases to justify his absence.

4

"STABBING BACK"

ON A QUIET SUNDAY MORNING, June 24, 1973, David Forden— "Daniel"—trim and well groomed and wearing wire-rimmed glasses and a summer suit, stood unobtrusively in the lobby of his Hamburg hotel. At 10:30, a car pulled up, and Colonel Henry got out. Although they had not previously met, Daniel knew from his briefings that Henry had been essential to the operation, and they shook hands enthusiastically.

They drove together to the popular Hansa Theater on Steindamm, where they hoped to make contact with Kuklinski. The *Legia* was moored for two days at Wedel, a marina west of the city. The plan was for Kuklinski to leave his boat, approach the theater, and make eye contact with Henry, who would lead him down into the U-Bahn, the subway system, and up again on the other side, to near a taxi stand. Henry reviewed the site with Daniel, who agreed that it offered an excellent route, including two vantage points for support officers to perform countersurveillance.

From the theater, they drove to a small apartment the CIA had rented as a safe house. In Daniel's experience, safe houses tended to be shabby and small—this room was spartanly furnished with a few chairs—but they had decided to sacrifice size and comfort for security. There would be no doorman or nosy porters. Daniel and Henry spent several minutes straightening and sweeping the room, then left separately.

The next day at noon, fifteen minutes before Kuklinski was to arrive, Daniel and Henry met at the theater. They blended easily into the midday crowd, and when Kuklinski did not appear, they returned again, at 2:15, 4:15, and 6:15, but did not see him. Daniel returned to his hotel, while Henry waited in a café. Shortly before 7:00 P.M., he spotted Kuklinski. Catching his eye, Henry led him along the agreed-upon route to the apartment, where Henry called Daniel and signaled that he should join them.

When Daniel arrived, he sensed that Kuklinski was expecting someone older. Daniel tried to put him at ease. "It's a great honor for me to meet you," he said in Polish, introducing himself. Unlike Henry and Lang, who had maintained the pretense of being military officers, Daniel said, "I'm from the CIA and I'm delighted to be here and working with you."

He explained that the U.S. Army lacked the authority or the ability to run such a clandestine operation overseas, and that the CIA was best equipped to handle the tradecraft, including the secure communications in Poland that would be necessary for their relationship to succeed. Offering belated congratulations for Kuklinski's forty-third birthday, Daniel noted that he was almost exactly the same age. "You and I are of the same generation," Daniel said. He said he had lived in Warsaw, knew the city well, and was determined to ensure that Kuklinski's already superb efforts would endure.

Daniel explained the route Kuklinski should use to return to the *Legia* and outlined their plans for meeting the next day. Daniel also asked for a list of car parts Kuklinski could plausibly have bought on the trip, in order to explain his disappearance from the crew. Henry would buy them. Then they went to work.

At one point, Kuklinski grabbed the microphone Daniel had placed on the table and spoke with great emotion and purposefulness. He thanked Daniel for his birthday wishes, which had meant a lot to him. On the General Staff, he said, birthdays were rarely celebrated; everyone was too busy. One day, a few years earlier, Kuklinski said, he had told a colleague that it was his fortieth birthday. "For me, it is a certain special moment—in the life of every man—40 years," Kuklinski recalled saying. "It seems that one is still young, but he is already 40!"

His friend joked cynically, "Don't fuck around. We've already had our drink. Get your ass out of here and back to work!"

Kuklinski laughed. It was typical of how people were treated on the General Staff, he said. "To a man from whom the last juices are sucked out." Any flicker of emotion or happiness was "extinguished." He added, "An individual counts nothing in our system."

Kuklinski said that he hoped the American people appreciated their freedom. "Since you have it every day, you will probably never be able to value it," he said. "Communist slogans are extremely deceiving and can turn everybody's head." He described their so-called utopia as "a feudal system simply adapted to contemporary times."

Kuklinski smoked heavily and sipped the fruit juice that Daniel had poured for each of them. "He can take his spirits clean as well as anyone, I'm sure, but I also feel that he sees no place for alcohol at these meetings, other than as a parting toast," Daniel wrote later.

At about 9:30 P.M., the men embraced, and after Kuklinski left, Daniel tidied up the apartment and returned to his hotel. The tape of the session was taken to Stan, the CIA translator, who had been flown in from Langley to make quick translations of the recordings of each session. Essential information was then cabled to headquarters in case there were immediate follow-up questions.

The next morning, Daniel returned to the safe-house apartment and was joined about thirty minutes later by Colonel Henry and Kuklinski. This time, Kuklinski said, he could stay for five hours, but they agreed to stop at 4:30 P.M. to allow him extra time to return to the boat. Henry set off to find an auto-repair store where he could buy an air filter for Kuklinski's Opel.

Kuklinski scanned a list of questions from the CIA and addressed each in detail, sometimes speaking to Daniel and other times talking into the recorder. Daniel marveled at Kuklinski's concentration and style and realized how effective he must be as a lecturer, a briefing officer, or a leader of troops. Kuklinski said he had recently been nominated to be a deputy chief in the operational training department.

The CIA had asked whether Soviet nuclear weapons existed in Poland. Kuklinski said he assumed they did. On an air force firing range in Czersk in northern Poland, on the boundary of the Soviet's biggest base near Borne-Sulinowo, there had been a presentation of nuclear warheads and of the Soviet troops who were trained to mount them on rockets. Kuklinski said he would try to learn more about the fenced-in compound, which was run by a Soviet general.

He stressed that Moscow's emphasis on an offensive military strategy not only was dangerous but also was crippling Poland's economy. The Polish armed forces chafed under Moscow's control. There was "constant friction" between the country's economic possibilities and program and those "as set forth by the war plans," Kuklinski said. There was also heavy pressure on Poland to upgrade its divisions, wartime weapons, and materiel reserves.

"Our equipment should match that of the Soviet Union," he said. "The aim is that we should have an immense war machine, conduct large and costly maneuvers, which we cannot afford."

Contrary to Moscow's claims that it treated Poland as its "best ally," the Poles were given outdated equipment, and all innovation was stifled. If the Poles improved a weapon, the Soviets would familiarize themselves with the documentation, and the same item would appear on the market as "Made in U.S.S.R." Whenever Polish and Soviet officials met in Moscow for consultations on the introduction of new weapons, the Poles found it almost impossible to get anything out of their Soviet counterparts. "They cover their files, half pull out a sheet, and read something that is surely doctored," Kuklinski said disdainfully. "I have heard directly from those who took part in such meetings." There was no free exchange of information.

He recalled that years earlier, in 1956 or 1957, he had visited a Soviet unit in Bialograd, a Polish town near the coast. The Soviet soldiers were living behind three rows of fences. "I almost offended a Soviet officer whom I asked, 'Were these fences left by the Germans, or put up by you?' He replied that the Soviets put them up. I then asked, 'Is it to prevent your own soldiers from going out without a pass, or is it against us, your hosts on this soil?'" It was all so bizarre, Kuklinski said, pausing occasionally to sip juice or draw on his cigarette.

After an hour or so, Kuklinski said he wanted to address the subject of war and peace and the contingency plans, which he said were "one-sided," only offensive.

"Defense is not at all included in these plans," he said. He and like-minded colleagues had pushed unsuccessfully for a new doctrine and war plan. "We have suggested that an alternate war plan should be developed—first, a defensive plan, and then an offensive plan." They had been told that they "do not know the situation, and should not butt in."

He said the Poles realized that Moscow held "the key to everything" in the Polish military. "Moscow can, at will, draw our armed forces into a conflict that might have nothing to do with our national interests." There was a split in the Polish military. The leadership did not see the West's intentions as benign, but many senior officers had more enlightened views, with many looking forward to a balanced reduction in the forces on both sides and to closer political and economic ties—"a rapprochement between East and West," Kuklinski said.

As for Poland's culture and economy, he went on, "We were always leaning westward. Of course, we have our own achievements, our own culture, but all this is much closer to the European, the West European culture."

He added: "Our present close relationship with the East is based on bloody experiences." But although the average Polish officer looked forward to the relaxation of tensions with the West, the regime had made it clear that its goal was not to exchange ideas and information, "only to attack the West, and accept nothing."

Later, Kuklinski grew solemn as he discussed his family. He

repeated the story he had told Hanka of meeting some Americans in Saigon and seeing them again in Europe.

"I did not tell her anything more, although I trust her infinitely, just as I trust myself. She does not know at all what I am doing." He would keep her ignorant of the true nature of his clandestine activity, so that she could not even accidentally reveal anything if she was interrogated by officials or even questioned by a friend.

Daniel asked, "Is your wife at home when you photograph?"

"She is not," Kuklinski said, citing her job as a factory bookkeeper. "She works just as I do. It is worse with the children because sometimes they are at home. This is why I turn loud music on, shut the inner door and tell them I have work to do."

Kuklinski described his darkroom and his renewed interest in the hobby. He developed all sorts of photographs "in order not to arouse suspicions. I am simply again interested in photography."

Once, when he came home to photograph at night, he explained to his family that he had urgent work to do and asked Hanka to sleep in one of the boys' rooms.

"She was nervous and urged me to get some rest," he recalled. "She asked why I played music. But then she gave up."

Kuklinski said he probably would not have even mentioned any relationship with the Americans, but had felt compelled to tell her something because of his moodiness after returning from the first European voyage. "I do not tell her any details, because she does not need it." Their sons would also remain unwitting.

As they talked, Henry burst in, laden with bags and boxes that included two air filters for Kuklinski's car and navigation maps of the North Sea and Helgoland Island, off the Danish peninsula. Henry gave receipts to Kuklinski and noted where each item had been bought. Kuklinski asked for reassurance that if he was arrested, the CIA would try to help his family. He did not believe that it would be possible for the family to leave Poland, but he asked that Daniel and his colleagues watch out for them. Kuklinski again said that in such a circumstance he hoped to be able to take a suicide pill, although the CIA had not yet acted on his earlier request for one.

Daniel asked whether Kuklinski had raised the issue because he felt more strain, and Kuklinski replied that although he had been afraid, he was reassured by the efficient and secure way the CIA had handled the exchanges and communications with him in Warsaw. "Of course, I'm careful not to let this more relaxed feeling lead me into mistakes," he said.

At about 4:30 P.M., Daniel brought the session to a close, telling Kuklinski that the Americans admired him for his personal and professional qualities and his convictions.

Kuklinski expressed concern that the quality of his documents had been less than promised, but Daniel said that was far from the case. They agreed to a final meeting on July 1 in Kiel. Five minutes later, Kuklinski, carrying his packages, left for the department store, where he would meet his crew and exchange stories about their shopping excursions.

On Sunday, July 1, the normally bustling Kiel Rathausplatz was almost empty. At 10:15 A.M., Daniel, Henry, and a third CIA officer stationed themselves around the square, but Kuklinski did not appear. Nor did he show up at the backup times, every two hours throughout the day. At about nine that evening, Daniel and the third officer joined the crowds strolling along the waterfront, watching boats and fireworks. Daniel could see the *Legia* docked in the harbor, and as they approached it, they saw Kuklinski through a window talking with a crewmate. Daniel returned again at 10:15 P.M., but Kuklinski had not left the boat.

Late the next morning, Daniel and his colleagues returned to the Rathausplatz, but did not see Kuklinski. The officers returned to the square at just after noon. From a distance, Daniel noticed a man crossing the square, but did not pay him much notice and paused outside the deserted Rathauskeller to examine the menu. Then it dawned on him that he had just seen Kuklinski. "I'm abashed to say," Daniel later cabled headquarters, "that I had seen Gull crossing the Rathausplatz at about 12:17 hours without actually recognizing him. He was just another nondescript figure moving along with a rather loping gait from my left to right front. He was wearing a khaki instead of a white shirt, and purposely did not come near me or even look at where I was sitting and scanning. While this doesn't say much for my powers of observation, it does, I think, underscore his ability to 'blend in' and to exercise discretion and alertness. He did not approach me until I was off center-stage!"

Daniel entered the hotel, with Kuklinski well behind him. It was only after both men were in the elevator, and the doors had closed, that they spoke. They proceeded to the hotel room, which was not air-conditioned. Both men were sweltering in the summer heat. Henry again left to shop for Kuklinski.

The CIA had questions about a particular secret Soviet military base. Kuklinski, who had visited the base, said it was in Ashuluk, which was located about 120 miles north of the city of Astrakhan on the Caspian Sea. The town was not marked on Soviet military maps and was used as a rocket range for Soviet air defense troops. Kuklinski said there were several battalions at the base equipped with various air defense systems, which were dug into a vast expanse of arid ground where only sparse vegetation grew. Soviet and Warsaw Pact troops trained there, as did troops from Syria and other Arab countries. The rocket firings occurred on Tuesdays and Fridays. Remote-controlled missiles were used as targets, and Kuklinski gave their range and speed.

In addition to the field battalions, Kuklinski said, there was an installation that included two hotels, with a third being built, the firing range command quarters, the officers mess, garages, quartermaster's warehouses, a boiler house, other buildings that housed serving crews, in all about forty buildings, about half of which were one-story wooden barracks. A dirt road, reinforced by a lane of cement slabs for vehicles up to fifteen tons, ran from the Ashuluk railway station to the range. Other heavy equipment used a parallel dirt road, about fifty meters south. There was a special airfield with a single runway, located six to seven kilometers from the range. "Only Soviet planes can land on this airfield," Kuklinski said. His plane from Poland had to land in Astrakhan.

Daniel was astonished by Kuklinski's command of detail. At about 1:25 P.M., there was a knock at the door. It was Carl Gebhardt, the Warsaw Station Chief who had first met Kuklinski in the cemetery the previous fall. "Both men greeted one another with the kind of enthusiasm that springs out of joint success at a delicate and dangerous game," Daniel later told headquarters.

Kuklinski and Gebhardt spent nearly three-quarters of an hour discussing potential operational sites for the future and reviewing sketches and maps. With Daniel, they discussed surveillance patterns by the SB, the manipulation of gaps, and how Kuklinski could recognize the CIA car as it arrived for an exchange. Kuklinski asked whether there were other officers watching their exchanges on the street. He was told there were not. Other than a partner or spouse inside the car, the officer was alone.

As the session ended, Kuklinski said he wanted to discuss his motivation for collaborating with the United States. "I consider the small contribution I make to the strengthening of your country, my duty.

"Your country does not represent strength only, but also serves as an example," he said, "and all the changes to the better in my country are generated by this example of yours, from your country and the entire West.

"I consider it the highest honor," he went on, "and my duty, to extend assistance in order to make your strength a formidable deterrent, which will ensure that the world will go in the direction in which it is now going. I consider myself a servant not of your country alone, because I work for the freedom of all, but since this freedom emanates mainly from your country, I have decided to join with you, and I shall continue as long as my strength lasts."

Daniel presented Kuklinski with a gold-plated German-made ballpoint pen. He said he hoped Kuklinski would think of him when using it to write to the Americans. Kuklinski promised to keep them informed of his plans for the following summer. Henry opened a bottle of Linie aquavit, the Norwegian liquor aged in oak casks and carried by boat twice across the equator (the change in temperature is said to provide its unique taste). He poured a glass for each of them, and they joined in a toast before Kuklinski left.

After the meeting, Gebhardt sent a brief cable to Langley saying that the meeting had been highly worthwhile:

> It provided an opportunity to establish a rapport that would never be possible during our brief encounters in Warsaw, and it seemed to erase any doubts Gull may have had about our abilities to deal with him securely, considering his personal welfare above all.
>
> It was an opportunity to explain subtleties that cannot come through in written exchanges, which normally cover the most important basics. And, though we didn't need a reminder, the meeting did serve to remind that we have a warm human being at the other end of our communications who is worth all the effort we expect to put forth.

For his part, Daniel prepared an extensive "Memorandum for the Record," reviewing the meetings and offering his impressions of the colonel. "He is a valiant, able, and dedicated man, who, in my view, does not consider himself a 'traitor' or the participant in some kind of 'dirty game.' He is 'stabbing back' at those who have made a shambles of his country, and he expresses deeply serious satisfaction in the fact that he can do this by cooperating with us."

Kuklinski seemed determined "to make this not only a secure and productive assault on the enemy, but a personal and *human* undertaking with us," Daniel wrote. For all of his military training and achievement, Kuklinski was "not a robot," he added. "He said sadly that he would like to get to know us better, to associate with us as human beings."

Kuklinski had exhibited a quiet sense of humor as well as consideration for Daniel and Henry, expressing concern that they had to wait for him to appear on the street. He had shown modest pride in describing how he had gained access to a particular classified report that was outside his normal assignments, and he appreciated Daniel's concern that the trail might lead to him, by pointing out that the document had come to him and that he had not asked for it. Kuklinski showed "a deep respect for his wife and for her unquestioned loyalty to him; a recognition that one can seldom read the thoughts of others—his crew might be talking about him—but establishing a solid reason for his absences is more intelligent than fretting over their possible suspicions and so on.

"Throughout all of this, he was articulate, enthusiastic, even excited—in a controlled way—at times," Daniel wrote.

Daniel described Kuklinski as compact, perhaps five feet, six inches and 145 pounds, with piercing eyes and a good complexion. He looked healthy and strong, his face clean-shaven, his fingernails clean, and his dress simple. "He has no phony or artificial mannerisms that I could detect. In short, he impressed me as an able and likable human being. I think we should do all in our power to help him realize that we see him in this light, not just as an efficient and daring provider of highly prized intelligence."

Daniel also recommended that future meetings with Kuklinski include Colonel Henry. "Briefly, he impressed me—and more important—I think he has impressed Gull with his calm, unruffled, modest, strong character.... It would be an error to count him out of this case."

After returning to Washington, Daniel drafted a three-page letter to Kuklinski, which would be translated and delivered in a forthcoming exchange. Daniel said he was profoundly moved by their meetings and hoped Kuklinski would feel free to express himself openly in personal correspondence between them.

For now, I hope you understand what a deeply rewarding personal experience it was for me to meet and begin to know you. I, too, can only regret that the circumstances of our relationship prevent us from spending relaxed hours and days together, talking of many things, our families, our hopes, our future. I wanted to tell you about this at our last meeting, but the clock was running fast, and so were we—with the sweat dripping off our brows. You are such a responsible, considerate, and articulate person that I knew it would be difficult for us to stop once we began talking about the things that have shaped us as human beings, and that make our lives worth living.

I received a letter from my wife—in a secure way—while you and I were in the same city. She wrote of many things that she and our children were doing, all of which have a special meaning to a father who values the present in its own right and as a path to the future for himself and the ones he loves. She wrote of our youngest daughter, five years old, who was conceived in your country and born in mine. We think she represents—or is—the best of both places. She is a happy and an intelligent child with many activities which, of course, are very important to her. She has been particularly busy in the past few weeks, but, my wife wrote, the little girl would stop every now and then, look up into the air where my airplane had disappeared many days ago, and say, "Oh, Papa, I miss you. Oh, Papa, I love you; I hope you will come home soon!"

A man "cannot be made of wood," or he ceases to be human. Even as we work with the plans or the programs or the schedules or the machines that are a part of our everyday life and profession, there must be a strong and vibrant current of humanity in each one of us, and there must be time to feel and savor, to express this current. You did this for me in many ways during our time together, in talking about the significance of a birthday, about the deep respect and loyalty which you share with your wife, about the friends who mean something to you, yet who cannot share what is probably the most significant decision of your life.

I would like to share all this with you in any way possible. Our time together was all too brief, but the experience we've shared so far causes me to say again, as you have said, that I hope we can come to know one another better, as human beings. It was with this thought already in mind that I gave you the gold pen at the end of our last meeting. I would be very happy if you would use it from time to time, at the quiet end of a long day, to write me about yourself, your youth, your parents—anything you wish to share with me.

Other parts of this message bring you again the evidence of our highest respect for you and the work that you are doing so superbly. Here, I simply want to repeat my deep personal satisfaction for knowing you, and for sharing with you the human thoughts and goals that give meaning to our lives. These thoughts, with you as their central focus, are constantly on my mind.

Daniel added a P.S.: "Please destroy this letter in the usual manner."

On September 20, 1973, Kuklinski was promoted to deputy chief of the operational training section of the General Staff. The job was created for him by General Jerzy Skalski, deputy chief of the General Staff, who was increasingly relying on Kuklinski for consultation and assignments. The new post would give Kuklinski more access to the leadership of the Polish and Soviet armed forces.

In an exchange on November 6, Kuklinski passed a letter to the CIA describing his new job, offering "hearty greetings" to Daniel, and thanking the CIA for its efforts to assure his and his family's security. He said he would also soon send along photographs and biographical data for his wife and sons, which the CIA needed to prepare false passports and other travel documents for the family. As the CIA car drove by for the exchange, Kuklinski handed over three roses along with his package.

But Kuklinski soon had renewed concerns about his security. One day, while visiting northwest Poland for a top-secret military exercise, he misplaced a document that contained the briefing program. His anxiety was compounded when he and others in attendance were told that a French diplomat had been detained nearby as he was taking photographs of the exercise. Over the next few months, the Polish counterintelligence officers conducted an extensive investigation at the General Staff into how the diplomat had learned of the exercise. A list was drawn up of all officers who had had access to the date and location of the event, and each person was questioned. "Somebody is transmitting here, but his days are numbered," one investigator had declared. Kuklinski had no idea how the French diplomat had learned of the exercise or why he had been in the area, and he wondered whether his missing document had somehow made its way into the diplomat's hands. Kuklinski barely slept for days.

Meanwhile, General Skalski was again trying to promote him, to be chief specialist for operations. And Jaruzelski had approved his nomination to attend the Voroshilov Academy in Moscow, an elite school where the Soviet Union trained the members of its General Staff. For a Warsaw Pact officer, a stint at the academy was an honor and was seen as a prerequisite for serving in military leadership positions. In early December, Kuklinski was appointed chief author of a major military exercise called "Summer 1974," which would be managed by Jaruzelski. The exercise, scheduled for early June, was to test the functioning of wartime field communications, and it would include senior officials of the Warsaw Pact Supreme Command in Moscow and air forces of the northern group of the Soviet Army. In writing up the exercise, Kuklinski would work closely with Russian officers in Legnica, where Soviet troops were based in Poland.

On another front, Kuklinski was invited to join a group of officers who were building townhouses on Rajcow Street, a quiet block on a slight hill in the Old Town, overlooking the Vistula River. They had formed a cooperative to complete the project, assisted by loans from the Defense Ministry. All members of the cooperative were to receive financial assistance equal to the value of their current apartments, plus long-term loans at little or no interest from the government. Kuklinski's current apartment was cramped, and he remained concerned that the Russian who lived above him would hear the sounds of his camera as he photographed documents. He needed more space and privacy. There were some risks, as his neighbors would include a deputy chief of army counterintelligence. In any case, the project would take several years to complete.

On December 31, 1973, Kuklinski invited his longtime friend Roman Barszcz and his wife, Barbara, to spend New Year's Eve with him, Hanka, and Waldek, their elder son. Their other son, eighteen-year-old Bogdan, who had joined him on the first voyage to Europe in the summer of 1972, was in the country with his girlfriend, Grazyna, whom he had been dating for about a year. Her father was General Wladyslaw Hermaszewski, a military colleague of Kuklinski's and a member of the cooperative of officers building homes on Rajcow Street. After their guests had left and his family was asleep, Kuklinski wrote a letter to the CIA, for delivery on January 2, 1974.

Dear Friends,

Today's meeting (if it goes smoothly) will start another year of our effective collaboration. This fact is highly satisfactory to me. To all with whose activities I am allowed to include my modest forces against militant communism, its utopian philosophy and aggressive practices, I express great esteem and thanks.

On the occasion of the new 1974 year I express my best wishes for all happiness to all those with whom I had the honor to get personally acquainted or met in those short contacts. At the same time I express my hope that the coming year will be good for the American nation and that the ideas which this nation has will have a beneficial influence on the formation of the world's face, including progressive and freedom-oriented changes in my own fatherland.

Kuklinski recounted his recent concerns, including the story of the lost document, the French diplomat's arrest, and the counterintelligence investigation in the General Staff. "Work conditions are very tense. I constantly live on my nerves," he said. He described being assigned to prepare the Summer 1974 exercise and how he would work closely with Soviet officers, "which I shall exploit for the purpose of obtaining information on the strength of their forces in Poland," he added.

Kuklinski asked for the CIA's advice on whether to attend the Voroshilov Academy, which would keep him on track for future promotions but would take him out of the General Staff, beginning in the fall.

"Please mark with a white chalk a slanted line on the electric box on Krzywickiego Street," Kuklinski wrote. "I shall await this sign between the 20th and 30th of January. If there is no such sign, I will start efforts to remove my name from the list of candidates for study."

Kuklinski said that another yacht trip was planned for the following summer, with possible stops in Denmark and West Germany. "According to initial plans, it is supposed to be a trip with families," he said, and Hanka would join him. Kuklinski concluded with a clarification about his request for a cyanide pill.

"In one of the initial messages I took up a rather unpleasant but difficult problem to avoid: of how, under conditions which would allow no way out and after careful consideration, to end my life." If he was arrested for espionage, he would be executed. "I would have no chances whatsoever," he wrote. But he did not want the Americans to misinterpret his dwelling on the issue as a sign of depression.

"This is not any obsession," he wrote. "I love life, and without [the most extreme reason] and utmost purpose, I would never part with it. I also believe that I will be saved by the almighty from such a final solution." He signed the letter with his pseudonym, Jack Strong.

He began a second letter. For some time, Kuklinski had wanted to reply to the letter Daniel had sent after their meetings in Europe, and he wrote that Daniel's words had brought him great joy. "I regret that it is only now that I can take up some of its threads," he said. He described the holiday with the Barszczes and Bogdan's desire to marry Grazyna, which Kuklinski said he supported "from the bottom of my heart."

Clocks and bells in a nearby church announced midnight and the beginning of the new 1974 year. In this beautiful elation, reciprocal cordiality and endearments, I thought about you, your great country, and the cause which I want to serve with all my strength. My thoughts were running fast. I made a quick summing-up. Yes, it is already a year when in a dark cemetery alley I spotted the expected car. A friendly "good evening" greeting. A year! It certainly is not a long period of time but long enough to take a breath and gain greater self-confidence. While toasting success, I already had a more realistic basis to see it.

In spite of dark clouds, which are not lacking, I endeavor to look at the world with my head raised high. I am happy about each success, even though some of them might not be that important. Great joys grow from small ones. Tomorrow I go to a sanatorium for a rest. There will be a possibility to do some interesting reading for which there is never time. I am looking forward to our eventual summer meeting. Perhaps fate will prove more generous, will spare us some sweat and make our thoughts more efficient. Accept a hearty handshake.

Kuklinski changed his signature when writing to Daniel. He signed the letter P.V.

At CIA headquarters, David Blee, who had helped end the agency's paralysis in the recruitment of Soviet spies as chief of the Soviet Division, was succeeded by John Horton, who had been Station Chief in Mexico City. Daniel also returned to headquarters and was soon placed in charge of clandestine operations inside the Soviet Union and East bloc. In that capacity, Daniel would be directly overseeing the Gull operation.

Daniel and his staff were delighted to hear that Kuklinski had been chosen for the academy in Moscow. It would also allow Kuklinski to slow down, a kind of "operational sabbatical," Daniel and his staff said in a cable to Warsaw Station. Because Kuklinski would be away from Warsaw for some time, he would need instructions on how to dispose of compromising materials, such as his camera and film, and how to resume contact with the CIA when he returned on holidays. Warsaw

Station was told to leave a signal for Kuklinski indicating approval of the Moscow trip by making a chalk mark on the electrical box.

Kuklinski's recent security concerns had convinced Daniel and his staff that they needed firmer contingency plans for exfiltration. The issue of the suicide pill was finally resolved after continued internal debate. Warsaw Station opposed providing Kuklinski with a pill, but Daniel disagreed, and in a cable to the field, the Soviet Division wrote:

> Gull has repeatedly come through as an exceptionally well-disciplined individual of strong military character. We definitely do not view him as considering terminal measures because he doesn't believe or understand that we can help....
>
> We see in his talk of possible self-termination the expression of a military man with a deep sense of honor who wants to guard against the possibility that he might be seized without warning and forced physically or psychologically to act in a way that would destroy his sense of self-respect and honor.

The CIA ultimately gave Kuklinski the pill, placing it inside a one-and-a-half-inch capsule that was hidden in a fountain pen.

In Warsaw, Kuklinski was working with a group of Soviet officers one day on a military exercise when he looked up and was astonished to see a man approaching him with the build, hair, face, and complexion—even the glasses—of Colonel Henry. Kuklinski got up and almost embraced the man before he realized this "twin" was a Soviet officer. Kuklinski walked straight by the officer, stealing a final glance as he realized his mistake.

Eager to learn the CIA's recommendation on whether he should accept the Moscow assignment, Kuklinski drove by the electrical box on Krzywickiego Street in late January looking for the CIA's chalk mark. He did not see it and assumed this meant he should not go to Moscow. (The CIA later concluded that the mark had been washed away by rain or cleaned off.)

Soon afterward, Kuklinski was relieved to learn that the mystery of the missing document had been solved. A colonel had borrowed it and forgotten to return it.

In a message to the agency in early March, Kuklinski told the CIA that he had removed his name from the list for the Voroshilov Academy. He noted that his decision "coincided" with General Skalski's view; Skalski was happy to have Kuklinski remain in Warsaw. Kuklinski expressed pleasure at the "unchanged character of our relationship," which he described as "warm, and marked with genuine personal concern." He also expressed satisfaction at the "flexible" and "very carefully considered instructions" by which he was to carry out communications and exchanges. He said the clandestine operation was "above all, a source of faith in the meaning of existence, and the purposefulness of my activities."

In an exchange with the CIA in early March 1974, Kuklinski received a letter thanking him for his latest package and letters. As for the mix-up concerning Voroshilov Academy, the agency said the result was probably for the best: "Although attendance at the academy is probably a good thing for your military career development, perhaps you can be considered for it again sometime in the future. In the meantime, as you point out, your access to information of great value to our mutual endeavors will certainly be enhanced in your new assignment."

At eight o'clock one rainy morning in early May, Kuklinski arrived at work and was called to see General Florian Siwicki, chief of the General Staff. Siwicki said that he was about to brief high level officials in the Polish leadership on "Project Albatross," one of the Warsaw Pact's most sensitive undertakings. Albatross involved the construction of three underground bunkers that would exclusively hold Soviet officers for command and control of Warsaw Pact troops in wartime. One such bunker was being built in southwestern Poland as a Soviet command post for the western theater of military operations in Europe. A second was being built in Bulgaria for the southwest theater of military operations. A third, near Moscow, would be for strategic command and control of the war. The locations and depth of the bunkers and the specifications of their walls, ceilings, and shock absorbers were closely held secrets. If the West was able to target these installations in wartime, Warsaw Pact military operations could be paralyzed. The project was so secret that when General Viktor Kulikov, chief of the Soviet military General Staff, went to inspect the bunker being built in Poland, he flew to a nearby base and changed into civilian dress before driving to the site.

Siwicki said he was dissatisfied with a paper he had received from another officer who had worked on the bunker project in Poland, and he asked Kuklinski to redo the report.

Kuklinski had been aware of the project, but the technical details were new to him. He called in the officer who had been working on the assignment. The officer, clearly upset as he handed Kuklinski a slim folder of papers, said that because of the sensitivity of the project, he would have to remain in the office while Kuklinski worked. Kuklinski, certain that the CIA would want the documents, said he would need some privacy. Finally, the officer agreed to stand outside, and Kuklinski closed the door but did not lock it, knowing that would raise suspicions. He placed the document on his desk, planted his elbows, and began using the tiny Tubka to snap pictures. He had almost finished when the door suddenly swung open.

Kuklinski looked up, and in the instant he made eye contact with the officer, he curled his right hand into a fist to conceal the camera. He then put his hand into his pocket and exchanged the camera for a lighter. In the same instant, he put his left hand into his other pocket, took out a cigarette, and kept both arms moving naturally as he lit it. "Look," Kuklinski said to the officer, "it's really difficult. I don't know if I can do anything with this."

Smoking the cigarette, he began pacing the room and expressing frustration at his inability to prepare the memo. Then he returned to his desk and studied the materials again. For fifteen awkward minutes, the officer stood by him. Finally he turned and left, saying he would wait in an adjacent office.

Kuklinski rubbed his face anxiously as he contemplated what to do next. There was no escaping the fact that he had been interrupted photographing classified materials. His shirt was matted to his back with sweat. He stowed the Tubka behind a radiator and walked to the next office where the officer was sitting. Kuklinski wanted to gauge his reaction. If the man looked away, it could mean he suspected him and was intending to report him. As Kuklinski entered, the officer looked up. Kuklinski told the officer he was prepared to tell Siwicki he was unable to produce the memorandum on Albatross, and he asked if the officer wanted to assist him in the report. The man shook his head and left.

Kuklinski returned to his office and peered out the window. A heavy rain was still falling. He saw the officer hurry across the court-yard and through a door into a gatehouse that was near a counterintel-ligence office. At that moment, Kuklinski considered taking his life: He had his pistol and his pill. But he tried to suppress his panic. There was also a barbershop behind the gatehouse door. Improbably, it seemed to come down to that: The officer was either reporting Kuk-linski or getting a haircut.

Shaking and sweating profusely, Kuklinski retrieved the Tubka and left his office. Fearing his office would be searched, he hid the camera behind a radiator in the stairwell on the top floor of the General Staff. Then he left the building and walked into the front courtyard. He stood there, letting the rain soak through his jacket and his clothes, and felt the tension leave his body. He returned to his office, wiped the water from his face, and tried to shake out his dripping clothes. Then he got to work on the report for Siwicki. At about 2:00 P.M., he was interrupted by a call from Siwicki.

"Is it ready?" the general asked.

"Almost," Kuklinski said. Soon after, he delivered the report to Siwicki's office, and a bit later, Siwicki stopped by to thank him.

"Why are you so wet?" Siwicki asked.

Kuklinski said he had gone outside to take a break from the assign-ment. "It was so hard, General," he complained. Both men laughed.

In a letter to the CIA later that spring, Kuklinski described the incident and said it had led him to question whether using a camera to photograph documents at work was too risky. But because some documents were available to him at the General Staff only for brief periods, he came up with an alternative idea of using a nearby conference room, which was normally kept locked.

Kuklinski also wrote that he and his crew were scheduled to leave for their next "surveillance" voyage through Europe on June 29.

On July 4, 1974, the *Legia* arrived in Copenhagen, and in the evening, Kuklinski and Hanka, who was one of several spouses on the trip, strolled from the harbor toward the main railroad station. It was unusually chilly for a summer night. Kuklinski said he was going to meet some old friends, and Hanka decided to go see a movie. But they arrived at the theater between showings, and patrons were not being admitted. Hanka agreed to wait at a nearby pub, and Kuklinski left alone for the railroad station. Daniel and Henry were waiting near a clock by Tracks 5/6 and 7/8.

Once the trio had arrived in a nearby apartment, Kuklinski described the near-catastrophe that spring as he was photographing documents in his office and his momentary consideration of suicide. He felt confident now that he was not under suspicion. He described Siwicki's reassuring comments and said General Skalski, Siwicki's deputy, continued to praise his work. In one recent exercise, Kuklinski's superiors made a big show of a presentation and a briefing paper that Kuklinski had prepared to party chief Edward Gierek and other "big fish," as Kuklinski put it, and he was introduced to them. Even the Defense Ministry's chief of counterintelligence shook his hand and offered compliments.

Daniel and Henry raised the matter of exfiltration—how the CIA would move Kuklinski out of Poland if he felt he was about to be arrested. Kuklinski reiterated that he had no desire to leave Poland. Daniel said he nevertheless should send the CIA photographs and biographical information for each of his family members so that false travel documents could be prepared for them.

After the ninety-minute session, Henry left first, leading Kuklinski back to where Hanka was waiting. As Henry approached the pub, he saw Hanka, in slacks and a knee-length cream-colored coat, shivering in the cold and pacing on the sidewalk. Henry could tell she was upset. It turned out that the pub did not serve coffee, and Hanka, who did not drink, had decided not to stay. As she had waited for her husband outside, several men had accosted her, mistaking her for a streetwalker.

The next day, July 5, Kuklinski met again with the Americans. Kuklinski had presents from Warsaw for both men, and the Americans gave him a pin for Hanka. Daniel later cabled to Langley that the sessions marked the "strongest personal and professional rapport yet with this remarkable man." On July 6 they met again for an hour and a half. As they finished, they embraced each other. Henry took out the bottle of aquavit and offered a toast.

After the July 1974 meetings in Europe, the CIA prepared a package for delivery to Kuklinski in Warsaw. Under "general requirements," the CIA noted that Soviet military plans and capabilities "continue to be of primary concern." A list of "general categories of interest" was included to help Kuklinski decide which documents to photograph. Among them:

1. Soviet instructions, orders, and directives (including exercise critiques) to Polish or Warsaw Pact forces.
2. Information and documents on new Soviet weapons systems....
3. Warsaw Pact War Plans. We prefer Soviet versions of these: Next we prefer any Polish documents concerning war plans (Secret or Top Secret) in Series "K" or "Of Special Importance."

The CIA's note was typically exhaustive: It sought the locations, staffing levels, and combat readiness data for Soviet air, naval, and missile units; the locations, descriptions, and control of Soviet nuclear warhead depots in the Polish towns of Borne-Sulinowo, Bialystok, and

Sulecin. The CIA also wanted "military budget data and specific cost figures for weapons systems;" details of Soviet activities and doctrine concerning chemical warfare, including information on research, production, testing, warhead fill, and storage; and classified articles from Soviet military journals.

"We would appreciate any information," the CIA added, on "Soviet or Pact negotiating positions for mutual balanced force reductions in Europe," a reference to the Vienna arms talks.

The CIA also had questions about Soviet weapons systems, for which the Pentagon wanted to develop countermeasures. One detailed question concerned the Strela, a Soviet surface-to-air missile that was not yet in American hands.

Daniel wrote separately to "P.V":

> I trust that the voyage home was a good one with clear sailing and that all continues well with you and your family. Your wife and son will soon celebrate their birthdays; although I do not know them personally, as I know you, I will be thinking of them on those occasions and wishing all the best for them now and for many years to come. Perhaps one day, God willing, we and our families can all know each other.

Daniel said that after returning to the United States, he had consulted with colleagues about ways to improve Kuklinski's "personal security."

He acknowledged the danger. "You realize, I am sure, that we were deeply concerned about the incident in your office," Daniel wrote. He explained that the agency had included in the package for Kuklinski several new concealment devices for the Tubka camera. Daniel said he wanted Kuklinski's opinion of the devices and "any suggestions you may have for their improvement." He moved to the issue of Kuklinski's security, "which will always be the most important consideration for all of us."

I understand and agree with your sentiments never to leave your native land; and I am sure that travel from there should never be necessary if we all continue to act with caution and follow good practices in our methods of communication. At the same time, both you and we recognize that unforeseen accidents, such as the incident in your office, can occur.

We have pledged to assist you and the members of your family in any adversity, to the very best of our ability, and we would like to be in a position to honor that promise. I ask then that you provide the details necessary to prepare travel documents for you and your family which can be held ready if they are ever needed. Hopefully you have included the photos and personal data in the package we will receive from you in September.

Daniel added that there had not been enough time in Copenhagen for him to offer "a complete assessment of the work which you have done since we began our association."

Eagle* has asked me to relay to you, along with his warmest regards, the following brief comments made recently at the highest decision-making level of our government.

1. [Soviet] General Staff lectures, especially Glebov's, are invaluable. They give the best view we have of Soviet tactical doctrine.
2. Of the latest documents received, the most valuable are the Southwestern [Theater of Military Operations]† exercise critique and electronic warfare manual. The manual is the best ever received by the government on this subject. The exercise critique was particularly valuable in planning for contingency of Soviet military actions in the Mediterranean.
3. The bulletins on NATO and Western Order of Battle are precisely

---

* Kuklinski had been told that Eagle was CIA Director Richard Helms.
† The Southwestern Theater of Operations included Greece, Turkey, Bulgaria, Hungary, Romania, and the southwestern part of the Soviet Union.

what the Secretary of State needed for preparing negotiations for
the Vienna talks.

Daniel added that Soviet journal articles on military exercises, tactics, doctrine, electronic warfare, and air defenses were all "especially
good."

I know you can be justifiably proud of the work you have done and
continue to do ... We and our associates [in Warsaw] look forward to
working with you in the future, just as we have in the past. Until we
meet again, I wish all the best for you and your family.
     Daniel

Early September 1974 was a time of political turmoil in Washington:
President Richard M. Nixon had resigned, and President Gerald R.
Ford would soon pardon him. Protesters were marching against the
war in Vietnam. Kuklinski followed the news in the Polish press, and
he was concerned that antiwar sentiment in the United States could
lead to the withdrawal of American troops from Europe.

By September 3, the day of the next CIA exchange, he had filled five
more rolls of film, which included the contents of two thick manuals
issued by the Soviet Defense Ministry on Soviet air force and navy
operations. He inserted photographs of Hanka and his sons and information about the dates and locations of their birth for the CIA to use
in producing false documentation. Kuklinski also sent the results of
his annual physical, which the agency's doctors wanted to review.

Kuklinski also said he had been pondering something the Americans had told him in the summer meetings. If the CIA did not have
backup officers on the street during exchanges, shouldn't he carry his
gun? He realized that he would be on his own, he wrote. His job
allowed him to have a sidearm. If he found himself in peril during a
moving-car delivery, should he use the gun to escape or to make his
way to the American Embassy?

He wrapped the letter with his rolls of film and headed for the exchange site. The location—a spot on the north side of Ladyslawa Street, near its intersection with Krzywickiego Street—had been chosen because it had good escape routes. It was a neighborhood where hundreds of military families lived in two-and three-story apartment buildings that were built around gated courtyards, which were accessible from the street.

As he looked up the street, Kuklinski saw a car turn onto Ladyslawa, adjust its beams, and reduce its speed. It was a Mustang, a model that Kuklinski knew Warsaw Station used. He stepped forward and made a quick exchange through the passenger window.

The Mustang accelerated and continued down the block. But before Kuklinski could step backward, he was caught in the headlights of another car, a cream-colored Fiat 125, which had quickly turned the corner and was tailing the Mustang. Two men in the front were leaning forward, as if they were trying to identify him. Kuklinski retreated, but the Fiat seemed to be heading right at him.

Terrified, he entered the gate to the courtyard and walked briskly down an alley to the next street, Langiewicza, which ran parallel to Ladyslawa. The driver of the Fiat appeared to have anticipated his move. The car, its high beams on, had also made two turns and was again heading in his direction.

Kuklinski almost ran to the next block, Sedziowska Street, but saw the Fiat again. He turned another corner and picked up his pace, finally believing he had escaped the pursuing car. But at the intersection of Koszykowa and Niepodleglosci Streets, the two men bore down on him again. Kuklinski did not believe they had seen his face, but he felt certain he had been caught in SB surveillance. He ran down Koszykowa Street, then disappeared up alleys and into buildings, zigzagging block by block: Wilcza, Poznanska, Hoza, Marszalkowska.

He entered a pedestrian tunnel that led into Warsaw's sprawling central railroad station near the huge Palace of Culture, Stalin's oppressive gift to Warsaw, and mingled in the crowd around the ticket booth. One man seemed to be looking at him with interest. Ignoring him, Kuklinski approached the ticket window. Suburban trains ran every few minutes. He bought a ticket to Rembertow and walked to the platform. He waited as several trains passed through the station. The train for Otwock arrived. Kuklinski watched as the cars filled with passengers; then he stepped into one just as the doors began to close. As he did, he saw two men, dressed in civilian clothes, enter the next car. Kuklinski turned in the opposite direction and began to walk from one car to the next. At the first stop, Powisle Station, Kuklinski paused as passengers disembarked, and as the train began to inch forward again, he opened the door with an emergency handle and leaped out. This time, he saw no one behind him.

He hurried down several streets until he saw a bus stop in front of him. He boarded a bus, rode for a while, and got off at the Chelmska stop. Kuklinski found a pay phone and woke up Hanka at home. He said he was stuck at a vodka reception, which was running late, and he might not be home until early in the morning. He then asked for Bogdan. When his son got on the phone, Kuklinski slurred his speech slightly, saying he was too drunk to drive. He told Bogdan where he had left the car and asked him to take the bus there, retrieve the car, and return it to their garage. Kuklinski said he would find a ride home.

Kuklinski boarded a bus at Chelmska and got off at a large square called Plac Unii Lubelskiej. There, he caught a taxi to Nowe Miasto Market, near where his new home was being built.

It was close to midnight, and Kuklinski was exhausted. He was still carrying his briefcase with the package from the CIA. He replayed the incident again and again in his mind: Had the SB men seen his face? Did they know whom they were chasing, or had they just seen a man acting suspiciously in a military neighborhood?

He walked to Rajcow Street, where his new home was being built. Picking his way through the dirt and debris, he found some tarpaper, which he wrapped around the box he had received in the exchange. He buried the package on his property, near the foundation of his home construction. Then he left, walking for a few blocks until he could hail another taxi to his apartment.

At home, he slipped in quietly, changed his clothes, and left again, driving several miles to a bridge that crossed the Vistula River. Halfway across, he dropped his empty briefcase over the side and heard it hit the water. It was the last thing he had been carrying that could connect him to the incident.

Kuklinski tried to analyze his situation objectively. If he had been observed, he probably had not been identified. At most, the secret police had an incomplete picture of him, his movements, and his outward appearance.

It was still dark, and Kuklinski decided to drive to Warsaw's other major railroad depot, the Main Station, where there was an all-night barbershop. The barber did not know him. Kuklinski wore his hair slightly longer than his colleagues and had been teased recently by one of his superiors, who said he was spending too much money on his new house and not enough on his hair. "Make it short," Kuklinski instructed the barber. When the barber finished, Kuklinski was not satisfied and asked the barber to cut off more.

Kuklinski got home before dawn, put on his uniform, and left for work. He did not feel he could risk leaving a chalk mark for Warsaw Station asking for an emergency meeting. He would have to wait until the next scheduled car exchange, in November.

Unaware of Kuklinski's close call, the CIA processed his latest documents and prepared a letter for delivery to him in November. The letter thanked Kuklinski for the materials he had sent on September 3 as well as the photographs and biographical information about his family. The only item missing was a photograph of Bogdan, the agency said, requesting that he include one the next time. The letter went on to ask Kuklinski for handwriting samples from each family member. "Such samples, for example clipped from notes or school papers, would assist us in preparing travel or other documents for your family's use if ever required," the agency said. CIA physicians had reviewed Kuklinski's medical results and concluded that Kuklinski was in excellent condition. "We are delighted, and wish you continued and long-lasting good health," the CIA wrote. The agency also devoted several paragraphs to Kuklinski's question about whether to carry his gun during car exchanges, recommending against it.

> Although that decision is one only you will be able to make if circumstances ever require it, and hopefully they never will, we suggest that any other possibility for escape and flight should be preferred.
>
> Our reasoning is that should you use your weapon to escape, should you be successful in eluding your captors but kill or injure one or more of them in the process, and should you then succeed in reaching us, then your government might be in a position to claim a legal jurisdiction over you, citing an alleged criminal act on its territory.
>
> Although we would of course deny their claim, the publicity might complicate our plans for your escape from Poland. However, should you succeed in eluding your captors by any means short of killing or injuring one or more of them with a weapon and then reach us, we would then be in a stronger position to help you escape clandestinely to the West.

Kuklinski waited fitfully for the November exchange, fearful that he might be arrested at any time. On the evening of the exchange, he wrote to the agency, describing in detail the incident with the Fiat. "My situation is unclear and uncertain," he said. "In spite of the fact that the exchange of correspondence was executed swiftly and flawlessly, it is greatly probable that it did not go without being observed."

He had been unable to elude his pursuers, he said, recounting how they had "cut into my way and put high beams on me."

He had given great thought to the incident. "I spent almost the entire night analyzing the situation," he wrote. In the darkness, he said, the surveillance team would likely have been able to get only a "general description," such as his movements and the clothing he was wearing, and not a positive identification. On that assumption, he said, "I decided to continue my pattern of life and work while applying special caution."

Since the incident, he had not noticed anything out of the ordinary at work that might indicate that his superiors, including Chief of Staff Siwicki, had any idea of his situation. It was possible an investigation was under way without his knowledge, which could explain why he had been allowed to continue to work. If so, he speculated, Polish counterintelligence would be quietly monitoring his activities, in order to trace his contacts and try to determine with whom he might be collaborating. Such an investigation, he wrote, would be "programmed for a longer period of time," and "carefully camouflaged." He asked for the CIA's advice on how to proceed.

"It is possible that my feelings—not void of strain and emotion— lead me to a subjective evaluation of the situation and improper conclusions." He described everything that he could remember, including the route he had taken to elude his pursuers. He wanted to offer as much detail as he could, he said, "in order to present you the fullest possible picture . . . and to make it possible for you to make an appropriate decision."

He added a pledge: "With full awareness of the danger, I am ready to continue the work undertaken, treating it as my sacred duty to my own nation and country. Without objections, I shall abide by any other decision which will be passed to me."

Kuklinski felt he could not wait for an answer until the next exchange, as it was several months away. He asked the CIA to place a chalk mark immediately at the regular location, using a number signal system, which would correspond with a list of options:

1. Continue activities using agreed upon communications system.
2. Continue activities [while] perhaps keeping equipment and materials outside of the house. Wait for signal or message

according to agreed upon communication system. Abandon
planned (regular) meetings and exchanges.

3. Immediately interrupt activities. Conceal equipment outside of
the house. Wait for signal or message according to agreed upon
communication system.

4. Interrupt activities. Destroy equipment. Wait for signal or message according to agreed upon communication system.

5. Interrupt activities. Establish contact while abroad (sailing
cruise) in accordance with the agreed upon system. Dispose of
equipment according to own decision.

6. Interrupt activities. Destroy all traces. Wait for clarification of
the affair. In case of arrest and interrogation deny all contacts.
Re-establish activities and contact in favorable conditions.

7. Leave the country [following] instructions concerning assistance.

8. Wait for detailed instructions which will be passed in accordance with the existing system of communications.

After finishing the letter, Kuklinski wrote to Daniel. He wondered
whether it would be their last communication.

I am grateful to you beyond words for your friendship.... I
intended long ago to share with you matters and thoughts of a
more personal character. Most unfortunately, even today, while
preparing materials literally on one knee, I shall be able to write
just a few sentences.
You should, however, know that in my personal thoughts, you
are often my conversation-partner. I do not know how my fate will
turn out, whether I shall ever be able to pass to you even a small
portion of the tale of my not-so-easy life, as well as the motives for
my activities.

In his mind, Kuklinski wrote, America had always been the homeland for people of all nationalities, including Poles, who "linked their

existence and progress with a concern for the existence of the entire human family."

He cited the Vietnam War as a factor in his life choices. "In my conscience," Kuklinski wrote, "the card 'for our and your freedom' was filled out with authentic and unselfish contents by your fathers and brothers, the people of the United States. Perhaps the Vietnam War was, for you Americans, a nightmare, and it is difficult for you to believe that precisely the experience of that war decided my present road in life." In Vietnam, he said, the American troops had made a strong impression on him. He realized many Americans were angry and cynical about the war, and he described his concerns about a backlash that could lead the United States to bring its troops home from Europe.

Kuklinski recalled the role of Polish troops in the 1968 invasion of Czechoslovakia and crushing of Prague Spring. He still felt bitter at "my almost direct participation in the infamous act of aggression of the socialist coalition against the Czechoslovak nation and its, after all, legal government."

He was satisfied that he had been able finally "to break with the utopian doctrine and practice of hate in order to join the forces of true progress and freedom.

"I hope that this letter will not be the last which will reach your hands. I also trust that my modest achievement will be multiplied and be more useful in the future.

"Confident of that, I shake your hand, Daniel."

After receiving Kuklinski's letter about his close call, Warsaw Station officers cabled headquarters to say that although the news was deeply troubling, it seemed that any agents pursuing Kuklinski probably did not actually witness his exchange or identify him. The station recommended advising Kuklinski to destroy his photography equipment and message pads and to cease activity until he was confident that his situation was secure.

Headquarters responded that whatever had occurred, Kuklinski's perception of events must govern. Urging Warsaw to exercise even greater caution, headquarters ordered several steps to protect Kuklinski, including the firming up of contingency plans for exfiltration. Warsaw was told to watch for Kuklinski in places he normally frequented, such as the yacht club and the site of his home construction on Rajcow Street.

The agency left a signal for Kuklinski that it was suspending the operation temporarily. Over the next few months, Warsaw-based officers kept an eye out for Kuklinski. Twice, officers reported seeing a man who fit his description on Rajcow Street, but there was still some uncertainty. Langley cabled out a new description of Kuklinski: Small, almost elfin build; shoulders square but not broad; sandy-colored hair; precise movements; direct but not rigid attitude; favors tan clothes; lips usually pursed; blue, penetrating eyes.

By February 1975 there were encouraging reports that Kuklinski had been seen carrying out the normal activities of his daily life. Headquarters suggested Warsaw Station try to contact him. A letter was drafted, which contained instructions for Kuklinski to resume contact by making a chalk mark on a street sign.

Daniel also cabled a letter to Warsaw Station on February 25, 1975, for delivery to Kuklinski when contact was reestablished.

> You must know that I have thought about you every day since I received your November message. I have had many conversations with Eagle about you, and about the ways we can support and protect you during a troubled time. We had to agree that the best thing to do during the past four months was not to interfere with your life and work in any way. This was a difficult decision, but probably a wise one....
>
> If you believe we should prolong further the period of waiting, we will understand and abide by your wishes....

Warsaw Station continued to try to observe Kuklinski, but by mid-May, it reported only one positive sighting of Kuklinski's car, and Daniel wondered where he was.

5

NEAR MISS

KUKLINSKI HAD BEEN SENT to Moscow. After a fretful autumn in which he feared Polish counterintelligence might confront him at any time, he learned he had been selected to attend a short-term intensive course on operational strategies for senior Warsaw Pact officers, which was given at Voroshilov Academy, the elite military school run by the Soviet General Staff. In 1973, Kuklinski had been nominated to attend a two-year course at the academy, but he had put it off. He felt that turning down such an honor again would raise too many questions. Hoping to inform the CIA, he tried to leave a chalk mark at an intersection he regularly used in Warsaw for signals, but discovered that the designated signpost was gone, apparently removed by a construction crew.

He flew to Moscow with a group of Polish generals on February 24, and for the next two months, he received an abbreviated version of the course given to high-ranking Soviet officers. He socialized with Warsaw Pact deputy defense ministers, chiefs of General Staffs, and Warsaw Pact and Soviet commanders. He also forged friendships with several senior Polish officers, including General Czeslaw Kiszczak, who recalled Kuklinski padding around in socks on large military maps and who was struck by his meticulous attention to detail.

Kiszczak thought Kuklinski had a gift for illustrating military operational concepts on maps; he drew them beautifully and exactly.

As cautioned earlier by the CIA, Kuklinski did not take his camera to Moscow, but he found another way to collect intelligence there. At the academy, he was issued a leather portfolio for classified note-taking. Sewn inside the portfolio were about 200 numbered and registered pages. The portfolio could be locked and sealed with wax and had to be turned in when Kuklinski left Moscow. But he was told he could ask that it be sent to him for review back in Warsaw. Kuklinski was a model student at the academy, taking copious notes.

One day he attended a speech given by a Soviet general, who claimed the Warsaw Pact would not need to use nuclear weapons first in Europe because of its superiority in conventional forces. "It is an illusion to think that the West has superiority, even in its air force," the general said. "We have superiority on land, in the air, and on the sea." He said that within ten to twelve days, the Warsaw Pact would be able to realize operational goals and eliminate the main European NATO countries without the use of nuclear weapons on the European war theater. "We have superiority in conventional forces," the general had said. "We shall not use nuclear weapons first. If the West uses nuclear weapons first, regardless of type, be it a nuclear mine or an accidental shot, there is only one answer—a global riposte." Kuklinski was stunned by the general's talk; he left no room for an escalating conflict with the West.

On April 29, 1975, Kuklinski returned to Warsaw with a dozen Polish generals and other officers who had attended the academy. General Jaruzelski invited the group to his office, where the officers were asked to talk about their experience in Moscow. During the discussion, Kuklinski candidly expressed the view that Moscow was exaggerating the threat NATO posed in Europe and overstating NATO's willingness to start a war against the Warsaw Pact. General Kiszczak interrupted, saying he disagreed. Nevertheless, Jaruzelski later singled out Kuklinski and another officer for praise, calling them "our youth."

Kuklinski received increasingly important assignments and assisted

Colonel Jan Zarek, who ran the strategic defense department and who had a heart problem, in drafting speeches for Jaruzelski. Kuklinski also received permission to organize a fourth surveillance voyage through Europe.

Still, he remained cautious. The Defense Ministry had become embroiled in a major scandal after Lt. Colonel Jerzy Pawlowski, a former Olympic saber champion, was charged with spying for the West. The General Staff was given lectures on security, with warnings that Western intelligence forces, notably the British, Israeli, and Dutch, with U.S. support, were increasing their activities in Poland. Kuklinski detected signs that an investigation was under way in the Defense Ministry.

It had been more than six months since Kuklinski had communicated with the agency, and he wanted to reestablish contact. In mid-May he spotted a signal indicating the agency intended to leave him a message. Kuklinski confirmed with a chalk mark that he had received the signal and went to the agreed-upon location. He picked up a piece of folded newspaper and a cigarette wrapper, but after examining both items at home, he realized they were just pieces of litter.

On June 10, after seeing another signal, he set out again, taking a long and intricate route to lose possible surveillance, and took the extra precaution of changing his clothes along the way. Tense and excited, he arrived at the signal location and only then discovered that he had left the chalk in the pocket of his other pants.

Kuklinski finally was able to exchange signals the next day confirming an exchange. "I am looking forward to today's meeting with suspense and impatience," he wrote on June 12. In his letter, he described his two months in Moscow and the missing street sign that had prevented him from signaling the CIA about his departure. He admitted that he had not followed the agency's instructions that he suspend his collection activities after the incident the previous fall. In his latest eighteen rolls of film, he had included his certificate for completing the course at Voroshilov Academy.

Kuklinski said that his security was "ambiguous and uncertain," although he admitted that perhaps he was not able to evaluate it objectively. Being sent to Moscow with "highly placed personalities in the Polish military hierarchy" certainly suggested that he was still well regarded, and he cited Jaruzelski's praise of him and the "full confidence expressed to me by the General Staff leadership."

Kuklinski informed the agency of the three-week yacht trip through Europe that was scheduled to depart on July 1. "I will expect Daniel or Henry in all ports." He said he needed another location to leave chalk marks, because of the removal of the street sign they had used in the past. Until then, he would leave signals on the reverse side of the sign for Kostrzewskiego Street, where it intersected with Sobieskiego. Driving north on Sobieskiego, he wrote, it was possible to see the sign from a car.

Usually he photographed his letters to the CIA and included both the film and the paper copy in his package. This time he destroyed the paper copy and sent his message only on film, marking the roll in red ink. He packed his film in a leather pouch, along with the requested photographs of his son Bogdan.

CIA officials were stunned to read that Kuklinski had disregarded their advice to suspend his clandestine activity, although Daniel saw one positive result: "We realized that he was still there, and able to tell us about it."

The first summer meeting in 1975 was held on July 6 in Kiel. When Colonel Henry first saw Kuklinski, a day before Daniel arrived, he appeared distracted and nervous, and his smile was forced. His handshake, his embrace, even his kisses on Henry's cheeks lacked the usual enthusiasm.

Kuklinski reviewed his difficult year. Even during the voyage, the *Legia* had been held up for almost eight hours by the Polish authorities. A crewmate had told him that another officer on the boat was under investigation by Polish counterintelligence. Kuklinski had taken the news impassively, but wondered whether surveillance might be tighter on the trip.

When Henry asked why Kuklinski had ignored the agency's instructions that he suspend his clandestine activities after being chased by the SB the previous fall, Kuklinski smiled briefly. The materials were "much too attractive to be ignored," he said, adding that he hoped the CIA enjoyed this "high-grade" intelligence.

"We had to admit, of course, that we certainly did," Henry wrote later. He noted that Kuklinski then "became serious again and solemnly promised to obey our signals in the future."

Kuklinski reaffirmed that he wanted to stay in Poland and, "nerves permitting," continue his secret work for ten more years. But he asked for some clarity regarding exfiltration procedures, wondering how long someone in his position could endure psychologically. Henry, who said that it wasn't the kind of question he was supposed to answer, acknowledged that the toll could be enormous. He cited the case of Oleg Penkovsky, the Soviet GRU colonel, who had spied for the West in the early 1960s for less than two years before he was arrested and executed. Henry thought someone could stay in place for about five or six years before the psychological toll became too taxing. Of course, Kuklinski could always stop for a while or slow down his activity.

Kuklinski also asked Henry whether he, like Daniel, worked for the CIA. Henry replied obliquely, "This operation could not be run without the participation and guidance of the CIA."

Daniel joined them the next afternoon and on July 11 and 12 at the meetings in Amsterdam. In their sessions, Kuklinski raised the Pawlowski affair, which he said was the talk of the General Staff. He did not know Pawlowski, but there were rumors that he had worked secretly for the West Germans.

Daniel said the rumors were wrong, that Pawlowski had been meeting with the CIA in the West for several years until 1973. It was possible Pawlowski had been in touch with the Germans as well, he said, but through their interrogations of Pawlowski, the Poles were probably aware of his cooperation with the Americans.

Responding to Kuklinski's concerns on exfiltration, Daniel reviewed the contingency plans to help Kuklinski and, if necessary, his family escape from Poland and build new lives in the West. They would be given language and professional training, and Kuklinski would probably receive a consulting position with the Pentagon. But Daniel also pointed out that there was no hard evidence Kuklinski was under suspicion, citing the "demonstrable fact of his undiminished success, vital work, and repeated expressions of confidence by his superiors in his work."

As Daniel and Henry drove Kuklinski from the hotel after the third meeting, Kuklinski suggested with a sheepish grin that they meet again that night. Daniel and Henry declined and suggested Kuklinski take his crew to a movie.

In the final meeting, which lasted two and a half hours, Kuklinski seemed much more relaxed, and he promised to remain alert and cautious so that he might be able to arrange another set of meetings in 1976. "Our farewell was capped by firm embraces and best wishes," Henry noted, with the ritual toasts and quaffing of aquavit.

It was Henry's impression, after the sessions ended, that whatever anxiety Kuklinski felt about security had not altered his resolve. "There is no doubt that subj is a political fanatic, whose strong anti-regime and anti-[Soviet] sentiments build the main portion of his motivation, and that he is willing to remain in place and work 'to the last drop of his blood,'" Henry told headquarters.

"Despite that, the wear and tear of his nerves is beginning to show, resulting in a creeping fear, which at times seems to deprive him of previous, so-clearly-displayed, logic—and he is starting to think of a 'way out.'"

Henry believed Kuklinski could remain in place "for some time to come, if we put his mind to rest by providing a package of clear-cut guarantees, and stress the human element of our relationship in personal messages to him." Daniel and Henry had urged Kuklinski to engage in constant self-analysis "and to inform us immediately if and when the psychological burden of his work on our behalf should become intolerable."

In a separate cable, Daniel and Henry wrote that Kuklinski seemed prepared to stay in place, although he "still claims—and shows—nervousness over something going on in the background."

The agency prepared a twenty-three-page single-spaced typed set of instructions concerning security and communications for Kuklinski to be delivered in the next car exchange, which was scheduled for the fall. The CIA also offered cautions because of the Pawlowski espionage case.

We have received evidence from a number of sources that the Pawlowski affair has had far-reaching repercussions in your country and that there is an extensive investigation going on among military personnel. We realize that you did not personally know Pawlowski, but as all military personnel may be subject to closer security, we want to remind you to be especially discreet in your personal behavior.

From our sources, we understand that there is much uneasiness among the military and that anyone who appears to be living [above] his means or who has access to western contacts becomes suspect. Even little things—unusual purchases—can bring one to the attention of the authorities....

We know that your professional work is very exhausting and demanding. This coupled with the special work you are doing for us must place a heavy strain on you physically and mentally. We hope this does not cause moods of depression, fatigue or nervousness which could draw attention to you. Your personal courage and dedication to our mutual cause are profoundly respected by all of us who work with you, but we do not want you to take unnecessary risks on our behalf.

Daniel wrote separately to Kuklinski:

You know that I will be waiting eagerly to hear that you received this package securely. Although it is by necessity so brief, even such human contact as that has great meaning to us, as I know it does for you, in the difficult mission that we are carrying out together.

[Henry] and I talked at length that day after you left, and I have returned in thought many times to the scenes of our most recent meetings. The truth is that they started on a difficult and anxious theme, understandably so because of what had happened the year before. It seemed to me that we faced this theme squarely, identifying facts, feelings and possibilities. . . .

By the end of our last meeting, I had the strong conviction that—together—we had reached an honest and positive conclusion. . . . Your record of increased access to materials, repeated praise from your superiors, training and travel abroad is not the kind of record that someone under suspicion can expect. In short, it was a difficult year, but it is over. You had the alertness, calm, and courage to remain steadfast when lesser men would have faltered in one way or another. All of us salute you most profoundly for this. But there are some very specific lessons to be learned from this. . . .

Daniel advised Kuklinski there was much to "read and study" in the CIA's latest package, and he hoped Kuklinski would not be offended if the security information repeated areas he already knew.

These "reminders" I ask you to accept in the spirit of their giving. The importance of your security, of your well-being and that of your family, is unmatched by any other consideration. Sure, we will labor over every package from you, to examine and benefit from the documents you have selected and copied so expertly. They will have, as they already have had, tremendous value to my government. But, always, our first concern in opening each package is to find the personal note from you, to learn that you are . . . OK!

"Czolem," Daniel closed, meaning "I salute you." A successful exchange took place October 12.

★

Over the next six months, Kuklinski felt the pressures alleviate somewhat; his work situation seemed stable, and his family was doing well.
Waldek, now twenty-two, had never learned to drive and cared little
about clothes or material goods. He remained a loner, rarely went out,
and at times appeared completely detached from the world. He never
asked for money, and when Kuklinski and Hanka offered to buy
clothes for him, he would refuse, saying it was too expensive and
reminding them they were building a new house. But he adored
books—he had a collection of more than 1,000 volumes, including first
editions—and he and Kuklinski spent many hours discussing various
moral issues Waldek confronted in his reading. Kuklinski told his son:
"I know the song in your heart and in your mind, and I'm proud of it."
Waldek was studying law at Warsaw University.

Bogdan, who was twenty, lacked Waldek's intellectual curiosity, but
shared his father's passion for adventure. He loved to drive cars and
motorcycles, had a knack for fixing them, and enjoyed sailing with his
father. For a long time, Bogdan had wanted to be a doctor, but his
grades had not been strong enough. Recently, they had begun to
improve; he had finished with the highest grade in biology and had
even participated in a national biology competition. Now he was
preparing for graduation and was hoping again to study medicine. His
girlfriend, Grazyna, General Hermaszewski's daughter, was studying
economics in Gdansk, but planned to transfer to Warsaw if Bogdan
was accepted to medical school there. They spent all their free time
together, usually at her house. Neither son showed any curiosity about
Kuklinski's work at the General Staff.

At work, Kuklinski occasionally dropped hints of marital problems.
Before heading to an exchange, he would buy roses or other flowers,
explaining to Hanka that he needed a cover for the occasional encounters with his American friends from Vietnam. Word even spread on the
General Staff of Kuklinski's surreptitious liaisons in parks around the
city. Within the male-dominated General Staff, this led to nothing
more than a few raised eyebrows, and Kuklinski did nothing to dispel

the rumors. If he was ever seen going to a late-night exchange, such gossip might explain his behavior.

On December 21, 1975, in a year-end letter to Daniel, Kuklinski said he had taken Daniel's cautions seriously and had not allowed the incident of the previous year and the chase by the SB to discourage him.

Dear Daniel,

Your personal letters and the entire pertinent correspondence are for me a special kind of reward for tensions and anxieties which, after all, I included in my thoroughly thought out and absolutely mature decision to initiate our cooperation. Although never, not even for a moment, did a thought come to my mind that my life's path should be different (during my efforts to break away from the chase, I only thought, why does it come so soon?).

Nevertheless, a feeling of wanting to live and act—because it is useful and helpful—is probably very necessary for me. I thank you for this, because while reading your letters I can indeed think that way. I also thank all those who in a non-personal manner steer my efforts in the right direction, who exert themselves in preserving the durability of established contacts, and who, to a no lesser degree than I, take a risk in contacting me for regular exchanges....

Daniel, although the recent period of time did not spare me shocks and psychological tensions, the state of my health is good and the feeling of security stronger than ever before. I think this is not only a question of routine and natural adaptation. The curing factor is mainly my murderous tempo of work, continued access to information which is subject to a specific and restricted kind of secrecy, and also further proof of deepening confidence of the leadership of the Polish Armed Forces General Staff.

The serenity in his family life was clearly a source of great satisfaction to him. He described Waldek's strong moral character and his deep immersion into philosophy, literature, and the law; and noted Bogdan's improved grades and rekindled dream of medical school.

Hanka's doctors had diagnosed pains in her limbs as arthritis, but despite her fragility, she worked diligently and maintained their household. "She is my true friend, and I cannot imagine that anyone could be her match," Kuklinski wrote.

In response to earlier questions about his decision to participate in the housing cooperative on Rajcow Street, Kuklinski said he had been reluctant at first, feeling that the project might draw him unwanted attention, and he wondered if he could afford it. But he eventually agreed to join under pressure from colleagues, including General Hermaszewski, who said it would be feasible over time. Kuklinski emphasized that he was careful to maintain his frugal lifestyle to avoid attracting attention. They had not added any furniture, rugs, or curtains to the apartment, and they had had the same refrigerator for seven years and the same TV for fourteen.

The General Staff was planning a fifth cruise in the summer of 1976 through Scandinavia. Because of the Pawlowski affair, Polish counterintelligence was now scrupulously investigating any military personnel traveling abroad, and Kuklinski had considered withdrawing from the voyage, under the pretext of needing to supervise his house construction. "But this can also arouse suspicions," he added, saying he had decided that he should not alter his plans. That night, he made the exchange in a heavy downpour. The agency's letters included a note from Daniel thanking him for his latest films.

> As you predicted, it appears that you have been incredibly busy since your return. Certainly the results in your last package showed the superb effort and product of long, arduous hours of work. We are deeply grateful. Still, as I wrote you, the first thing we look for in opening each package from you is your personal note, to learn that all is well.

Daniel and his staff paid keen attention to the tone of Kuklinski's messages, in part because they had a new reason for concern. The CIA had been under harsh scrutiny in the news media, and Senator Frank

Church had initiated a series of investigative hearings in Congress to look into a wide range of abuses by the agency, including plots to assassinate foreign leaders and the surreptitious opening of mail sent by American citizens. Daniel and other officers worried that sources like Kuklinski would be following the news of the investigations and might fear that their own activities would be exposed.

A copy of Kuklinski's letter was sent to the Deputy Director of Operations (DDO) by the Soviet Division chief, who noted that Kuklinski's last letter made "no mention at all of the investigations of the CIA, nor has he done so in earlier messages."

> We can take his silence on this score as a sign of his trust in us, or as further evidence of his resolve—under any and all circumstances—to follow the path he has chosen. Although he has had some chilling experiences, and even proposed a suspension of internal contact last year, he has never stopped collecting and copying documents in the three and one-half years of his work with us.

The DDO wrote back, saying Daniel's letter had been shown to Director William Colby.

As it turned out, Kuklinski had indeed been aware of the investigations but seemed more concerned about the burden they were on CIA officers than about any risks to himself. On February 15, 1976, he wrote to the Americans:

> It is with great concern that I follow the daily reports sent by the Polish Press Agency about the blind hue and cry against this organization. It is not for me to evaluate these facts, nor do I fear that this may affect my security (which is not certain in any case).
>
> I am, however, amazed by the fact that in a situation where the forces of violence are extending even farther [in the world] that such actions are being undertaken. I believe, however, in the American peo-

ple, in their enormous creative powers and instinct, which will not permit the strength and effectiveness of its state and its executive authorities to be weakened.

I send to all of you, gentlemen, expressions of my highest respect and esteem along with best wishes and regards to Daniel.

Jack Strong

Warsaw

One day in April, Kuklinski was in his office secretly photographing a map that had been prepared for Warsaw Pact maneuvers planned for the fall when he was called by a counterintelligence officer who wished to see him. Kuklinski hid his camera and placed the map in his desk. The officer questioned him for ninety minutes about the surveillance voyage planned for June and about the previous trips. He wanted to know the original reason for the voyages, what intelligence was gained, how long the voyages took, how the crew was chosen, what the trips cost, how much time was spent abroad, and whether there was contact with foreigners.

Kuklinski responded matter-of-factly to each question. The officer then asked about the yacht club, Atol, of which Kuklinski recently had been elected president, wanting to know who were members and how they joined. Kuklinski wondered whether the interrogation was related to the Pawlowski investigation, and a few weeks later, he was called in for two more hours of questioning. But nothing more came of it, and Kuklinski dismissed the matter as routine fact gathering.

On June 5, 1976, Kuklinski arrived in Copenhagen, leading another voyage through northern Europe. When Daniel and Henry met with him in a hotel room, he seemed considerably more relaxed and confident than in earlier meetings. Kuklinski was in his third year as chief specialist for operations, overseeing all operational planning on the General Staff. He had regular contact with military officials in Moscow and throughout the East bloc and had recently begun working on a five-year plan for the armed forces through 1980.

He conceded there had been difficult moments. Pawlowski had been convicted and sentenced to twenty-five years in prison that spring. "The vigilance in the army, in my institution, was greatly sharpened," he said. He described the visits by the counterintelligence officer. "I must admit that I was shaken, because he called me immediately after my return from photographing a map." Kuklinski had even discovered that the telephone line in his apartment had been bugged, but only by a clever neighbor who did not have his own phone. The incident reminded Kuklinski of how little privacy he had. "I do not conduct any conversations which could suggest the character of my 'second personality,'" he added.

They met twice more in the ensuing days, discussing topics ranging from Soviet military capabilities to the after-hours love-life of one of Kuklinski's General Staff colleagues. Kuklinski said that the plumbing, heating, and electrical work on his new home had been completed, the walls should be plastered within a month, and the roof tiles would soon be laid. The construction was going slowly, but his family might be able to move in by Christmas.

Daniel cabled headquarters after the final session with Kuklinski: "Consensus here is that [Gull], while very much aware of the pressures he [is] working under, has achieved [a] remarkably fine balance of alertness, endurance, and naturalness to carry out his work with us during [the] next year."

Over the summer, Kuklinski had to cancel a family vacation after he was assigned to complete the Defense Ministry's directives for the armed forces for 1976–1980. The work brought him into extensive contact with the Defense Ministry leadership, including Jaruzelski and Siwicki, who were friendlier than ever toward him. On August 22 he appeared for a moving-car delivery, writing to the CIA that he felt "an atmosphere of peace, previously unheard of for me." Warsaw Station cabled headquarters two days later to say Kuklinski seemed "smiling and relaxed, almost nonchalant." He "may be a shade too relaxed," the cable said.

Daniel wrote to say that he was grateful for the personal meetings. "They are especially valuable for the human contact they give us, something without which our relationship could not be so deeply satisfying." In a postscript, he praised the performance of Polish athletes in the recent Summer Olympics in Montreal, "particularly their victory over the Soviets in the volleyball finals."

That fall, Kuklinski received a series of commendations. His superiors cited him as "Leading Worker of the General Staff of the Polish Army." General Siwicki awarded him a medal, Amor Patriae Supreme Lex, with a written dedication and letter of commendation. On October 12, Army Day, Jaruzelski awarded him the Cavalier's Cross of the Order of the Rebirth of Poland. About thirty colleagues attended the ceremony, and Jaruzelski and Kuklinski spent a few minutes discussing Kuklinski's ideas for innovations in military planning. Siwicki also announced special honors for Kuklinski's work on the Defense Ministry directives. "This type of public show of interest and consideration for me ... would probably not be possible if there were even the least shadow of suspicion," Kuklinski wrote to the CIA on October 31. He said he understood that the smallest indiscretion could cost him his life, and that total safety was unattainable within the borders of his country. He added:

> The recognition recently accorded me in no way weakens my desire to continue cooperation. I nourish only the hope that as a result of my good position in the General Staff, as well as good feelings, in the future I will be able to provide more information on the potential and the actual intentions of the combined armed forces of the Warsaw Pact and especially of the Armed Forces of the U.S.S.R.

On November 3, 1976, portions of Gull's most recent letter were sent to then–CIA director George Bush through the DDO. "We, too, are planning to award him a medal when next we meet in person!" the Soviet Division chief said in a memorandum.

In a letter to Kuklinski the following month, Daniel wrote that the CIA could not "match the public honors that you received recently.

But I assure you that the enormous value of your work (and of your anonymity) is recognized at the top levels of our government."

Throughout the summer and fall of 1976, public discontent in Poland grew. In late June, after the government announced it would raise food prices on average by about 60 percent, riots, work stoppages, and other protests broke out across the country, resulting in the deaths of two demonstrators, injuries to seventy-five police officers, and millions of dollars of damage. The increases in food prices were postponed, but dozens of workers were arrested and many were tried and sentenced to prison. In August, Cardinal Stefan Wyszynski, the revered Polish primate, criticized the government's decision to fire and imprison the demonstrators, saying the punishments were too severe.

On December 9, Kuklinski decided to carry a particularly large collection of classified documents out of his office to photograph at home, but had little time to do so. He hid the material in a large briefcase that he kept in his office. Such briefcases were practically standard issue for General Staff officers, whose perks included access to an exclusive shop that sold sausage and other meats that were in otherwise short supply. Kuklinski had always felt the shop was a symbol of the double standard in Poland, but it was a useful cover for his secret work. He shopped there regularly, filled his briefcase with groceries, and put the documents beneath them.

That day, clutching the briefcase, Kuklinski barely acknowledged the guards as he left, heading toward his car and driver. Preoccupied, he walked briskly and collided with a massive concrete column.

Kuklinski staggered blindly, his face bleeding. He stumbled to his knees and felt as if he might pass out, but he steeled himself to stay alert. Other military personnel and guards rushed to his side, and one man reached for his briefcase. Kuklinski, dizzy, swaying, and blinking back tears, yanked it back, sputtering, "Leave me alone!"

He struggled to his feet and reentered the General Staff building. Shaking off solicitous security personnel, he hurried to his office, where he left the briefcase, and entered the bathroom. He ran cold water over his hands and splashed his face in an attempt to stanch the bleeding from his nose, lips, and forehead. Still shaken, he returned to his office. He had lost valuable time. Trying to calm himself, he left the building again, this time without incident. At home, he cleaned up and put powder on his face, but winced when he glanced in the mirror. He looked dreadful, caked up as if he were going to a masquerade ball.

Three days later, he was still feeling the effects of his encounter with the pillar. A CIA officer who met him on December 12 for a car exchange noted in a cable that although he was smiling and seemed fit, "his face appeared somewhat fuller than usual." His written account of what had happened to him, the officers wrote, "leaves our knees weak."

Kuklinski wrote that despite his close call, he was satisfied that the exchanges were being conducted without detection. He apologized for not responding when American officers offered him a quiet hello in the exchanges. "The tension during these few moments is so strong that words of sentiment such as I would like to express remain somewhere in the background," Kuklinski wrote.

He regretted he had not provided even more material, but he was obsessed with trying to avoid missteps, although, as he put it, "concentration on fine points nearly ended in disaster," a reference to the incident with the pillar.

In a response to Kuklinski, the CIA expressed sympathy: "We are still marveling at your great presence of mind in protecting your briefcase of papers when you had your accident," and added, "Please don't worry about not returning our greetings. We understand completely that the moment of passing is very short and filled with many details. We know that, in your thoughts, you return our good wishes, and appreciate it."

In January 1977, President Jimmy Carter took office and appointed Admiral Stansfield J. Turner to run the CIA. Daniel had been promoted as well: After three years overseeing internal operations inside the Soviet Union and East bloc, he was named chief of operations worldwide for the Soviet Division. He wrote to Kuklinski:

Dear P.V.,

The earnest rivalry and rhetoric of our political campaign are long since over, and three weeks ago Mr. Carter spoke for the first time as president to the American people and to the world. As I listened, and again as I read and reflected on his inaugural address the next day, my thoughts turned repeatedly to you. In our talks together, and in many of your letters, you have touched on the same themes of human rights, liberty and opportunity that formed the basis of Mr. Carter's address.

It was a simple, straightforward, and moving address. I knew that Polish Radio was going to broadcast it the next day (Friday, the 21st of January)—or portions of it, at least. But I wondered if you would be able to hear it. If you did, I hope that you can understand why I was reminded so vividly and in so many ways of you and the goals that bind us together.

President Carter said that "the American dream endures.... We have already found a high degree of personal liberty, and we are now struggling to enhance equality of opportunity. Our commitment to human rights must be absolute, our laws fair, our natural beauty preserved; the powerful must not persecute the weak, and human dignity must be enhanced ... the world itself is now dominated by a new spirit ... people are demanding their place in the sun—not just for the benefit of their own physical condition, but for basic human rights ... because we are free we can never be indifferent to the fate of freedom elsewhere. Our moral sense dictates a clear-cut preference for those societies which share with us an abiding respect for individual human rights. We do not seek to intimidate, but it is clear that a world which others can dominate with impunity would be inhospitable to decency and a threat to the well-being of all people."

In the exchange on February 13, 1977, Kuklinski appeared grinning and hatless. His letter included a positive security assessment, saying there was nothing indicating any danger. "Nonetheless, in accordance with a saying that storms are preceded by tranquillity, I try to act very carefully."

For a long time now, my official workload has exceeded my work capacity. I am continually forced to work after hours and during weekends and holidays. Continuous sitting at work—although it is not connected with our cooperation—might, in the end, arouse somebody's interest in the negative sense. I presented my case of overwork to General Skalski, but he probably is not capable of understanding that human capabilities are limited.

He also reported sad news: Colonel Jan Zarek, who was in charge of the strategic defense department, had died of a heart attack. "I want to have an EKG examination," Kuklinski wrote. Although only forty-six at the time, he thought it might be prudent because of his workload and the stress in his life.

In a separate note to Daniel, he reported approval of another General Staff voyage, including a stop in Britain. A counterintelligence officer would join on the trip. "There are still countless details to be taken care of, but I nevertheless hope that it will materialize," he wrote.

He added:

You were and are for me a symbol of the country with which I associated myself and, seen in a wider national and social perspective, my feelings and hopes. In the now beginning fifth year of our cooperation, they seem to be still more rational and possible to achieve.

I do not know how much more my physical strength will suffice, but one thing is certain: that I would like to maintain this bond till the end, or at least as long as it will effectively serve the cause of freedom for Poland, Poles, and of other nations.

Yours,

P.V.

6

"Standing on Ice"

Daniel was heartened to learn that Kuklinski had received permission to sail again into ports in Western Europe, including a possible stop in Britain. But responding in a letter in April, Daniel said the agency would not meet Kuklinski there. Under long-standing agreement, if the CIA met a source in Britain, the agency had to notify British intelligence officials and invite them along.

"We share many things with them, but you and your product are not among these," Daniel wrote. He suggested that they meet instead in Copenhagen, Amsterdam, or a smaller port along the coast. He and Henry would appear outside the city hall of each city Kuklinski visited, except in Britain, at 12:15 P.M. each day. If they did not see Kuklinski, they would reappear every two hours thereafter, until 10:15 P.M.

In his letter, Daniel asked about Kuklinski's family. "It seems clear from your letter," he said, "that your sons follow the example of their father—they work hard, successfully, and have the strength of character to bounce back when there's been a disappointment...."

Meanwhile, Daniel and other Soviet Division officers urged that Kuklinski be recognized with the Distinguished Intelligence Medal, the agency's highest honor, which is generally bestowed only on CIA officers. On April 18, 1977, the Soviet Division chief sent a memorandum to the DDO requesting such approval, declaring, "For the past five years, Gull has been this agency's best placed and most productive source within the Soviet Bloc." Since 1972, Kuklinski had provided about 20,000 pages of "Secret" and "Top Secret" documentary intelligence, resulting in more than 1,200 disseminations to the intelligence community.

His access remains undiminished and his career potential is excellent.... Gull continually reiterates his dedication to the principles of peace and often comments that he hopes to be able to assist the United States Government even more in the future. He has never given any indication of a desire to resettle in the West, and believes that he can perform the greatest service by remaining in his homeland and continuing to provide us high-level documents.

Citing his "demonstrated dedication and extraordinary service," the chief recommended awarding the medal to Kuklinski during their next meeting. "Following the presentation of the medal, we would return it to headquarters for safekeeping."

In April 1977, Kuklinski was promoted to succeed the late Colonel Zarek as chief of the First Department for Strategic Defense Planning. In the new post, he would continue to work closely with Siwicki and his deputy, Skalski, and would have a range of other responsibilities. Kuklinski's department was also the one in the Defense Ministry that had a continuing and exclusive relationship with the Warsaw Pact command in Moscow, led by General Viktor Kulikov. The Soviet general had been appointed commander of the Warsaw Pact forces just a few months earlier and had been elevated to the rank of marshal. Virtually everything Kulikov and his staff sent to the Polish Defense Ministry went though Kuklinski's office.

Kuklinski would also be a member of the Polish delegations to each of the three critical Warsaw Pact committees, preparing speeches and acting as secretary. These included the Political Consultative Committee, or PCC, which included the party secretaries of the seven Warsaw Pact countries; the Warsaw Pact defense ministers committee; and the military council, which was made up of deputy defense ministers. Kuklinski would also be in charge of Polish armed forces development, which included long-term armament planning.

Shortly after assuming his new post, Kuklinski learned of a massive and unscheduled command-staff strategic exercise, called "West 77," which was being organized under tight secrecy by Soviet Defense Minister Dmitri F. Ustinov and the Soviet General Staff. The exercise, to be held in May, would include the Poles, Czechs, East Germans, and Soviets and was designed to demonstrate the need for Moscow to have centralized command of Warsaw Pact forces in wartime. Moscow had controlled the Warsaw Pact armies since World War II, but the arrangement had never been formalized legally. It was just another step in the eradication of Polish sovereignty.

Worse news followed. Siwicki told Kuklinski that the summer cruises were being canceled. Polish counterintelligence had come to believe they were too risky and had decided to restrict future trips to the coasts of Poland, East Germany, Finland, Sweden, and the Soviet Union.

Kuklinski was dismayed, but he tried to sound upbeat when he wrote to the CIA on April 17. "The events of the past two months can be compared to this year's spring. Although there is no shortage of shocking winter recurrences, spring comes in the end, enlivening the world with the beauty of life."

He said his new post would afford him greater access to sensitive materials, and he described the forthcoming West 77 exercise, which he said was under preparation in great secrecy "on a hitherto unencountered scale."

Daniel and his colleagues in the agency saw the canceled voyages as a major setback and contemplated a future without the personal encounters. On the list of permissible countries, only Sweden seemed feasible. Finland was too risky. "Chances of an outside meeting with

Gull this summer appear dim," Warsaw Station cabled Langley on May 10, 1977. The station suggested that as a result of "the increasingly heavy psychological pressure on Gull," there was a "need to take some kind of action that will bolster his morale on a routine basis."

It proposed holding "black," or clandestine, meetings inside Poland, but headquarters rejected the idea as too dangerous and unlikely to "substantially alter Gull's mental attitude." In a message prepared for Kuklinski in June, the CIA expressed its disappointment at the cancellation of the cruises, but said it was pleased to hear of his new job responsibilities, which would give him greater access to Soviet plans, research, and development.

One morning in May, Lt. Colonel Jozef Putek, an officer in the Wojskowe Sluzby Wewnetrzne (WSW), the military's counterintelligence arm, barged into Kuklinski's office. "Comrade Colonel," he declared brusquely, "tell me, please, why do Western diplomats know about the West 77 exercise?"

Kuklinski had no idea. Putek had not said military counterintelligence knew of a leak or that one had actually occurred, and Kuklinski wondered if he was being put to a test. On June 13, Kuklinski described Putek's visit in a letter to the CIA. "Fortunately, I was able to preserve my cool and react calmly," he wrote. He was not overly worried, because Putek's questioning seemed to be directed at him simply because he was in charge of organizing the army's role in the initial phase of exercise.

A few weeks later, with assistance from the army quartermaster's office, Kuklinski moved his family into their new home at 11 Rajcow Street. His neighbors on the block were all military officers, including General Hermaszewski, whose daughter was still romantically involved with Bogdan.

Kuklinski's townhouse measured about eighteen feet wide and stood like a small fortress, built of stone and stucco, with hardwood floors and steel beams within its walls. Kuklinski was proud of the design and workmanship, much of which was his own. Beneath the house was a two-car garage, which led into a finished room with a stone fireplace. On the same floor, next to the garage, Kuklinski had built a darkroom. A stairway led one level up to the kitchen and living and dining areas and the front entrance to the house. From the windows in the front of his house, Kuklinski had a panoramic view of the eastern part of Warsaw, including the Wislostrada and the Vistula River.

On the third level were the master bedroom and bathroom, a family room with a television, and Kuklinski's study. Waldek had the fourth level, where Kuklinski had built a library for his son's book collection. Bogdan slept on the fifth level. The room had a skylight and was flooded with light. The room quickly became strewn with clothes, books, fishing poles, and photographs of cars and motorcycles.

The family had no heirlooms; all had been lost in the war. But they decorated their home with symbols of Poland, such as a chandelier featuring an eagle and a crow, and a saber that dated to the Polish-Soviet war in 1920. They also hung paintings of maritime scenes throughout the house. The move "gives me much joy," Kuklinski wrote to the CIA on July 24.

The exchanges with the CIA continued through the summer and fall. On October 14, 1977, Kuklinski wrote that his frame of mind was as good as it had been in five years; he felt secure, and his new post made him feel that he would be able to improve his "modest efforts on behalf of our great common cause of human freedoms."

He also cited President Carter's inaugural address. "Carter's political dynamism and his involvement and unprecedented offensive in the questions of human rights place special obligations on those in whose name the struggle is being waged," Kuklinski wrote. He closed with a greeting to all his friends in the United States—"that distant and, at the same time so uniquely close to me, great country."

In early December 1977, Kuklinski traveled to Budapest for the Tenth Warsaw Pact Defense Ministers Committee Meeting. Of particular interest were presentations by Soviet officials about the strengths and development perspectives of the Warsaw Pact air defenses, projected through 1985, and a new and highly sophisticated command-and-control system for the Warsaw Pact. During a break, in which a detailed chart of the air defense systems remained on the wall, Kuklinski stayed back as the participants were ordered out of the room. Standing alone, he began to copy the chart on his pad. Suddenly, he felt a hand on his shoulder. "Colonel, what are you doing?" a Russian officer said brusquely.

Kuklinski froze. "You see what I'm doing—I'm drawing," he said.

"It is prohibited," the Russian snapped.

Kuklinski insisted that he had authority from Jaruzelski to make a copy of the chart.

"Get lost," the Russian said.

Kuklinski had been bluffing about Jaruzelski, who was attending the meeting, but he was supposed to have detailed knowledge of the chart so that he could answer his superiors' questions.

Eventually, he was able to prepare a report on the Budapest conference—for his bosses and the CIA.

Late in the year, the CIA told Kuklinski it was canceling an exchange in December because President Carter was going to be in Poland at that time. The agency did not want to risk a diplomatic crisis if the operation was exposed during Carter's trip. Carter landed in Warsaw on December 29 and was greeted by party chief Edward Gierek and hundreds of other Polish officials. President Carter declared that Polish and American ties were "ancient and strong."

At about 9:30 P.M. on Saturday, January 7, 1978, Kuklinski was scouting an intersection where an exchange was scheduled for the following night when he noticed a Fiat 125 parked on the southwest corner. From the spot, people in the car could see the exchange site. Kuklinski returned the next afternoon and again saw the Fiat, and two men standing on the corner. "I left the area after about one hour, not in the best of moods," he wrote later. He left a signal that he was aborting the exchange and would try a backup site.

But when he went the following Sunday, January 15, he spotted three militia cars at the corner. Perhaps it was coincidental, he thought, but he refused to take the risk. He would try for a third time in a week.

Kuklinski also was coping with a near-tragedy at home. In early January, Bogdan dropped his father off at the General Staff and drove on to a consignment shop to buy parts for their car. Along the Wislostrada, a young man darted into the street. Bogdan braked quickly but hit the man, who was seriously injured.

On Thursday, January 19, Kuklinski drafted a letter to the CIA, saying he agreed that canceling the exchange during Carter's trip to Poland was a good idea. Carter's visit was "an extremely desirable act, and there should not have been even the slightest shadow on the way to its realization. I am deeply impressed by that event just as are millions of other Poles, including high military personalities."

Kuklinski wrote that he had much to report and had taken advantage of "particularly favorable circumstances presented by late evening and night work" to photograph documents. "Leaving work at night, often with my superiors, I kept taking out more important documents and photographing them at home, without drawing my wife's and children's attention."

Among the forty classified documents he had photographed since the last exchange were the minutes and decisions of meetings of the Defense Ministers and Political Advisory Committees and the Military Council of the Warsaw Pact members from 1969 to 1977. There were presentations from the recent Defense Ministers Committee meeting in Budapest on Warsaw Pact air defenses and command-and-control systems. And there was a proposal by Warsaw Pact Commander Kulikov to bring the Warsaw Pact armies exclusively under Soviet control during wartime. The proposal, which became known as the wartime statute, had deeply angered Kuklinski.

They are also irrefutable proofs of the limited sovereignty of the Warsaw Pact countries. They are proof of the indolence and of the puppet functions, contradictory to the state's interests, and activities of the Polish People's Republic's authorities.

It is my hope that, in case my present mission comes to an end, these matters will get through to our society. Perhaps these materials could constitute some type of bargaining factor.

On January 20, 1978, two days before the planned exchange, Marshal Kulikov made a surprise visit to the General Staff, accompanied by his chief of staff, General Anatoly Gribkov. Kulikov wanted to discuss his plan for putting Warsaw Pact armies under exclusive Soviet control in wartime. Each Warsaw Pact leader would be asked to sign the proposal, which was being drafted as a treaty. Kuklinski found Kulikov to be bombastic, swaggering, and tactless and suspected he would push the plan through with little debate.

In a letter to Kuklinski delivered in the January 22 exchange, the CIA wrote:

As you will recall, our first truly clandestine meeting took place just about five years ago in the vicinity of the Powstancow Warszawskich cemetery which honors those heroes of the Polish nation who sacrificed their lives for their beloved Poland during the Warsaw Uprising. Little could they have known or even dreamed that their struggle for the ideals for which they gave their lives would be carried on by others in subsequent generations....

As we begin our sixth year of cooperation for our common cause, we respectfully bow to you and salute you, wish to convey to you our deepest gratitude and admiration. Through you, Poland lives and will continue to live.

Daniel also wrote, expressing his disappointment that Kuklinski's voyages had been ended:

Even had we not been able to meet for some reason or other, I would have been happy to know that you had the freedom to move, to explore, and to enjoy—if only for a few weeks—a respite from the burdens of your work.

I have not given up hope that the decision will be reversed, and that we will again meet along the way—you, Henryk, our colleague from Warsaw, and I. Time passes, but friendship is sustained over any obstacle of time or distance. You will recall that at our last meeting, Henryk spoke of retiring. He did so this past summer (after learning that we would be unable to meet with you). He then moved to California, bought a new house, and was just about to settle down when the doctors told him he needed a rather delicate operation.

I have not seen him since then, but he called me several nights ago to assure me that he is once again in good humor and approaching good health. He also assured me that—retirement or not—he is ready to come back when I call with a sign that we will once again travel to meet you.

Daniel said that he was writing before President Carter's trip to Warsaw, adding, "We will be with him in spirit."

At headquarters, the Soviet Division sent CIA director Turner a memo describing the significance of Kuklinski's latest haul; it had amounted to 600 pages of classified material.

On February 3, 1978, during a strategic war game in Warsaw, General Teodor Kufel, chief of military counterintelligence, briefed the participants in the game on foreign espionage activities inside Poland. Kufel said his officers had established camouflaged surveillance posts in Warsaw, in areas where spies were believed to be operating, and on the routes diplomats used on their way to and from work. The surveillance posts had "passed the tests," Kufel said. He also said that a "spy film" had been found and was under investigation.

In early February, Kuklinski contracted pneumonia and was sick for several weeks. Hanka, still in frail health, had decided to take a year's leave without pay and would stay at home. Kuklinski returned to work in March. Over the next month, he obtained important Soviet documents on the outfitting of Warsaw Pact armies through the 1980s, including materials on the new T-72 battle tank. The Soviets were in the earliest stages of fielding the T-72, which had armor designed to be impervious to NATO tank rounds. The Pentagon could envisage 4,000 such tanks crossing into Europe in a war. Obtaining accurate data about the tank's armor, the quality of its fire-control system, and the lethality of its projectiles was a priority for the Pentagon, which wanted to devise countermeasures.

Kuklinski also attended a weeklong exercise with the Soviet General Staff that included a demonstration of wartime command-and-control procedures for the Warsaw Pact. He secretly photographed documents on a new four-stage combat-readiness system designed to harmonize the transition of the Warsaw Pact militaries from peacetime to wartime under Soviet command. The documents gave a step-by-step explanation of how the Soviets and Warsaw Pact would prepare for war.

"I recommend that two documents be meticulously analyzed," Kuklinski wrote to the CIA, citing the Soviet combat-readiness materials. He noted that film roll number seven "contains real data from the system introduced recently into the Soviet Armed Forces. It will be introduced, with some supplements, into the Warsaw Pact forces towards the end of the current year."

He also described a question-and-answer session that had taken place in the exercise: Who will be in command of war conducted in Europe? What would be the structure and relationships in the command of operations in the European war theater? How and when will the Warsaw Pact armies become subordinate to the Soviet high command?

Kuklinski listed the officers who attended the exercise. "The strictest rigors of secrecy were imposed," he added. For him, he said, the recent period had been marked by moments of tension and anxiety, even bouts of depression. He realized that these were "inseparable elements in activity of this kind," he wrote, and would try to cope.

He also responded to several earlier questions from the CIA. One asked for up-to-date information about Soviet troops in Poland. Kuklinski said that except for some basic information about locations and status, the Polish military had no information on their combat readiness, personnel, and equipment changes. "The Soviets do not comply with agreements on the status of Soviet troops in Poland," he wrote. "They inform no one of strength and equipment of their units in Poland."

The country's economic crisis was growing more severe. "Only a small elite in power knows the true situation," he wrote, adding that the government's strategy had been to implement price increases selectively and quietly, so as not to stir disorder among the people. Kuklinski said there was widespread apathy in the General Staff about Poland's political and economic problems. But with everything else going on, Kuklinski was enjoying his new home. The fact that his precarious relationship with the CIA made him feel sometimes as if he were "standing on ice," he wrote, "does not bother me too much. I enjoy its every warm corner."

Writing separately to Daniel, Kuklinski said that although he had not written to him as often as he had hoped to, "believe me that in my thoughts, I did address to you much more. You are a frequent guest in my home, and I talk with you openly about my ups and downs."

Of the news that Henry had retired, Kuklinski wrote, "As you know, he was the first American whose outstretched hand I was able to shake heartily."

So, at first Henry, and later you, Daniel, are basically the only representatives of your great nation of freedom with whom I have a right to believe that I do have a personal and sentimental contact. Your carefully considered remarks and advice are an inspiration for me, and assist me in my difficult road of life....

Before I retire, western countries are closed to me. I hope that I retire in the 1980s and will sail alone on the yacht to the United States.

I think that our friendship will last till that time, and that we shall then be giving each other more time and attention. . . .

Yours,

P.V.

On Sunday, April 16, 1978, Kuklinski turned over his letters and nineteen rolls of film in a car pass, and he received, among other things, an updated exfiltration plan. Over the next two months, he continued to receive visits from Colonel Putek, the overly inquisitive counterintelligence officer. On April 3, Kuklinski's "Name Day," a holiday celebrated like a birthday in Poland, Putek had arrived with a bouquet of flowers, embraced Kuklinski, and lavished him with praise. Kuklinski was baffled by Putek's flagrant attempts at ingratiation, but he did not want to seem unpleasant and played along. Twice he recommended Putek for cash bonus awards. Putek thanked him profusely.

One day in May, Kuklinski discovered that he could not account for a roll of film the CIA had given him. At first, he thought he had mislaid it, but he searched his closets, drawers, and other hiding places without success. He could also not remember whether he had used it yet for photographing documents. He recalled General Kufel's comment about the discovery of a lost "spy film."

He grew more worried. General Siwicki had assigned him to write a speech to be delivered in Sofia, Bulgaria, for a combined meeting of the chiefs of the General Staffs. The session was to focus on weapons development from 1981 to 1985 as well as Marshal Kulikov's proposal to place the Warsaw Pact armies under Soviet control in wartime. But Siwicki ordered Kuklinski to avoid including any hard data on Poland's armed forces in the speech. Siwicki said Moscow had complained that information from recent meetings was being leaked to the West. He implied that the Romanians were to blame, but Kuklinski wondered whether the leaks could be traced to him.

★

In June, Daniel prepared a new letter for Kuklinski, acknowledging that the course Kuklinski set out to take in 1972 had now become more lonely and difficult, as they could no longer see each other.

Robert Kennedy, younger brother of President John Kennedy, was assassinated 10 years ago this week. Just before that, he wrote that "Every generation has its central concern, whether to end war, erase racial injustice, or improve the condition of the working-man." Today's young people appear to have chosen for their concern the dignity of the individual human being. They demand a government that speaks directly and honestly to its citizens. We can win their commitment only by demonstrating that these goals are possible through personal effort.

I know very well that you are not alone in your "central concern" in the course you have chosen. Others like you in Poland, in the other nations of Eastern Europe, and in the Soviet Union, have the same concern. They, too, accept the dangers, control their outward manner, and know inwardly that they are fulfilling a responsibility that Robert Kennedy and his brother felt so deeply. The difference is that they, like you, must act alone. Your personal effort is not publicly known, shared, or praised by broad masses of society. It is known, in fact, by only a very few persons in my government. Yet, the results of your efforts have had, and continue to have, a deep impact on our capability to understand and counter the objectives and tactics of the Soviet Union....

You wistfully mention a lone cruise across the Atlantic to the United States. I wish nothing else for myself, and all those of us associated with you, than exactly this. We would welcome you with wide-open arms and a brotherly embrace. Our friendship will last not only until those days, but far beyond them. I do not have to assure you of that.

On June 18, in advance of the next exchange, Kuklinski drafted two letters to the CIA. "I await tonight's exchange with impatience," he wrote in one. He described Putek's visits and Siwicki's comment about leaks to the West. The implication that the Romanians were to blame did not exclude him "from the circle of suspects," he said. He asked for "an analysis of my situation, honest clarifications, and eventual instructions." He described General Kufel's briefing on surveillance traps in Warsaw and the discovery of the so-called spy film. "Initially, I did not attach much weight to it because I was convinced that this matter does not concern me," he wrote. But then he had discovered his own lost roll of film. "The fact is, one . . . film got lost somewhere, and I have not found it."

He continued to maintain strong relationships with his superiors and colleagues, and when Jaruzelski had asked General Skalski about him recently, Skalski had commended his work. "In sum, everything goes very well, but at the same time, there is a serious tension and concern. I feel a bit trapped," Kuklinski wrote. He needed to know what he should do.

> I reserve the final decision for myself. I would like to express my profound desire to continue our cooperation. I realize that, in fact, it is only now that [our cooperation] can be fully effective for my homeland and the cause of freedom in general.
>
> I have a heavy heart and I realize that in the end I shall have to leave this post, accepted out of free choice. However, I would like to close the matter concerning wartime statutes of the Combined Armed Forces, which aims at the sacred cause of independence of millennial Poland. I would like to pass possibly full information on the perspectives of developments of the Warsaw Pact forces within the next five years, on the new system of combat readiness, and also the entire data (still not accessible) from manuals of the USSR forces.
>
> In light of the tasks I have laid down for myself, my [collaboration] should last to at least the beginning of the 1980s. I am still against my leaving the country. Sooner or later, due to specific traits of my character and also circumstances, this would probably mean self-annihilation.

He said he was about to leave for a General Staff cruise along the Baltic coast, followed by a vacation with Hanka in Varna, a Bulgarian town on the Black Sea. "I ask for an urgent reply," he wrote.

In a second letter, Kuklinski said that his twenty-one new films included new materials "of a rather great importance" from the recent meetings in Sofia, including the Warsaw Pact's comprehensive weapons development plans for 1981–1985, and additional documents pertaining to Kulikov's new wartime statutes proposal.

That night as he waited at the exchange site, Kuklinski saw the CIA car being followed closely by another vehicle, whose headlights nearly blinded him. Kuklinski stepped back, and both cars passed without slowing. Kuklinski waited fifteen minutes, but the CIA car did not return. As he left the area, he realized a man was following him. It was several blocks before Kuklinski was able to lose him.

In an exchange on June 25, Kuklinski finally delivered his materials, including an account of the latest incident.

Warsaw Station officers, after reading the letters, cabled headquarters that Kuklinski was "very upset and needs our reply." At Langley, Daniel expressed concern about the investigation into the lost film and asked whether Kuklinski should be exfiltrated immediately. But the Soviet Division concluded that Kuklinski could not be a suspect, given his continued access to high-level materials.

Daniel and his colleagues decided Kuklinski should temporarily halt his activity. On June 28, headquarters cabled Warsaw saying Kuklinski should be told to destroy his "spy equipment"—cameras, special paper, and "commo" (communications) instructions—and "cease all activity on our behalf until early next year." Writing to Kuklinski, the agency said:

> We want to tell you that we sincerely believe that you are, at present, under no specific or special observation or suspicion. We are convinced that you would not be allowed to retain your access to high-level documents and conferences if there was the slightest hint of active suspicion directed at you, nor would you enjoy the high confidence of your superiors.

However, we should be very careful at the present time in order to keep any possible suspicion away from you. In the recent past, the WSW has conducted some successful investigations and made some arrests of persons working for the West. This has undoubtedly whetted their appetite to do even more and to be even more alert. Probably everyone who has had access to information on the defense ministers' meetings is being looked at. We want to be sure that when they conduct their investigations, no suspicion is directed at you.

Kuklinski was given new procedures to "call out" Warsaw Station for emergency contact and was asked to provide a VRS, or visual recognition signal, at 4:00 P.M. on a Sunday every other month, to alert the CIA that he was all right. He was told to pretend to make a call from a phone booth across from a particular fish shop. A CIA officer would drive by at that time. Emergency exfiltration procedures were "always in effect," the letter said.

His latest materials, the agency added, were invaluable. "The films in the last delivery are particularly excellent, perhaps the best and most significant material ever received." Saying it looked forward to renewing its contact with him in January 1979, the agency encouraged Kuklinski to take a well-earned rest. "After destroying your materials, please completely forget about us for a while," the CIA said.

The agency passed its letter to Kuklinski in a car pass on July 2. In the same exchange, Kuklinski delivered new films and a response to Daniel's last communication.

Your letter—as always characterized by cordiality and consideration, reached me—I shall not hide it—at times rather difficult for me, about which you undoubtedly are already informed through my last correspondence.

It was for me not only a boost (which I cannot enjoy, for obvious reasons, in my own milieu), but also strengthened my slightly wavering determination with new force. I thank you for all your thoughts, hopes, and words which you passed to me in this way.

The Polish nation, martyred by a not-so-distant war, pays dearly for its doubtful sense of stability brought about by submission to the communist indoctrination and dependence on the USSR. Studying materials which I pass according to my modest possibilities, you certainly had many occasions to realize what a thousand-year-long independence of Poland means, and how far and how deep the hands of Moscow are reaching. A clear proof of this are the wartime statutes—now being prepared for the Combined Armed Forces—through which the USSR demands full political, administrative and military powers over all the Warsaw Pact countries. The silent (except for the Romanians) approval of these authentically Socialist-imperialistic plans should be, for those who understand them, not only a shock, but also an alarm signal for action.

I do understand that the secrecy of negotiations does not permit telling the world public opinion about this. However, the preparation of grounds for rejection of these provocative demands is an indispensable necessity. I am proud of the fact that I find myself on the other side of this unnoticeable-for-the-average-citizen barricade, and that I am able to inform competent authorities of the power that was never indifferent to the cause of oppressed nations—the United States of America.

The governing team in Poland does not represent the nation's interests, and will have to go sooner or later, but this will mainly depend on the national consciousness of the Poles. I believe that I still have enough strength in order to act in this main, though deeply hidden, stream of events.

Daniel! In my last correspondence, I shared with you my observations and concern about security, but in my subconscious I await one answer only—that everything is okay, and that there is no red light to further cooperation. Wish this to myself most of all. . . .

Yours,

P.V.

This time, when asked to cease his activities temporarily, Kuklinski dutifully tried to erase all traces of his collaboration. He destroyed the

CIA's letter, the microfilm that contained the communications plans and communications sites, and his pad of water-soluble stationery. He placed his Olympus camera and rolls of unexposed film inside a box along with a sealed envelope. It contained his last will and testament. In it, he wrote a short account of his secret life and what had motivated him. He wrapped the box in plastic and paper and sealed the package with tape. He then affixed his military seal to the outside in wax and signed his name on it.

Kuklinski drove to the home of an old friend, Leon Barszcz, who lived in Bialobrzegi, a town about seventy miles south of Warsaw. Barszcz, whose younger brother Roman was Kuklinski's childhood friend from Niedabyl, was about eight years older than Kuklinski. Leon had served in the Polish underground and had managed to survive even after being arrested by the Gestapo and later the SB. After World War II, Leon Barszcz managed his family's fifty-five-acre farm in Niedabyl and later moved to a smaller farm in Bialobrzegi.

Kuklinski knew Leon still despised the Polish Communist regime and asked him if he would hold a sealed package for him. Kuklinski said nothing about what was inside the box, except that it contained no money or personal items. But he stressed that the contents meant everything to him and to Poland, and that it had to remain secret. He implored Leon to protect it with all his means. Leon said he was proud to help.

Kuklinski told Leon that if he ever heard a report that something untoward had happened to him, he should deliver the box to the American Embassy in Warsaw. Barszcz placed the box in a hiding place beneath a concrete terrace where he had also stowed some guns.

At headquarters, Daniel raised Kuklinski's latest security concerns with Soviet Division chief George Kalaris. A CIA counterintelligence officer was asked to investigate whether there had been leaks of Gull's material and to assess "the nature and severity of the security threat."

The task was a formidable one, given the large amount of intelligence Kuklinski had provided and the number of disseminations of his material by the Soviet Division's Reports and Requirements Staff. Sally Boggs,* the veteran officer who conducted the review, studied files and debriefed officers. On July 14, 1978, Boggs filed a seventeen-page single-spaced memorandum stamped "Eyes Only." She wrote that Gull "is by a wide margin the most valuable agent we are currently running against the Soviet/East European target, and possibly the most productive single human source against the Soviet/East European military the Agency has ever had." Over six years, Gull had provided more than 25,000 pages of classified Soviet and Polish documents concerning Warsaw Pact forces, plans, and equipment, resulting in roughly 1,300 disseminations. And there was still "a considerable quantity of documentary material yet to be processed."

> Much of this reporting has been of the highest intelligence value and has been sufficiently damaging to Warsaw Pact interests to eliminate any suspicion that it has been fed to us deliberately. Gull's production has established his bona fides beyond any reasonable doubt, and there is nothing in the operational record of the case or from collateral sources tending to refute this.
>
> The cause for concern in this case is recent reporting from Gull which indicates that the Poles and Soviets are aware that there has been leakage of important Warsaw Pact military information to the West, and that intensive counterintelligence efforts are underway to identify the source of such leaks. Although there is no indication that Gull is, as yet at least, under specific suspicion, the fact that he is one of those with access to material which is thought to have been leaked puts him within the circle of persons who are or could become targets of investigation.

The memo said a vital element in the assessment was whether Gull's intelligence had come to the attention of the opposition through leaks from "customers" in the intelligence community or

---

* Pseudonym.

through misuse. But to answer that would require extensive investigation within several U.S. government agencies to determine the actual—as opposed to the intended—dissemination of Gull's reporting, and a determination of how Gull's information had been used in negotiations with the Soviets, as in the Vienna arms control talks.

After an extensive analysis, Boggs laid out her conclusions. The best news concerned Gull's continued superior production. "As of 25 June 1978," she wrote, "when we received our last major delivery from Gull, his access and excellent standing within the Polish General Staff seemed undiminished...."

Boggs noted that "a preliminary assessment of the 21 rolls of film he passed on 25 June indicates it is some of the most valuable material he has ever provided. It seems unlikely that his extraordinary access would have been allowed to continue if he were under active suspicion at the time."

But Boggs cited the series of troubling incidents, from the evening in 1974 when Kuklinski was chased after being caught in surveillance to the most recent occasion involving the two cars. Although it was unlikely the SB had witnessed a handoff or identified Kuklinski as the man on the street, she wrote, the incidents suggested that he had been followed and was a marked man.

> Although Gull seems to have eluded his surveillants, his evasive actions must have convinced the surveillants that their target had been guilty of something and his description made matter of record for future reference.
>
> In addition to these two incidents, there have been problems with casuals [bystanders] on several of the exchanges, one or more of whom may have been sufficiently suspicious to report the incident, i.e. an unidentified man in furtive contact with a momentarily stopped diplomatic vehicle, and furnished a physical description. It thus seems to me probable that [Polish counterintelligence] has on file a physical description of Gull as a person possibly in clandestine contact with [foreign intelligence].

Fortunately, Gull is a rather slight individual of unprepossessing appearance and no singular or prominent physical characteristics. Moreover, in civilian clothes he would be unlikely to be taken for the senior military officer he is. His description, in itself, has not and probably will not lead to Gull. However, were suspicions to be directed at Gull for other reasons, a damaging comparison conceivably could be made.

We have no way of knowing on what grounds the Poles and/or Soviets believe that there have been significant leaks of important information on Warsaw Pact matters, but there seems little doubt that there is serious concern about this, and that counterintelligence activity to identify the source of such leaks has intensified. On at least four occasions, known or suspected leaks have involved material which Gull's office was in some way involved in preparing, although these documents apparently had fairly wide dissemination within the [General] Staff, and the suspected leakage would not necessarily be attributed to Gull's office on that basis....

I consider it vital that we make every effort to determine exactly what is happening to Gull's substantive reporting after it is disseminated, and to do whatever is possible to ensure that it does not go beyond those who have a genuine and compelling need for it. We should also, if possible, try to ascertain just how Gull's reporting has been used in any negotiations with Warsaw Pact governments, and whether our possession of Gull's material could have inadvertently been tipped off in this manner.

This, I recognize, constitutes a difficult task and perhaps an impossible one, but I feel we owe it both to the U.S. national interest and to this truly remarkable and dedicated agent to do everything humanly possible to protect him. Until we have thoroughly looked into what has been and is being done with Gull's reporting following formal dissemination, we will never have a full picture of his overall security situation.

After reviewing the Boggs memo, Kalaris alerted CIA director Turner to Gull's security situation. Kalaris said the agency was prepared to exfiltrate him on short notice, although Gull "has always stated that he wishes to remain in Poland unless there are specific indications that he is about to be arrested." On Sunday, August 6, 1978, an officer spotted Kuklinski in the phone booth near the fish shop—the visual recognition signal—and cabled Langley that he "appeared relaxed and healthy."

Two days later, the CIA informed the FBI that classified documents provided by Gull may have been "mishandled, either deliberately or otherwise."

In the half decade since Daniel had first met Kuklinski in Europe, he had risen from case officer to chief of operations for the Soviet Division. But his recent five-year stint at headquarters was relatively long for a field officer. In August 1978, at the age of forty-seven, he was asked whether he would be interested in going to Vienna as Chief of Station. Vienna, a lively, beautiful city, was a busy place for the CIA, which had more than thirty officers posted there. But the transfer would remove Daniel from the Gull case and would also raise family issues. His wife, Sally, had joined him on his four previous overseas postings, in Germany, Argentina, Poland, and Mexico. She was not excited about a fifth. They had a lovely house in Potomac, Maryland, and their children, Caty, Daniel, and Sara, who were then ten, twelve, and eighteen, had settled into school and the community. Sally also wanted to resume her career as a journalist. Daniel finally decided to go to Vienna alone.

In August 1978, Kuklinski and Hanka enjoyed their brief vacation in Bulgaria, but he returned to some uncertainty. Over a period of several nights, he found cars parked outside his home for hours, with people remaining inside them. Then one day at work, a military counter-intelligence (WSW) officer visited Kuklinski's office and said the WSW was conducting a broad investigation into intelligence leaks to the West. The officer had asked Kuklinski for a list of officers who were involved in weapons planning and development, command systems, and combat readiness. Kuklinski was relieved later when he learned that Chief of Staff Siwicki had requested the investigation. Since Siwicki regularly entrusted him with sensitive duties, Kuklinski concluded that he was unlikely to be under suspicion.

Upon his return from vacation in Bulgaria, Kuklinski was assigned to prepare materials for the continuing Vienna arms negotiations. The instructions from the Soviet Union were to conceal the true manpower of the Warsaw Pact ground forces.

In September, Kuklinski was enormously relieved when he found the missing roll of film in the pocket of a flannel workshirt that he had not worn in a while.

Feeling more confident, Kuklinski retrieved his sealed package from Leon Barszcz and began photographing documents again.

In late 1978, the CIA prepared to resume contact with Kuklinski. As requested, he had appeared at 4:00 P.M. on Sunday, October 1, in the phone booth near the fish store, to signal that he was safe. That month, a memo summarizing the operation said that Gull had been producing intelligence "at a prodigious rate," and the exchanges were to begin again in two months. The memo repeated earlier assertions that he was "the best-placed source now available to the U.S. government in the Soviet bloc, in terms of collection of priority information."

In late December or early January 1979, Kuklinski left a signal asking for an exchange that night. In it, he delivered twenty rolls of film, which contained around 500 pages of documents. "I will not attempt to hide the fact that I lived through some difficult days," he wrote in a five-page letter, adding that he hoped the crisis was over. He described his relief at finding the missing film. "I considered the possibility of informing you about this important discovery, but a sober evaluation of the still-complex situation restrained me from taking this step. Any contact with me could have been dangerous for both sides."

Kuklinski said he had begun to collect documents again in August. They included materials from the Warsaw Pact command in Moscow on weapons development, his notes on Project Albatross, and a draft directive from Kulikov concerning the new combat-readiness system. "This document carries the highest grade of classification," Kuklinski wrote.

He also described the misleading figures being submitted in the Vienna arms talks. "It was a matter of the Poles (on instructions from Moscow) concealing the actual manpower of the ground forces," he wrote. "While working on this problem, I gained normal access to documents which might once and for all dissolve your doubts concerning Soviet intentions and, under pressure from them, those of the other Warsaw Pact countries, to deceive and swindle the West regarding the numerical strength of the forces under negotiation."

At Langley, Kuklinski's materials—his first document delivery in six months—produced relief. Kuklinski, meanwhile, received a letter commenting on several documents he had delivered the previous summer.

"The Russian-language document you provided in your last delivery on the development of the Warsaw Pact forces from 1981–1985 was an outstanding acquisition," the letter said. "However, the Russian-language document which provided the tactical and technical specifications of Soviet military material to be introduced into the Warsaw Pact forces during the period 1979–1985 is potentially the single most important document that you have provided us in our long and productive association, because it will not only impact on all branches of the U.S. military establishment but will also impact on NATO force structure in the forward area."

The CIA reminded Kuklinski that in resuming his activities, his safety should remain paramount. "If there is ever any question in your mind as to whether you can securely manage an act, please make your decision in favor of safety, even if this means you are not able to photograph an important document or that you must abort a scheduled exchange," the CIA said.

The agency warned of an investigative tactic sometimes used to track leaks. A test document, often genuine but also marked in some covert way, would be given to an official who was under suspicion, and a Soviet agent in the West would then be used to determine whether the document was passed to the CIA. "This is a technique which the KGB has used, for example.

"Therefore, we ask that you be particularly attentive to circumstances when documents to which you and your immediate working colleagues do not have normal access or which, for one reason or another, seem suspicious or unusual become available to you. If such a situation arises, please exercise special care in deciding whether or not these documents can be securely copied. Please also identify the specific document or documents to us."

The CIA advised Kuklinski not to be overly concerned about surveillance on Rajcow Street, although he should exercise caution. "Remember that all of your neighbors are also military officials and the surveillance may have been directed against any one of them, or no one in particular."

A letter from Daniel was also cabled to Warsaw for delivery to Kuklinski. Daniel said he felt recurring frustration over not being able to do more to ease Kuklinski's lingering concerns about security. Over the past six months, he wrote, the CIA had conducted "an exhaustive study of what the Soviets might have learned, and in what way."

We have also examined what they know and speculate we learned from the Romanians—Gen. Pacepa.* Putting all this together, we find nothing that in their eyes points at you. Moreover, they have many more directions in which to look before they can begin to solve their problem of restricted information "leaking" to the West.

Even so, I am satisfied that our mutually agreed suspension of contact was a wise decision. You needed a period of normal activity in

* Lt. General Ion Pacepa, the former deputy chief of Nicolae Ceausescu's foreign intelligence service, defected to the West in 1978.

which there would be no risk at all of attracting idle curiosity. We needed time for our investigation. It was deeply rewarding for us, however, to see you during that period at the recognition site. Your timing was perfect....

P.V.—you are seldom far from my thoughts. In a complicated and changing world, there is no one I know who has shown greater courage and dedication than you in the successful pursuit of our common goals. In the loneliness of your work, know that the bonds of friendship, respect and shared purpose bind us together—and will do so always.

Sincerely,
Daniel

Warsaw Station, after reviewing the draft, made only a minor alteration, and the letters were delivered to Kuklinski in early 1979. But there would soon be a significant change in how Daniel's letters were prepared. With Daniel now stationed in Vienna, it would be impractical for him to continue the highly personal correspondence with Kuklinski. But because his letters were a critical part of the Gull operation, the CIA felt it was too risky to stop them, and the agency did not want even to suggest to Kuklinski that Daniel was no longer at Langley, for fear it would concern or distract him. The Soviet Division thus assigned a group of officers, including Stanley Patkowski, the translator who had adeptly handled Daniel's correspondence with Kuklinski, to produce letters under Daniel's name. They consulted with Daniel, studied his earlier letters, and became thoroughly familiar with his voice and style.

Daniel was not troubled by the idea. His friendship with Kuklinski was genuine, but so was his concern for Kuklinski's security and morale. Daniel agreed that it was essential for the letters to continue, but they had to be germane and contemporaneous. Keeping him in the loop would be a strain on the operation and could lead to mistakes. For the several years Daniel expected to be away from Langley, he was confident his colleagues would find his voice and keep the conversation going.

7

TREMORS OF CHANGE

ONE NIGHT IN FEBRUARY 1979, Ruth Brerewood,* who ran the CIA's Polish desk at Langley, was in Warsaw dining with a CIA colleague and his wife at a fashionable restaurant called the Duck. Brerewood had never served in Poland, but she had agreed to fill a two-month vacancy in Warsaw Station until a new full-time officer arrived. In a way, it was appropriate for her to be there. She had done just about everything else in the Gull case.

A former high school librarian from Ogdensburg, New York, Brerewood had joined the CIA in 1963. As the Polish desk officer, she played a quiet but critical role in support of the Gull operation. After Daniel went to Vienna, for example, she helped to coordinate the preparation of "Daniel" letters that were sent to Gull. She read the final version of each draft to make sure the secretaries had matched word for word what the translator, Stanley Patkowski, had written. When Kuklinski's film was shipped to Langley, Brerewood hauled the special lead-lined containers to the photo labs run by the Office of Technical Services, and soon there was so much film coming in that the lab technicians

* Pseudonym.

taught her how to make prints. After the rolls were developed, she logged in each negative, matching it with its corresponding print. Although she could not read Polish or Russian, she could usually determine by examining a series of images where each document began and ended.

And because Brerewood was privy to the dates of exchanges with Kuklinski, she experienced them vicariously. On Sundays, when she knew Warsaw Station would be meeting him in the evening Polish time, she grew tense in the afternoon, waiting, wondering, looking at her watch, knowing the exchange was taking place. She did not relax until she got into work the next morning, had checked the cables, and knew Gull was safe.

That night, as she and her colleagues sat in the Duck restaurant, she did not realize how close she would come to encountering Gull. As she and her friends studied the menu, her CIA colleague suddenly looked up and remarked, "You know, I don't think I want duck tonight." He glanced at a nearby table occupied by a group of men wearing the khaki uniforms of the Polish Army. The Americans got up and left. Later, the colleague told her that one of the officers at the nearby table was Gull.

In early March, Sue Burggraf joined Warsaw Station, the first woman to serve as a full-time CIA operations officer in Poland. She had initially turned down the job. A single woman in her early thirties, she had assumed that Warsaw would be a grim and lonely place, and she did not relish the notion of being the target of constant surveillance, in her apartment and car and on the phone.

Burggraf loved to travel, had visited every state except Alaska and Hawaii, and had spent a summer working as a chambermaid in a tiny village in the Black Forest in Germany. She craved adventure. As a senior at Ohio University in 1967, when she heard a CIA recruiter was on campus, she went to meet him. He told her she'd "be doing some spy-type things," she recalled. "It sounded pretty sexy to me." She wasn't told she would be hired as a secretary. Burggraf, whose father worked as a postman and whose mother was a church organist, was the first member of her family to attend college, and she felt out of place as the only college graduate in her training class of about two dozen secretaries-to-be. By the time she completed her training, about half of the women in her class had become pregnant and dropped out. Burggraf persisted and was sent overseas as a CIA secretary. She eventually returned to Langley and worked her way up.

But even as an officer, she encountered resistance. When she was first offered the Warsaw posting, the job was described as "station support," one step below an officer's slot. She would have no interaction with sources and would be allowed only to scout new operational sites and to watch for chalk marks and other signals on her way to and from work. Infuriated, Burggraf refused to take the position. One CIA official reminded her that she had signed a commitment to go anywhere the agency sent her, and another supervisor, Peter Earnest, urged her to reconsider. Earnest made some calls and assured her that she would be a full case officer by the time she arrived in Poland. Burggraf was given six months to prepare. She spoke no Polish and immersed herself in language classes, pausing only on Friday afternoons, when she would go to headquarters to familiarize herself with the Polish case files.

After her arrival in Warsaw, she bought a white Polski Fiat for $2,500, figuring it would be easier for sources to see in the dark. But like all new officers, Burggraf was told she would have to wait six months before she could carry out an exchange on the street. She would have to get to know the city and establish daily driving patterns to get a feel for surveillance. As she had expected, life in Warsaw was challenging. For months, her home phone rang repeatedly, and when she answered, she would hear different female voices, speaking in Polish. Burggraf didn't yet know the language well enough to converse with the callers, but she knew how to say "wrong number." When she hung up, the phone would ring again.

On March 23, after several aborted exchange attempts with Kuklinski, the CIA drove by the phone booth near the fish shop, where he had agreed to appear for a signal, but he was not there. A month later, Warsaw Station left a chalk mark signaling Kuklinski to appear for an unscheduled exchange, but again he did not show up. "Disappointed but not yet alarmed," Warsaw cabled Langley. The CIA decided to wait for a signal from Kuklinski.

At 8:30 A.M. on April 30, an officer spotted a chalk mark, an indication that Kuklinski would leave a message at ten o'clock that night. Warsaw Station retrieved the message, in which Kuklinski requested a car exchange on May 6.

Kuklinski had skipped the March 4 exchange because he had nothing significant to pass on to the CIA. He had intended to visit the phone booth on March 23, but the night before, he learned that one of his closest friends, Barbara Jakubowska, had died of ovarian cancer. She and her parents had been close friends of Kuklinski and Hanka. Barbara's father, Czeslaw, doted on Kuklinski, and reminded him of his own father, who had the same slow walk and temperament. Barbara, who was in her late twenties, had been employed by an electronics company and was studying economics. She was close to Kuklinski's son Bogdan, loved their dog, Zula, and enjoyed sailing with the family. In the early 1970s, when Barbara became ill, her parents asked Kuklinski for advice about the best doctors. His mother had died in 1963 from the same illness. Kuklinski accompanied Barbara to the hospital and stayed involved in her case. When her cancer went into remission, her parents, who were deeply religious, credited Kuklinski with performing a miracle.

Barbara continued her recovery, but one day her parents called Kuklinski to say she had suffered a stroke and lost her speech. In mid-March, after a second stroke, she had died. Her death, which saddened Kuklinski enormously, came at a time of difficult family issues for Kuklinski as well. Hanka's arthritis and back pain, which had been diagnosed as spinal degeneration, had forced her to quit her job as a factory bookkeeper. Bogdan had gone to trial in the case involving the pedestrian he had struck. He was convicted, fined, and received a suspended sentence of one year.

On May 3, Soviet Marshal Kulikov led a highly classified training exercise that involved small teams of Warsaw Pact officers and was intended to simulate the transition of Warsaw Pact military forces from peacetime to wartime status. Kuklinski was outraged that his superiors were not resisting Kulikov's proposal to place the Polish General Staff under Soviet control in wartime, and within the General Staff he openly expressed his hostility. He had heard scuttlebutt that the proposal also deeply offended Prime Minister Piotr Jaroszewicz, who was apparently unwilling to say so publicly.

On the night of May 5, as the exercise ended, Kuklinski wrote to the CIA describing the materials he had photographed under tight security. "It was forbidden to take any typists or draftswomen. All documents had to be executed by hand by generals and officers," he wrote. In a delivery the next day, he provided more than seventy documents, which filled more than 800 film images. One twelve-page report, dated January 12, 1979, was about Soviet chemical warfare training; a memo from Polish intelligence was about the collection of data on an advanced U.S. communications satellite system called Marisat. There was new material on the battle-readiness plan for the Warsaw Pact militaries, sent by Kulikov's staff.

Kuklinski said he felt secure enough to criticize Kulikov's proposed wartime statutes, and he suspected some of his colleagues silently agreed with him.

> I continue to belong to the circle of persons who are favored with the greatest trust in spite of my opposition to all solutions which menace the sovereignty of the state which I serve. Words of disapprobation about my bitterness toward pro-Soviet and servile attitudes are swallowed. It is possible that in the majority of cases, we all think the same but differ only in tactics of action.

Kuklinski, unaware that Daniel was no longer at headquarters, wrote him a separate letter, in which he expressed his fury at Kulikov's aggressive and presumptuous approach to the wartime statutes. The training exercise, which lasted up to twenty hours a day, had made clear that for the first time in a thousand years, Poland's leaders were to approve a procedure that would deprive the nation of its sovereign rights and relinquish them "to the hands of a foreign power which is stretching its greedy paws into all corners of the world in order to reign supreme over it." Kuklinski found it deplorable that except for Romania, no Warsaw Pact leader was objecting to "this shameful decision."

Daniel: The purpose of activities I assumed on my own free will seven years ago was and still is active counter-action against such a development of events as is described above. Facing you with these matters I wish to hope that knowledge of them will allow the highest authorities of the United States to take appropriate blocking counter-measures. I do not feel competent to voice any proposals in these matters.

Kuklinski described his sadness at Barbara Jakubowska's death. "She was extremely modest and inconspicuous, but a woman of enormous generosity who offered everything and asked nothing in return." He said he had visited her grave at Wolski cemetery, which was only fifty meters from the cemetery where he had first met the Americans. "Passing by there, I feel at this moment my only encouragement that our road, which had its good beginning at this very spot, has still not ended," he wrote.

Daniel—ending this, I would like to thank you cordially for your last letter, and for everything that you have done for me lately. I am grateful to you for your friendship, which you invariably sustain, caring about and doing everything for my security. I do not lose hope that it will be given to us not only to shake friendly hands but also to establish closer contacts, either in your or my country. Everything indicates that

last year's tensions have been completely conquered and that there is a
chance for continuation of a secure and effective cooperation.

Yours,

P.V.

The CIA considered the nineteen rolls of film Kuklinski provided
on May 6 highly significant. One CIA memo said that one document, a
fourteen-page letter from Jaruzelski to Kulikov on the proposal to
place Polish forces under Soviet control in wartime, would be held in
strict secrecy. Outside the CIA, it would go only to the chief of the
Defense Intelligence Agency, Lt. General Eugene F. Tighe Jr.; the director of the National Security Agency, Vice Admiral Bobby Ray Inman;
and the Army's assistant chief of staff for intelligence, Major General
Edmund R. Thompson.

Over the next two months, the General Staff continued to feel pressure from Kulikov and his staff on the wartime proposal. "I feel as if I
were in the eye of a cyclone," Kuklinski wrote to the CIA in a letter he
delivered in an exchange on July 8. He also turned over fourteen rolls
of film, including a twenty-seven-page Russian draft of the proposed
wartime statute that had been given to Jaruzelski. Only Jaruzelski,
Siwicki, and one other officer were aware of the contents, Kuklinski
wrote. "Please use information on this subject very sparingly."

He also provided a detailed analysis of Soviet weapons systems,
including the T-72 tank, "which I obtained during a demonstration of
this tank for the leading personnel of the Polish General Staff." He had
photographed a table that compared the combat capabilities of Soviet
aircraft, including the Su-24, Su-17 M2, and MiG-27. Most had not yet
been introduced into the Polish military. "I copied these tables from a
notebook of one of the Russian generals participating in bilateral talks
at the Polish General Staff (of course without his knowledge)."

He noted that Colonel Putek, the counterintelligence officer who
had visited him so frequently, had been transferred to Egypt. "He even
sent me a postcard from Cairo," he noted wryly.

In the exchange, he received a sympathetic response from "Daniel" to the news of the death of Barbara. The CIA also told Kuklinski that Stan, the officer who had translated the correspondence between him and Daniel, was retiring, so Kuklinski therefore might notice some differences in style and expressions in future letters.

"Because of his highest esteem and admiration for you, he postponed his retirement several times in order to follow closely our activities and take an active part in them," the CIA said. "Through this letter, he sends you his expression of highest respect and wishes you every success in all aspects of your life. His replacement is a long-time highly trusted colleague who feels honored to become a member of our small, exclusive group."

In August 1979, Ted Gilbertson,* an amiable thirty-seven-year-old West Virginian with a small mustache and boyish face, arrived in Poland, joining Burggraf in Warsaw Station. Gilbertson, an eight-year CIA veteran, had two children and was in the midst of a complicated divorce, but was pleased that he could work out the assignment. He had an uncommon background for a CIA officer. After graduating from Pennsylvania State University, he worked as a reporter at WPSX, a local educational station, where he started an innovative children's news program. After serving in the army, he applied to the CIA, and while waiting to hear from the agency, he became a traveling salesman for a pharmaceutical company. He seemed always to be in his car, making calls on offices and clinics, which turned out to be good preparation for Warsaw Station, where he spent hours on surveillance detection runs.

Before leaving for Warsaw, Gilbertson met with George Kalaris, the serious and at times mercurial chief of the Soviet Division at the time. Kalaris told Gilbertson that Gull was the most important case the Directorate of Operations had running against Moscow. "If you do nothing else, do not fuck up on this tour," Kalaris said.

* Pseudonym.

A third new officer, Michael Dwyer, thirty-three, arrived in Warsaw in early September for his first posting in a denied area. A native of Buffalo, New York, Dwyer* was an Asian expert who had served in Vietnam in the navy and was fluent in Vietnamese.

Some years earlier, Dwyer had been interviewed by Daniel about his next assignment. Dwyer was ready for a challenge and made clear that he wanted to be sent to Moscow Station. Daniel puffed slowly on a Camel, his lids half closed in the smoke, and sat silently. Dwyer watched the ash on Daniel's cigarette grow longer and longer, as the smoke billowed upward. Daniel finally spoke.

"Warsaw would be a terrific assignment," he said. "We *really* have some operations there." He held out his palm. "In one meeting, you can pick up in your hand more intelligence than most guys could get in their hands in their whole career."

Dwyer landed in Warsaw on September 2, 1979, three months after the historic visit of Pope John Paul II, the former Bishop of Krakow, who had celebrated a mass in Victory Square with 250,000 Poles. He had declared to thunderous applause, "There can be no just Europe without the independence of Poland marked on its map!"

As Dwyer drove around the city, he could feel the tremors of change. Buildings and walls were covered with slogans heralding resistance. Many signs displayed a "P" superimposed on a "W" for "Polska Walczaca" (Fighting Poland), the symbol of the Polish Home Army, and Dwyer was reminded of how proud and independent the Poles remained. Some of the slogans were quickly painted over by the Communists, but the paint never seemed to hold in the rain, and the slogans reappeared. On September 17, the fortieth anniversary of the Soviet invasion, Dwyer and a colleague drove past the Russian trade mission in Warsaw, where someone had scaled a thirty-foot wall in front and painted in large Polish letters "We will never forget!"

Later in the year, on November 11, the holiday that commemorates Polish independence in 1918 after nearly 125 years of partition by Prus-

* Pseudonym.

sia, Russia, and Austria, Dwyer went to hear the Polish primate, Cardinal Stefan Wyszynski, give a homily before thousands of Poles in St. John's Cathedral in the Old Town. Afterward, Dwyer moved with the crowd into the streets, where banners were unfurled reading "Freedom" and "Bread" and others quoting the pope's challenge that there could not be a just Europe without a free Poland. As Dwyer watched, SB agents moved through the crowd, tearing down banners. Just as quickly more went up. Dwyer was deeply moved by what he was seeing—the Poles' obvious courage in an evening of national defiance.

He joined the crowd as it marched in the chilly evening through the narrow streets of Old Town to Castle Square and up Krakowskie Przedmiescie, the main boulevard in Warsaw, to Victory Square and the Tomb of the Unknown Soldier, a national symbol that predated the Communist regime. That night, Dwyer learned the historic Polish national anthem as the crowd sang it over and over.

In early September, Jaruzelski ordered that the General Staff comment on the Soviet draft of the wartime statute before it was presented to party chief Gierek and Prime Minister Jaroszewicz. When Siwicki and his top officers met to discuss it, the group remained silent when asked for its views. Kuklinski finally spoke up, saying he felt strongly that the proposal should be rejected. "We should turn it down in this form. We're giving everything to the Soviets," he said.

Asked to draft a response for Siwicki, Kuklinski produced a highly critical document but was ordered to soften it. Kuklinski revised the document several more times, but each time he was told to eliminate criticism of the proposal, and to find that the proposal was in the interest of Poland and should be accepted. Finally, Kuklinski drew up a version that included only marginal objections and reached the conclusion that his superiors wanted.

When Jaruzelski and his deputies met on September 10 to discuss Kulikov's proposal, there was no dissent. Jaruzelski said that the issue was a difficult one that "requires comprehensive research and study."

Siwicki offered no criticism of his own, but handed Jaruzelski the paper Kuklinski had prepared.

On September 21, Marshal Kulikov returned to Poland to meet with Gierek and Jaruzelski. The Poles offered a muddled and weak compromise. Kulikov rejected the Polish ideas and said he would return for further talks. That day, Kuklinski began an angry letter about Kulikov's rigidity and the cravenness of the East bloc, including Poland. In the General Staff, he knew there were officers who saw the proposal as "a brutal attempt to cancel the sovereignty of the member countries of the Warsaw Pact." But it was clear that criticism would get nowhere. "All this week," Kuklinski wrote to the CIA, "we were backing out of specific stipulations and positions, and finally a very trimmed-down version was presented to Kulikov."

> I'm certain that the leadership of the MON [Ministry of Defense] will be ready, if Moscow demands it, to back out of the rest of their proposals, and support the draft of the statute.... Kulikov has already discussed these matters in Czechoslovakia, and according to his words, he received full support there. From Poland, he will go to the German Democratic Republic for the same purpose.

Kuklinski noted that his responsibilities had also increased. While remaining chief of the General Staff's First Department for Strategic Defense Planning, he would also assume the duties of deputy chief for the entire operational directorate. "Taking everything into consideration, I evaluate the situation as very favorable," he wrote.

Writing separately to Daniel, Kuklinski recalled the loss of Barbara and offered a meditation on "the delicate nature of friendship, brutally disrupted by death."

> There is no parting with real, devoted friends. There is no way to part with them even when they are not among us anymore. I don't

know if I will ever be able to pull myself together from this loss. . . .

Dear Daniel, I agree with you that we cannot reverse irreversible events. From personal survival and experiences, I also know that time heals even the most severe wounds, strength and faith permitting. Despite my continuing state of depression, I see ahead many unattained goals, both the great ones related to Polish aspirations for liberty, and the lesser ones pertaining to family and myself.

Kuklinski said that he felt he enjoyed the trust of his superiors, as evidenced by his inclusion in the narrow circle involved in the wartime statutes and his apparent ability to openly criticize the proposal within the General Staff.

Even though I know that my efforts to reject this disgraceful document, in the end, will not be crowned with success, this work gives me much satisfaction because for the first time in over 30 years I can speak what I think on this subject and how I evaluate it. Not all the evaluations, conclusions and proposals are being accepted. However, I hope that the language which aims at finalizing the transfer to the hands of Moscow of the inalienable right of the Polish nation to reach decisions concerning how to use its own armed forces will be changed, and the other provisions of this document, which attempt to destroy what is left of Polish statehood, will be considerably moderated.

Of course, preventing the destruction of one's own statehood, and total subordination to Moscow, is the business of the concerned nation and its government.

Kuklinski added a note of appreciation to Stanley Patkowski, the retiring translator, and said he was including "a token of my remembrance"—the pen used to sign the resolutions of the defense ministers committee meeting in Budapest. "Daniel, shake his belabored hand for me," Kuklinski wrote.

He delivered the pen, his letters, and twenty-seven rolls of film in an exchange on September 24.

Over the next few weeks, Kuklinski was assigned to coordinate the final negotiations regarding the wartime statutes with Kulikov and his staff, who were making visits to each Warsaw Pact capital, pressing for agreement.

In mid-October, Kulikov, accompanied by Gribkov, his chief of staff, and other deputies and officers, returned to Poland for two days of secret talks at Omulew, a town in the lush Mazurian Lake region in northeast Poland. As the sessions began, Kulikov made it clear that he considered any opposition to his proposal to be unacceptable. Bulgaria, Germany, and Czechoslovakia supported the draft "without reservations," he said. Hungary had been more difficult to win over. In fourteen hours of negotiations, he said, Hungary's defense minister had expressed numerous reservations, only to back down on every point, surprising even the Soviets, Kulikov said.

The biggest problem was Romania, Kulikov went on, accusing Romanian officials of leaking information to the West. He bristled as he described his visit to Bucharest. As his plane arrived, the Romanian air-traffic controllers had refused to communicate in Russian. Once on the ground, the Romanian secret police had surrounded him and followed him everywhere. Worse, he said, he was placed in a hotel room next to some Chinese officials. Kulikov said that he expected Jaruzelski to maintain the united front against the Romanians when the Warsaw Pact defense ministers met in Warsaw in December, in a session being led by Jaruzelski. The statutes were to be approved at the meeting. Gribkov added at one point that although he appreciated Jaruzelski's general support for the statutes, it was time for the Poles to give their "detailed substantive and editorial agreement."

During the meetings, Jaruzelski, Kulikov, and Gribkov went hunting, telling Kuklinski to work out the remaining disagreements between the Poles and the Soviets. When they returned a few hours

later, Kulikov had killed three stags, Gribkov two, and the Polish generals none. Kulikov demanded to know what progress had been made.

When Kuklinski reported that the latest Soviet draft did not adequately deal with Polish concerns, Jaruzelski looked unhappy. But
Siwicki said that the Soviets had to take Poland's positions seriously, a
stance that caught Kulikov by surprise. After another day of talks,
compromises were worked out in all but two areas. The most important disagreement was over Moscow's insistence on having unilateral
authority to move the Polish air defense systems beyond Poland's borders to protect Soviet troops as they moved westward in an offensive.

Kuklinski was told to go to Moscow with a two-star general who
served as the Polish air defense commander to resolve the issue. Before
leaving, Kuklinski met with Siwicki, who agreed that Poland should
not surrender control of its air defenses in wartime. At the very least,
Siwicki said, no such act should occur without Poland's agreement.

In Moscow, Kuklinski and the Polish air defense commander met
with a Soviet negotiating team led by the deputy Soviet air defense
commander, a General Podgorney. After a day of talks, Kuklinski felt
that they had won concessions on two points: The air defense of each
Warsaw Pact country should be used to protect only that country, and
if it became necessary to move air defense forces beyond the country's
borders, the decision should be made by the political and military leadership of that country, not Moscow. Second, the air defense commander of each Warsaw Pact country should have authority within
that country's territory.

That night, during a reception in Moscow in honor of the tentative
agreement, Podgorney rose and raised his glass. He gave a series of
toasts, to the Communist Party, party leaders Leonid Brezhnev and
Edward Gierek, Defense Ministers Ustinov and Jaruzelski, and others.

"I want to raise one more toast," he then said. "We respect Poland.
Poland stood behind us, supported us. We respect our friends." He
said he was proud that Poland had backed his country in wartime.
"We admire our friends who support us.

"But we also respect our enemy," Podgorney continued, offering a toast to the health of "Comrade Colonel Kuklinski," who he said had a bright future and was so highly respected by his superiors. "We know that he is not with us, but against us. Despite this, let us drink to his posterity."

Kuklinski, who had been sitting impassively, was stunned. The Polish air defense commander smiled grimly. The next morning, Kuklinski and the other negotiators were summoned to a meeting with an enraged Kulikov, who ranted about Poland's obstinacy on the air defense issue and said he was canceling the agreements reached by his own staff. Then, as Kuklinski and the others watched, Kulikov grabbed his telephone and spoke to Jaruzelski in Warsaw.

"Everyone wants a statute for time of war, and while they are at it, to put obstacles in my way," Kulikov snarled. "Everyone agrees that there should be one command, only everyone wants to be in command!"

Kulikov told Jaruzelski that further negotiations would be fruitless. It was clear Jaruzelski was backpedaling.

"Yep. Yep. Yep," Kulikov snapped. He turned to Kuklinski and held up the phone. "Listen to your boss," Kulikov said. "We've reached full agreement." Jaruzelski had conceded on every point.

Kuklinski was angry when he returned to Warsaw. He told Siwicki about the critical toast by the Soviet general and asked whether he should resign because it might be hard for him to deal with the Soviets in the future. Siwicki laughed it off and said the Russians probably criticized him, Siwicki, even more than Kuklinski; and he should just ignore it.

Throughout the fall, the CIA had been refining its exfiltration plans for Kuklinski and his family. On November 12 headquarters prepared an updated version of the instructions and cabled it to Warsaw for delivery. The document said that if Kuklinski ever felt he was in imminent danger, he should proceed immediately to the American Embassy. "We are prepared to receive you day or night at any time," the CIA wrote. If he arrived between 6:00 A.M. and midnight, he should enter the compound by the open driveway gate.

If you do come after midnight, you should use the entrance to
Piekna 14b, to the east of the driveway, because the lock on the
door of this entrance was damaged during recent renovations. A
new lock has been installed. We have included a key in this package which will open the new lock. Please throw the old key in the
river or return it at our next exchange.

He was told to prepare a short note in English identifying himself
as Jack Strong. "If you are stopped by anyone in the embassy compound, this note will assure that you are immediately taken to the
Marines at the Piekna entrance."*

Meanwhile, the CIA was studying ways to speed up communications with Kuklinski in the event he had to make an emergency escape
or report critical news. One form of technology under development,
known as Discus, was an electronic transmitting device that would
enable Kuklinski to send short encrypted messages to a receiving unit
in the American Embassy or carried elsewhere by a Warsaw-based officer. One September 5, 1979, cable from Warsaw Station to headquarters pointed out that the complex system of signals with chalk marks
on lampposts or electrical boxes required at least a thirty-six-hour
turnaround. "Gull learns of imminent hostilities one morning. He
makes signal at 'Szkola' that night, and we retrieve his package [the]
next night," the cable said. It all took too long. The cable noted that
when Discus eventually "goes into operation, this 'early warning' time
should be cut to almost zero."

By the late fall, Burggraf, Gilbertson, and Dwyer were in place. Dwyer,
the most recent arrival, was living in Warsaw with his wife and infant
son. Because he had not been in Warsaw for six months, he was not

---

* The agency included phone numbers if Kuklinski felt that he needed to call the embassy
in advance of his arrival. On any weekday, from 8:30 A.M. to 5:00 P.M., he could dial the
embassy's main number and request extension 220. At nighttime and on weekends, he
should dial CIA officers at home.

yet allowed to make exchanges with sources and had completed only one operational act in the Gull case: He had erased a chalk mark.

Dwyer had spent most of his time studying surveillance and casing for operational sites. On the night of November 25, Dwyer drove to retrieve a package that he had left on the ground for a source (not Kuklinski) but that had not been picked up. The source had volunteered his services to the Americans relatively recently, and his bona fides were not yet established.

Dwyer arrived at the site in his 1979 Italian Fiat, which had American diplomatic plates, and picked up the package, which had been left in the grass along a one-way street. As he began to pull away, he saw an unmarked car turn the wrong way out of a driveway before him and head in his direction. Hearing the wail of sirens, Dwyer began to slow down. He knew he had been ambushed. A half dozen police cars appeared, and as they surrounded him, Dwyer managed to toss the miniature earpiece he wore for countersurveillance out the window into the tall grass by the side of the road. He then reached down and stuffed under the seat the package he had retrieved and a transistor radio he kept beside him as a backup to listen for SB surveillance.

Within seconds, he was ordered out of the car at gunpoint and was surrounded by SB agents. One held a gun under his chin as another frisked him. The agents also took the package he had put under the seat. Then he was pushed into the back of a car and driven to a militia headquarters where he was interrogated and held for about ten hours in an office whose most notable feature, he would later recall, was a bust of Felix Dzerzhinsky, the Polish-born founder of the KGB, which sat at eye level on a bookshelf glaring at him.

"I am an American diplomat, my name is Michael Dwyer, and I have the right to contact my embassy," he said repeatedly, refusing to answer other questions as a camera rolled. The Poles, who were desperate for American grain and loan assistance, did not mistreat Dwyer while they held him.

It was clear that the source had at some point come under the control of the SB, and that the site had been under surveillance for some time. At about 3:00 A.M., Dwyer's frightened wife, who was at home with their son, called the embassy to say her husband had not yet come home. The next day, in an open telephone conversation that the Americans knew would be overheard by Polish intelligence, an embassy official told Washington that Dwyer was being withdrawn. He was released, and two days later, he and his family left Poland.

There was nothing good about being "wrapped up," Dwyer later recalled, but at least he knew that while Polish officials were celebrating the arrest of a CIA officer who had been in Poland for all of three months, they were being diverted from the greater intelligence coup: Gull, who had been working against them for seven years, was stealing them blind.

In early December, the Warsaw Pact defense ministers committee met in Poland under the leadership of Jaruzelski. During the session, the members, with the exception of the Romanians, voted to approve the wartime statutes, the first step to ratification. Afterward, Kulikov offered lavish praise for Jaruzelski, and Soviet Defense Minister Ustinov embraced him, saying, "Wojciech, you have made a historic and distinguished contribution for the Soviet Union." Jaruzelski's face turned ashen. Kuklinski sensed that he was embarrassed at being honored in front of his fellow Poles for helping the Soviets.

Even Kulikov's anger at Kuklinski seemed forgotten by the time the Soviet delegation prepared to depart. In a farewell address on December 6 in the military sector of the Warsaw Okecie International Airport, Kulikov praised Kuklinski and wished him well.

On December 16, Kuklinski wrote to the CIA and to Daniel. He felt drained by the negotiations over the wartime statutes. "My thirteen-man crew had to be in two or three places at once in order to cope with everything connected with this task," he wrote. Kuklinski, citing the sixty-six Americans taken hostage in Iran the previous month, asked whether any of them were people he had worked with.

I am stunned by this act of illegality, violence and impudent provocation, obscured beneath the spiritual leadership of Khomeini, who is striving not only to turn back the historical course of his own society but also to bury everything which mankind has been able to achieve in its natural, civilized development.

In a package for the CIA, Kuklinski included official photographs taken at the conclusion of the meetings of defense ministers in Warsaw. "I am enclosing them with the view that they record an unprecedented moment in the history of military alliances, when conditions were approved which, in their essence, result in the transfer of the inalienable national rights of the Warsaw Pact countries to make decisions on peace and war into the hands of a foreign power, the USSR." Kuklinski also enclosed the final negotiated version of the statute.

All sides (unfortunately!!!) with the exception of the Romanians approved the draft of the statute. In keeping with the prearranged tactic, everyone opposed the Romanian proposals, including the suggestion that further consultations be held in 1980 with the goal of reaching a solution which all members of the Warsaw Pact would be able to accept. And so this infamous document was approved for ratification.

Kuklinski responded to earlier questions from the CIA concerning the T-72 tank's ability to penetrate NATO tank armor. "At the price of repetition," Kuklinski wrote, "I would like to ask you to handle carefully the information relayed by me. Any sort of press and journalistic reports in the West are the subject of detailed analyses and investigation."

He said that despite the considerable tension of "this double-life," he was optimistic about the future. In addition to sending holiday greetings to Daniel, he wrote, "I extend my expression of highest respect and regard for the American citizens in Iran as well as the hope for their release."

After an aborted attempt to make a delivery on December 16, 1979,

Kuklinski carried out a successful exchange two days later. His films contained more than 830 images (the list of documents he sent ran eleven pages.)

The CIA's package included a list of proposed new exchange sites and an enthusiastic commentary on his previous delivery, which included one thousand pages of documents from the Soviet General Staff Academy on Soviet front offensive operations. Calling the information "an outstanding addition to your previous contributions on this subject," the agency said it would provide "our intelligence community with significant new information and insight regarding Soviet doctrine and tactics, particularly in the field of nuclear operations, combat employment of front rocket troops, etc." Kuklinski received the updated exfiltration instructions and the embassy key. There also was a note from Stanley Patkowski, the retiring translator, thanking him for the pen.

"Dear and esteemed colleague," Patkowski wrote. "I have been deeply moved by the words of your message and the wonderful gift. It [is] one of [the] most treasured gifts I have ever received."

Patkowski said he was sending a present to Kuklinski. It was a small flask, used as a canteen by Allied paratroopers who dropped into Poland during the Nazi occupation in World War II. This flask, Patkowski wrote, was one of the last of the originals in existence.

There were several score of them. Therefore, it is possible that such specimens could still be found in Poland.

Its contents—a bit of French cognac.

I would like to add that my work with you, Sir, will remain in my memory as a chapter of my life shared with one of the most distinguished Poles whose efforts and achievements are not limited to Polish interests alone, but are measured on a global scale.

With a sincere Polish handshake.

8

"OUT OF THE SHADOWS
OF DARKNESS"

IN A WELL-LIT CORNER suite on the fourth floor at Langley, a group of CIA translators came to work each morning, picked up folders in rooms lined with locked file cabinets, and spent the day hunched over desks in two offices, both sealed with two locks. They were the Russian and Polish translators who handled the Gull material, which, as one CIA analyst recalled, was "curling the hair of the analysts in the intelligence community." The two groups of translators knew each other, but they were barred from discussing their work and did not know they were translating material from the same human source.

Early on, the Reports and Requirements Staff used a half-dozen Russian translators and five Polish ones for the Gull material. Some of the Russian material was so complex that it took a full day for a translator to complete one and a half to three pages. It eventually became clear, as Kuklinski's materials poured into the agency, that more translators would be needed. Robert Lubbehusen, a veteran Soviet specialist who had succeeded Katharine Hart as chief of the staff, brought on several Russian-language specialists. His deputy, Hal Larsen, who oversaw the Polish translators, added more of those as well. Larsen borrowed one from CIA's Foreign Broadcast Information Service, an office that translates international news reports. The translator was supposed to stay for several weeks; he ended up joining the staff.

Some afternoons, when the Polish translators needed a break from their often tedious work, they would convene in the file room, where they kept a bottle of mead in the bottom drawer of a locked cabinet. They looked for any occasion, such as birthdays and holidays, for a toast. One day, Larsen opened the door and found the group in a circle with their glasses raised.

"What's the occasion today?" Larsen asked.

"Rosh Hashanah!" the translators shouted back. Larsen smiled: Not one of the translators was Jewish.

Much of the intelligence Gull was providing was highly technical and included military terminology that did not appear in any of the CIA's reference books. Over time, the translators developed a glossary of Russian and Polish terms derived solely from Gull's documents. The thousands of pages of English translations were later scanned into a computer in the translations branch; the system allowed the huge volume of material to be searched by individual word or topic.

On January 14, 1980, Kulikov, Gribkov, and other top Soviet officials returned to Warsaw for Poland's formal ratification of the wartime statute. Kulikov had hoped to secure the signatures of all Warsaw Pact leaders in a single ceremonial session, but Romania had refused to participate, so he decided to visit each East bloc capital. The Polish leadership appeared in full force and met with him for two hours and forty-five minutes, two hours longer than scheduled.

After the meeting, the Poles and Soviets met in strict secrecy in the small conference hall in the Central Committee building to sign the wartime statute. Kuklinski presented the documents for the signatures. Later, he packaged fourteen rolls of film with his letters to the CIA about the ratification. Kuklinski wrote that his role in "this deplorable act" had been limited to verifying that the documents presented for signing had not been altered from what Poland had origi-nally agreed to. After the document was approved and signed by the other Warsaw Pact countries, Kuklinski said he would try to photo-graph it for the CIA. He wanted to forward "a true copy, containing each word, period, and comma."

He also noted that he had received a black Volga as a new official car, and he provided the plate number. Warsaw Station could observe him as he commuted to work, making the turn from Ulica Pulawska onto Rakowiecka between 7:40 and 7:55 A.M., or at midday, when he often went home for a meal with Hanka. "I always sit on the front right seat next to the chauffeur," he noted.

Kuklinski said he believed he had again misplaced a roll of film. By his own calculation, he should still have six unexposed rolls, but he could find only five. He was also having trouble concentrating at work and admitted he was making mistakes he never made before. He sent greetings to Daniel and thanked the retiring translator, Stanley Patkowski, for the gift of the flask. The "present gave me tremendous satisfaction," he wrote.

After two aborted attempts to deliver his package to the CIA, Kuk-linski finally made an exchange on February 17. In a letter to him, the agency asked about Afghanistan, where Moscow had just sent 90,000 troops, inquiring if the Polish leadership knew how long the Soviets intended to remain there and what their long-term role would be.* Kuklinski's recent materials on the T-72 tank were "of immense value to our common cause," the CIA wrote, and it also covered the usual security issues. The letter reassured Kuklinski that his materials were being handled "with the greatest possible discretion" and advised him to be careful about signing for documents.

"We would rather occasionally miss some important information

---

* The CIA also provided Kuklinski with an updated list of vehicles being driven by its offi-cers so that he could recognize them in moving-car deliveries. Warsaw Station said it had disposed of a blue 1978 Fiat Brava and a white 1979 Volkswagen camper, and Kuklinski should not expect to see them again. It said its officers still had a dark blue VW Dasher and white and green Fiats.

than have your name registered for a document for which you cannot explain your need," the agency said.

The CIA encouraged Kuklinski to continue commenting on the sensitivity of documents he provided so that the agency could adjust its handling procedures accordingly, and it thanked him for his expression of concern about the American hostages in Iran. "Fortunately, we can tell you that none of those persons with whom you have worked are involved."

On February 21, 1980, Warsaw Station cabled headquarters that given Kuklinski's continuing stress and his grief over the death of his friend Barbara, the CIA should work to alleviate the pressure on him. The "best way to do this is to write him more personal letters from 'Daniel,'" the station wrote, "the only real [CIA] officer Gull knows well, and whom he probably pictures in his mind as he composes his messages to us. Effort and difficulty in regularly writing Daniel letters [are] far outweighed by good they will bring Gull (and us)."

Meanwhile, Sally Boggs, the CIA counterintelligence officer who had conducted the 1978 inquiry into whether Gull's materials had been leaked within the intelligence community, was retiring in February. Before leaving, she prepared a memo on security issues in the case for a colleague who had undertaken a broader review of Polish operations. Her colleague incorporated her observations in a memo to senior officials in the Soviet Division, expressing concern about control of the Gull intelligence, especially those documents that had limited distribution in Poland and to which Gull had access because of his position.

"The single gravest hazard in this case probably always will be the one inherent in any operation producing unique high priority hard intelligence—control of the product," the officer wrote. "Once 'positive' intelligence reports of which Gull is the source are in the hands of the consumers it is virtually impossible to know whether the controls will be respected or whether the reports will be mishandled, discussed with inappropriate individuals, leaked, or misused in some other way which could adversely affect Gull's security situation."

He advised assigning someone to monitor day-to-day operational decisions, Polish counterintelligence efforts, and dissemination and specific use of Gull's materials.

I have spent most of the last four months reviewing compromised and ongoing Polish operations. (We prefer examining cases while they are still active for whatever guidance can be given to prevent their compromise.)...

Considerable CI [counterintelligence] attention is presently being devoted to Polish operations. However, given the present bleak personnel situation in this Branch and our commitment to support the other IO [internal operations] branches, there are limitations on what we can do with regard to Gull. We will of course pay as much attention as possible to the case, which is obviously one of the Division's best. It would be of help if outgoing cables were coordinated with us.

The officer recommended that a review session be held to consider what steps, if any, might be taken to protect and enhance Gull's security. He said that such sessions had often been held in the past and had proved useful. "But, insofar as I know, none have taken place since August 1979," he wrote.

By April 1980, Sue Burggraf had completed a full year in Warsaw Station, and after some initial tension with her colleague, Ted Gilbertson, they had grown close. (Gilbertson had clumsily welcomed her when they first met as if she were a secretary.) Both officers were single, and their social lives were limited. Only fifty to sixty people worked in the embassy, and most of the diplomats were married. There were also strict rules on which foreign diplomats they could socialize with or date. As a result, they tended to see the same friends in the same hangouts: the American Club in the embassy, the Marine House bar across the street, and bars in the Canadian and Australian embassies, which were nicknamed "Eager Beaver" and "Fluffy Duck" respectively. Some CIA managers were leery about sending single or divorced officers into the East bloc because they might be susceptible to entrapment. The standing joke among CIA officers was "Sleep NATO." Burggraf became friends with several Marine guards and also fell in with some singles in the Australian Embassy.

Like all new officers in Warsaw, Burggraf and Gilbertson had been told they could not execute street exchanges for the first six months. But Burggraf had become infuriated when, after six months passed, the station chief still barred her from going out alone to make exchanges; Burggraf assumed it was because she was a woman. Finally, she was allowed to make a solitary exchange with Gull. Headquarters cabled Warsaw Station saying Kuklinski should be told that a single female officer was being sent out "because they draw less surveillance. So he should not be surprised or put off should a singleton female officer appear for an exchange."

Burggraf, who was just over five feet, five inches, felt like a contortionist during her first moving-car delivery. In the momentary gap in surveillance as she made the final right turn, she had to shift the Fiat into low gear to avoid stalling and dim the high beams to parking lights, both to signal her arrival and to keep from blinding Gull as he tried to read her license plate. As she glided up to him, she then had to reach over to roll down the passenger's window, all the while watching in the rearview mirror, and hand over the package.

After an exchange, Gilbertson and Burggraf would wait until the next morning to take the package from Gull into the embassy. The placing and reading of signals also had to be mastered. Sometimes Burggraf would drive past one of the sites where Gull would leave his chalk marks, and she would find her view blocked by a parked car or van. She could not slow down, because the brake lights would signal a trailing SB car that she might be up to something. So she would return later on foot to check for the signal. Luckily, she found a greengrocer near the embassy, and she began to leave the office at lunchtime for shopping trips.

Burggraf and Gilbertson, like everyone in Warsaw Station, spent much of their time casing potential sites for future exchanges. Once they found a promising location, they would prepare a written description, a sketch, and instructions for both the case officer and Gull. The instructions explained precisely where Gull was to arrive, stand, and leave and which alley or gate would serve as his escape route. Each site was photographed. Because the officers could not leave their car, they took pictures through the car window or used a concealment device, though they could not risk looking through the viewfinder for fear of being seen. Thus even a slight tilt of the camera could mean a wildly missed shot. Burggraf, who became expert in the station's darkroom, frequently teased Gilbertson for the quality of his pictures: *Hey, you've got a picture of the sky!*

Warsaw Station would eventually produce a kind of architectural drawing of the site, with lines designating roads and railroad tracks, arrows to show the traffic flow, and other lines, in red and blue, for approach and escape routes. Each proposed site was then sent for review to Langley and Gull. At headquarters, the sites were studied for suitability, and Kuklinski could also veto a proposed location if he knew, for example, that it was too close to the home of a Polish official or a known SB surveillance post.

On the surveillance detection runs that Gilbertson and Burggraf made in Warsaw, they usually carried a bottle of water. The idea was that if they were in an accident or were stopped by the police or SB, they could quickly try to douse any incriminating material in the car, such as a letter written on water-soluble paper.

When Burggraf went on an SDR, she left the embassy at 5:00 P.M., when virtually everyone else was leaving for home. Since the exchanges with Gull took place at about 10:00 P.M., she had five hours to "clean" herself of surveillance. As she began driving on an SDR, she would turn on the radio and listen for the scratchy sounds of SB transmissions, which could be heard on the FM dial. She could also hear

Ryszard Kuklinski in 1947, his first photograph in uniform. Kuklinski was seventeen, had just joined the Polish Army, and had begun officers school.

Kuklinski, twenty-two, and his wife Hanka, nineteen, at their wedding ceremony on July 16, 1952, in the town hall in Wroclaw, Poland.

The *Legia*, the wooden vessel Kuklinski and his crew sailed through Western Europe on military surveillance missions in the early 1970s.

Kuklinski and his son Bogdan, then seventeen, during Kuklinski's voyage in the summer of 1972 through Europe, when he made his first secret contact with United States officials.

Kuklinski's older son, Waldek, in his early twenties, while a law student at Warsaw University around 1976.

Colonel Kuklinski in a photograph taken for his last military identification. At the time this photo was taken, July 1981, Kuklinski had been working clandestinely with the CIA for nine years.

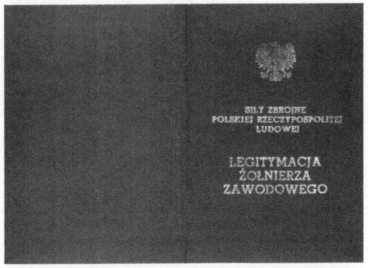

Colonel Kuklinski's last military ID, made in July 1981, just months before the martial law crackdown.

David Forden, the longtime CIA case officer who developed a close relationship
with Kuklinski. This photo was taken
around 1984 when Forden was Chief of
the Soviet/East European Division.

Forden (left) and his two roommates, Peter Falk (center)
and Alan Goldfarb (right), around the spring of 1953, while
graduate students at the Maxwell School at Syracuse University, a few months before Forden applied to the CIA.

Warsaw, December 1979: Kuklinski presents Soviet Defense Minister Dimitri Ustinov with the so-called wartime statute for signing. The agreement formally placed Polish Armed Forces under Soviet control during wartime.

Kuklinski (foreground) and the Polish Defense Minister, General Wojciech Jaruzelski (left), at a Defense Ministers Committee meeting in Budapest in 1977.

Kuklinski between Soviet Marshal Viktor Kulikov (left), the Warsaw Pact commander, and General Anatoly Gribkov (right), the chief of staff, at the Defense Ministers Committee meeting in Bucharest in December 1980, shortly before Kuklinski left a critical message for the CIA about preparations for a Soviet and Warsaw Pact invasion of Poland.

Kuklinski receives a blessing from Pope John
Paul II on a trip to the Vatican in 1997.

Kuklinski receives honorary citizenship of Gdansk on May 3, 1998.

them through a small earpiece she wore under her hair. A receiver was held in place in the small of her back by the waistband of her clothing. After a few hours in the car, the device could become painful, as it dug into her back.

Gilbertson, too, memorized various routes around Warsaw, including the so-called break-off and recovery points, such as certain bars, where officers could have a plausible reason to stop. Initially, Warsaw Station ordered its officers to spend three or four hours on SDRs, including a mandatory restaurant stop for "break-off and recovery." As surveillance began to intensify, the rule was three or four hours without the stop. On weekends, when many exchanges were scheduled, the officers were to drive all day.

This task was easier in Warsaw than in other East bloc capitals. Budapest had checkpoints at the edge of the city, and the Hungarian police made note of drivers with diplomatic plates as they entered and left. Warsaw had no such checkpoints, but there were unexpected hazards. For example, CIA officers on SDRs tried to avoid bridges because of concern that the SB had attached magnetic devices to the underside of their cars; the devices could trip a stationary beacon on a bridge and reveal the officers' position. Even heavy traffic could pose a problem. One night, Gilbertson was driving through the countryside before an exchange with Gull when he saw a convoy of Russian military vehicles blocking traffic. Gilbertson sat anxiously as the minutes passed. When the convoy finally moved, he sped back to Warsaw but was three minutes late for the exchange, and Gull was gone.

In another exchange, Gilbertson saw the headlights of an approaching car in his rearview mirror just as Gull extended his hand inside his window. Gilbertson hit the accelerator as Gull yanked back his hand. Gilbertson turned at the corner and almost hit a Polish police car.

One Friday, before an exchange, Burggraf visited the Fluffy Duck, the bar in the basement of the Australian Embassy. As patrons played darts, Burggraf talked with friends and drank ginger ale. Before long, she realized the miniature radio receiver in her ear was gone. She had not heard the device hit the ground, but she knew she had entered the bar with it. She told her friends she had dropped "an ear thing," trying to sound a bit embarrassed as she explained that a doctor had given her something for an earache. Soon her friends and other bar patrons were on their knees helping her look for it. Finally, Burggraf stood up, lifted her glass, and realized the earpiece had fallen into her ginger ale. Excusing herself to use the restroom, she cleaned off the device and was relieved to find that it still worked.

Burggraf did not always know the details of the intelligence Gull was providing to the CIA. As she once put it, "Washington controlled the operation. They were the history and the memory. We were the facilitators on the stage."

In early March 1980, Kulikov arrived again in Warsaw, this time with a resolution appointing Leonid Brezhnev as supreme commander of the Warsaw Pact. Unlike the way Kulikov had handled his proposed wartime statute, which underwent extensive debate in the Warsaw Pact militaries, he was pushing the Brezhnev resolution through without prior consultation. He had the signature of the East German leader, Erich Honecker, and Kuklinski was told to prepare a "talking points" paper for Edward Gierek, who became the second East European leader to sign the document. Kuklinski made a copy for the CIA.

On April 13, Kuklinski gave the CIA seventeen new rolls of film that included more than 555 images from twenty-eight documents. One nineteen-page paper, stamped "Secret of Special Importance," summarized what he had learned in Moscow on a recent trip to review war-planning matters.

He described another set of Russian documents, totaling ninety-two pages, that listed recommendations from the Warsaw Pact command dealing with the organizational structure of armies and fronts in wartime. "It is a very detailed report containing a complete list of people, methods of communication, automation, security and so on," he wrote. "This system will be implemented in all the armies of the Warsaw Pact in the next five-year period (1981–1985)."

Kuklinski said that the past two months had been exhausting, and that he was still having trouble concentrating. But he claimed he felt "safer and surer" of himself, his superiors continued to praise him, and at times, he had thought about retiring. He was looking forward to a five-week vacation starting in July, when he hoped to travel with Hanka and participate in a yacht race to Soviet ports. "Please accept my assurances," he wrote, "that on my part, I will continue to do everything in my power, in accordance with my strength and capabilities, to support activity for true freedom and progress. I extend very warm greetings to all my friends, with Daniel at the top."

The April 13 car exchange was "all in all, the smoothest we've done in the past 21 months," Warsaw Station cabled Langley. The CIA reassured Kuklinski that all of his films were accounted for. With greater economic and political tension in Poland, the agency wrote, American Embassy personnel were under increased surveillance by the Poles. The agency reminded Kuklinski that if an officer detected surveillance or observed something on the way to an exchange that might interfere with a smooth and unseen hand-off, the officer would drive past the site.

If, however, while making our final approach we should suddenly detect surveillance or anything suspicious we will continue on by the site without hesitation. We continue to ask that you be particularly cautious and observant in the immediate area of the exchange point, which we cannot see until the final moments of our approach. If you note anything suspicious, please leave at once.

In a "Daniel" letter, the agency said it shared Kuklinski's frustration over the approval of the wartime statute. "It's probably very little consolation," the letter said, "but I realize, and I'm sure that you agree, that no matter how many compromises must be made in the name of practicality, no document, including this one, can ever break the indomitable spirit of the Polish people."

In the spring of 1980, Soviet Division Chief George Kalaris sent a memo to the CIA's Qualitative Step Increase/Honor and Merit Awards Panel and asked that a Distinguished Intelligence Medal be struck, though nameless, for presentation to a sensitive source. "The medal will be retained at headquarters for safekeeping," Kalaris wrote. According to a CIA document, John N. McMahon, then DDO, endorsed the idea directly to Director Stansfield Turner. Turner responded: "I herewith concur in your oral suggestion that a Distinguished Intelligence Medal be awarded to Gull."

In April, Warsaw Station and Langley continued to explore ways to reduce pressure on Kuklinski. One memo proposed decreasing the frequency of exchanges with Gull, which Warsaw Station called the "most dangerous aspect of our cooperation together." The operation had averaged six exchanges a year, or one every two months, plus the exchanges for which Kuklinski prepared but that had to be aborted. "It is probably last-minute preparations, both physical and psychological, that wear out Gull," Warsaw Station wrote. The CIA weighed a temporary suspension of the operation, for up to six months. Warsaw Station said it believed that with Kuklinski's confidence and "healthy ego," a brief halt in the operation might upset him, but headquarters wrote to the field: "Do not believe he will react badly to our expression of concern for his well-being, and our suggestion of brief respite."

In late April the Soviet Division cabled Daniel in Vienna. "Wish to inform you that we have just received the director's approval to present a Distinguished Intelligence Medal to your old friend," the message said. Daniel responded the next day.

"Deeply grateful for ... news about an old friend," he wrote. "Thank you very much. Daniel will be ready to go anywhere, anytime."

On April 24, General Siwicki, the chief of staff, asked Kuklinski to join him on a trip to Moscow, which had been approved by party leader Gierek. Siwicki was going to raise an issue of major concern to the Polish leadership: that Soviet negotiators had understated Polish troop strength in the Vienna arms talks. Siwicki carried with him a document that said Poland, "guided by a desire to contribute to the progress of the negotiations," wanted to correct the record. The number of Polish troops should be increased by about 13,000, to take into account the soldiers attached to military academies, rear-echelon elements, depots, warships, and railroads. But in May, Moscow rejected Poland's request. Kuklinski felt the rejection was frustrating, if typical. But Siwicki's invitation to Moscow had reassured him that he was still in good standing.

On Saturday, June 7, the night before his next exchange with the CIA, Kuklinski was in his study watching the popular American miniseries *Rich Man, Poor Man*. When it ended, he picked up his pen and began a note to Daniel.

> This film is one of the few shows on TV for which I wait, and time permitting, enjoy. I am sure that you know that I am not talking about the interesting plot, fascinating heroes, acting of the actors or technical mastery—even though these are important—but that above all, I am talking about that certain topography, customs, and landscape of a country in which I have sincere friends, to whose fate I have tied my own fate, for better or worse, forever.
>
> From here, it is only a step to recollections and reflections, to the exchange of thoughts with you.

Kuklinski wrote that Daniel's last letter, with its encouraging view of the future, had boosted his morale.

> This is a beautiful vision of the future, but will the world, poisoned by the message-bearing doctrines, have enough common sense and strength to resist them, not speaking even of pushing them back into a position of defense? As you know, Daniel, from my many statements on these matters, I do not belong to the optimists, even though I must admit that when eight years ago I made some sort of statement to the representatives of the U.S. armed

forces, my perception of developments on the global political stage appeared to be even of darker colors.

However, taking this step in 1972, almost five years after the Tet Offensive in Vietnam, and not quite four years after Soviet aggression in Czechoslovakia, I was fully aware that I was actively committing myself on the side of the constantly shrinking forces defending the free world against the expansion of communism—and this was the main reason for my decision concerning permanent cooperation.

The subsequent run of events, whether in Indochina, Africa, on the American continent or the latest in Iran and Afghanistan, not only are unable to weaken my spirit—of which you mention in your letter—but I can assure you to the utmost, they strengthen my will for further and even more effective activity.

Dear Daniel! It was a great honor and at the same time a tremendous satisfaction to learn from your letter that the materials which I have forwarded in the course of years did not end their lives in CIA safes, but were the source of inspiration for many important decisions made on the highest level of American leadership circles and aimed at stopping Soviet aggression in the world. I thank you for this, and I can only reassure you, that I shall endure in these efforts and endeavors to the end, as long as this will be possible and serving a purpose.

Kuklinski expressed confidence in the security of their "magnificent collaboration." He had been hearing from others that he might be promoted to brigadier general, which he knew should fill him with optimism. He admitted that this was not always the case.

Frequently sleep comes at the time when it is time to get up and go to work. And again, four large mugs of coffee, two, three packs of cigarettes—and the cycle repeats itself. The only harbor where I really feel good is my home, which with my wife, and children already grown, creates a climate of warmth, peace and relaxation not possible to duplicate. We all enjoy this but only I am aware of how little is needed to lay in ruins this peace and family happiness.

My dear, cordial friend: study my situation calmly, show me the ways to overcome the crisis in making. I know only that I see no chance to lessen our friendship. I would not want to terminate our collaboration. I don't believe that I would feel well in the role of a retired colonel watering flowers in his garden. On a more distant horizon, yes. I am dreaming of venturing into the world on a yacht, reaching your great country and meeting you. But this is a very distant perspective.

Kuklinski reported that his car was in a repair shop. "It is costing me quite a sum of money and health. However, I would like to keep it for a few more years." He continued to enjoy his house. "I am completely satisfied. There is a small garden and much joy when plants get green and flowers begin to bloom."

In the exchange on June 8, Kuklinski delivered a new set of films, which included a critique of a Warsaw Pact General Staffs exercise called "Spring 80," notes from consultations in Moscow concerning Soviet airborne divisions and their communications equipment, and a twenty-eight-page document detailing Jaruzelski's talks in Moscow with Defense Minister Ustinov.

Over the next few weeks, the CIA tried to analyze Kuklinski's psychological state, and on June 30, headquarters cabled Warsaw Station that "Kuklinski's continuing commitment to a mutual cause" was evident in his last letter to Daniel. "However, what also is very obvious is the fact that he is physically and mentally exhausted. And this, of course, is a threat to his security," the CIA said.

On July 18, 1980, headquarters recommended sending another "Daniel" letter and said that because Kuklinski might need "some bolstering of spirit," the agency should bestow on him the Distinguished Intelligence Medal.

*

In July 1980, the Polish government announced that it would sharply increase the price of meat, a staple of the Polish diet, which prompted wildcat factory strikes across the country. Food prices, always an explosive issue, had led to protests and violence in 1970 and again in 1976. Workers' meager earnings provided barely enough for their families to subsist. There were also widely known inequities in the system: The party elite had access to stores where food was plentiful; and factory managers could receive special allotments of meat and other groceries to share with family and friends.

By early August, the work stoppages had spread to more than 150 factories, and workers had begun demanding higher pay, an end to press censorship, and other freedoms. The historic strike in the Lenin shipyard in Gdansk, led by Lech Walesa, occurred on August 14. Kuklinski was excited by the burgeoning revolution in Poland. As he watched and read news accounts, he was filled with admiration for Solidarity. He was particularly moved by Walesa's bravery.

On August 14, the day of the Gdansk strike, Kuklinski was asked by Skalski to supervise a small group whose principal task would be to monitor the strikes, brief the General Staff leadership, and respond to any requests from the Interior Ministry.

Kuklinski heard debate in the General Staff about whether the army should be deployed against the strikers; the officers agreed that such a strategy would only embolden the strikers and make it harder for Poland to resolve the situation internally. There was even concern that the Soviet Union would send troops based in the westernmost republics across the border to restore order.

On August 20, Polish authorities arrested more than a dozen leaders of the dissident organization KOR, a committee of workers and intellectuals created after the food riots in July 1976 to defend people involved in labor actions. On August 22, Polish workers won a major victory when the Polish government agreed to negotiate with their representatives. The strikes had closed more than 300 factories in Poland and involved more than 150,000 workers. Within days, the prime minister and three other members of the ruling Politburo were dismissed in a government shake-up. The Soviets issued sharp criticism of the workers, announcing that Poland was being destabilized by "anti-socialist elements." In early September, the regime signed agreements at Gdansk and Szczecin, and then at Jastrzebie, that promised critical reforms, such as the legalization of trade unions, the right to strike, more press freedoms, and better social services. "We have not won everything that we hoped for and dreamed about," Walesa declared, "but we have achieved as much as we could under the circumstances, including respect for certain civil rights." Several days later, Gierek was ousted as Communist party chief and replaced by Stanislaw Kania, a fifty-three-year-old member of the Polish Politburo who had been responsible for the Ministry of Interior, the army and the police.

During the turbulent summer of 1980, a new Chief of Station, Tom Ryan, arrived in Warsaw. A Bronx-born U.S. Army veteran, Ryan, who was turning forty-nine, was about to celebrate his twenty-fifth wedding anniversary. He and his wife, Lucille, had looked forward to the assignment, in part because Tom promised Lucille they could celebrate by taking romantic vacations around Europe. But, as Lucille recalled, "We got there in July, and by September, everything was going down the tubes."

In Washington, meanwhile, President Carter's national security adviser, Zbigniew Brzezinski, was convinced that Moscow would see the turmoil as a major threat to both Poland's political structure and Moscow's authority. On September 3 he asked Turner for the CIA's assessment of whether Moscow would intervene with troops.

On September 13, Kuklinski wrote a sixteen-page letter to the CIA, in which he described a debate within the General Staff about the government's capitulation to the workers and the potential for an invasion by the Soviet Union. The General Staff leadership was following the crisis "with utmost apprehension."

It was realized that an eventual decision to use troops against the strikers could not only strengthen the determination of the strikers, but also lead to a state in which a solution on the internal plan would not be possible. At the peak phase of the conflict, just before signing the agreements at Szczecin and Gdansk, even though there was no specific information, the possibility of bringing into Poland a dozen or so, and even tens of Soviet divisions from the western regions of the U.S.S.R. was taken into consideration.

There also had been discussion of East Germany's and Czechoslovakia's possible participation in an invasion, because the conflict in Poland posed a threat to their countries. Jaruzelski appeared to be trying to orchestrate events. When Gierek legalized the union and the right to strike, Jaruzelski "allegedly expressed disapproval not only of those who were responsible for it, but also of Gierek." Kuklinski was convinced that Jaruzelski and Kania, the new party leader, in concert with Moscow, had been behind Gierek's dismissal.

"The election of Kania already indicates a decisive influence of Jaruzelski on Party operations," Kuklinski wrote. "At this stage, he preferred to remain the power behind the throne. However, this does not rule out his greater ambitions, as long as they were not fulfilled under conditions of a party coup."

Kuklinski speculated that Jaruzelski aspired to be party secretary. "In any event, the Party and Soviet leadership can depend on one more anchor," Kuklinski wrote. "All that I have said here does not in the end rule out the positive role of this man in resolving the conflict. However, it is regrettable that Jaruzelski's strong position in the party, his ability to influence Kania—a man of a low power of independent thinking and acting—will create for the country yet many misfortunes, and possibly nullify the step forward."

Kuklinski noted that he had been asked to oversee the special group to monitor events. He added that the events in his country had only reaffirmed his commitment to the secret collaboration. "I must say this, without beating around the bush, that this cooperation has me totally under its spell," he wrote. "I am happy, almost like a child, with the acquisition of every important document and piece of information; the fact that I am constructing a means of safely sending information from Poland to the West, and with knowing that this material is indeed from me."

He said he grasped the concern behind the agency's suggestion that he take another break from his collection activities, which had been communicated to him recently.

> I understand the reasons which motivated you gentlemen, especially—I am guessing—my personal friend Daniel, proposing temporary curtailment (for a period of four to six months) of our activities. Thank you for the noble intentions. I realize that the proposal stemmed from a desire to give me rest from tension, help me to regenerate strength. At this time. I feel much better, in fact, very well. Today, I need our collaboration as much as any other function of normal life.

Kuklinski placed his letters in a container with thirteen rolls of film, which included a forty-one-page Russian document on the Warsaw Pact's radio-electronic warfare capabilities; a fifty-one-page Russian document on defending against the U.S. cruise missile; and a seven-page paper laying out tactics for the Vienna talks. On September 14, at 10:37 P.M., Kuklinski passed his materials to the CIA, and after returning home, he read the agency's letter to him.

The CIA took note of the eighth anniversary of their collaboration. "Our greatest hope," the CIA wrote, "is that we will one day, once again, be able to sit down with you and discuss our mutual interests." A separate letter from "Daniel" told Kuklinski that he had been awarded the Distinguished Intelligence Medal.

> This is the highest award in our profession, and only given for performance of outstanding service and for achievement of a distinctly exceptional nature, the results of which constitute a major

contribution to the goals of our nation. The awarding of such a
medal is usually the subject of much ceremony; however, this was
awarded in secret with no one knowing your name—only that you
have made an extraordinary contribution to the policies of the free
world. I would like to tell the world about your efforts and contributions; but, of course, it cannot be done. I only hope that someday in the future, history will be able to acknowledge your
tremendous courage and dedication to principle. I offer you my
sincere and heartfelt congratulations on receiving this honor and
hope someday I may present it in person. In the meantime, I will
keep it for you with my most cherished and secure possessions.

"Daniel" expressed sympathy with Kuklinski's health concerns and
wished him a relaxing vacation.

I know how easy it is to fall into the coffee and cigarettes habit, and I
hope you can reverse the trend because I do want you to be well and
happy....
    I agree we must also begin to think about retirement from our
work together, but find it very difficult to offer you advice on this matter. Our cooperation is such a large part of both of our lives, I'm
afraid we'd both feel unfulfilled without it. As you recognize it's not
time yet to sit at home and tend the garden. Someday, however,
younger men must take over and continue our work. The exact timing of retirement is very difficult and, really, only you can make that
decision, knowing what your physical and mental capacities are and
how much longer they will last. I don't want you to retire too soon (it
would leave a tremendous gap in our knowledge). But even more
upsetting would be if you waited too long to retire and were not able
to enjoy your well-deserved peace and quiet. What I am saying is that
timing is critical, and you are the best judge of what time is appropriate. I don't think I have to say that our friendship is forever, no matter
when your decision is made....
    Esteemed friend, in this complicated and changing world, no one
shows greater courage and dedication than you do. I only hope that

you are not asking too much of yourself. Remember, we all have our limits, although yours appear to be endless. Always remember, no matter what the future brings, our friendship cannot be terminated and will endure and grow in strength forever.

For always,

Daniel

On September 19, 1980, CIA Director Turner, responding to Brzezinski's request for an assessment of the chances of a Soviet invasion of Poland, sent an "Alert" memorandum to President Carter and his senior advisers. "Soviet military activity detected in the last few days," the memo said, "leads me to believe that the Soviet leadership is preparing to intervene militarily in Poland, if the Polish situation is not brought under control in a manner satisfactory to Moscow." Kania, the new Polish leader, might be allowed some time to try to resolve the matter, Turner wrote, but if he failed, and "Poland's role in the Warsaw Pact is called into question, the Soviets will threaten or employ military force."

On September 21 a scheduled exchange between the CIA and Kuklinski was aborted because of the presence of "casuals." The backup date was the next night. Before going out, Kuklinski wrote to Daniel expressing gratitude for the intelligence medal, the news of which he received "with unconcealed emotion."

In this award, I find one more strong confirmation that my choice of the difficult but noble mission was justified and correct. I would also like to assure you that I am deeply aware of the enormous need for pulling out of the shadows of darkness of the tightly closed communist system everything which does not serve peace of the world and freedom of nations. In this conviction, I once more want to confirm my readiness to serve our common cause to the limits of my strength and capability.

Dear Daniel!

During the last months, I reanalyzed my situation again, and I came to the conviction that any kind of attempt to escape realities is much too early. Speaking of retirement, I never had in mind interruption of our collaboration, because this collaboration has become not only the essence but the highest goal of my life. I can truthfully say that only now, after eight years, I feel like a normal human being, and not a suicidal type.

My first step and outstretched arm toward collaboration were based primarily on spiritual premises void of sober calculation, and even of the slightest hope, for long-lasting success. This feeling of confidence (if in this kind of operation one can speak of confidence) developed only over a period of years. I never feel that I am a spying ace, but I have some basis for sober evaluation that during this span of time I succeeded in shaping certain character traits favorable to accepting and performing intelligence tasks.

Of course, I never feel safe. However, the acute feeling of a state of threat passed fairly long ago. Today, I am much better prepared for operations on behalf of our common cause than I was in the past. It would be a pity therefore to waste this capability. (More importantly, I would strongly resent any weakening of our ties.) . . .

Dear Daniel!

I value your friendship so much, the friendship you call "firm, immovable, forever." I hope that regardless of circumstances which may cause your transfer to another sector of your responsible job, our contacts will be maintained. During those many years shared, you had the opportunity to learn, better than anybody else, all of my weaknesses as well as my strengths. You know that my family was always to me the most important concern. So in the name of our friendship, I charge you personally with the responsibility for their fate in an extreme case. I believe that the need will not arise, but I also believe that in the event of bad luck, I can depart with peace of mind.

In order not to end this letter on a gloomy note, I hasten to assure you that I view the future with optimism. I feel completely well and

composed. I will try to take into consideration—but I cannot guaran-
tee the results—your advice concerning breaking the habit of drinking
coffee and smoking cigarettes.

Sincerely,

P.V.

On September 23, top White House national security officials met to
review the current intelligence on Soviet troop movements. CIA director Turner gave a briefing, noting that worker strikes were spreading
and that Moscow feared a ripple effect, in which the prodemocracy
movement could threaten the entire Communist system. Most of
those attending agreed that the Poles would resist any invasion.
Brzezinski, who was leading the meeting, suggested that a Polish
resistance, along with a powerful Western reaction, would be the best
means of deterring the Soviets.

Kuklinski and the CIA, after two failed attempts, made a successful
exchange on September 25. About a week later, Polish workers staged
a one-hour national strike as a warning that the regime was moving
too slowly in carrying out the reforms promised in the recent agreements. "Solidarnosc" banners hung in factory windows, and demonstrators marched, shouting, "Solidarity today, bread tomorrow!" On
October 12, Polish Armed Forces Day, Polish generals, who usually
received a flurry of congratulations from their counterparts in
Moscow, got only a few messages. Kuklinski noticed that Soviet officers who were in regular touch with the General Staff were appearing
less frequently, and when they did appear, they were reserved and dis-
trustful. One day, during an airport ceremony for a Polish military delegation returning from Prague, Kuklinski listened as a Russian
general, who was Kulikov's representative in Poland, openly disparaged the workers movement. "Democracy, yes! But only as dictator-
ship of the proletariat while adhering to the principles of democratic

centralism. What you are doing is pure, rotten, and compromised liberalism," he said.

On October 22, Kuklinski was summoned to the office of General Skalski, who said Jaruzelski had an urgent request. The General Staff had to begin secret preparations for imposing martial law. It appeared that Moscow was in the final stages of planning an invasion, and an internal crackdown by the Poles was the only way to forestall outside intervention.

Kuklinski, who was already leading the group monitoring events in Poland, listened as Skalski asked him to oversee another small cell of officers who would plan the military's involvement in martial law. Skalski knew Kuklinski would be troubled by the request. "This order you have the right to refuse," he said solemnly.

Kuklinski had always admired Skalski, a slim and powerfully built man with deep blue eyes and a noble face. He felt certain that Skalski, who clearly hated the Soviets, was as troubled as he was by the idea that the Polish Army might be directed to move against the Polish people.

When Kulikov and his patronizing entourage visited Warsaw, Skalski could barely hide his anger. Spending as little time as possible with the Russian visitors, he stood with his jaw clenched and his faced flushed and tried to dispatch them as quickly as possible to Kuklinski's office.

Skalski had been fifteen years old in September 1939 when the Soviet Army entered Poland. He awakened that morning on the veranda of his home outside Grodno (in what is now Belarus) to the sound of a heavy storm. Then he realized he had been hearing the thunder of Soviet troops marching in the street. For the first time, Skalski saw Russian soldiers, who wore gray uniforms and conelike hats with a red star in the center and carried rifles with exceptionally long bayonets. The local schools were quickly transformed into Russian schools. Skalski and his classmates had to study Russian several hours a day and were indoctrinated in Moscow's version of history that condemned Poland's prewar past to oblivion. Eventually, Skalski's father, a prewar Polish officer, was taken prisoner by the Soviets and never returned to Poland. Skalski saw him only once more, after the war. Skalski's older brother, a Polish military academy graduate, had been captured and was one of thousands of Polish soldiers ordered massacred by Stalin in the Katyn forest in 1940.

As for Skalski, he joined the so-called Berling Army of Polish soldiers created in the Soviet Union and led by a Polish officer. Skalski became an antitank artillery officer—a job requiring the ability to make quick mental calculations about distance, elevation, and wind speed—and he was awarded the highest Polish military order of merit for destroying a German self-propelled gun. Skalski gradually rose in the Polish Army. Kuklinski knew him to be demanding and impatient, and at times he made subordinates cry. But he was decisive, and he knew what he wanted.

Skalski relied increasingly on Kuklinski, whom he found tireless and meticulous, a man of imagination who had the "outstanding ability to transform ideas into written form." He was also adept at dealing with the Soviets. "He had all the features which enabled him to gain the trust of people, to conciliate people," Skalski recalled years later. "His subordinates had great esteem for him. He was a good and friendly boss. I have to tell you that his positive features made him very popular among the party ranks—whenever delegates to party meetings were elected, he was chosen unanimously."

Kuklinski could not imagine assisting in a plan to suppress Solidarity. He admired the strikers and their supporters. "They were my heroes," he said later, "starting from Walesa and ending with the last lady on the line yelling slogans." He had also not forgotten the experiences of his friend in the army who had been ordered to shoot at striking workers to put down the 1970 demonstrations on the Baltic coast, an incident that contributed to Kuklinski's decision to collaborate with the West. But he realized that if he took on the task, he might be able to influence events and perhaps prevent violence—and, of course, keep the CIA informed. "If you see nobody better, I agree," Kuklinski told Skalski.

*

In Washington the next day, October 23, Brzezinski led a meeting of the Special Coordination Committee, a small cabinet-level group that was monitoring events in Poland. Among those also present were CIA Director Turner, Secretary of State Edmund S. Muskie, and Secretary of Defense Harold Brown. "Participation was restricted because of the sensitivity of the meeting," Brzezinski wrote later in an account of the meeting. "The agenda was how to respond in the event of a Soviet intervention in Poland."

In four years as national security adviser to President Carter, Brzezinski had regularly asked the CIA to provide him with raw intelligence reports, from which he could make his own assessments even before the analysts processed them. Brzezinski was one of the few people in the administration who knew the agency had a vital source in the Polish Defense Ministry. From the earliest stages of the crisis, Brzezinski felt, the White House had to take an unambiguous stand against Soviet intervention in Poland. In 1968, he recalled, the White House had indications the Soviets would invade Czechoslovakia, but failed to act. He believed Washington's passivity had contributed to the Soviet decision and had encouraged further Soviet control throughout Eastern Europe. Brzezinski told Carter it was important not to make the same mistake with Poland.

On October 26, Kuklinski began a six-page letter to the CIA distilling the events of the past month. Within the General Staff, he noted, there was a widespread view that only the CIA was capable of formulating "a reliable prognosis" concerning further developments in Poland.

> This opinion reflects not so much esteem for the U.S. intelligence services, which have called the attention of world opinion to the concentration of Soviet Armed Forces in the vicinity of the Polish borders, as a conviction that Polish authorities are incapable of directing the destiny of the nation, and particularly of standing up to possible U.S.S.R. intervention.

As to the plans that were under way in the Polish Army in case Moscow sent troops across the borders, Kuklinski wrote:

> I am embarrassed to confirm that nothing is planned. This topic belongs to the taboo subjects, which prevent everybody from taking any kind of action. The leadership of the Polish General Staff recognizes the gravity of this threat....
>
> As of today, the Polish Armed Forces General Staff has not undertaken even the slightest steps intended to oppose military intervention by the U.S.S.R.

Just a few days before, he wrote, "a small group of us began preparations of a plan for introducing a condition of wartime readiness on Polish territory"—martial law.* He included a memo and a draft of the resolution and decrees of the government pertaining to martial law and other details:

> The plan proposes that, because of national security, a condition of wartime readiness will be introduced only as a last resort, after exhausting all options for cooling off social unrest. In addition to suspension of civil rights and granting the authorities extraordinary powers, a decree on labor relations will be issued. Also the provision of the law on compulsory military service will go into effect, along with partial mobilization, broad militarization, and service in civil defense as well as services rendered in the interests of defense. It is proposed that troops be used for protection and defense of special installations and for patrolling the cities. The allies will be notified of the introduction of a condition of wartime readiness *ex post facto*....
>
> Everybody fears this step. Among people in the know, there is a

---

* In Kuklinski's reports on martial law, he used the Polish term *stan wojenny* to describe the crackdown, a phrase the CIA initially translated as "wartime readiness." The CIA soon switched to "martial law." I have used "martial law" from the start, as Kuklinski intended it.

rather popular belief that introduction of a condition of wartime preparedness could signal the beginning of the end.

Kuklinski said there was increasing anger in the Polish military. "Accusations against the present leadership of the Ministry of National Defense are more and more openly and loudly voiced," while the Defense Ministry "is doing everything it can to calm the troops, to hold them on a tighter leash." He warned of the possibility of a Russian takeover of the military in Poland and said somewhat scathingly that some Polish generals had acknowledged to one another that their positions would probably be taken by Russian generals. "Their apathetic posture makes organization of any kind of resistance impossible," Kuklinski wrote.

He and his colleagues had little direct knowledge of Soviet deployments at the borders. "I would like to emphasize that the question of martial law in Poland at this time is in a planning stage, and the plan may be implemented only as a last resort," he wrote.

On October 29, the day before the next exchange, Kuklinski received a visit from two Soviet officers from the Warsaw Pact command. Kuklinski asked about any invasion plans. They knew of none, the officers said, although a "psychological conditioning" of Russian officers had begun. At meetings of Russian generals, there was talk of providing "military assistance to Polish communists." And recently, Russian officers had been told they would serve alert duty during nights and weekends. In Moscow, the Soviets told Kuklinski, officers often gathered to listen to Radio Liberty and Radio Free Europe, and many expressed anger at Solidarity's assertiveness.

On October 30, Kuklinski wrote to the CIA describing his conversation with the two Russians as well as recent talk among General Staff officers about the need for massive arrests of trade union leaders across the country.

"Once more I ask you to use the data I send very sparingly," he wrote. "Recently in my institution we were commended for safeguarding the secrecy about the [wartime] statute because 'if the West knew about it, they could strike at a very sensitive spot, and they would certainly do it.'"

In an exchange that night, Kuklinski delivered his letters and five rolls of film, which contained 215 pages of documents. These included the first documents pertaining to martial law that were sent to the United States.*

In Washington, National Security Adviser Brzezinski believed the crisis was escalating dangerously. He had special access to the detailed satellite photographs of Poland and other intelligence that had documented the large concentration of Soviet troops on the border, Soviet transport planes at airports in the region, and military convoys lining the roads. But it was difficult to be certain of Moscow's intentions. For one thing, the ability of U.S. spy satellites to monitor events in Poland and the western Soviet Union was hindered by a vast cloud cover over the region. Brzezinski asked the CIA for another assessment of the chances of an invasion. "I am becoming increasingly concerned that this is likely," Brzezinski wrote in his diary on October 29.

---

* These documents included:

Note on the Subject of Martial Law with Consideration for State Security. Secret. Polish. 5 pages.

Resolution of the State Council Concerning the Introduction of a State of Martial Law. Secret. Polish. 2 pages.

Law on Amendment of the Constitution of the PPR. Secret. Polish. 1 page.

Decree on Protection of State Security and Public Order During the Existence of a State of Martial Law. Secret. Polish. 8 pages.

Decree on Supplying the Population During the Existence of a State of Martial Law. Secret. Polish. 5 pages.

Decree on Labor Relations During the Existence of a State of Martial Law. Secret. Polish. 5 pages.

Proposals Pertaining to the Procedure for Introducing a State of Martial Law with Consideration for State Security. Secret. Polish. 5 pages.

Initial Draft. Decree on the Administration of Justice During the Existence of a State of Martial Law. Secret. Polish. 8 pages.

Decree on Protection of State Security and Public Order During the Existence of a State of Martial Law. Secret. Polish. 8 pages.

In early November, the group working with Kuklinski on developing the army's preparations for martial law sent its report for review to the KOK, a special committee in the Defense Ministry chaired by Prime Minister Jozef Pinkowski. Details were kept vague because of the fear of leaks. But the central theme was this: Because of the disastrous events of 1970, when Polish soldiers shot at striking workers, the army would be restricted to large cities and industrial centers and would avoid direct confrontations with workers. That task would be left to the Interior Ministry and the SB. The army would maintain "internal law and order in the cities"and protect critical buildings and installations. To ensure that the Interior Ministry was equipped to carry out its tasks, the army would provide it with the necessary weapons, ammunition, armored transports, and helicopters.

In November, the KOK met to discuss the plans and a separate set of directives from the Interior Ministry. During the meeting, Interior Minister Miroslaw Milewski took a hard line, indicating that his goal was nothing less than the broad internment of activists, the establishment of special courts to punish violators of the crackdown, and the suspension of all civil rights. Milewski said he wanted direct assistance from the army in confronting striking workers. Kuklinski and some of his colleagues on the General Staff said Milewski's proposal was unacceptable.

The KOK reached no final decision on the plans, but recommended that the Defense and Interior Ministries work with other civilian ministries that controlled the country's communications, power, and transportation. The KOK concluded—correctly, in Kuklinski's view—that imposing martial law inevitably would lead to Soviet armed intervention.

During a meeting of senior officers in Skalski's office, Kuklinski said the army should resist Soviet intervention, and he suggested the Polish government not broadcast news, such as reports of sabotage by the Polish opposition, that could give Moscow a pretext to invade. But there was little support for his position.

*

On November 25, the CIA sent President Carter another "Alert" memorandum, stating, "The Polish leadership is facing the gravest challenge to its authority since the strikes on the Baltic Coast ended in August," adding that "the present situation moves us closer to coercive measures by the regime or possibly a Soviet military invasion."

Three days later, Robert M. Gates, the new national intelligence officer responsible for the Soviet Union and Eastern Europe, wrote to Turner that "the situation in Poland is intolerable to the Soviet Union." Even without new demands by Solidarity, Gates said, "I believe the Soviets cannot and will not settle for the status quo."

Inside the CIA's Soviet Division, there was concern that in the event of an invasion or martial law, Kuklinski would be unable to drive freely about Warsaw, which would make it much harder for him to communicate with the agency. The CIA's technical experts had been working on a project known as Discus, a sophisticated communications device that would allow Kuklinski to transmit short encrypted text messages to Warsaw Station. It was almost ready for deployment.

The agency, meanwhile, prepared a special note for Kuklinski. The information he had provided on the development of martial-law plans "was of outstanding intelligence significance," it said. "We limited the dissemination to the President and several select members of the Department of Defense."

The agency posed several follow-up questions: Where had the martial-law plans originated? Who, besides the officers working on the plans, were aware of them? Was there any dissent? Did Moscow know about the plans? Was it aware of the attitudes of Polish soldiers that might affect Soviet planning with respect to possible intervention?

"We do not want you to even attempt to answer them if you cannot do so securely," the CIA wrote.

On Saturday, November 29, as Kuklinski was preparing to leave with the rest of the Polish delegation to the defense ministers committee meeting in Bucharest, he learned that two officers—Colonel Franciszek Puchala, who led the combat-readiness department, and General Tadeusz Hupalowski, the first deputy chief of staff—were being sent urgently and confidentially to Moscow. From quiet discussions with his superiors, Kuklinski gleaned that their trip was related to Moscow's preparations for an invasion. The rest of that day and on Sunday, Kuklinski picked up more information, although some of it was impossible to verify. One rumor was that Defense Minister Jaruzelski, in talks with the Soviets, was resisting Moscow's plans. Jaruzelski was said to be upset that Moscow wanted Polish troops to remain in their barracks as the invasion began, and that East German troops would be included in the intervention.

To Kuklinski, it seemed unlikely that Jaruzelski could summon the courage to resist the Soviets. Jaruzelski had recently taken to closeting himself in his office, locking his doors and even shutting out his closest advisers. He was said to be so paralyzed by the crisis that he was not even going to attend the meeting of defense ministers in Bucharest and was sending General Eugeniusz Molczyk, a pro-Soviet hard-liner, instead.

Kuklinski had been assigned to write the speeches that Jaruzelski (now Molczyk) would be delivering at the meeting, and he decided to visit Jaruzelski, on the pretense that he needed approval of the speech drafts. If he sensed that Jaruzelski really was objecting to Moscow's plans, Kuklinski could try to reinforce his resistance and even suggest Jaruzelski quietly enlist the United States in a diplomatic solution. It was a highly risky, even desperate step. Kuklinski had his driver take him to Jaruzelski's compound on Klonowa Street. When he arrived, a guard who knew Kuklinski told him, "The minister is not in his office." The guard smiled, and as he left, Kuklinski suspected that Jaruzelski was indeed behind the closed door, but was not seeing anybody.

At the airport the next morning, December 1, as Kuklinski waited for the plane to Bucharest, he encountered Hupalowski and Puchala, the two General Staff officers being sent on the secret mission to

Moscow. He took Puchala aside and quizzed him. Puchala said he had been asked to bring back certain documents from the Soviet General Staff, although he was uncertain about the details. Both men agreed to talk again when they returned.

The bad weather over Eastern Europe continued to prevent U.S. spy satellites from tracking Soviet troop movements. But the East German–Polish border had been closed, and there was evidence that Soviet troops on the Polish border were on higher stages of alert. On December 2, Turner sent President Carter another "Alert" memo.

"I believe the Soviets are readying their forces for military intervention in Poland," Turner said in a cover note. "We do not know, however, whether they have made a decision to intervene, or are still attempting to find a political solution."

Brzezinski, meanwhile, urged Carter to send Brezhnev an unambiguous warning against intervention. At noon on Wednesday, December 3, Brzezinski met with Turner, Muskie, and Brown. All agreed the president should issue public and private warnings to Moscow. Brzezinski dictated the draft of the private warning that would be sent under President Carter's name on the "hot line," the special link between the White House and the Kremlin. The United States did not wish to exploit the events in Poland, the message said, nor did it seek to threaten the Soviet Union's legitimate security interests in that region.

"I want you to know that our only interest," the message said, "is in the preservation of peace in Central Europe, in the context of which the Polish government and Polish people can resolve their internal difficulties. At the same time, I have to state our relationship would be most adversely affected if force was used to impose a solution upon the Polish nation."

The hot-line message was transmitted to Moscow, and at 4:21 P.M., Washington received confirmation of its receipt. President Carter issued a public warning that "foreign military intervention in Poland would have most negative consequences for East-West relations in general and U.S.-Soviet relations in particular."

Meanwhile, that same Wednesday morning, after the conclusion of meetings of the Defense Ministers Committee, Kuklinski was at the Bucharest airport preparing to fly back to Warsaw. Typically, the Warsaw Pact delegations left airports in the order of the Russian alphabet, which placed Poland after Bulgaria, Hungary, and East Germany. But that day, Kulikov told the Polish delegates that they should leave first, saying, "You have serious business at home."

At the Warsaw military airport, as the returning Polish delegation was being greeted, Kuklinski was approached by General Waclaw Szklarski, his direct superior, who briefed him on the events of the past few days. Szklarski confirmed what Kuklinski had feared: A Soviet invasion was imminent. Hupalowski and Puchala had returned from Moscow with documents showing the intervention was to be carried out under the guise of a military exercise called "Soyuz 80." Szklarski offered many details, including the number of divisions and countries involved. He said the General Staff had analyzed the plans and was convinced that Moscow had misread the situation, and that an invasion would be counterproductive. The previous day, Siwicki, encouraged by his deputies, had tried to persuade Jaruzelski to renew talks with Moscow aimed at forestalling intervention and to say that Poland was prepared to impose martial law.

But Jaruzelski refused even to entertain any such discussions, Szklarski said. He insisted that Kuklinski keep the information confidential.

When Kuklinski arrived at the General Staff that night, he found Puchala and asked him what had occurred in Moscow. Puchala was evasive at first, then began to laugh nervously. Kuklinski confronted him, reminding him angrily that they had agreed to exchange information. Kuklinski made it clear that he already knew many details.

Puchala said that Hupalowski had met privately with Marshal Nikolai Ogarkov, chief of the Soviet General Staff, while Puchala had been relegated to meetings with lesser officers, who were developing Soyuz 80 as a cover for the action. No one used the word "invasion," Puchala said, only "exercise."

Kuklinski had his driver take him home and then drove his own car to a mailbox, where he drew a half circle in white chalk to signal that he would be leaving a message the following night, December 4.

The night of the exchange, Kuklinski printed a message to the CIA, filling both sides of one sheet of paper and one side of another.

"Bardzo pilne," he began. "Very urgent."

Dear Friends,

On the instruction of Defense Minister Jaruzelski, Gen. Hupalowski and Col. Puchala agreed in the General Staff of the U.S.S.R. Armed Forces in Moscow to a plan for introducing (under the pretext of exercises) the troops of the Soviet Army, the Army of East Germany and the Czech Army to Poland. From prepared plans which were presented to them for viewing and partial copying, it is apparent that three armies consisting of 15 Soviet Army divisions, one army comprised of two Czech divisions and the staff of one army and one division from East Germany are to be sent to Poland. Altogether, the group of intervening forces in the first phase will consist of eighteen divisions. An additional four divisions are to be attached to the armies of Czechoslovakia and East Germany (the Polish 5th and 11th Armored and the 4th and 12th Mechanized Divisions). Readiness to cross the Polish borders has been set for 8 December.

At the present time, representatives of the "fraternal armies" in civilian disguise are carrying out reconnaissance of marching routes, training areas and regions of future actions. The Czechs and East Germans are to operate in the Western part of the country, while the Central and eastern parts of Poland fall to the troops of the Soviet Army.

The operational scenario for the intervention foresees a regroupment of troops into all main training areas of the Polish forces and the conduct of live-fire exercises there, and then, contingent on how the situation develops, the blockading of all larger and industrial cities in Poland. From laconic and imprecise statements of highly placed military figures, it appears that the political decision on this matter was made much earlier and the leadership (Kania and Jaruzelski) was not put under pressure at the present time.

General Siwicki under pressure of his deputies has attempted to influence the Minister of Defense in the direction of opposing the endeavors of the allies, but that terribly trembling servant of Moscow has not even permitted discussion of this topic. At yesterday's extraordinary meeting of the Military Council, the Minster of Defense presented assignments to military districts and branches of services commanders. The leadership of the General Staff is hurriedly working out details of implementing the plans for intervention.

Prodded by Siwicki and General Molczyk, Jaruzelski had approved "working out an alternative plan for using solely Polish forces to 'secure internal security.'" Jaruzelski would personally present the plan to the "allies" in Moscow on Sunday, December 7, and ask that the introduction of Warsaw Pact forces be postponed "until the actions of Poland's own forces have proven ineffective." Kuklinski offered an excoriating picture of Jaruzelski, suggesting he was only appearing to resist Moscow's invasion and was presenting the alternative plan because of pressure from others. Writing with great emotion, Kuklinski said that Jaruzelski was "unworthy of the name Pole" and called him "the greatest coward in this land."

His partial buckling under pressure from Siwicki and Molczyk can only have the aim of throwing a smoke screen up against the judgment of those who could some day accuse [him] of national treason. . . .

In conclusion, with bitterness, I must report that as much as a small group of generals and officers of the Polish Armed Forces privy to the planning of the intervention are dispirited and crushed, there hasn't even been thought of military opposition by Polish forces to the military action of the Warsaw Pact. There are even statements that the very presence of such a large force on Polish territory can lead to increased calm.

Kuklinski folded his letter repeatedly, wrapped it inside cellophane, and taped it shut. Snow had been falling for several hours, and Kuklinski began a wandering drive through the city. At about 10:00 P.M. he reached the designated site beneath the streetlight on the Wislostrada and skidded the car into the curb. He got out and dropped the package on the ground.

That morning on his way to work, Ted Gilbertson spotted the chalk mark. Knowing that any message from Gull would be critical, he checked the list of dead-drop sites in Warsaw Station. He was not pleased to see that the Wislostrada was next on the list. The four-lane highway lacked a shoulder, and there was nowhere to park. With the streetlights on and the trees bare, the site was too exposed for a wintertime exchange. The Wislostrada had been envisaged for summer use, when an officer could park elsewhere and approach on foot. But the CIA had depleted suitable operational sites with Gull faster than expected.

That night, Gilbertson left work at the usual time, around 5:00 P.M., and headed home. There, he waved courteously to the militiamen who stood nearby, guarding the Iranian Embassy and the American ambassador's residence. Divorced and single, Gilbertson ate his habitual meager supper, peanut butter on bread and a beer. Around 8:00 P.M., he put on a tan parka and went outside again. He drove into the city center and began his own journey to be certain he was not being followed. Gilbertson had let his hair grow longer so that it would cover a small earpiece he wore to monitor the scratchy sounds of SB officers communicating on their radios. He also listened for SB transmissions on the FM band of his car radio. Despite his precautions, he felt conspicuous. With the snow falling fast, it seemed that only the diplomats and police were out on the empty streets.

As the gleaming lights of the Wislostrada loomed in the distance, Gilbertson drove slowly, passing a boat club, the park, and the monument for fallen heroes. A police car passed in the opposite direction and disappeared. Gilbertson kept his defroster on high to melt the snow on his windshield. As he made the final turn onto the boulevard, he began counting lampposts, knowing where he had to stop.

He had timed his arrival for about 10:30 P.M., estimating that the snow would be no more than a few inches deep. But as he approached the site, Gilbertson was dismayed to see a snowplow chugging ahead of him, sweeping mounds of snow off the street and onto the curb, where the package was supposed to be. Gilbertson realized that whatever he was searching for—an old yogurt container, a glove, a piece of crumpled foil—would be almost impossible to find. As the spot came into view, Gilbertson, as Kuklinski had before him, braked and skidded into the snowbank as if he had lost control. Seeing no cars approaching, he pushed open the door and stepped outside. His boots sank into the snow. He nervously checked his watch: 10:32 P.M. He walked around to the other side of the car and pretended to fiddle with something on the windshield. Then he knelt down and began to search under the streetlamp, pushing clumps of snow to the side as he dug. Soon he had made a hole about a foot deep and had found nothing. He plunged his arms deeper into the snow.

Five minutes passed. The snow was soaking through Gilbertson's pants, and his chest was matted with sweat. He scooped up clumps of snow, crushing them between his fingers, while watching for passing cars. *Where is it?* he muttered, swearing under his breath. He continued to dig, beginning to despair. Finally, he felt something crinkle in his grasp and pulled out a snow-covered cellophane package. He got back into his Fiat, skidded out of the snowbank, and began to drive down the Wislostrada. Suddenly he thought, *I'd better make sure.* Steering awkwardly with his knees, he fumbled with the package until he could unwrap it and found the tightly folded sheets inside. He recognized Gull's distinctive handwriting. Exhilarated, he wanted to drive to the embassy and cable Washington immediately, but he returned home and poured a glass of vodka. He turned off the lights and slipped into bed with a Polish-English dictionary and the letter attached to a clipboard. As a sharp wind rattled the windowpane and the snow continued to fall, Gilbertson pulled a large wool blanket over his head, switched on a flashlight, and began to translate the message.

Gilbertson took several hours to prepare a rough summary of the text, then placed the letter under his pillow. The next morning, he arrived at the embassy at about nine o'clock and reported immediately to Station Chief Tom Ryan. Ambassador Francis J. Meehan would be briefed. Another officer used a Selectric typewriter to type the Polish text of the message, along with a rough translation, onto a special form. A communications officer then scanned the form and cabled it to Langley. It was not yet dawn in Washington. The cable asked that the CIA officer for the Polish desk be summoned from home immediately. Less than two hours later, a cable was sent to Warsaw Station:

> Report is of critical importance and due [to] your prompt handling, translated version was in the hands of DDO and DCI [Director of Central Intelligence] by opening of business. It will be disseminated to the President and his closest advisers this morning. . . .
> Please stress to ambassador that, within the Department, only Secretary of State will receive report.

At Langley, a summary was prepared of Kuklinski's message, which was to be hand-carried to the White House. It said:

> The following information was received from a long-time reliable source who has proven access to it. The date of the information is 4 December.
> Moscow has developed a plan for intervention in Poland which was delivered to the Polish General Staff and agreed to by Polish

military leaders. The intervention is to take place under the pretext of joint Soviet, East German and Czechoslovak exercises in Poland. Readiness to cross the Polish frontiers was set for 8 December.

The memo recounted Gull's description of the invasion plans, reconnaissance missions, live-fire exercises, and blockades of Polish cities. Some sentences were lifted almost verbatim from Kuklinski's message. "The political decision to intervene was evidently taken some time ago, and there appears to have been no resistance to it from Party Leader Kania and Polish Defense Minister Jaruzelski," the memo said.

At 9:10 A.M. on Friday, December 5, Brzezinski received a phone call from Turner, who told him that a reliable source had said "18 Soviet divisions will enter Poland Monday morning."

About five minutes later, Brzezinski went to see President Carter, who was scheduled to go to Camp David for the weekend. The president said he would return on Sunday morning to lead a special session of the National Security Council on the crisis.

On Saturday, at 4:00 P.M., Brzezinski and Turner briefed senior White House advisers on the new information. "Stan Turner gave us his assessment," Brzezinski later wrote in his diary. "It is the Agency conclusion that the Soviets will be ready to go within 48 hours." Turner also reported that the Poles would "crack down heavily on Solidarity" and that "there will be bloodshed."

Carter met with Brzezinski, Turner, Muskie, and Brown in the Cabinet Room on Sunday morning, December 7. Brzezinski said he believed Polish security forces would begin rounding up Solidarity leaders late that night, when the activists would least expect it, as a way of eliminating any possibility of organized resistance. Soviet troops would enter the country throughout the night and early Monday morning, catching the country off guard.

Carter agreed that the White House should immediately issue a public statement, which would deny Moscow the element of surprise and alert the Poles to the threat.

"Preparations for a possible Soviet intervention in Poland appear to have been completed," the president's statement said. "It is our hope that no such intervention will take place." There would be "very adverse consequences for U.S.-Soviet relations of a Soviet military intervention in Poland."

Separate messages were sent to the leaders of Germany, France, Britain, Canada, Italy, Australia, and Japan as well as to the U.N. secretary-general. Brzezinski briefed the press and congressional leaders and passed word to Polish dissidents so that they could hide. He also spoke for ten minutes by phone with Pope John Paul II, a Pole and the former bishop of Krakow.

Brzezinski and other administration advisers waited tensely for news throughout the night and into Monday morning. Soviet troops did not cross the border.

After leaving the package in the snow, Kuklinski continued to gather intelligence about Moscow's plans. One colonel told him a delegation of East German generals was traveling through western Pomerania, the area near Poland's German border. Another described a similar group of Czech generals traveling in the Silesian military district, near the Czech border. A Polish general reported he was to meet several Soviet generals in eastern Poland. A fourth officer said he had just returned from Minsk, where he had accompanied a number of Soviet generals inspecting airfields in central Poland.

General Szklarski told Kuklinski that Jaruzelski had ordered the General Staff to put aside all other work and begin preparations for "internal peace," as Jaruzelski had described the martial-law crackdown.

On Monday, December 8, General Skalski called Kuklinski and other top aides into his office and said Jaruzelski and Kania had flown to Moscow over the weekend to present Jaruzelski's alternative plan to liquidate Solidarity.

Skalski gave a briefing about what Jaruzelski had said. Jaruzelski had been convinced that Moscow was now persuaded that Poland had to solve its own problems. "Our country, in view of its importance within the Warsaw Pact, cannot allow itself to be devoured by the enemy," Jaruzelski said. "We ourselves, with the moral, political, and economic support of our allies, will resolve the difficulties."

Jaruzelski also said he believed that a new wave of young soldiers, who not long ago had participated in the Solidarity strikes and more recently had been drafted into the army, "have been exposed to military discipline." One of the main tasks, Jaruzelski said, was to isolate "the Solidarity leaders from the main body of workers, bringing their hypocrisy to light. The period of humiliating the government will be brought to a close. The law will restrain the outbreak of strikes. . . . A stricter course is needed."

Jaruzelski added: "The No. 1 matter for the armed forces is to maintain high combat readiness, political and moral unity, and fitness for political combat. The most critical period has passed. We are being hit, but we are not defeated. The Polish Armed Forces are in good condition. This is the result of good work in the past years." Jaruzelski was proposing the liquidation of Solidarity as an alternative to a Soviet invasion.

Jaruzelski had admonished Siwicki to treat his description of the summit as confidential and summarize it in only the most general terms for the lower ranks.

On that same Monday, December 8, Warsaw Station received a cable from Langley saying that the "weekend's high meetings here, and subsequent White House statements on Polish situation, were prompted by report from Gull." The CIA said it was preparing a note for Kuklinski expressing its appreciation for his work.

Warsaw Station cabled headquarters: "It is difficult to find words to adequately thank Gull for his efforts, dedication, and sense of duty."

Over the next two weeks, Kuklinski, battling exhaustion and a severe cold, fell ill with the flu. Still, he showed up at work, collecting and photographing new documents, trying to keep abreast of the latest news. On December 14, one week before the next exchange, he started a long letter to the CIA, offering more details about the plans for invasion and the debate within the General Staff over what the Polish Army would do if ordered to help put down Solidarity. Kuklinski believed Polish troops would resist:

> In the final analysis, nevertheless, the troops will not permit a massacre of the nation. They will choose death rather than to live in disgrace on their knees.... It would seem that both the Soviet leadership and the traitors from the Polish United Workers Party, with Jaruzelski in the forefront, are aware of this. And the fact that, in the planned intervention, it is proposed to deploy five armies, which will be commanded by Russians, Czechs, and Germans, with the Poles being excluded, testifies to this emphatically....
>
> It is not possible to exaggerate the value of sharp U.S.A. reactions to threats made to Poland. Many Poles are well aware of this, but especially those who may have been called up to defend the nation, and are not in position to fulfill this most sacred obligation because of the power of the enemy, and also because of the duplicity contributed to it by our own traitors.

On December 21, Kuklinski collected fifteen rolls of film containing his latest intelligence—thirty-four documents running more than 450 pages.

All day there had been a light fog and a steady drizzle. Kuklinski drove to the exchange site, but concluded that the poor visibility made it too risky. The next day there was a broad shakeup in the Defense Ministry, with a group of hard-liners assuming new positions. Kuklinski wrote another note to the CIA saying that the "preparations for pushing the proverbial 'last button'" of a Soviet invasion had been delayed.

Among the documents Kuklinski delivered in an exchange on December 23 was a secret agreement between Poland and the Soviet

Union dating to the 1950s, detailing the numbers, locations, and movements of Soviet troops based in Poland. There was also a bulky attachment of more than 100 maps, with handwritten notations giving more details, including barracks locations, patrol boundaries, and the communications equipment the troops were allowed to possess.

In the exchange Kuklinski received a letter from the CIA, which thanked him for the invasion plans he had left in the snow.

> Your information was of extraordinary value and timeliness. Upon receipt of it and following translation, it was immediately hand-carried to the President. Further, your report played a very important role in U.S. Government decisions and actions during the following several days.
>
> We again thank you for your devotion and contribution to our mutual cause. We wish there were some way we could lighten the burdens you carry during this critical period.
>
> You are constantly in our thoughts.
>
> Your friends

9

PREPARING TO CRUSH SOLIDARITY

THE SOVIET DIVISION had long felt there was a need to develop a way for sources in denied areas to pass timely and perishable intelligence more quickly and securely. Car passes were scheduled too infrequently to be useful in crises, and the thirty-six-hour turnaround time for a dead drop and the signals involved were too unwieldy. But now Discus was ready. Langley had developed a compact, short-range, two-way transmitter that could send encrypted messages in electronic bursts. The agency built a version for the Gull operation and codenamed it "Iskra" (*spark* in Russian and a play on the title of Lenin's journal, "Iskra").

The Soviet Division sent an Iskra and twenty pages of instructions to Warsaw Station and told the officers to get it to Kuklinski as soon as possible. In a letter prepared for Kuklinski, the CIA said the Iskra could be used to send "information of extraordinary importance and urgency (for example, imminent state of war, Soviet intervention, personal danger to yourself because of your activities) that cannot wait even for a few hours."

For its time, the Iskra was a major advance in miniaturization. The size of a pack of cigarettes, it weighed about a half pound and had a keyboard and memory. Kuklinski could type in a message at home, place the device in his pocket, and carry it somewhere else. There, he could push the transmission button without removing the Iskra from his pocket. The device had a small window through which a single line of text could be read, from an outgoing or incoming message. If he transmitted directly into the embassy, an alarm would sound in Warsaw Station. As a rule, Kuklinski was asked to leave a signal in the morning that he would transmit in the night, and an officer would take another Iskra outside to receive the message. The CIA did not want Kuklinski to transmit too often into the embassy, fearing that the SB was monitoring the compound for electronic transmissions and could pinpoint the sender's location.

Kuklinski received the Iskra soon after leaving the message in the snow in December 1980. Not long after, he learned from a neighbor, General Wladyslaw Hermaszewski, that a Soviet-inspired conspiracy was developing among hard-line Polish officials who wanted to replace Jaruzelski and Kania. Kuklinski tried to convey the information, carefully typing a message into the Iskra, but he could not get it to work.

On January 2, before leaving for Moscow on a short trip with Siwicki, Kuklinski requested an unscheduled car exchange and returned the Iskra, along with a somewhat teasing note: "The indicators begin to blink a few seconds after I turn the power on," he wrote. "Despite many attempts to turn the power off and then on again, and changing the batteries for new ones, this phenomenon keeps occurring. The set is marvelous. The instructions are clear. Now if it would only work."

Although the plot against Jaruzelski and Kania did not develop, Hermaszewski remained a good source of information about Soviet intentions and plans. Kuklinski's bond with him was more than just professional. Although Bogdan's romance with the general's daughter, Grazyna, had cooled, Kuklinski and Hermaszewski were still neighbors on Rajcow Street and friends. Hermaszewski had also proposed that Kuklinski join him and about twenty officers in the purchase of property in Wiazowna, a village southeast of Warsaw. They intended to subdivide the land and build summer homes for their families. Kuklinski liked the idea of having some land in the country, where he could hide film and other supplies. He hesitated when he learned that among the participants were Poland's chief military prosecutor and other government officials, but he decided to buy his share, which he then resold to his friend Roman Barszcz.

Kuklinski used the proceeds to help his son Bogdan buy a twenty-two-acre farm a short drive away. Without Bogdan's knowledge, Kuklinski decided to use some parts of the property as a hiding place for his clandestine activity. The property, which was long and narrow and surrounded by a fence, was crossed by two country roads and filled with hundreds of trees. There was also a dilapidated farmhouse in which an elderly woman lived (she had the right to reside there until she died). Without her knowledge as well, Kuklinski created a hiding place behind some bricks in an outer wall of the house, where he was able to secrete film rolls, cameras, and even some of his writings. He then moved the bricks back into position, sealed them with a filler material, and smeared the outside with dirt. (The bricks could easily be pushed aside and resealed when necessary.) The house was not visible from the road, and the wall where he created the space was shielded by bushes. The property also had a tall barn, where Kuklinski hid the sheet of microfilm given to him by the CIA that listed the locations of sequence of operational sites. Over time, Kuklinski said, the property became an important facilitator for the operation.

Bogdan, meanwhile, who had finally given up his dream of medical school, took some agriculture courses and moved into a trailer on the farm. He expanded a small apple orchard, built an irrigation system, raised rabbits for sale, and assembled motorcycles that he sold to collectors in West Germany.

Bogdan had also fallen in love with a woman he had met in 1979 in a popular Warsaw discotheque called The Barn. Iza was twenty-three years old, had a master's degree in microbiology, and worked as a researcher in a government institute studying the production of protein. Slim with large blue eyes and brown hair that brushed her shoulders, Iza was an ardent Solidarity supporter and helped to deliver underground newspapers and magazines. She was aware that Bogdan's father held a senior military post, yet she felt at ease at their home, even when she discussed politics. Iza was unsparing in her criticism of the regime, yet Kuklinski always listened patiently, never taking offense.

Langley sent another Iskra to Kuklinski, and on January 21, at 10:00 P.M., Kuklinski successfully used it for the first time to transmit a message about new plans to use troops to blockade cities and naval forces to blockade the seacoast and ports.

> The highest party-government circles appear to be resolved to employ directly the Polish military for internal settlement. . . . On Jan. 20, the commanders of the military districts and of the branches of the armed forces were summoned to the General Staff. In special rooms, isolated, they are working out plans for the use of the military in the event of martial law.

The Soviet Division chief cabled a congratulatory message to Warsaw Station for its successful use of the Iskra. "I hope this is the first of many, many more to come," he wrote. On January 23, Langley cabled Warsaw to say that Kuklinski's message had been placed in the "President's Daily Brief," the highly classified intelligence document provided to the president each morning.

On January 29, Kuklinski transmitted his second Iskra message, with more details about the military's role in "the political resolution of the crisis" and some rumors that Jaruzelski might be promoted to prime minister. "Gull obviously likes his new toy," Langley cabled Warsaw.

In early February, Kuklinski learned that two dozen Soviet generals had arrived in Poland for an unannounced five-day visit, ostensibly to prepare for a new military exercise, "Soyuz 81," which was to begin in the spring. But it was clear that the underlying mission was to sound out Polish officers about the evolving crisis. Individual Polish commanders were summoned to meetings with the Soviets, who also visited military units around the country. The encounters were tense. In Wesola, a deputy of Kulikov's asked a Polish regimental commander what he would do if he had to remove strikers from a local plant. General Siwicki had peremptorily interrupted, saying that such a question should be directed to him. The two men got into a shouting match.

On Monday, February 9, Jaruzelski was promoted to prime minister, replacing Pinkowski. In one of his first acts, he ordered a secret war game to be held to rehearse the implementation of a crackdown. Kuklinski transmitted another message that night at 10:29. "Hurried preparations are being carried out to introduce martial law," he wrote.

Conclusions drawn from this exercise will be presented to Kania and Jaruzelski the following day. It is assumed in the plans that 12 hours before introducing the state of martial law, security forces will conduct a special operation arresting approximately 200 activists [in Warsaw] of the opposition and Solidarity. Six hours before introducing the state of martial law, Polish troops will enter operations.

Four days later, in Jaruzelski's first speech as prime minister, he asked for ninety days of peace to give the government time to deal with the country's economic crisis. Criticizing the "hostile forces" working against socialism, Jaruzelski declared: "Our place is and will remain in the socialist camp. Poland will remain a faithful member of the Warsaw Pact."

The next day, more Soviet generals arrived in Legnica under the guise of preparing for Soyuz 81 and began making reconnaissance visits to major industrial plants throughout Poland, shipyards in Gdansk and Gdynia, and the radio-TV center in Warsaw. Forests near Warsaw were chosen as bases for two Soviet divisions, and public buildings in Warsaw were selected as the *wojenna komendantura* (headquarters) for the military administration during an eventual invasion.

The secret war game ordered by Jaruzelski was held on February 16. The four dozen officials from the Defense and Interior Ministries who attended had to sign a secrecy oath. Only two officers—Kuklinski and one from the Interior Ministry—were allowed to take notes. The war game offered a vivid look at how a crackdown would be carried out. The participants agreed that the key to liquidating Solidarity was the swift detention of as many as 6,000 activists in the hours before martial law was formally introduced. The best time would be a holiday or weekend, when most Poles were at home. The SB would infiltrate Solidarity in order to learn its plans and influence its actions. Other militarized forces from the Ministry of Interior would enter factories and schools, while the army would send tanks and troops into cities.

Kuklinski summarized the war game and the official conclusions in a report for his superiors, which was presented to Jaruzelski. The prime minister gave his approval and ordered that a briefing paper be prepared for Moscow.

On Sunday, February 22, Kuklinski wrote to the CIA describing the visits by the Soviet generals, their tense encounters with Polish officers, and the war game. It was clear, he said, that Moscow would impose its will on Poland one way or the other. In preparation for Soyuz 81, Moscow was sending in troops, tanks, helicopters, and planes. "There exists a serious uneasiness among the leadership of the General Staff, who recognize the danger of transforming an exercise into a pre-planned military intervention," Kuklinski wrote. He included film of the notes he took during the war game. "I must add that the plans in these documents are the most closely guarded secrets," he wrote. He passed the letter and films to the CIA that night at 10:34.

On March 5 headquarters cabled Warsaw to say of Kuklinski's most recent documents on martial law: "They are of outstanding importance to our understanding of the current situation and interpretation of future events. [In] view of extreme sensitivity of these documents as they relate to [Gull's] security, dissemination will be limited to the President, Vice-President, Secretary of State, and Secretary of Defense."

That day, the Reagan administration issued a public statement of concern about Soyuz 81. "Outside intervention, in whatever form, would have the gravest consequences," a State Department spokesman said.

On March 11, five days before Soyuz 81 was to begin, Kuklinski tried to use the Iskra to report that Marshal Kulikov was to lead the exercise from Wunsdorf, East Germany, and that 44,000 Polish troops would be involved. But he again had trouble getting the device to work. So he left a chalk mark signaling for a car pass in two days.

On the night of the exchange, he wrote a letter providing an update on Soyuz 81. Jaruzelski had ordered troops to "bypass large cities" to avoid confrontations. Moscow was also keeping key details from the Poles. In a briefing in Moscow, "everybody participated except the Poles. For us there was a separate briefing."

Kuklinski included films of the war-game summary that had been the basis for Jaruzelski's briefings when he had gone to Moscow, and he enclosed the defective Iskra. The CIA officer who went to meet him almost missed the exchange after becoming stalled about a half mile away by a religious festival. The officer drove through a throng of celebrants and arrived just in time to find Kuklinski.

On March 19, three days after the beginning of Soyuz 81, 200 riot police brutally beat more than twenty activists in Solidarity and an affiliated organization, Rural Solidarity, which represented more than 3 million farmers, who had occupied a local government hall in Bydgoszcz. Three people were seriously injured. The incident prompted Solidarity to consider calling a nationwide strike. Meanwhile, Marshal Kulikov told the General Staff that the Soyuz 81 exercises would continue indefinitely. Polish ground, air, and naval forces were placed under Polish General Eugeniusz Molczyk, a strong ally of Moscow, for the duration of Soyuz 81. The decision infuriated Kuklinski. He received frantic calls from officers at front headquarters in Bialobrzegi, southeast of Warsaw, asking, "Don't the people at the top understand what is going on?"

In an exchange March 27 on a rainy night, Kuklinski wrote that he had become convinced the Soviets were creating the conditions for an invasion and for establishing an independent command center that would not keep the Polish General Staff informed. In the exchange, the CIA delivered a new Iskra to him.

On April 1, Kuklinski was able to use the new Iskra to send a message about Moscow's reaction to Jaruzelski's martial-law plans. Moscow had deemed the plans unsatisfactory and presented its own strategy. Kuklinski said that four days earlier, thirty Soviet defense and KGB "functionaries," led by Kulikov and a first deputy to Soviet KGB chief Yuri Andropov, had flown to Warsaw to act as "consultants" on martial law. "After familiarizing themselves with our plans," he wrote, "the Soviets deemed them unsatisfactory and presented their own proposals." He explained the Russian assessment:

> Introduction of the state of martial law is dictated by the necessity to defend socialism. Its introduction should also be accompanied by suspension of the Constitution, with the total power being put into the hands of the military command. In the provinces the authority should be in the hands of garrison commanders and in areas where there are no garrisons, the authority should be in the hands of appointed commanders of the Polish Armed Forces.

Kuklinski described proposed activities during preparations for martial law:

> We should concentrate our effort on unmasking counterrevolution in Solidarity [and the] identification of leaders and elements who are extremist, determination of where they live, introduction of agent networks into hostile organizations and the location of underground radios and printing presses. Fourteen hours before the state of martial law is introduced, we should complete detentions and start investigation and emergency courts. In order to stifle counterrevolution and strikes, we should use the security forces together with the armed forces. Soviet advisers should be brought into the Polish Armed Forces General Staff, to the military district commands, and branches of the armed forces.

Kuklinski wrote that the Polish military leadership had generally rejected the Soviet suggestions. "Our leaders—Jaruzelski, Kania, and in the Polish Armed Forces, Siwicki—have no intention of introducing this state. During the visit the Soviets in a provoking manner appealed to the generals in the General Staff to revolt," he added.

Over the next few days, Soviet combat helicopters buzzed repeatedly over Polish air space, ignoring the Polish air-traffic controllers and frightening the population. When General Siwicki demanded an explanation, he was told that the flights were carrying food and were part of a normal troop rotation. Kuklinski also learned that on the evening of April 3, Jaruzelski and party chief Kania were flown secretly on a Russian military aircraft to the U.S.S.R. for talks with the Soviet leadership; they returned the next morning. A few days later, Marshal Kulikov and his chief of staff, Anatoly Gribkov, flew into Warsaw, asking if Polish officials had incorporated their "corrections and additions" into the martial-law plans. After a briefing, Gribkov demanded that twenty key documents be translated into Russian and sent to Moscow.

The Soyuz 81 exercise ended in the first week of April, but the threat of outside intervention or martial law remained. On Saturday, April 11, Jaruzelski visited the General Staff to meet the small group of officers, including Kuklinski, working on "Operation Spring," the code name for the martial-law plan. Jaruzelski seemed depressed as he studied the documents. He stated, "I am not acquainted with matters on which you have worked for the past several months, but I must finally learn them."

Jaruzelski was by turns reluctant and impatient. "In the darkest corners of my mind," Jaruzelski added, "I could not find the thought that we could do such a thing. I do not want to be the Prime Minister if I must sign these documents so that they may be implemented."

As Kuklinski listened, Jaruzelski blamed the crisis on provocations by Solidarity activists, and he lamented that "the bloodying of three noses" in Bydgoszcz had put Poland on the edge of disaster. He was still searching for an intermediate solution before ordering the mass internment of Solidarity activists. On Sunday, April 13, he met with Kulikov and "categorically refused" Kulikov's demand to set a date for introducing martial law.

On three occasions—April 10, 12, and 16—Kuklinski tried without success to alert the CIA with the Iskra. On April 26 he wrote to the CIA that the Iskra's malfunctions were "regrettable, since this communications system appears to me to be indispensable in the present situation which approaches a confrontation."

He said he awaited that night's exchange impatiently, "so I can give you a timely alert about the danger of military intervention in Poland." He went on to describe Moscow's continued "air war of nerves against Poland." In a single night, April 25, he said, the Soviets had conducted 280 flights into and within Poland.

Under Moscow's pressure and supervision, the basic planning for martial law had been concluded. He enclosed sensitive General Staff documents, including one pertaining to the use of army troops against the workers. "The General Staff, chiefly Skalski and Siwicki, could not entertain the possibility," Kuklinski wrote. "On the other hand, the Russians and General Molczyk saw the armed forces as the main force which should deal with the 'counterrevolution.'" The process was being conducted under "the greatest secrecy."

Kuklinski expressed increasing concern about security: "There is a new list of persons who know the plans in the parts pertaining to them," he wrote, "and also those who have access to the whole. This list is kept together with the only copy of the planning documents by the chief of the Polish Armed Forces General Staff [Siwicki] in his own safe. My name is one of three who had seen the complete plans. I beg that you continue to handle reporting on these matters with care."

Kuklinski said that if the Poles realized what was happening, they could formulate strategy and tactics in the struggle for "their inalienable rights." But he saw little evidence of preparations for armed resistance by the Polish military if Moscow invaded. "In conclusion," he wrote, "I greet you with the hope that just as during the entire course of the crisis in Poland, my country will not be left to itself."

In a letter to Daniel, Kuklinski described a meeting in which a Polish general had criticized the United States for not doing more to oppose Moscow. The general claimed America had sold out the Poles, allowing Moscow a free hand. Kuklinski had remained silent, confident the materials he was providing the CIA "would be properly utilized" for the Polish cause.

"We Poles are deeply aware that for freedom, we ourselves must fight, even if we had to pay the ultimate price," he wrote. "I continue to believe that the assistance which your country gives to all who are fighting for this freedom may speed up the attainment of such a goal."

The Soviet presence in Poland remained an issue. One day, Kuklinski heard from the commander of the Polish Third Division in Lublin that Soviet soldiers with communications equipment had landed at a nearby airfield, and that a Soviet major had approached the Polish officer, looking for food. The Soviet major said that his contingent was waiting for a Soviet Army air echelon to arrive in three days. The Soviets had also informed Siwicki that during Soyuz 81, eighteen communications sites were secretly deployed in Poland, with eight Russian soldiers stationed at each. Kuklinski made a list of the sites and their locations.

Tom Ryan, Warsaw Station Chief, was worried. He had been engaged in continuing discussions with the Soviet Division at Langley about what would happen to their communications with Gull if the Poles imposed a crackdown or if the Soviets invaded. In one cable to Ryan, the Soviet Division said it shared his concerns. But, the cable noted, "We must face stark reality that a HUMINT [human intelligence] source such as Gull is a key contributor to our evaluation and reactions to a crisis such as this. [Station's] and Gull's security are uppermost in our considerations, but Gull remains a unique source of critical and perishable information as he has clearly demonstrated."

Ryan responded that Gull still had "the best view" of his situation and had so far correctly assessed his status, but he insisted that the agency had "a moral obligation" to instigate "changes in operational

M.O. or frequency of contact if at any time we determine that the value of the information Gull can provide does not match the risks to his personal safety."

Ryan said Gull would have more freedom "under a Polish-declared, Polish-enforced state," even with curfews, than he would if the Soviet Union invaded.

> Under Soviet intervention, believe Gull's usefulness and security will be in question.... Gull has reported to us he has an anti-Soviet reputation, and on at least one occasion, a Soviet general made pointed note of this attitude in a meeting. If the Soviets come, there could be a purge of the Polish military, especially those with anti-Soviet sentiments. It is quite possible that Gull could be among those purged. If not, he certainly could be shunted off to some unimportant duty. Sustained contact with Gull under such circumstances would be unrealistic and dangerous for his personal security.

On June 17, Kuklinski was ordered to prepare a speech for Siwicki to deliver to the KOK, the highest-ranking Polish defense body. Kuklinski worked into the night and gave copies of the speech the next morning to Siwicki and his three top deputies—Generals Skalski, Hupalowski, and Antoni Jasinski, who oversaw organization and mobilization. Siwicki offered his suggestions for revisions and said he needed the speech by 6:00 P.M. The final version, which was eight pages, was classified "Secret, of Special Importance." Kuklinski made four copies but could find only Siwicki and Skalski. He gave each a copy. He placed the third copy inside his private safe and the fourth copy in his briefcase.

At home, Kuklinski photographed the speech. But he was so tired that he overslept the next morning and did not reach the General Staff until 7:45. Rushing upstairs, he was stunned to see General Waclaw Szklarski, his direct superior, and three aides standing in his office. His safe was open and in disarray, and one of the aides was reaching into it, rifling through the papers in search of the missing document.

"Ryszard, where do you keep the fourth copy?" Szklarski asked, holding out the third copy that had been in Kuklinski's safe. He said the fourth copy had to be delivered to General Jasinski immediately.

"Where's the fire?" Kuklinski asked sarcastically, pretending to be annoyed. He asked the major searching the safe to leave. He then strode toward the safe and grabbed the first document he could find. "It's right here," he said briskly. He quickly placed the document in a folder. "I will deliver it."

He was almost paralyzed by fear, but his bluff seemed to work. After the other officers left, Kuklinski returned to his office, opened his briefcase, and exchanged the document in the folder with the copy he had taken home.

Although Kuklinski did not attend the KOK session on June 19, he was given a full account of what happened, which he described in his next letter to the CIA. Jaruzelski had criticized the United States, blaming "American imperialism" for Poland's troubles. Kuklinski also noted that the latest documents showed how differently the Poles and Soviets viewed the crisis.

"In the leadership of the General Staff," Kuklinski wrote, "the opinion prevails that the Russians would want at all costs to avoid military intervention in Poland." But Soviet activity showed that "very intensive concrete preparations" were being made in this direction.

He cited the increasing number of Soviet troops in Poland and the revealing comments of Soviet and Polish officials. In one heated exchange, Soviet Marshal Kulikov had demanded to know why martial law had not yet been implemented. General Siwicki blamed the Interior Ministry, saying it had "fallen apart." Kulikov retorted that it was the whole government, not the Interior Ministry, that had fallen apart. Kulikov added that the ministry wanted to take action, but was being blocked by Jaruzelski's unwillingness to make a decision.

Kuklinski described the incident involving his safe, which had almost resulted in "an immediate tragedy." He said he had been elected Communist Party delegate from the General Staff and the Defense Ministry, and some of his colleagues were suggesting he stand for election as a delegate to the big party congress in July. "Of course," he added sardonically, "all this takes place without any say on my part."

At 10:37 P.M. on June 21, Kuklinski passed the letter to the CIA, along with twenty-one rolls of film that held some 880 pages of documents, including a map of Soviet Army communications sites in Poland.*

It is likely that few people appreciated the secrets spilling out of Warsaw Pact and Soviet vaults more than Aris Pappas, a junior CIA analyst who had been assigned to monitor martial law. In his job, he saw a broad array of information. Much of it came from satellites, electronic eavesdropping, diplomatic cables, and even foreign news reports. The human intelligence was different. Pappas would get calls as new documents arrived. *You've got to come down and look at this now.* It was, as he liked to say, intelligence that was "hot and wet." He had no idea who the source was, or if there was more than one. But after months of immersion, he appreciated its value. The details were intimate, the observations incisive, and the tensions palpable. It was clear the Polish General Staff was in emotional turmoil, and a source was among them, deeply engaged.

Pappas had been with the CIA for five years, in the Directorate of Intelligence's Office of Soviet Analysis, commonly known as SOVA. He worked in the Theater Forces Division, an office that along with the rest of SOVA had been moved to a nondescript building in northern Virginia because of construction at the CIA compound. One day in the spring of 1981, Ben Rutherford, the tall, gaunt, and highly respected division chief, assigned Pappas to focus exclusively on martial-law developments. Other analysts were following the issue, but no one else had primary responsibility for the military's preparations.

---

* Kuklinski had new construction details about a second Project Albatross installation, the underground wartime Soviet command post that was to be built in a former hunting lodge in the forests near Opole. The two bunkers, to be built near an abandoned brickyard containing two small man-made lakes, would be able to withstand a force of fifteen kilograms per square centimeter. The usable area would be suspended inside a chamber on nitrogen-filled cylinders. "The chamber has a 3-meter-thick reinforced concrete foundation and protective shields against explosion and shock. The inside wall of the chamber is covered by steel plates and fortified by cushions made of glass wool."

A tall thirty-five-year-old with a mustache, glasses, and dark hair, Pappas was born in Astoria, Queens, to a family of confectioners. As a child, he would sit on Rockaway Beach, Queens, watching the airplanes leave from Idlewild Airport. He became familiar with the markings on each plane—Air France, BOAC, Alitalia—and he liked to imagine their destinations. He read everything he could about airplanes and built models as a hobby. His friends liked building gas-powered models, but they often had to make compromises, such as distorting the shape of a wing, so that the planes would fly. Pappas appreciated the fineness of scale and the precision of detail and preferred constructing models that did not fly, since they could be built as precise replicas. There were no compromises.

Over the years, Pappas constructed and painted hundreds of models of fighters and passenger planes (some were later displayed in the Smithsonian National Air and Space Museum in Washington, D.C.). He spent hours in the library researching their assembly and history. He attended conventions of the International Plastic Modelers Society and judged their contests. After graduating from City College in New York, he would have joined the Air Force ROTC, but was not qualified for pilot training because he had imperfect vision. So he joined Army ROTC, and later earned a commercial pilot's license.

Army service took him to Korea and Germany, where he was introduced to military intelligence. An extroverted and amiable man, he was offered a job in CIA operations when he was hired in 1975. But he turned that down, knowing even then that he wanted to be an analyst. He liked nothing better than immersing himself in documents. After joining the CIA, he was thrilled when he was shown the trove of materials provided by Oleg Penkovsky, the Soviet spy who provided critical intelligence during the Cuban missile crisis.

Pappas and his SOVA colleagues were divided into three sections: political, economic, and military. The military group was, in turn, separated into two areas. The first was strategic forces, which focused on Soviet nuclear weapons and long-range missiles that could directly threaten the United States. The second area was theater forces, which dealt with the threat of the Soviets launching a massive war in Europe. In theater operations, where Pappas worked, the analysts were responsible for such issues as command-and-control matters, chemical warfare operations, General Staff theory and doctrine, and large-scale armor, artillery, and infantry exercises.

His job sounded a good deal like Kuklinski's.

Pappas had studied Russian in college and kept a Russian grammar book on his desk, for he occasionally found it useful to do his own translation of a word in a Soviet document. Like many analysts, he looked beyond words; he studied how articles were grouped in Soviet journals, whether they were ghostwritten, and how they were footnoted. Analysts learned to take a holistic approach; frequently what they found was not what they had been searching for.

In his early years with the agency, which were also the early stages of the Gull operation, Pappas came to realize that a steady stream of documents was giving the CIA the best insight it had, in documentary form, of the structure and intentions of the Warsaw Pact and, by extension, the Soviet Union. The materials had allowed him to see how powerfully Moscow controlled its Warsaw Pact allies; the fact that they were puppets of the Soviets made them no less important. For one thing, Moscow could not mount a successful war in Europe without their participation. And because of the nuclear parity between the superpowers, a sudden attack remained the Pentagon's greatest fear. If Moscow started a conventional war, the Warsaw Pact countries, particularly the Poles and East Germans, would play a critical early role. Indeed, the only elements of Soviet war plans that did not involve Eastern Europe were Moscow's strategic operations, such as the use of nuclear weapons or launching long-range missiles from deep inside Soviet territory. Almost everything else would involve the Warsaw Pact, whose armies would have to be trained, equipped, and accounted for at the front. As Pappas and his fellow analysts saw it, the more the United States knew about the Warsaw Pact, the more it understood Soviet intentions and capabilities.

Gull's intelligence had been incorporated into national estimates, used to counteract Soviet weaponry, and employed to help the Pentagon determine where it needed to spend money for weapons and where it did not. "We have a critical need for information on the armor of the T-72 tank," the CIA wrote to Kuklinski one day in 1981, "inasmuch as several billions of dollars of our defense programs are contingent on acquiring this information." Gull's intelligence had allowed the United States to direct satellites with extreme precision at Warsaw Pact military exercises in order to check the accuracy of other sources and to understand not just what the Soviets were doing, but why they were doing it. As Pappas later put it, Gull's material on the Soviet and Warsaw Pact militaries "virtually defined our knowledge. It was the touchstone. It was the basic standard." One of Pappas's colleagues said of Gull: "He held that window open for a long, long time, and gave us a look at the entire landscape."

In Pappas's mind, everything returned to the central question faced by all intelligence analysts: the difference between secrets and mysteries. Secrets were facts that existed somewhere—like the nature and wiring of the Warsaw Pact air defense system or the thickness of the skin of the T-72 tank. But analysts also had to divine mysteries. What events would trigger the westward movement of the Second Strategic Echelon? Some answers lay in knowing the sequence of events that led to war, events that could be observed and measured. So when Pappas was assigned to focus exclusively on martial law, he continued to rely on the stream of intelligence from the Warsaw Pact. Wherever it was coming from, it was affording the CIA an exceptional insight into mysteries as well as secrets.

By the summer of 1981, Sue Burggraf had completed more than two years in Warsaw, and she saw the city as a profoundly tragic place. In the winter, women shuffled through the snow wearing sandals and two or three pairs of socks. Meat shortages were also acute: Poles often waited in long lines at grocery stores only to find bare hooks hanging from the ceiling and the shelves empty except for vinegar and fish paste. Polish citizens who worked in the American Embassy had been fired for stealing toilet paper. There were long lines at bread and fabric shops. But the current political crisis, the Gull operation—and the arrival of summer—had instilled in her an intense loyalty to the country, and she would not have considered leaving.

In the normal rotation of officers, Sue Burggraf had succeeded Ted Gilbertson as deputy chief to Tom Ryan. She and Ryan were joined by a third case officer, Evan Davis,* who was in his first tour abroad; a fourth operative, Jason Wilcox,† soon joined them.

All but Davis worked from a spartan suite in the embassy's political section. Ryan, whose cover was first secretary, had the largest office, overlooking the front plaza, the public entrance, and a large American flag. Burggraf, who had an adjoining office, had just enough room for a metal desk and a chair, and she hung a reproduction of a Matisse print on the wall. Davis, who had a different cover as a consular officer, worked on the ground floor where Poles applied for visas. Cables were hand-carried to a CIA communicator in a restricted part of the embassy.

Given the troubles with the Iskra device, Warsaw Station remained concerned about obtaining timely intelligence from Kuklinski. The CIA had noticed an increase in the number of "casuals" where exchanges with Kuklinski were scheduled, and several exchanges had to be aborted. The heightened security also meant that officers had to extend their surveillance detection runs.

One Sunday, Burggraf was scheduled to make a car exchange with Kuklinski at 10:30 P.M. at the Gdanski Bridge, which spanned the Vistula River. She packed a lunch and took with her a bottle of water, a book, a travel guide, and maps. By late morning, after driving through the countryside, she arrived in Zelazowa Wola, the birthplace of Chopin, about sixty kilometers from Warsaw. Burggraf enjoyed the pastoral setting, where piano concerts were held in the summer and people sat on blankets on the lawn. She stayed through the afternoon, eating her lunch and reading. Then she set out in her car again, winding through the countryside before she drove back to Warsaw. She had seen no signs of surveillance all day. As night fell and the streets grew quieter, she contin-

* Pseudonym.
† Pseudonym.

ued to act like a tourist, but maintained her vigilance, frequently check-ing her rearview mirror and stopping occasionally.

As the hour of the exchange approached, Burggraf had been free of surveillance for more than twelve hours. The exchange was to occur at the base of the bridge on the west side of the river. Gull was supposed to be on the bridge above and would descend a flight of steps to the roadway below as she cruised by.

But as Burggraf arrived, she spotted a man sitting on the wall, right by the base of the steps. She circled the block, cursing under her breath. He was still there when she returned. *Will you go home?* she muttered. She knew that any pedestrian had to be treated as hostile surveillance, and she aborted the exchange. She never even saw Gull.

As the July party congress neared, pressure from Moscow intensified. Kulikov announced that Soviet troops would continue to carry out maneuvers in Poland, and Siwicki received regular calls from Russian officers alerting him to the latest developments. "You see, sometimes I have to listen to this for hours," Siwicki told Kuklinski after one such call.

A day or so before the congress was to begin, Kuklinski wrote a six-teen-page letter to the CIA, saying he had detected a hardening of Jaruzelski's position toward Solidarity and a growing readiness to impose martial law. Kuklinski said a Polish colonel had reported to him that Moscow had tripled the number of T-55, T-64, and T-72 tanks at the largest Soviet base in Poland, at Borne-Sulinowo, to about 1,000.

There was "understandable anxiety" about the Soviet presence, Kuklinski wrote, adding that Kulikov "believes that the best medicine for all Polish problems is military pressure."

Kuklinski had photographed a secret speech Jaruzelski had made to defense officials in late June, in which the general said that if Poland could not resolve its crisis, "this would be the signal for starting inter-vention by U.S.S.R. forces. In this scenario, civil war on a broad scale would be inevitable." Thousands would probably be killed. Polish leaders "think that the wave of fascination with Solidarity has largely ebbed." Jaruzelski was "exhausted physically and mentally."

Kuklinski noted that Jaruzelski remained steadfast, however. "He now smokes up to 40 cigarettes daily (he did not smoke before). He uses energy pills. Despite this pressure, he appears presently to have decided to retain his government post even after the Congress."

On July 14, the day the congress began, Kuklinski drafted another note. He said Skalski had recently offered him a short vacation. He would return on August 1 and would pass along any new information with the Iskra, "if there is one," he added.

As a postscript, Kuklinski said he was considering switching to a typewriter for his letters. "What do you gentlemen think? . . . Is that necessary? I have certain reservations that my handwriting is not very legible."

In the exchange at 10:33 P.M., Kuklinski handed over the letters and two rolls of film.

The party congress was held July 14–18 in the Palace of Culture and Science, a huge Stalinist-era structure that dominates the Warsaw skyline. The delegates chose themselves in secret and cast secret ballots for their leaders. Kania became the first party leader of a Soviet bloc country elected by secret ballot. Jaruzelski also received strong backing.

On August 11, Kuklinski left a chalk signal for the CIA. As he was returning to his car along Plac Jednosci, an orange Fiat 125 slowed as it passed him, then stopped. The two occupants appeared to be trying to see his face. Kuklinski got into his car, pulled away, and drove a random route until he was certain he was not being followed.

The next night at 10:32, Kuklinski turned over films that included the minutes of the recent KOK meeting on martial law and a five-page Russian document entitled "Announcement About the Introduction of Martial Law." (This document, which Kuklinski's staff had translated into Russian for the Soviets, was the text of posters that would be placed around Poland on the night martial law was imposed.) On August 14, Langley sent a cable to Warsaw that included a message for

Kuklinski thanking him for his latest intelligence and replying to his question about switching to a typewriter. "Absolutely not. It is too great a security risk. Your handwriting and printing are both very legible and we have no problems reading your messages."

The CIA had another reason it did not disclose: Kuklinski's style was distinctive; he printed in small Polish letters. If he were ever arrested and ordered to communicate with the CIA under the control of Polish authorities, the CIA believed it could detect his situation by changes in his handwriting.

On September 4, Moscow began maneuvers in the Baltic and in the western Soviet republics with more than 100,000 troops, clearly intending to intimidate Solidarity, which was holding its first national convention in Gdansk. The next day, Lech Walesa welcomed 900 delegates to the Solidarity convention, which went on to call for more control of industry by workers, open elections, and access to the mass media. Perhaps most provocative, the convention also sent a message of support to "working people of Eastern Europe."

On September 6, Kuklinski prepared an eleven-page letter to accompany his latest eight films, which included a near-final version of the martial-law plans and highly sensitive correspondence between Jaruzelski and Kulikov on the introduction of Soviet "advisers" into the Polish military. "As you gentlemen know, since 1957 there have been no Soviet Army military advisers in the Polish Armed Forces." Marshal Kulikov wanted to insert them down to the lowest levels and had gotten into a heated disagreement with Jaruzelski. "Allegedly Kulikov got up from the table, and without saying good-bye, left the Prime Minister's office, slamming the door," Kuklinski wrote.

Kuklinski described the unsettling incident involving the Fiat and said he often saw cars with antennas on their trunk lid parked on his street; the cars occasionally remained there all night.

Kania's election at the party congress was seen by Moscow as a disaster, and more rumors were circulating that Moscow wanted Jaruzelski replaced, although as Kuklinski noted: "It finally got through to the

Soviet comrades that in order to declare martial law in Poland, it is necessary first to prepare the 'house front,' that is, it is necessary to have the support of at least part of the population. However, Brezhnev recommended holding a hard, uncompromising course."

Kuklinski said that in his view, the Kania-Jaruzelski leadership seemed resigned to a crackdown. "While rattling the saber, they realize that using force will be the beginning of the end."

He then made a prophetic statement: "It is a pity, because the success of the Polish experiment could have a chance of a chain reaction, not only in the weak satellite countries of the U.S.S.R., but indeed, in the U.S.S.R."

In a short letter to Daniel, Kuklinski touched on his personal life. The grueling pace had allowed him little time for his family, he said, "which constitutes for me the highest goal in life and ultimate value."

I am indeed fortunate and rewarded by the Providence that when frequently I leave them alone, they maintain with each other cordial relations and share with me their mutual love and family ties.

I give much thought as to how to protect my dearest ones from calamity in the most difficult moment. Also I desire that the image of the husband and father never be disgraced, so they will never be ashamed of it. I believe that they never even suspect that when I leave on my risky short meetings, I bid them a discreet farewell every time. I find it difficult to conceal my happiness when all goes well and I return safely.

Despite all of this, I have boundless faith in the rightness of what I am doing. Nobody and nothing could possibly change my mind or lead me off the chosen path. After August [1980, the creation of Solidarity], I was additionally convinced that I am not alone traveling the road, that the nation desires freedom from the shackles of communism imposed from the outside. After all, today I am able to do more for this country, for the cause of freedom, than nine years ago; from the effort of individuals the strength of a nation is formed against which even the greatest power is powerless.

Kuklinski admitted that his years of constant vigilance and tension had affected his psychological state. Sometimes, he wrote, he had "dreams of a quiet harbor" and of seeing Daniel again. "Is it possible for this dream to ever assume a real form? How many more years will it take?" At 10:33 P.M., Kuklinski handed over eight rolls of film and his letters. He did not know that for the first time in three years, Daniel would be in a fifth-floor office at Langley, once again reading the letters himself.

Daniel had served three years in Vienna with mixed emotions. Professionally, the assignment had been satisfying. But as close as he was to Warsaw—about an hour's flight—he had felt very far from Kuklinski. It had been almost five years since they had last seen each other and shared a toast of aquavit. Daniel had been briefed only occasionally on details of Gull's progress.

Daniel also missed his family. Sally and their three children had not come with him to Austria. They had visited him for the 1978 Christmas holidays, and Daniel had hoped they might consider staying permanently. His apartment on the top floor of a converted palace in the historic center of the downtown was large enough for all of them. But Sally had no desire to move, and the visit turned out to be their last as a family. Their marriage could not sustain the prolonged separation, and eventually they divorced.

In his years in Vienna, Daniel had focused on a broad array of operations, covering such areas as terrorism, the Middle East, the Soviet Union, Eastern Europe, and the arms talks. On January 20, 1981, he was alone in his apartment watching Ronald Reagan's inaugural address on television. The new president spoke about America's economic problems and declared, "Government is not the solution to our problem. Government is the problem."

Daniel was outraged, feeling a kind of unity with government workers everywhere. He also thought of the embassy hostages in Iran; his old friend Richard Welch, Chief of Athens Station, who had been assassinated by terrorists in 1975; and the Warsaw-based officers working to keep Kuklinski alive. To Daniel, Reagan's remarks were insulting.

Daniel had kept abreast of events in Poland through the intelligence summaries that crossed his desk and perhaps even more vividly through Austrian radio and television, which had sent teams of journalists into Poland. Daniel felt exhilarated as he walked through the historic Stefansplatz in the central district of Vienna and saw Poles and Austrians selling "Solidarnosc" buttons and T-shirts to raise money.

In spring 1981, Daniel had received word that he was in line for a promotion: He would return to headquarters and become chief of the Soviet Division.

He was briefed on the status of the CIA's Soviet operations worldwide. He also read the files, including an updated case history of the Gull operation. It stated that in the event of Gull's death or arrest, the agency was committed to establishing contact with his wife and assisting her and her two sons "to the extent that it can do so securely." The CIA was prepared to exfiltrate and resettle Gull and his family in the United States, if necessary. But it added, "Gull has never expressed any wish for resettlement; this would only be in an emergency situation." The document said that as of July 1981, there had been fifty-four scheduled exchanges and nine others initiated by Gull or Warsaw Station.

"Gull has regularly produced highly classified Soviet documentary intelligence at a prodigious rate (approximately 40,265 pages)," the report said. The writer of the case history reiterated an observation made first in the earliest stages of the operation, describing Gull as "the best-placed source now available to the U.S. Government in the Soviet Bloc in terms of collection of priority information." His intelligence offered "the best existing potential for early warning of Pact hostile actions and priority information on the U.S.S.R., Soviet air defense systems, and other military equipment capabilities."

On September 7, Jaruzelski interrupted a visit to the Soviet Union and returned to Poland. Three days later, after meeting with Jaruzelski,

Siwicki told a select group in the General Staff that martial law was imminent. That same day, Kuklinski signaled the agency that he would fill a dead drop that night. He had concluded he needed to communicate more frequently with Warsaw Station. He wrote a letter describing Siwicki's comments. "This can happen as early as next week," he noted. "If the radicals decide on confrontation, we will declare the state of martial law. If this is unsuccessful, will we receive help? (the Russians)," Kuklinski added.

In a few days, he said, there would be an extraordinary session of the KOK to evaluate Poland's state of national preparedness. All military personnel on leave were being recalled, and specific units envisioned for operations in Warsaw, such as the Fifty-fifth Mechanized Regiment of the Sixteenth Armored Division and the First Mechanized Regiment of the First Mechanized Division, would be brought up to full strength. At Rynia and Bialobrzegi, receiving centers had been set up for families of higher-ranking officers to preclude their use as hostages. Kuklinski added: "Iskra is not working. The symptoms are the same as previously occurred."

He included film of ninety documents pertaining to martial law, including legal papers that Polish officials had demanded to justify the impending action, and left his package for the CIA that night, September 10.

Kuklinski's recent messages intensified concerns within the CIA and led to a series of cables between Daniel and the Soviet Division and Warsaw Station. "Gull's concern for his security is justified," the Soviet Division wrote in one in early September. "Gull's report of probable surveillance vehicles in the area of his home is also worrisome."

Daniel had considered and rejected asking Gull to suspend contact temporarily until matters were less cloudy. As for the Iskra, the Soviet Division wrote on September 11, "Frustration, disappointment—we are beyond words at this point as far as the Iskra is concerned."

*

One day in early September, General Skalski took Kuklinski aside. The people involved in the preparations for martial law would be divided into two groups, planning and command-and-control matters. Skalski asked Kuklinski whether he would be willing to manage the planning group, which included about thirty officers from the military, the Interior Ministry, the propaganda section of the Central Committee, and other ministries. Colonel Franciszek Puchala would oversee the command-and-control group.

Skalski again offered Kuklinski the opportunity to decline, but Kuklinski decided the position would give him continued access to key documents.

Around the same time, he was summoned by Siwicki, the chief of staff, and asked to write his speech for the September 13 meeting of the KOK. Siwicki outlined what he wanted to say. Kuklinski knew that General Kiszczak, the new interior minister, would also be addressing the group, and he concluded that the two men were trying to put concentrated pressure on Kania to make the necessary political decision to implement the crackdown.

He decided to broach a sensitive subject: If Siwicki was going to argue for such a profound step, he should address whether the military would be allowed to use arms. Siwicki replied irritably that that was not his concern. Kuklinski thought it was dishonest to avoid the issue. Privately, Kuklinski hoped to scare Kania, in hopes that, fearing bloodshed, he would refuse to proceed with martial law. To that end, Kuklinski inserted a sentence in the draft that said the question of arms was still open. Siwicki, reviewing the draft, crossed it out. "I told you I would not say that," he told Kuklinski.

On the evening of September 13, Kuklinski prepared another letter for the agency. "Intensive preparations for martial law are in progress," he wrote, describing the two teams set up by Skalski, which were led by him and Puchala. "Planning, headed by me (Oh! Horrors!)," he noted.

He commented on his superior's hint that he could refuse the assignment:

Skalski, who discussed this matter with me, stated that if I should decide that performing duties in this position collide with my conscience, I have the right to decline it. To tell the truth, I was at [a] loss as to what to reply. Guided by a higher need for obtaining information on decisions and plans of operation of the traitors to the national cause, I did not refuse. Only you know the truth, that every chance I have, I will spare no effort to give support to those forces which undertook the struggle, so that "Poland remains Poland."

As he had expected, the SB had infiltrated Solidarity's leadership "and has a good grasp of what is going on." But there was a sharp split between party chief Kania, who "will not listen to any solutions using force," and the defense and interior ministers. Jaruzelski, perhaps being pushed by the Soviets, had "changed his position, and currently favors more decisive solutions." Siwicki, the chief of staff, believed martial law, although late, "is inevitable, and the sooner it is declared the better." General Kiszczak, minister of interior, was pressing for "an immediate and surprise declaration of martial law, mainly for the purpose of interning the Solidarity radicals." His ministry even had "photographs of their future victims."

The Soviet maneuvers in the Baltic region were seen as a big success, Kuklinski said. "The maneuvers were of an extraordinary, greatest-ever show of thrust and dynamics, as well as employment of the most modern materiel," he wrote. Soviet Defense Minister Ustinov, in a critique, had said, "The U.S.S.R. will not allow us to fall behind the U.S.A. in the field of armaments."

On the evening of September 13, Kuklinski left a package containing his letter, a roll of film, which included Siwicki's speech, and the faulty Iskra in a dead drop. He wrote "B. Plne" (very urgent) on the outside of the film canister. Warsaw Station immediately cabled the letter to headquarters and sent the film to Langley by special courier.

★

In Washington, Daniel continued to be concerned about the frequency of Gull's exchanges and dead drops. "No one is to blame," Daniel wrote in a September 14 cable to Warsaw, "and I am hesitant to suggest to Gull that he slow down. However, I'm afraid operational security dictates a note to him at our next exchange suggesting that we hold down the frequency of our meetings."

Daniel was very attuned to the possibility that Kuklinski might take offense: "Clearly, we must be careful as to how we say this," Daniel wrote, "since we don't want him to think that his reporting isn't needed and greatly appreciated. What are your thoughts?"

In another cable that same day, Daniel also told Warsaw Station that Kuklinski's last two messages had been included in the "President's Daily Brief," and the most recent one was cabled "Eyes Only" to Secretary of State Alexander M. Haig Jr., who was traveling, and General Bernard W. Rogers, Supreme Allied Commander, Europe. "In both of the latter cases, we received cabled notification that the report was destroyed, and Haig and Rogers had read the messages," Daniel wrote.

On September 14, Kuklinski had a visit from a counterintelligence officer, who stressed the importance of preventing leaks. What had prompted the visit was a mystery, but the next day, Kuklinski learned more from a general, one of the pro-Soviet hard-liners who had attended the special meeting of the KOK. During the session, Interior Minister Kiszczak had announced that his ministry was investigating a leak. Solidarity had learned details of the martial-law plans, including its code name, Operation Spring.

That night Kuklinski left a signal at a site called Zaspa (snowdrift) that he would leave a message the next day. He drafted a letter describing Kiszczak's revelation. The Ministry of Internal Affairs "was ordered to find the source of the leak urgently," Kuklinski wrote.

At the KOK session, the blueprint for martial law had been finalized, he wrote, and he offered new details. The crackdown would be imposed at night, from Friday through Sunday.

That is when factories will not operate. The detention operations would begin around midnight, six hours before the proclamations of martial law on radio and television. In Warsaw, about 600 people will be detained by about 1,000 policemen, using their own private cars.

The same night, the Army will block the most important parts of Warsaw and other major cities. Initially, the operations are supposed to be carried out only by the Interior Ministry forces. In order to "improve the troops' situation," i.e., to relocate entire divisions in the vicinity of major cities, a separate political decision is expected to be made.

This will take place only after the major resistance centers flare up. It has not been ruled out, however, that divisions which are stationed far from the areas of their future operations could begin their relocation with the moment of the imposition of martial law, or even earlier, e.g., the 4th Mechanized Division needs about 54 hours in order to move in the vicinity of Warsaw.

Kuklinski paused. He had no idea if the leak under investigation by Kiszczak was due to his activities, but any investigation would inevitably lead to him and the small group working on martial law.

He made three large X's on the sheet, for emphasis, and continued to write:

Due to the investigation in progress, I have to stop providing daily information about the situation. I ask you to use data provided by me cautiously, because, I think, my mission is nearing its end.

That data could easily reveal its source. I do not oppose the idea—and that is even my wish—that information provided by me serve the cause of those who struggle for Poland's freedom with their heads up. I am also ready to pay the highest price, but we can accomplish something only by action, not by sacrifice.

Long live free Poland! Long live Solidarity, capable of bringing freedom to all oppressed nations.

Kuklinski photographed the letter. He then opened his camera, removed the roll of film, and wrapped it in paper and cellophane. He then placed his tiny package inside an old glove, which he dipped into hot grease. Finally, he took the glove outside and rubbed it in the dirt.

Usually, before leaving for an exchange or a dead drop, Kuklinski checked the list of sites the CIA provided him on a sheet of microfilm, which he read with a magnifying glass. The microfilm, when rolled up, was no thicker than a match. During his house construction, he had hidden the microfilm beneath some bricks. Later, after he moved in, he secreted it behind a piece of wood in the barn of Bogdan's farm in Wiazowna. As Bogdan and Iza were spending time on the farm, Kuklinski often drove there and visited the barn to confirm the location of the next site.

That day, Kuklinski trusted his memory. He was certain the next dead-drop site was Kaftan (jacket), the code name for an overgrown lot strewn with garbage and rocks. The lot was often used as a shortcut to a nearby bus stop, so it was not unusual for people to cross it. After a long drive, Kuklinski parked at Kaftan, walked through the lot, and dropped the glove on the ground.

On September 16, Sue Burggraf headed out in her Fiat on an SDR. She drove toward the next site on the list kept by the CIA, Przelot (passage), which was located near the Jewish cemetery. After parking a few blocks away, Burggraf walked to the spot and searched under a specified streetlight, but found nothing.

The next morning, Burggraf reported to Ryan that she had come back empty-handed. She assumed Gull had aborted the run. The CIA had worked out signals to confirm to Kuklinski whether it had received his packages. An officer parked a car in front of an ice cream store on Pulaski Street (a site code-named Dublet) with its wheels turned inward. That meant a package had not been received.

But as Kuklinski passed by the ice cream store the next morning, he failed to see the car with its wheels turned in. He drove on, assuming that his package had been retrieved.

As the days passed, the glove containing Kuklinski's declaration in support of Solidarity and a free Poland lay in the overgrown lot, and neither he nor Warsaw Station realized a mix-up had occurred.

In mid-September, the Soviet ambassador to Poland had delivered a personal message to Kania and Jaruzelski, warning that Poland must "take determined and radical steps" to end the anti-Soviet actions in Poland. On September 18, when the letter was made public, the U.S. State Department publicly criticized the Soviet message, calling it "interference in Poland's internal affairs."

Kuklinski, feeling the strain of recent weeks and worried that he might become a target of investigation, decided to take a short break. He and Hanka drove to Krakow, his favorite city. Its beauty had survived World War II intact. For centuries, Polish kings had lived in Krakow's glorious Wawel Royal Castle, and forty-two of the royals were buried under the cathedral. There, too, were the burial sites of Poland's greatest heroes–Tadeusz Kosciuszko, the dashing military engineer who helped the Americans win the Revolutionary War and later led Poland's uprising against the Russians; General Wladyslaw Sikorski, who led Poland's government-in-exile after the Nazi invasion; Marshal Jozef Pilsudski, who fought the Russians in 1920 and was Poland's first head of state; and Adam Mickiewicz, the legendary poet and patriot. Kuklinski felt energized whenever he was in Krakow.

Daniel soon had another reason to be concerned. For more than a decade, a Polish colonel named Wlodzimierz Ostaszewicz, deputy chief of Polish military intelligence, had been cooperating with the CIA. Now he had decided to leave Poland and seek protection in the West. Colonel Ostaszewicz lacked Kuklinski's access to sensitive operational intelligence, but he had provided valuable information on what the Polish military intelligence knew about NATO. More recently, he had served as an adviser to the Polish delegation to the arms talks in Vienna and had worked with Daniel when he was posted there. By

coincidence, Ostaszewicz was also a member of the military cooperative on Rajcow Street, and a neighbor of Kuklinski's. They knew each
other slightly, although neither realized the other was cooperating
with the CIA.

Daniel and other CIA officials were prepared to exfiltrate Ostaszewicz, but they were concerned about the implications for the Gull operation. Once Ostaszewicz's defection became known, the SB would
investigate and clamp down tighter on security. "We are all in agreement
that the recent flurry of activity is dangerous," the Soviet Division
cabled Warsaw on September 21. "We also all know that Gull is aware of
this danger but apparently has resolved his concerns for his security, and
has no intention of suggesting a cutback in contact with us."

Daniel's cable advised that Warsaw Station vary the timing of contacts and exchanges with Kuklinski. On October 5, the Soviet Division
cabled a message to Warsaw, to be delivered in the next car pass.

> We have carefully considered your recommendations for increased
> Iskra exchanges and the addition of sites where you can securely
> leave packages. As we have told you in the past, there is no ade-
> quate way to express our gratitude for the timely and invaluable
> information you provide, and we are aware of the urgency you feel
> to give us information on a timely basis in this period of crisis.
> However, the very fact of the crisis makes it imperative that you
> exercise great caution in your contacts with us.

On October 7, Daniel and his colleagues decided Kuklinski should be
informed of the Ostaszewicz matter and given the opportunity to suspend contact. If he concurred, he would be asked to destroy his supplies. The CIA wrote to Kuklinski to reveal the news about Ostaszewicz.

> We want to alert you to the fact that your neighbor traveled to the
> West in September and requested asylum for himself and his wife.
> His son also has decided to remain in the West. We have carefully
> considered this matter and, in our judgment, and with the proper
> precautions, we do not believe this matter will adversely affect

your security. You, your neighbors and many of your colleagues will undoubtedly be interviewed concerning [Col. Ostaszewicz]. But at this time, there is no reason to believe you yourself would be the subject of any heightened interest.

In your office, you should exercise extreme caution. It is possible that the random inspection of briefcases and parcels you told us about previously will be increased. If that is the case, you should immediately stop removing documents from your office to photograph at home. We would prefer you not photograph any documents until you are positive the situation has returned to normal. We do not wish to unduly alarm you, and hope that this alert will enable you to put the expected security investigation in proper perspective. That is, it is a result of [your neighbor's] decision and not a result of your activity. However, we believe you should be prepared to witness a very active investigation by the WSW [military counterintelligence] who will follow through the slightest suspicion.

[Your neighbor] is, as a matter of course, being debriefed concerning colleagues, neighbors, etc. He speaks highly of you, characterizing you as a colonel with a very good future who "knows more about his business than most generals."

Daniel sent Kuklinski his first personal letter since returning from Vienna.

With our officer who delivers this to you, I shake your hand with esteem and affection. The ever-present need for vigilance and alertness and the resulting tension that you wrote of are burdens in your life I wish I could share. Unfortunately, they are the penalties a great man must bear. How fortunate, however, that you have the love and honor of your family. This must be a great comfort to you, and your devotion to them surely must be evident to them.

P.V., your invaluable information is carefully studied at the highest levels of our government and I can assure you it is an important factor in the planning of our government's policy to stem Soviet aggression.

Dear friend, do not despair of the work that is ahead. You indeed are one of the few who can accomplish much in our mutual struggle. We stand ready to help you, but our role is insignificant in comparison to your role. We thank you.

Both letters were cabled to Warsaw Station for delivery at the first opportunity.

On his way to work on Friday, October 9, Kuklinski spotted a chalk mark calling for a car pass that night. He was still unaware that Warsaw Station had not found the message he had left at Kaftan three weeks earlier. At 3:00 P.M., Siwicki called, asking Kuklinski to begin working immediately on a speech Siwicki would deliver at a party meeting the next week. He wanted to take a hard-line stance attacking Kania and defending Jaruzelski. Siwicki said he was ready to criticize party officials for failing to move faster against the "internal opponent."

That evening, Kuklinski began a letter to the CIA. He said he now had more evidence of the divergence in views between Kania and Jaruzelski. "Today I have proof that their paths have parted completely." Kania had rejected the idea of imposing martial law as a way of eliminating Solidarity, but Jaruzelski had accepted Moscow's arguments and ordered the Defense and Interior Ministries to begin making final contingency plans. For days, there had been intensive deliberations concerning the possibility of leadership changes. Kuklinski described Siwicki's planned speech and its central message that it was time for "radical measures—martial law." Kuklinski said he had been told to "stand by" for new orders on the use of force. He also learned that handbills and posters announcing the crackdown, which had been printed in Moscow to avoid leaks from Polish printers, had been delivered to Warsaw.

Soviet leadership maintains contact with Jaruzelski. Brezhnev had many telephone talks with Jaruzelski. These talks were reportedly very unpleasant. Kania is left out completely. The new military attaché of the U.S.S.R. armed forces in the Polish People's Republic stated during a confidential talk in which Gen. [Wladyslaw] Hermaszewski was present that before he started his mission he had a talk with Ustinov. Ustinov stated that U.S.S.R. has decided under certain situations to intervene militarily.

Kuklinski asked the CIA to leave a signal confirming that it had retrieved his package at Kaftan. He noted that he had not seen the car at Dublet with its wheels turned inward. At 10:32 P.M., at a site codenamed Skok (jump), Kuklinski smiled broadly as he handed over a package containing four rolls of film. His message was summarized and included in the "President's Daily Brief" of October 14.

Kuklinski received an Iskra in return, with new batteries and instructions, twelve rolls of film, an updated list of exchange and dead-drop locations, a new set of signals to use to indicate he was safe in the event communications had to be suspended, and the letters from the agency and Daniel. "We have called you to this exchange tonight," the CIA's letter began, "to give you this message discussing our communications agreements, to return the Iskra to you, and to inform you of a recent event which has bearing upon your security," a reference to Ostaszewicz's defection.

Kuklinski was surprised to read of the news about Ostaszewicz, but was thunderstruck by what he read next: "We observed what we thought was your signal at Zaspa on 16 September and our officer went to Przelot that night but was unable to find any message from you. Our cars were parked at Dublet the following day to advise you that we did not find any message."

Kuklinski suddenly realized that he had left the glove containing the film at the wrong dead-drop site. A whole month had passed. He considered the possibilities. His biggest concern was that someone had found the glove, inspected it, and taken it to the police or the SB. Kuklinski knew that the "Jack Strong" signature would not give him away. But the contents of the letter would reveal that its writer had knowledge of the September 15 session, which so few had attended.

At that moment, Hanka entered the study and saw Kuklinski's stricken look. "I did something wrong," he murmured. It was far too risky for him to return to the lot himself, but he had to find out whether the glove was still there. After considering his options, he felt he had only one choice.

The next morning, Saturday, October 10, he called in Bogdan, then twenty-six years old. Kuklinski could not disguise the sense of urgency in his voice. Without elaborating, he asked Bogdan to drive to the lot, park nearby, and take a walk. Bogdan should establish that he was not being followed and casually look around to see if the glove was still there. Kuklinski warned Bogdan not to pick up the glove. If it was there, Kuklinski would ask him to return at night to get it. Kuklinski knew the plan was risky, but he felt Bogdan would be safe because his son knew nothing of his activities, and if he was questioned, he would have no answers.

Kuklinski paced in his living room for more than an hour after Bogdan left. Hanka sat in silence. Suddenly, the door opened, and Bogdan entered with a smile on his face and the glove in his hand. He pulled out the wrapped film canister and drop-kicked it to the ceiling. Bogdan did not ask for an explanation, but assured his father that he had not been seen or followed home. Kuklinski practically fell into his son's arms.

That night, Kuklinski typed a message into his newest Iskra, describing the mix-up in the sites. "It was my fault, because I left it at Kaftan instead of at Przelot. The absence of cars at Dublet . . . reassured me that all is well. Today I recovered my package, which was undisturbed."

As for Ostaszewicz, he was still undecided about whether to suspend contact. Warsaw Station received the message and cabled it on to Langley.

At 11:30 A.M., on October 18, just before a meeting of the Communist Party Central Committee, Kuklinski transmitted another Iskra message. "The military are on alert status in case matters at the plenum take an unfavorable turn," he wrote. "In the event a liberal leadership is appointed, the military will not support it."

Kuklinski said he had still heard nothing in the General Staff about his neighbor's defection. "Did the West reveal this fact? Is the current leadership covering it up because this defection is too embarrassing to the Ministry of National Defense and the Ministry of Internal Affairs?" Warsaw Station cabled headquarters the same day, including Kuklinski's message and the news that Kania had been ousted at the plenum and replaced by Jaruzelski. The result "would seem to indicate a victory for hardliners," the station told Langley.

At 11:15 A.M. on Sunday, October 25, Kuklinski used the Iskra to send another message that the military was taking steps to "penetrate all fields of life in the country. . . . At the same time, orders were issued for preparation of activities under conditions of martial law." The biographies of several hard-line generals had been sent to Moscow for consideration. Kuklinski observed that the Iskra was finally functioning properly. "No garbles. Thank you," he added.

As he transmitted, he received the CIA's latest Iskra message back, which said the West had not yet revealed his neighbor's defection. Kuklinski was also reminded to be sparing in use of the Iskra, transmitting "only when necessary."

At about 1:00 P.M. on Monday, November 2, Kuklinski was summoned to an office of one of his superiors. He arrived and walked in to find Skalski sitting at a large T-shaped table, looking pale and grim. Seated around the table were General Szklarski and two colonels working on martial law, Franciszek Puchala and Czeslaw Witt.

Skalski barely nodded and directed Kuklinski to take a seat across from him. There was an awkward silence. Skalski looked straight at Kuklinski and then at the others. There had been a disastrous leak, he said, an act of treason.

10

"EVERYTHING IS POINTING TO THE END OF MY MISSION"

KUKLINSKI SAT IN ASTONISHED SILENCE as Skalski continued. The Polish leadership had learned that the CIA—Skalski said "Langley"—had obtained the latest version of the martial-law plans. The information came to them from "Rome sources." Skalski said he was confident that Polish counterintelligence would be able to trace the source of the leak. It was only a matter of time.

Kuklinski's colleagues around the table were aghast and angry. General Szklarski spoke first, saying he was willing to offer himself up for questioning and suggesting that any leak must have come from the Interior Ministry. Colonel Puchala went next and protested his innocence. Colonel Witt said it was clear that Solidarity had an ally in the center of power, but he declared he was not it and that he, too, would submit to interrogation if necessary.

Kuklinski listened, his mouth dry. His name was on the classified control forms for the most sensitive martial-law documents, including perhaps the one most closely held. Referred to as the "final version," it was the most complete set of plans and included the latest revisions ordered by Jaruzelski. There were only two copies, and only several officers had access. Kuklinski had prepared the original in his office and kept it in his safe. Puchala had the other copy in his safe.

As the others turned to him, Kuklinski began to speak. He said he agreed with Witt. Solidarity must have a high-level source in the Polish government. He paused, leaving an awkward silence. Inexplicably, he suddenly felt an urge to confess. But Skalski interrupted him.

"*Enough!*" he barked, waving his hand to cut off discussion. "I am not a security services functionary to screen you gentlemen." He said the proper authorities would carry out any investigation. Even he might come under scrutiny. Meanwhile, they had work to do.

He has saved my life, Kuklinski thought as the meeting ended. Unable to concentrate, he left work at 5:00 P.M., thinking about the message he would send that night.

Entering his house, he gestured for Hanka to join him. Speaking softly, he told her they were in danger, revealing that he had been involved in an operation against the Soviet Union that he had believed was vital to Poland's security. He was about to be found out.

Kuklinski described their limited options: He could await further developments, hoping he would not be arrested. He could ask for help in leaving Poland. "I have a chance to get assistance from the Americans," he said, but he could not imagine leaving without his family. Or he could take his life.

Hanka was shocked and frightened, but she quickly regained her composure. She said that she was proud of Kuklinski, trusted him, and knew he would never do something wrong. Suicide was out of the question, as was doing nothing. She had sensed her husband's anxiety in recent months and wondered whether he could withstand the ordeal of a long investigation. Without hesitating, she declared that he should seek help from the Americans in leaving the country. "You must try," she said, "and if there is any chance, we go."

Kuklinski embraced his wife and wept. He then went into his study and began collecting materials—his address books, photographs, soluble paper, communications plans, Iskra instructions, film canisters (some still unexposed and in their foil wrapping), and personal papers—that could incriminate him or link him, however innocently, to anyone else in Poland. He saved a few critical documents; he burned the rest in the fireplace.

Next he sat down and typed a message on the Iskra's small keypad.

Today [Skalski] declared in front of a select group of persons that from a Rome source it is known that CIA is in possession of the latest version of the martial law document. He also reported on passing of other data to American intelligence which will make unmasking the agent possible.

I urgently request instructions for evacuating from the country myself and my family. Please take into consideration that the state border is possibly already closed for me and my family.

I am waiting for personal contact on 3 November at Straz; 4 November at Klatka, 5 November at Skok, or for "call out" at any day at Chmura. End.

About an hour later, Waldek arrived. As Kuklinski explained what he had done and said he hoped they could escape as a family, Waldek listened in silence. Then he expressed uncertainty about leaving, and asked whether they could trust the United States. "The Americans might get all the information from us, then abandon us," he said.

Kuklinski said the American military paid attention to every human life. It tried to rescue its pilots behind enemy lines and never stopped searching for soldiers missing in action. He cited the attempted rescue of the American hostages in Tehran. "America is the only country in the world which does *not* abandon its people," he explained.

Waldek said he would go.

About eight o'clock, Kuklinski left to see Bogdan. Kuklinski knew his younger son faced a difficult choice. Living on the farm in Wiazowna, Bogdan was building a new life, and he was deeply in love with his girlfriend, Iza.

Kuklinski arrived at the farm, embraced Bogdan, and began to talk. His son did not hesitate when his father asked whether he would try to escape with the family.

"Dad," Bogdan said, "I will go through fire and water with you."

Kuklinski felt a surge of love and pride but also considerable guilt. Although he had anticipated the possibility of this day for years, he had not been able to prepare his family at all. He told Bogdan he would need his help. He removed the Iskra from his pocket and explained how it worked. They drove together into Warsaw, with Kuklinski teaching Bogdan how to watch for surveillance and how to operate within the gaps. They arrived at the tree-lined Plac Trzech Krzyzy (Square of the Three Crosses), the site of St. Alexander's Church. Kuklinski's parents had been married in this church; nearby was the orphanage where his mother had been placed as a child. It was just a few blocks from the American Embassy, close enough for Kuklinski to send a message directly into the compound. As Bogdan provided cover from a distance, Kuklinski walked to the northeastern corner of the plaza, reached into his jacket pocket, and pushed the button to transmit.

When Kuklinski and Bogdan returned home, Kuklinski went into his study to read the latest Iskra message to him. Written without knowledge of his troubles, the CIA's message included a list of new transmission sites and future exchanges. Kuklinski took his camera and a few items he had not burned—a half dozen rolls of exposed film and some personal papers. He asked Bogdan to hide the items at the farm.

The next day, Tuesday, November 3, Sue Burggraf arrived at the American Embassy. Tom Ryan and his wife, Lucille, were in Berlin with their daughter Maureen on a long-planned vacation. That made Burggraf the acting station chief. She joined a group of embassy officers at Ambassador Meehan's daily meeting in the "bubble," a room designed to be safe from outside monitoring. After the meeting ended at about 10:00 A.M., Burggraf returned to her office and noticed that the switch on the Iskra that signaled receipt of a message had not been flipped. She flipped it and immediately heard a beeping sound. Lacking confidence in her language skills, she summoned her colleagues,

Evan Davis and Jason Wilcox, to translate. Davis, who spoke Polish fluently, and Wilcox carefully copied the words from the screen.

After Burggraf read the translation, she sent a "Flash" cable—the highest priority—to headquarters with Kuklinski's news: "Field [officers] in process of considering options left open to us at this point. If borders are indeed closed to him that leaves us with no choice but to exfiltrate not only Gull but wife and possibly both sons."

Burggraf realized she had no idea whether Gull's sons were married. "Don't know if this will include sons' wives too," she wrote. "Request HQ's guidance ASAP."

When Daniel read the cable a few hours later, he was incensed: How could the agency have failed its best source? He was convinced there had been a leak of Kuklinski's intelligence. What had gone wrong? Without question, Kuklinski would now have to be exfiltrated. But the timing couldn't be worse. Martial law was imminent, and surveillance on American diplomats in Warsaw was tighter than ever.

Langley initially instructed Ryan to return to Warsaw, but both Ryan and Burggraf recommended that he remain in Berlin. For the station chief to return to town before he was expected would only arouse the SB's suspicions and result in even tighter surveillance. At Langley, Daniel received similar advice from a deputy, Steve Weber. "Why don't we leave him there for now?" Weber said. "It might give us another option."

The Ryans were told to stay in Berlin.

Daniel briefed John Stein, the DDO, and his deputy, Clair George. They approved the exfiltration, as did Director William Casey and his top deputy, Admiral Bobby Ray Inman. A CIA cable under Casey's name went to Ambassador Francis Meehan in Warsaw, saying that Secretary of State Haig had been apprised of the situation involving "our prime source."

Kuklinski was on everyone's mind. "We appreciate your cooperation," the cable said. "I wish to confirm that the Secretary authorizes you to do all possible in support of our efforts to protect and possibly exfiltrate this valuable man and his family."

Daniel and his staff cabled Warsaw with a message to be delivered via the Iskra to Kuklinski: "Your message received. Prepared to assist you. Will meet you at Klatka on 4 November. However, before taking irrevocable step to exfiltrate you and your family from Poland, we need your best estimate of situation. Is it possible, for example, that suspect person is [Colonel Ostaszewicz] and not you? Have you learned any more details today on the investigation?"

Headquarters knew that everything would depend on the ability of Kuklinski and Warsaw Station to carry out the prearranged steps with absolute precision. Burggraf told Davis and Wilcox that neither officer should change his daily routine. Headquarters sent another "Flash" cable to Warsaw that said if Burggraf was free of surveillance, she should be prepared to meet Gull, and perhaps the rest of his family, that night at the site named Straz. Headquarters had included a list of questions for Gull, including a Polish-language version:

A. Were you present when [Skalski] announced the leak of information? If not, who told you about the announcement? Is his info to be trusted?
B. What is the situation as of tonight?
C. Are you positive you can be identified as the suspect?
D. Could the [SB] be sending out feelers to trap the agent into a hasty move?
E. Is it possible that suspect person is [Colonel Ostaszewicz]?
F. Do you know anything more about the Rome source?

The cable outlined the steps Warsaw Station should take to assist Kuklinski:

Please reassure Gull that we stand ready to assist him. If Gull feels that his security is in serious jeopardy and needs to be given safe haven, we are ready to do so. Would like field officer [Burggraf] to be prepared for possibility that Gull will show for tonight's meeting with wife and two sons. We have no record of either son being married. Therefore, we ask that officer and field be prepared to take Gull's family into [embassy] tonight.

If Gull shows by himself and asks that he and family be assisted ASAP, but not necessarily tonight, please arrange for 4 November at Klatka, with alternative 5 November at Skok. If we have surveillance on 4 and 5 November, Gull should come to Klatka on 6 November or to Skok on 7 November.

Headquarters included a Polish translation of the message for Kuklinski.

Burggraf asked Davis to hand-print the Polish version of the CIA's questions for Kuklinski on a small card in letters large enough to be read under a streetlight. She would try to read the message to him and then hand him the card to take home. If Gull's family was with him, she would be prepared to escort them to the embassy. She waited impatiently for evening to fall.

At one point at headquarters, Daniel telephoned a friend who was chief of the Office of Communications. "We desperately need one of your communicators for a tricky job," Daniel said, asking to borrow the officer in Warsaw Station who was in charge of sending encrypted cables. The officer would be needed to help drive a family out of Poland. If the assignment didn't go well, Daniel added, "It's going to be a big mess." The officer was made available.

That Tuesday morning, as Kuklinski was driven to the General Staff, he noticed two people standing outside the historic Najswietsza Maria Panna Church, just fifty meters from his house. He had seen them there before. He guessed he was already under surveillance, but figured it would be a few days before the investigation focused on him. At work, Kuklinski found the mood somber, as if a collective depression had set in, but he greeted colleagues and secretaries cordially, masking his own terror. His closest colleagues continued their work, and even in private conversation, no one raised the issue of the leak Skalski had described.

Inside his office, Kuklinski checked his safe. The martial-law plans were undisturbed. He found blank sheets of paper bearing the oval imprint of the General Staff that were to be used to issue field orders in wartime. Years earlier, before even contacting the Americans, Kuklinski had obtained these papers, hoping that in the event of war, he could use them to organize his conspiracy in which Polish troops would lay down arms and not join a military offensive against the West. One day, he had hoped to forward these to the CIA, but he had not done it. Now he would destroy them.

Around noon, Colonel Witt stopped by to discuss the martial-law preparations. Moments later, a counterintelligence officer knocked on the door and invited himself in. Kuklinski could tell that Witt was anxious, but they talked amicably with the CI officer. He asked both men to come to his office the next morning for coffee.

For the rest of the day, Kuklinski tried to concentrate on the details of assignments and movements of troops in the martial-law preparations, but he could think of nothing but that night's meeting with the CIA. He arrived home at about 6:00 P.M., greeted Hanka and his sons, patted Zula, and entered his study. He began a three-page note to the CIA.

Dear friends,

Everything is pointing to the end of my mission. I have a choice of taking my own life, early arrest, or the help which was once offered me.

Yesterday via Iskra, I asked for instructions for evacuation of my family, first of all, and then for myself. I know that it is not an easy operation, the more so in view of the probability that the border is closed for suspected persons and their families. However, I see no way of saving even my own head. That is why I request that an attempt be made to evacuate to the West, in first order, my wife, son Waldek and son Bogdan, and only then, giving me assistance.

. The family can leave the country at any time, even immediately, and I, by Thursday; any day between 1700 and 0800 of the following day, or during days free of work beginning at 1600 hours on Friday.

Kuklinski said that to Polish officials, "it is clear that in the close and confidential circle of the leadership, an agent of American intelligence is operating. However, it will not be difficult to identify him because also known are other data transmitted by him."

Kuklinski described the meeting with Witt and the Polish counterintelligence officer and the invitation to coffee. "Could this be the beginning of the end?" he wrote. He concluded with a demand, which he felt entitled to make, given that the leak of the martial-law plans he had passed to the United States had placed him in peril.

Pure chance, and to certain degree careless handling of data provided by me, places me face to face with the most difficult test. I have decided to leave the country as soon as this is possible. The condition for fulfilling this step is giving assistance to my family, equal to that given me.

He went downstairs and embraced each member of his family. He then had Bogdan drive him around the city and drop him near the Warsaw fire academy in northern Warsaw. While Bogdan drove off in the direction of Iza's apartment, hoping to draw any possible SB surveillance in that direction, Kuklinski, wearing a drab dark parka, walked toward the Straz site. At precisely 10:30 P.M., he entered a path that led into a cement courtyard in the center of a quadrangle of apartment buildings. A small-framed blond woman appeared before him in a beige coat. She approached with a confident smile.

"*Dobry wieczor,*" she said cheerfully. "Good evening."

"*Dobry wieczor,*" Kuklinski replied.

Gull was shorter than Burggraf had expected. Of course, she had always viewed him from the vantage point of a car seat in the dark.

He seemed courtly but was shaking noticeably. Burggraf put her arm around his waist and drew him closer. She could see his face closely for the first time. He seemed to be much older than she was, and he looked drawn and tired. She whispered two words—"Jack Strong"—and pulled him into an embrace as if they were lovers. Gull was whispering rapidly in Polish, and Burggraf found him hard to understand. She tried to communicate in her stilted Polish, then switched to German, which she knew well. But Gull did not appear to understand her. Finally, Burggraf placed the card in his hands so that he could read the message in Polish. Kuklinski looked frantic: He gestured that he did not have his reading glasses. She took the card back and began to read in Polish. They fell into a natural gait, with Burggraf keeping her arm around Kuklinski's waist. "Please be assured," she read, "that we are ready to assist you if you feel your security and that of your family is in serious jeopardy."

Kuklinski said he could not go without his family. Could he return with them all, and they would leave immediately? He slipped Burggraf his three-page letter. Burggraf said she could take him with her now, but it would take another twenty-four hours to move the entire family. She did not express her real fear—that if the family somehow was seen moving into the embassy, the SB would surround the compound, and the result would be a dangerous standoff. Burggraf continued to read from the card: The CIA would appear the following night, Wednesday, November 4, at a site code-named Klatka to pick up the family. The backup plan was Skok, Thursday, November 5. If Kuklinski felt he was under surveillance both nights, he should try Klatka on Friday, November 6, with the Skok again as the backup on Saturday, November 7.

Burggraf described the emergency chalk signals that both sides should use to communicate with each other. She gave Kuklinski the card and asked him to show it to his family. She kept her face close to his.

"We will be there tomorrow night," she said. "If not me, someone else. If we have surveillance, do not worry. We will continue until we are able to meet."

The rendezvous lasted no more than ten minutes. She pulled him closer and hugged him. "See you," she said, turning and leaving.

Kuklinski crumpled the card in his pocket and left the quadrangle. He returned to where Bogdan was to meet him, but saw only a Polski Fiat containing two men parked about fifty feet away and three other men standing near the car. Feeling nervous and lightheaded, Kuklinski changed plans: He crossed the street, boarded a bus, rode a few blocks, changed to a second bus, rode again, switched to a third bus, and got off at Ulica Marchlewskiego and then began to walk home.

Several blocks away, at Ulica Freta, he noticed another man, perhaps in his forties, wearing glasses, who was slowly approaching him. Without warning, the man abruptly turned around so that he and Kuklinski were walking in the same direction. Kuklinski slowed in order not to overtake the man, but the man slowed down as well. The man suddenly stepped sideways into the archway of a building entrance and watched Kuklinski's face as he passed.

Kuklinski reached home at about 11:30 P.M. Bogdan had not yet arrived, and they waited nervously. It occurred to Kuklinski that even if he was the only suspect, the SB might not confront him immediately. It seemed possible that they would watch him for several days, in hopes he might lead them to others involved in any conspiracy.

Bogdan finally arrived and explained that he had gone back to meet his father, but had also seen the Fiat and the three men on the street. Bogdan had waited about 100 feet away, and after fifteen minutes, he decided to drive away alone.

Kuklinski was awed by his son's performance under pressure. He showed his family the card he had received from the CIA officer that evening. They studied it together, and then Kuklinski destroyed it in the fire. Kuklinski gave Bogdan the Iskra and asked him to hide it at the farm.

After Bogdan left, Hanka mentioned that their neighbor, General Wladyslaw Hermaszewski, had left a message asking Kuklinski to stop by. Because of the late hour, Kuklinski called first, but his friend urged him to come over. Hermaszewski greeted Kuklinski and led him into his basement, a handsome room outfitted with rustic wooden furniture and the walls adorned with hunting rifles, bugles, and antlers.

Hermaszewski said he wanted to discuss the defection of their neighbor, Ostaszewicz. How would the Russians react? He surmised that Ostaszewicz had been preparing his defection for some time, because his house appeared neglected. Kuklinski nodded politely as Hermaszewski talked. Finally, Kuklinski said he had to go home and get some sleep.

Before the family left the country, Bogdan had wanted to see Iza, and he picked her up at her mother's house. As they drove toward her apartment, Bogdan swore her to secrecy. His father was in trouble, he said, and the whole family was going to try to leave Poland. When they had arrived safely somewhere else, he said, he would send word to her.

Iza was caught completely off guard. She pulled her green wool jacket tightly around her body, shivering in the night air. What a time for such news! Her father was ill with cancer, and she was about to make a special trip to West Berlin to obtain a chemotherapy drug for him that was not available in Poland. She would be back in Warsaw in a few days, but by then Bogdan and his family would be gone. They both realized that once the regime learned Kuklinski had fled Poland, she would not be allowed to leave to join him.

They drove for a while as she tried to make sense of the news. Might she want to go? Bogdan asked tentatively. No, she replied. She could not. They sat in silence, both devastated.

The next morning, Wednesday, November 4, Daniel and his staff reviewed the cable from Burggraf describing the meeting with Gull and his note. Daniel immediately sent a message back directing Burggraf to send all further cable traffic by "Flash" priority.

"We are prepared to be here around the clock to assist you," Daniel wrote, "and try and answer/respond to any question or problem. Sending further instructions, recommendations re: exfiltration within next hour."

Daniel knew the undertaking would be a challenge. He remembered Kuklinski's personal appeal in one of his letters that Daniel take care of Kuklinski's family in such an emergency. Kuklinski had written: "In the name of our friendship, I charge you personally with the responsibility for their fate."

That day in Warsaw, Kuklinski decided he had to find a home for his beloved dog, Zula, who was thirteen years old. Kuklinski thought immediately of Czeslaw Jakubowski, the elderly father of his late friend Barbara. Czeslaw was now a widower, and the dog would be a good companion for him. Kuklinski whistled Zula into his car, packed some food and supplies, and drove to the Jakubowski house. The old man greeted him warmly and was surprised to hear that Kuklinski was being sent on an overseas assignment that would last several years.

"I can't take her," Kuklinski said. "But I know your wife and your daughter loved Zula, and she can't get better care from anyone else."

"Ryszard, I will try," Czeslaw said.

Kuklinski knelt and hugged Zula tightly, then left quickly in tears. As he climbed into his car, he could hear the dog yelping and scraping her paws on the door.

The Kuklinski family members went their separate ways until they were to meet at night. Bogdan drove his pickup truck from the farm to the outskirts of Warsaw in the evening and parked in the lot of a restaurant on the south side of Ulica Bronsilawa Czecha. From there, he caught a bus into the city. Waldek spent the afternoon browsing through Warsaw bookstores. Hanka went to see an Andrzej Wajda film, *Man of Iron*, and slipped out of the theater after about thirty minutes. Kuklinski left work, telling his colleagues he was going to dinner. They all then headed for Klatka by taxi or tram, getting on and off and reversing direction. At 10:30 P.M., the four convened at Klatka.

They waited in the dark for fifteen minutes, but no car arrived to pick them up. Kuklinski, Hanka, and Waldek took separate routes

home. Bogdan, carrying the Iskra, took a taxi to where he had parked
his truck and drove it to the farm, where he spent the night.

Burggraf was anguished that Warsaw Station had been unable to pick
up Kuklinski and his family Wednesday night. She and Davis had left
the embassy on separate surveillance detection runs, and she had
driven around Warsaw for almost two hours. Just as she concluded she
was free of surveillance, she spotted a car that appeared to be following her. Davis also had surveillance. Neither of them got near Klatka,
and the run was aborted. Burggraf spent another restless night in her
apartment.

On Thursday morning, November 5, Burggraf arrived exhausted at
her office. She cabled Langley, recounting her frustrations at the events
of the previous night and saying they would try again that night at
Skok. A few hours later, she heard from Daniel and his staff: "Share
frustration over conditions last night that prevented run to Klatka but
you made the right decision. Concur with plan for tonight.... Good
luck tonight. We are thinking of you every moment of this anxious
time, and wish you well."

That morning, Kuklinski was summoned to see Skalski. The general
did not mention the leak investigation, but asked how Kuklinski was
progressing on the Defense Ministry's five-year plan, which detailed
the military's requirements from 1981 to 1985. Consumed by the
martial-law preparations, Kuklinski had tried to squeeze in his work
on the plan, but he had not finished, he said. Skalski said he needed a
report by the following day at 8:00 A.M. because it was supposed to be
presented to Jaruzelski.

Kuklinski could not refuse Skalski's request, but the prospect of
working through the night unnerved him. The whole family was supposed to be at Skok at 10:30 P.M. Kuklinski decided to prepare an abbreviated version of the paper, which took him into the early evening. At

eight o'clock, he thanked his secretary, who had been typing the report, and asked her to be back the next day at 6:00 A.M.

At home, he drafted a short note to the CIA asking that the exfiltration be postponed until the following night at nine, with Saturday and Sunday as backup dates. He instructed Hanka and Waldek to remain at home and had Bogdan drive him to Skok, hoping to pass the message to the CIA. Bogdan dropped Kuklinski off near the site, and Kuklinski walked alone to Skok, waiting in the darkness for the car to appear. No one came.

After fifteen minutes, Kuklinski returned to where Bogdan was waiting, and they drove home. Kuklinski said they would try to send a message by Iskra the next day.

That night, Burggraf and Davis had gone out hoping to meet the family at Skok, but again had to abort after both found they were being trailed by SB officers. Back at her apartment, Burggraf prepared a scotch and resolved to try one more time on Friday. If they were unsuccessful, she concluded, Tom Ryan would have to make a final attempt to pick up the family on Saturday night on a drive in from Berlin. Burggraf mused that Berlin to Warsaw would be the longest surveillance detection run in history. If they were still thwarted, they would switch to yet another plan, an "exfil package." A suitcase containing disguises, false travel documents, and currency was being sent from Langley via the CIA station in another East bloc country. It would be left at a dead drop, and Kuklinski and his family would use the contents to try to get out of Poland on their own.

The next morning, Friday, November 6, Burggraf cabled Langley to report the lack of progress. "The continuing presence of heavy surveillance [on the officers] made pickup of Gull and his family impossible last evening," she wrote. "[Station] will plan to try once again this evening with a similar plan."

Copies of the cables between Warsaw and Langley were being sent to Tom Ryan in Berlin. When he and his wife had been advised to stay there, Ryan had set a cover story in motion. Using an unsecured phone in the American consulate in Berlin, he called the chief of the political section in the U.S. Embassy in Warsaw. Ryan, whose cover was as a political officer, said that Lucille had seen a doctor in Berlin and would require further tests. Their return would be delayed by a few days. Their daughter, Maureen, would return sooner with friends. Since Poles would be monitoring the call, Ryan knew the SB now would not expect him back immediately or Maureen to be with her parents.

Kuklinski arrived at work on Friday at 6:00 A.M., greeted his secretary, and fortified himself with a cup of Turkish coffee. He put the final touches on the report for Skalski and handed it in well before 8:00 A.M. Skalski beamed. He would have extra time to review it before presenting it to Jaruzelski.

Kuklinski had not slept and was subsisting largely on coffee and cigarettes. Later that morning, he was visited by General Rakowski, a hard-liner on the General Staff. As they talked, an officer entered with a package for Kuklinski from Moscow. Kuklinski opened the carton and found cigarettes, vodka, and a jar of herring inside, an unexpected present from a colonel on the Soviet General Staff.

"So, you also have an agent in Moscow!" Rakowski cracked.

"I have them everywhere," Kuklinski replied. Rakowski laughed heartily.

That afternoon, Kuklinski attended a party meeting and sat beside Stanislaw Radaj, his friend and classmate from military school who worked on the General Staff. Radaj noticed that Kuklinski seemed distracted. "You don't look well," Radaj said, concerned about his friend's health.

"We've been working hard, night after night," Kuklinski said.

Radaj said he understood and advised Kuklinski to take care. He reminded him of an old Polish adage: Work as hard as you want, but they'll still spit in your grave.

Kuklinski arrived home early that evening. Although he had not heard from the CIA in two days, he tried to reassure his family. He was certain they had not been abandoned. He guessed that surveillance had been too tight. Privately, Kuklinski worried he was asking too much of his family. The situation seemed hopeless. He considered breaking contact with the CIA and dropping his plans to escape. He even contemplated taking the suicide pill. He quietly consulted with Hanka about their options. She cut him off. The family was completely behind him, she said. They would go together.

They were to try again that night. Kuklinski wanted to send another Iskra message first. He reviewed the device's operation again with Bogdan, and they left for Iza's apartment, where Bogdan was expected. Iza was not yet home, and while Bogdan stood guard, Kuklinski knelt in the stairwell of the apartment building, removed the Iskra from his jacket pocket, and typed in the message he had planned to deliver in his note to the CIA the previous night: "Security situation unchanged. We are prepared to meet the car on Friday at Klatka, the following night at Skron, and Sunday at Rabata. Friday, Klatka, Saturday Skron, Sunday Rabata."

He gave the Iskra to Bogdan and asked him to transmit from the block near St. Alexander's Church at the Square of the Three Crosses. Kuklinski went to a restaurant at Plac Komuny Paryskiej and waited for his son to return.

Bogdan took a bus to the square and transmitted the message toward the American Embassy. He met up with his father at the restaurant about eight o'clock. Smiling, he said the device appeared to have worked. They ate sandwiches and drove back to Iza's apartment, where they could see from the lights that she had arrived. As Kuklinski waited outside, he read the CIA's message that had arrived in the Iskra.

Our officers had heavy surveillance night of 4 November. Could not meet you at Klatka. Prepared to meet you and your family if we are surveillance free 5 November at Skok, 6 November at Klatka, 7 November at Skok, 8 November at Straz.

Current plan entails immediate evacuation to west. Destroy all compromising material. Bring [Iskra] with you, or if not possible, throw in river. End X. End X. End.

Kuklinski felt enormous relief as he read the message. Bogdan spent an emotional hour with Iza, who was about to leave for Berlin to buy the medicine for her father.

At about 10:15, each member of the family went separately to Klatka. But again, the CIA car did not arrive. Kuklinski, Hanka, and Waldek returned home; Bogdan went to the farm, carrying the Iskra with him.

When Burggraf arrived at the embassy on Saturday morning, she cabled headquarters to report on the latest failed attempt. "Unfortunately, both teams heavily covered last evening and had to abort," she wrote. It was time for the Ryans to drive in from Berlin.

But there was a new problem: confusion about where Kuklinski would turn up. In his last message, Kuklinski had proposed Skron as the site for the pickup on Saturday night. The station's last message to him had proposed Skok. It was decided that the Ryans would go to Skron, and that Davis would drive by Skok, with Burggraf as a backup in her own car in case Davis was drawing surveillance.

At Langley, Daniel and his staff were concerned that the repeated attempts to meet the Kuklinskis were only exposing them to more danger. The problem was that the Warsaw officers were drawing surveillance wherever they went. "Looking at it from here," headquarters wrote in a cable that would later be sent to the station, "we wonder if the heavy surveillance Warsaw Station is experiencing is because the Poles know there is a source reporting to the Americans, but they still do not have positive identification of the agent, and stepped up surveillance on us may lead them straight to him."

The Ryans made a good team. Tom and Lucille had trained together, and although Lucille was not a full-fledged case officer, she was as adept as any officer at reading and placing signals and looking for new operational sites. She happily took on the task and established cover stories for her frequent trips. Her favorite activity was shopping. She shopped for clothes, pottery, household items, and decorative wooden eggs, which always made good presents. She also joined a committee for the American School, which was in a different part of Warsaw, and helped run a Girl Scout troop, which met in different homes. After a few months, SB surveillance on Lucille slackened a bit. By one count, she found and cased almost half of the usable operational sites that Warsaw Station submitted over a year to Langley for approval.

Tom and Lucille regularly made long surveillance detection runs through the Polish countryside, and if they noticed surveillance behind them, they would change their plans and go bird watching, picnicking, or hiking. As Tom said, "There were times when we went dancing that we didn't want to go dancing, times we went drinking when we didn't want to go drinking. Because you needed a plan for every single move you made."

It was a chilly Saturday morning in Berlin as the Ryans prepared for their return to Warsaw. They dressed early and packed their car, a dark green four-door Volvo with diplomatic plates. They filled a can of gasoline and placed it in the trunk. They would have to prolong the drive, which usually took about eight hours, to perhaps twelve hours. They knew from experience that the SB tended to initiate surveillance on the outskirts of Warsaw rather than at the Polish border, so they could drive through the countryside and into the forests and kill time there. They had to arrive at Skron at 10:30 P.M. sharp. There could be no accidents, delays, or diversions.

But as Ryan read a cable describing Skron, he realized he did not recognize its location. He turned to Lucille. She studied the map. She had not been to the exact place, she said, but she knew the neighborhood. She was there two weeks earlier, casing new locations. "I think we can find it," she said.

That morning, Kuklinski's neighbor, General Hermaszewski, was standing in front of his garage, packing his car for an overnight hunting trip. As he placed his rifles in the car, he looked up and saw Kuklinski being picked up by his driver. Hermaszewski waved, and Kuklinski waved back.

Kuklinski arrived at the General Staff and was summoned to join a group of officers in a conference room for a routine briefing by Siwicki on martial-law planning. Kuklinski mentioned to a few colleagues that he was taking his family to southwestern Poland to visit Hanka's ailing mother, who was celebrating her seventy-fifth birthday.

The meeting ended about 11 A.M. Kuklinski returned to his office, retrieved his briefcase, and called for his driver. Usually, the soldier drove him home in a black Volga by the same route—Ulica Rakowiecka, Pulawska, Armii Wojska Polskiego, Trasa Lazienkowska, and then the Wislostrada.

"Today, we do not have to hurry," Kuklinski said.

Kuklinski watched through the window as they passed the familiar landmarks—Lazienkowski Park, the Vistula River, the Royal Castle that loomed over the Old Town—and even the trees and homes of his beloved city.

As they turned off the Wislostrada and onto Sanguszki, nearing his home, Kuklinski's driver asked him what time he wanted to be picked up the next day. Kuklinski said he would not need him Sunday because of his trip to see his wife's mother; the driver should return to the motor pool in case anyone else required his services. Kuklinski would call him on Monday.

As they passed Ulica Przyrynek, Kuklinski saw two young people on the street watching his Volga pass. On Rajcow Street, Kuklinski saw two others standing by Najswietsza Maria Panna Church.

At home, Kuklinski embraced Hanka and immediately built another fire, in which he placed the last cache of files he had in his home. There were so many that the smoke began to billow through his house. Coughing and terrified that he might attract the attention of neighbors or even the SB, Kuklinski opened some windows, trying to clear out the smoke. He decided to take the rest of the papers with him out of Poland.

That night, Kuklinski and Hanka had been invited to dinner at the home of Barbara Barszcz, whose husband, Roman, was Kuklinski's childhood friend. Roman, an engineer, was in Athens on his way home after two years in Libya, where he had worked for a Polish company that was building bridges.

Kuklinski and Hanka decided to make a brief appearance at the Barszcz residence, where they had cold cuts and salad. Barbara felt at ease with Ryszard and Hanka, although that night she sensed some tension in her friends. They told her they were preoccupied by the drive they were taking the next day to see Hanka's mother. At 7:30 P.M., as Barbara was carrying a tray of tea, Kuklinski said he had to leave to finish some work. He hugged Barbara and departed. Hanka stayed for a few more hours, and then she, too, said good night.

At home, Kuklinski gathered some personal possessions, including some photographs and the small World War II flask the CIA translator had sent him. Kuklinski considered it his lucky token, his symbol of survival. He poured into it a small amount of cognac. Waldek had already left for his usual run through the Warsaw bookstores. Bogdan was at the farm. When Hanka arrived at home, they left separately for Skron.

Hanka met Waldek in the city and went to a movie. They slipped separately out of the theater before the film ended. At the farm, Bogdan wrote a letter to Iza, who had left for Berlin to buy the medicine for her father. In the note, Bogdan said he had to leave Poland unexpectedly but, as their relationship had soured, "it would not matter to you anyway."

Bogdan belabored his farewell. "Please forget about me," he wrote. "Don't write. Don't call. Don't look for me. When you read this letter, I'll be already far away. Good-bye."

The note was a fake, meant to mislead the SB.

He then wrote a second letter, which instructed Iza to hand the first note to the SB if she was questioned. The second letter should be destroyed immediately. Bogdan drove into Warsaw, stopping at Iza's empty apartment and slipping the fake note under her door. He gave the second one in a sealed envelope to a trusted friend, asking that it be given to Iza when she returned.

At 10:15 P.M. Kuklinski arrived at Skron, a location on a sidewalk near a sheltered alley that ran between an apartment building and a garage. Within minutes, the rest of his family arrived. They hid in the dark, waiting by the garage.

It was midmorning as the Ryans began their long drive to Warsaw. They sped down the autobahn, as they could not leave the main highway in East Germany. Once they crossed the border, their usual practice was to stop in Poznan, the first major city in western Poland, where there was a consulate and they could refill their tank. Instead, they turned off the main road and cruised into the countryside, into parts of Poland where Americans rarely went. They knew these woods from one of their "bird-watching" trips. They turned off their lights and parked the car, covering themselves with wool blankets because of the cold. They took turns napping, and after dusk, they started up again, driving toward Warsaw. They entered the city limits and continued toward Skron. With Lucille holding the map, Tom drove on carefully, so as not to violate any traffic laws. As he made the last right turn, Lucille put down the map.

A figure emerged from the darkness, and Ryan slowed down. Kuklinski rapidly gestured to Hanka and his sons to follow. They clambered into the Volvo, squeezing into the backseat and onto the floor as Lucille and Tom leaned back and covered them with wool blankets and raincoats. As Tom began to drive, Lucille handed back a flashlight and a short note in Polish, cautioning the family to remain as quiet as possible.

They drove in silence. Kuklinski, his body wedged close to the floorboard, could feel every bump in the street, and he imagined the route they were taking. Ten minutes passed, and the Volvo glided through the gate to the American Embassy and pulled into a dark corner of the compound, where Ryan parked in his regular space, which was sheltered by a carport. As the family got out of the car, Kuklinski embraced Ryan and handed him a bag containing the Iskra, his camera, his Polish military identification documents, and the cyanide pill. He and Hanka and their sons were introduced to two officers—Wilcox, who would drive the van that would take them out of Poland, and the communications officer who had joined the operation. Each family member was then helped into a large packing carton that had been placed in the rear of the van. Kuklinski had to lie flat on his back; Waldek, Bogdan, and Hanka were able to crouch in their cramped spaces. The van, which had American diplomatic plates, would appear to be making a routine delivery of packages to West Berlin, where there was a military post office that was used for large shipments.

At 10:55 P.M., the van pulled out of the lot. The officers talked to the family as they drove, offering reassuring accounts of their progress. At one point between Warsaw and Poznan, Kuklinski heard the officers discussing the route they were taking, and he tried to help them with directions.

When the van reached the East German border, Polish guards motioned it out of line, and Kuklinski could hear them barking orders. It turned out that the license plate of the van, which had been recently obtained by the embassy, was not yet on a list of updated plate numbers kept at the border. The guards were calling Warsaw to see if the van was authorized to leave the country.

For twenty-five minutes, the family waited in the dark in terrified silence. They could hear the Polish guards walking around the van, but no one looked inside. Then the engine started again, and the van hurtled forward. They began their drive through East Germany.

At 9:55 the next morning, they arrived at an American military base in West Berlin. The next day, Kuklinski and his family flew to Frankfurt, where they were examined by physicians and given a few days to recover. At one point, the Kuklinskis were taken to a small office, where an American diplomat greeted them. "Don't tell me who you are," he said. "I don't want to know anything about you."

He pointed to an aerial photograph of Washington, D.C., that hung on his wall. The Mall and the monuments were clearly visible. "The next time you see this, it will be for real," he said.

The family boarded a military plane and landed under a gray sky at Andrews Air Force Base in Suitland, Maryland, on the morning of November 11—Veterans Day in the United States and Independence Day in Poland. The runway was protected by Air Force guards and CIA security officers. After the plane taxied to a stop, a small door opened near the cockpit. Kuklinski poked out his head and walked down the stairs, followed by Hanka and their two sons. On the tarmac were Air Force ground crews and security officers. Standing somewhat to the side by himself was Daniel.

Kuklinski smiled and burst into tears as he embraced his friend. It had been five years since they had last seen each other. He proudly introduced his wife and sons for the first time.

As security officers whisked the family to a safe house in suburban Virginia, cables flashed between Berlin, Warsaw, and Langley. "Well done, Warsaw!" declared one.

At General Staff headquarters, General Skalski asked an aide to summon Kuklinski. The aide returned to say Kuklinski was not in his office and no one had seen him at work. Skalski instructed the aide to call Kuklinski at home, but there was no answer. Skalski summoned General Szklarski. "We must find out what is going on," Skalski said. He was afraid Kuklinski was ill, and he needed him. Several officers were sent to Kuklinski's home on Rajcow Street. They reported that the doors were closed, and no one seemed to be home.

"Break down the door," Skalski ordered. He was told the house was empty, and the family gone. An investigation was opened, and the authorities questioned Kuklinski's friends and colleagues. Iza was repeatedly called to the SB offices in Warsaw, where she was interrogated a half dozen times. She turned over Bogdan's phony letter and said she had no idea what had happened.

Zula, meanwhile, barked and cried for days, and on November 10, Zula's new owner took her to a dog pound on Paluch Street. Three weeks later she was put to sleep.

When Kuklinski and his family arrived at the CIA safe house in Virginia, they found a full refrigerator and a bouquet of flowers on the dining room table, prepared by Ruth Brerewood, the Polish desk officer. On their first evening in America, the family was in shock. Kuklin-

ski felt drained, and Bogdan broke down in tears. Waldek was withdrawn. Only Hanka seemed to hold herself together. In the following
days, the agency helped the family settle in, providing them with new
names and identification papers.

Kuklinski also had a present for Daniel, a piece of art that had once
hung in his home. It was an 1899 etching of a once-splendid sailing
ship that lay on its side, half-submerged off a sandy shore. It was called
After the Storm.

Kuklinski's arrival remained a closely held secret within the U.S.
government. One person who knew, Zbigniew Brzezinski, the former
national security adviser, met Kuklinski at the Four Seasons Hotel in
Georgetown and solemnly addressed him with words traditionally
conferred when a Polish soldier is decorated: *"Pan sie dobrze Polsce
zasluzyl.* You have served Poland well."

Debriefings of Kuklinski began soon after his arrival. The CIA sent
Aris Pappas, the martial-law analyst, to meet with him. Victor Kliss,
who had handled the correspondence between Kuklinski and the CIA,
acted as the interpreter.

Pappas was not told the identity of the man he was debriefing, but
merely that a new Polish defector had arrived, as if there had been no
previous relationship with him. But as the interviews progressed, Pappas felt a growing sense of recognition.

On December 11, Pappas, who had continued the debriefing, concluded the Poles had made a final decision to declare martial law and
were merely waiting for the appropriate opportunity. He summarized
his views in a short memo, which was intended for the president.

In the early morning hours of Sunday, December 13, Pappas was driving south on Route 95 in his white Volkswagen Rabbit, returning from
a Christmas party in Baltimore. His wife, Eva, a schoolteacher, was
asleep next to him; their infant daughter, Lara, slept in a car seat in the
back. Pappas fiddled with the radio and heard the news. A reporter
was announcing that martial law had been imposed in Poland.

Holy shit, Pappas thought. *They can't do it when I'm not on duty.* He roused his wife and said they would have go to his office, which was located in a satellite building off the Langley headquarters compound. As they pulled up, Pappas ran up to the guard's desk, realizing he did not have his CIA badge. "I'm coming from a party," he explained to the guard, who recognized him and let him in.

Pappas ran to the door to his office, dialed the combination, and entered. It was empty. He called the agency's operations center and reached Ben Rutherford, who ran Theater Forces Division. "We've been trying to get you all night," Rutherford said; he started to relay what was known about the crisis. The crackdown was unfolding just as the documents said it would. "We need you right here," Rutherford said, instructing Pappas to bring his files—Kuklinski's material.

Pappas grabbed one of the paper bags with red stripes that signified it as a "burn bag" (contents to be destroyed). He unlocked the safes, took the folders of sensitive martial-law documents, and filled the bag. Under different circumstances, a person could get shot for doing this, he realized. After locking up, Pappas returned to the guard desk and said he had to take the material to headquarters. As he jumped into his car, he handed the files to Eva. "What's this?" she asked. Pappas could see the absurdity of the situation. With all this material, he joked, they could get a dacha on the Black Sea.

As he drove to headquarters, Pappas had visions of being rear-ended and classified documents flying around the Tysons Corner intersection. At headquarters, Pappas kissed Eva and Lara and ran to the operations center.

There were no surprises as the reports filtered in from Poland. The Polish people had awakened to find tanks in their streets and communications disrupted. More than 6,000 Solidarity activists, including Lech Walesa, had been detained. Every hour, interspersed with the music of Chopin, Jaruzelski's speech announcing the imposition of martial law was rebroadcast for the nation.

Jaruzelski declared, "Our country is on the edge of the abyss."

11

PATRIOT OR TRAITOR?

ONE MONDAY EVENING in September 1986, an unusual procession of guests arrived at a two-story brick house in the suburb of Oakton, Virginia. The visitors were all intelligence officers and their spouses. They had organized car pools to reduce the number of vehicles parked on the quiet street. And though the night was warm and the garden spacious, the festivities were kept indoors.

The owner of the house greeted each guest at the door. His neighbors knew him by an assumed name, a fictional identity created for him soon after he had left Poland. His guests knew him by his real name, Ryszard Kuklinski, and they had come to celebrate his initiation as an American citizen, which had taken place earlier that day in a secret proceeding at a local courthouse.

It had been almost five years since Kuklinski and his family had been exfiltrated from Poland. Now fifty-six, Kuklinski vigorously shook the hands of his guests or embraced them. Many had worked on the Gull operation at CIA headquarters and were meeting Kuklinski for the first time. Others, including officers who had been based in Warsaw and seen him only furtively on the street or who had helped engineer his perilous escape, were renewing old ties. Someone broke out a bottle of champagne. David Forden—"Daniel"—clinked his glass and offered a toast to Kuklinski and his new life. Then Kuklinski began to speak. His voice was barely audible, for he was still self-conscious about his heavily accented English.

"There are moments in a person's life, when your heart almost stops beating," he began, "and you can't find the words to express your feelings." He recalled the thrill of seeing the American flag outside the U.S. Embassy in Warsaw during his nine years of cooperation. Today, he said, he was proud to call that flag his own. "I take the oaths, the obligations, related to this."

He paused briefly. "But forgive me," he said, his voice beginning to break. "In my heart, my body, I will always remain a Pole."

Kuklinski's first years in the United States after the exfiltration were not easy for him or his family. Hanka and their sons had to adapt to life under new names and identities. Hanka had left her elderly mother without saying goodbye. They had abandoned friends and had left behind virtually all of their possessions, including Waldek's entire library. The family had to take intensive English, as none of them knew the language. With the CIA's assistance, Kuklinski's physical appearance was altered. He grew a beard and mustache, and a doctor removed the "Atlantyk" tattoo that he had imprinted on his arm as a teenager during the war. There was concern for Kuklinski's safety in the United States: Poland's embassy in Washington, D.C., and its consulates around the country were staffed with agents of the SB, and Poland had issued a warrant for Kuklinski's arrest. If caught, he would face execution. Of course, there also was the KGB, whose officers in the United States were undoubtedly interested in the Polish colonel.

Bogdan tried to stay in touch with Iza, calling her at the homes of trusted friends in Warsaw, but they missed each other desperately. Kuklinski, longing for another dog, saw a classified advertisement in *The Washington Post* for bichon frise puppies shortly after his arrival.

The breeder in Maryland had one white-haired puppy left. Kuklinski and Hanka named her Gemini.

Forden and his colleagues and their spouses tried to alleviate some of the burden on the Kuklinskis, seeing them regularly, inviting them to dinner, offering pep talks.

One day shortly after he arrived in the United States, Kuklinski was invited to CIA headquarters for a ceremony in the office of Director William Casey. As Forden and other CIA officials watched, the agency finally bestowed the Distinguished Intelligence Medal on Kuklinski. Because Kuklinski's English was still poor and Casey tended to mumble, the CIA had Victor Kliss, the translator, act as an interpreter. Kuklinski received a Polish version of the citation on the medal, and Kliss read it aloud in English:

> While facing great personal danger, Col. Kuklinski consistently provided extremely valuable and highly classified information about the armed forces, operational plans and intentions of the Soviet Union and the Warsaw Pact members. Having accomplished the above, he made an unparalleled contribution to the preservation of peace, especially in crisis situations. Throughout all that time, Col. Kuklinski was motivated by the most noble patriotism, a deep sense of duty and dedication to the ideals of freedom.
>
> Unfortunately, his dedication and sacrifice must remain a secret forever. This medal, secret as well, reflects the appreciation—which he greatly deserves—of the legions of people worldwide who share his ideals.

In the months after his arrival in the United States, Kuklinski became a valuable consultant to the government on Soviet and Warsaw Pact issues, writing a critique of the Pentagon's AirLand Battle doctrine and preparing a lengthy paper, written from the perspective of the Soviet General Staff, on how Moscow might react to the new doctrine. He also prepared a report on Soviet and Warsaw Pact arms planning. Aris Pappas, the CIA analyst who had specialized in martial law, debriefed him regularly. Kuklinski was given an office near Langley with a computer and a secretary, and one officer's wife took him shopping for supplies like a Selectric typewriter ball with Polish letters and symbols.

Key defense and intelligence officials in the United States were informed of Kuklinski's arrival. One of them, Les Griggs, a colonel in the Pentagon, joined the debriefing team. Kuklinski was delighted to learn that he finally would be working with a military officer. "I've been looking for you—we need to talk," Kuklinski said when they were introduced.

Griggs, Pappas, and other officers, with Kliss as the interpreter, debriefed Kuklinski for six months on Soviet and Warsaw Pact issues. "It soon dawned on me that I'd been reading his stuff for years," Griggs recalled later.

A small team of analysts in the Pentagon supplied questions through Griggs, who would summarize the debriefing sessions in memos to the group. The analysts went back through the tens of thousands of pages of material Kuklinski had sent in the previous nine years, trying to clear up ambiguities and questions they had long had.

The CIA continued to keep Kuklinski's arrival a secret within the larger intelligence community. But in December 1982, the first account of his role in clandestine activity became public. *Newsweek* magazine reported that the CIA had obtained the martial-law plans before Poland's crackdown on Solidarity had occurred. "In fact, the CIA had a longtime secret agent who by 1981 had risen to the rank of colonel at Polish Army headquarters," the article said. It quoted one unnamed source as saying, "For a very long time there were very few things that went on at the upper levels of the Polish military that the CIA didn't know about."

The *Newsweek* article suggested that the CIA, having obtained the martial-law plans from Kuklinski, could have warned Solidarity's leaders, which would have given them time to go underground before they could be arrested. But it went on to note that "Solidarity was riddled with government spies," and a specific warning would have risked Kuklinski's life. The article said: "One of the legends of World War II is that Churchill decided not to defend the cathedral at Coventry against a Nazi air raid in order to protect the Ultra secret: that the Allies had broken the German code. In the Cold War of the 1980s, Solidarity may have served as Coventry."

Kuklinski's name appeared nowhere in the article, but it didn't matter. He feared the article would be used against him by his enemies, as propaganda, even as evidence in the Polish military court. He saw the disclosure of his role by unnamed American officials as a betrayal, and he was angry at being described as an "agent" for the CIA. He had always seen himself as an agent working for Poland. Using a tape recorder, he dictated a one-hour monologue, which he called his life's confession. He wanted to make contact with a Polish church in Maryland and ask the priest to present the tape someday, if Kuklinski was not alive, to whoever was elected as Poland's first free president.

Forden, learning of Kuklinski's anguish, rushed to his home and found him overwhelmed by despair. He had shaved off his beard and mustache, and he told Forden he wanted to return to Warsaw and offer himself up to Polish military authorities. Forden said that made no sense. In the United States, the press was free, he explained; it was not controlled by the government or by the political parties. A few days later, Kuklinski received a two-page letter from Casey, which he was told was written on behalf of President Reagan, in which the CIA director promised that "everything legally possible will be done to find and hold accountable the person who leaked information for this article."

Casey said the article was "unwanted, unfortunate, and yet, in a certain way, it was well-meaning. Let me explain: America has had many heroes in its history. The American people are constantly seeking more heroes to help add positive meaning and strength to our democratic creed. Those of us who know you personally regard you as a friend, a man of high character and courage, as a Polish patriot—a hero."

Forden persuaded Kuklinski to stay in the United States. Kuklinski increasingly relied on Forden for advice on personal matters, and Forden looked for ways to ease the family's transition. At one point, aware of Bogdan's depression at being separated from Iza, Forden and John Stein, the CIA's deputy director for operations, had dinner at Kuklinski's home. The discussion centered on the possibility of carrying out another secret operation, this time to bring Iza out of Poland. A plan was eventually developed and run through the CIA station in Bucharest, Romania.

In early September 1983, a group of Polish tourists flew south for a week to the Romanian resort of Mangalia on the Black Sea, not far from the Bulgarian border. Iza, then twenty-seven years old, was among them.

One morning, she slipped out of the hotel, leaving behind her luggage and clothes. She wore red pants and a T-shirt and carried a tiny leather pocketbook and a passport. She walked several blocks to a corner near a bowling alley, where she had been told to look for an American couple. She saw two people who seemed to fit the description. They smiled, and one held out a photograph. Iza looked at it and saw herself.

The two—they were the chief of Bucharest Station and his wife—led Iza to a nearby van. The rear seat had been replaced with a rectangular box in which Iza was to hide. She climbed in and lay on her back, with her face almost touching the closed lid. Although there was an airhole, she felt as if she were in a coffin.

She lay in the dark, her body taut. It took less than twenty minutes to reach the Bulgarian border, and when the van stopped at the border, Iza could hear the guards talking and dogs barking. The driver and his wife got out of the van. An hour passed, and she began to hyperventilate. She could hear the dogs circling the van. Finally, the Americans returned to the van and started the motor, and they drove off through Bulgaria. Iza called out that she had to pee. The officers pulled to the side of the road and allowed her to get out of the box, but not out of the van. They handed her a plastic bottle. After several hours, the van reached the Turkish border, where they were again stopped before being allowed to cross into Turkey. The van soon pulled off the road and into a wooded area. There, Iza finally got out of the van and was welcomed by a group of CIA officers and their families, who had set up a picnic in her honor. Iza spent the night in a hotel in Istanbul, where she was given new identification documents and a change of clothing that had been flown in from Britain. Iza had to laugh as she examined the new outfit: The bra seemed several sizes too big.

Iza was flown to Frankfurt, where Bogdan and his mother were anxiously waiting for her. The reunion was tearful and joyous, and when she arrived in Virginia, she received a hearty welcome from Kuklinski, who later drove her through the countryside, showing her the scenery as the fall colors changed. In October, Iza and Bogdan were married in the family's home in a ceremony attended by Forden and other new friends of the family from the agency and the Pentagon.

Kuklinski's other son, Waldek, began to collect new books to replace those he had left in Poland, and he retreated once again into his reading and writing. He also grew close to a graduate student at Georgetown University, and eventually they moved in together. In November 1983, he finished a manuscript, which he dedicated to his father. It was a highly allegorical 200-page account of the family's life. Waldek wrote the manuscript under a pseudonym and omitted details that could reveal he was Kuklinski's son. Nonetheless, as Kuklinski read the work, he could see Waldek was still distressed about the uprooting of the family.

In the final chapter, "Fulfillment," the narrator enters a large used bookstore and discovers every book he has ever wanted. He approaches the shelves labeled "History": "Twenty centuries stared at him. . . . Each title captured his attention. . . . He found himself at a loss as to which book he should reach for first. And so he came to the letter 'P.'"

He grasps a book and embraces it. Nobody would take it from him. But he finds that he cannot buy it. He asks why, and where he is, and how he arrived there. And why can't he take the book?

Waldek ended his story with a poem, titled "Postscript," in which he described a book lying open, its pages caught in a gust of wind.

> *The wind turned over only one page*
> *And your city disappeared*
> *And you are left with the cold night in your eyes*
> *And the echo of footsteps in your ears*
> *And a handful of air in your palms.*
> *Even though the streets of the city are in your blood*
> *And the stones of the walls are in your bones*
> *And the sky is like a protective shield.*
> *The diary of your mind stops abruptly*
> *And only a river of memories remains.*
> *Over, over and over again, until your face is buried in the ground.*

Waldek had titled his book "Dog in the Ruin of the City."

Polish officials said nothing publicly about Kuklinski's disappearance, but in May 1984, Kuklinski was tried in absentia in a secret proceeding in a Warsaw military court. The military had conducted an extensive investigation, obtaining statements from at least a half dozen witnesses ranging from senior military officials to Czeslaw Jakubowski, the elderly friend whom Kuklinski had asked to care for Zula.

On May 23, 1984, the court declared that Kuklinski had deserted the Polish Army, convicted him of "treason of the Fatherland," and sentenced him to death. Saying that it had found no mitigating circumstances, the court also ordered the seizure of Kuklinski's property and stripped him of some of his rights as a citizen.

In a detailed explanation, the court described Kuklinski's participation in "the fundamental defense matters of the Warsaw Pact" as well as his role as author of Poland's military doctrine and of documents pertaining to martial law. "Those projects, classified as top secret, were of the utmost importance," the court said. "To reveal them would

jeopardize Poland's defense and security in an incalculable manner."
The evidence "unequivocally indicated that Col. Ryszard Kuklinski
had deserted the Polish People's Army."

> While passing out the most severe sentence onto defendant
> Ryszard Kuklinski, the court took into account the fact that the
> treason was committed by an officer who occupied such a high
> post in the General Staff of the Polish Army, and whose knowl-
> edge about Poland's defense and security was therefore particu-
> larly broad. The defendant unscrupulously passed that information
> to the U.S. intelligence in a period especially difficult for the exis-
> tence of the Polish People's Republic, that is, prior to the imposi-
> tion of martial law. The damage caused by defendant Ryszard
> Kuklinski is immeasurable, given the scope of his knowledge and
> the fact that he works now as an adviser on Eastern Europe for a
> country that is hostile to the Polish People's Republic. The results
> of that activity cannot be foreseen in the future.

There is no evidence that the military court was aware of the tens
of thousands of pages of Soviet documents Kuklinski had provided
the West. But the court speculated, "One may safely suspect that
defendant Ryszard Kuklinski had cooperated with the United States
intelligence for a long time."

The CIA eventually informed Kuklinski of the verdict, but he did
not tell Hanka or his sons. His only surprise was that the Jaruzelski
regime had waited so long to act.

During Kuklinski's first three years in the United States, David
Forden—still "Daniel" to him—called the family regularly and tried to
visit once or twice a week. Sometimes he stayed for dinner, and other
times he just talked, offering any guidance he could and working to
help the family understand America's often startling culture and
media. Kuklinski was astonished at what he saw on American televi-

sion: the nightly accounts of shootings and murders in Washington, D.C., for example, and a program in which people swallowed goldfish in return for money.

Forden was also undergoing a transition: After three years running the Soviet Division, he was being named Athens Station Chief. He was also getting married. He had fallen in love with a vibrant Austrian woman named Aurelia, whom he had met toward the end of his posting in Vienna, where she worked as the protocol officer at the American Embassy.

Under the rules, the CIA must give its approval to officers wanting to marry a foreign national. As part of that process, Aurelia had to undergo a polygraph examination, and Forden had to submit a request for permission to marry her and a letter of resignation. If the CIA approved the union, they could marry, and Forden could stay with the CIA. If it did not, Forden would have to resign.

Forden did not tell Aurelia about Kuklinski—he could not reveal classified information to people who were not cleared to know it.

Aurelia passed the polygraph, and the CIA gave its blessing. In mid-1984, Forden decided it was time to introduce her to some of the most important people in his life.

He invited the Kuklinskis to dinner at his modest townhouse in Falls Church, Virginia. That night, Forden gave Kuklinski some startling news: "My name is really David."

Aurelia, who had lost her father at a young age, asked Kuklinski to give her away at the wedding. Kuklinski agreed and invited the couple to have the wedding at his home. One day in August 1984, he led Aurelia down the stairway into his living room, where David and a crowd of well-wishers had gathered. David and Aurelia were married before Kuklinski and his family and David's three children, including his twenty-year-old son, Daniel.

In early June 1986, Aris Pappas, the CIA specialist on Polish martial law, and James M. Simon Jr., a senior military operations analyst, accompanied Kuklinski to Norfolk, Virginia, to meet General Al Gray, then Commanding General, Fleet Marine Force, Atlantic, and Commanding General, II Marine Expeditionary Force.

The gruff fifty-seven-year-old Gray was responsible for all Marines east of the Mississippi, in the Atlantic, and in Europe. One of his responsibilities in wartime would be to reinforce the northern flank in Europe, which included Norway, Denmark, and northern Germany— one of Kuklinski's areas of expertise.

Gray greeted Kuklinski in Polish, explaining that he had once played quarterback at Lafayette College, and that some of his Polish-American teammates called out their signals in Polish. Kuklinski was pleased to meet the high-ranking military officer. After a daylong discussion in the company of admirals, generals, and other officers, Gray invited Kuklinski and his entourage to his home for a cookout. "We're going to continue this," he said.

Gray's home overlooked the waterfront on Dillingham Boulevard, which is known as Admirals Row. He introduced Kuklinski to his wife, his ninety-three-year-old mother, and their five dogs, including his miniature poodle, Cozy. Gray also showed Kuklinski his large library.

The general put some steaks on the grill, and noticing that Kuklinski was chilly, he brought him a World War II–style leather flight jacket, on which was imprinted "Papa Bear," Gray's call sign during the evacuation of Saigon, where he was the last commander to leave. Kuklinski enjoyed himself, and the party did not break up until almost 1:00 A.M.

Later that morning, while he was still in his hotel room in Norfolk, Kuklinski got a frantic call from Hanka. The *Washington Post* had published a front-page article revealing Kuklinski's name and his role in providing the martial-law plans to the CIA. The article, by Bob Woodward and Michael Dobbs, said the CIA considered the Kuklinski operation one of its "most important intelligence successes."

At one point, the article reported, a copy of the martial-law plans sat on President Reagan's desk. The article said that Jerzy Urban, spokesman for Polish leader Wojciech Jaruzelski, had volunteered information about the case to a *Post* reporter in Warsaw, using it to attack the United States. The article cited the death sentence imposed by the Polish military court, and indicated that Urban believed the case showed why the United States and Kuklinski, not Jaruzelski, had betrayed Solidarity.

"The U.S. administration could have publicly revealed these plans to the world and warned Solidarity," Urban said. "Had it done so, the implementation of martial law would have been impossible."

Urban said Polish authorities had assumed the CIA withdrew Kuklinski from Poland so that it could publicize "his information on the preparations for martial law without jeopardizing his safety." Jaruzelski had waited for an announcement from the Americans, Urban said, but after hearing nothing, the plans were put into effect.

Two days later, Urban held a news conference in Warsaw to discuss the article, which came at a time when Poland was chafing under tight economic sanctions imposed by the United States as a response to martial law. Urban's tone was harsh and sarcastic.

> The fact that President Reagan's administration did not warn its friends in advance also points to the insincerity of the surprise and holy indignation expressed by the U.S. authorities at the introduction of martial law.... Hypocrisy also lies at the foundation of the anti-Polish restrictions. The U.S. government cheated not only its ardent Polish allies but also its own society. Such are the undertones of the case of Kuklinski, who was sentenced in absentia to death by the Polish Military Court.

Kuklinski was deeply wounded by the article and frustrated by his inability to respond. He told Hanka he had to get away, and he decided to go sailing. After arriving in the United States, Kuklinski had taken up sailing on Chesapeake Bay, and he had bought a forty-four-foot sailboat, which he christened the *Shadow Line* after the Joseph Conrad novel.

Kuklinski sailed in the direction of Norfolk, Virginia, planning on a leisurely trip of about a week. But after several days, the weather grew stormy, and the boat's anchor was damaged. He sailed back up the Potomac to the small town of St. Marys City, Maryland, where he stopped for repairs. As he arrived, he saw two young women reading on the dock. They jumped up and offered to help with the ropes. "What a beautiful boat," one said. They were students at the local college and loved sailing.

Kuklinski, who had regrown his beard, welcomed them aboard. As they chatted, Kuklinski offered them a tour of the cabin, pointing out his boat's library, which included a collection of Conrad's works.

One of the women looked up, saying, "I only love spy stories." Unsettled, Kuklinski cursed under his breath and abruptly ushered them off the boat.

The *Washington Post* story and Urban's attack still rankled. The next year, Kuklinski decided to enter the debate, and gave an interview to a Polish émigré journal, *Kultura*, in which he detailed his clandestine activity in the year before martial law and his motivation for acting as he did. He only hinted at the extent of his earlier cooperation and offered no details of how he had escaped from Poland. He said it was "premature to describe the circumstances of how this occurred."

He maintained that warning Solidarity about the impending crackdown would have accomplished nothing. By then, martial law was inevitable, and had Jaruzelski refused to implement it, other Polish officials would have. Moreover, a warning would have provoked Solidarity to even greater levels of resistance, barricading factories and fighting in the streets. "There is no question that . . . the whole matter would end with an incredibly bloody massacre," Kuklinski wrote.

"Today, despite the sentence of death issued against me," Kuklinski said, "I sleep soundly, and this is not because I have some specific personal protection, but because my conscience is not burdened with the loss of any human life."

The *Kultura* essay spurred broad debate in Poland, which Kuklinski followed closely in the Polish press. Meanwhile, the CIA moved him to another location in Virginia after a car with a Soviet diplomatic license plate was observed parked outside his house.

Over the next few years, Kuklinski began to feel reason for hope as Poland underwent a fundamental change. The breakthrough came in spring 1989 with the roundtable talks between Communist authorities, led by Interior Minister Kiszczak, and Solidarity, still an illegal organization, led by Lech Walesa. The talks resulted in semifree elections to the Polish parliament in June 1989, and in September, a Solidarity-led government was created, the first government in the Communist bloc led by a non-Communist prime minister, Solidarity activist Tadeusz Mazowiecki. The events began a process of profound systemic change in Poland and had a ripple effect throughout Eastern Europe. But even as Solidarity assumed control of all government ministries by the middle of 1990, there remained an entrenched bureaucracy in the military, which had come up under communism.

In mid-November 1990, during a visit to Warsaw by CIA director William Webster, his DDO, Richard Stolz, raised the Kuklinski case with several high-ranking Polish intelligence officials at a reception and asked why Kuklinski was still being treated as a criminal. They replied that they had no problem with clearing his name. "But it's the military," they said.

Late that month, with Poland ready to hold its first nationwide presidential elections, Kuklinski was caught up in the enthusiasm. Hearing that Poles all across America were invited to go to their consulates and exercise their freedom by casting an absentee ballot for the president of Poland, Kuklinski wanted to participate and vote for Walesa. Some years after Kuklinski's arrival in the United States, he had sent Walesa a present through an intermediary: the flask the retiring CIA translator had given him. The flask had once helped a World War II Polish paratrooper, and it had helped him as well, Kuklinski wrote in a letter to Walesa. "This is a symbol of survival." He had never heard from Walesa, but he was prepared to vote for him now.

On November 24, he boarded a plane to Chicago, where he rented a car and drove to the Polish consulate on North Lake Shore Drive. He strode through the gate with dozens of other Poles who were arriving to vote.

Inside, he approached an election official.

"Do you have a Polish passport?"

No, Kuklinski said.

"Some ID?"

"I have," Kuklinski said, pulling out his old General Staff photo ID, which he had taken with him from Poland.

"Ah, Kuklinski," the official said, recognizing him.

The official said that it would be impossible for him to grant Kuklinski permission to vote. Did Kuklinski want to see a higher consulate official?

Kuklinski decided not to risk it; he hurried out of the building in tears.

In the second round of voting in December, Walesa was elected president of Poland with nearly three-quarters of the votes. That year, as part of a general amnesty for political prisoners, Kuklinski's death sentence was reduced to twenty-five years, but little else changed for him. Zbigniew Brzezinski, the former U.S. national security adviser, made appeals through the Polish news media for Walesa to invalidate Kuklinski's conviction and decorate him as an officer. Walesa refused, writing to Brzezinski in January 1991: "I am deeply concerned with this matter, but it will take time and preparations to resolve it. I hope you understand this."

In July 1991, Polish television broadcast a documentary on Kuklinski's case. Among the Poles interviewed was Jacek Szymanderski, a member of the Polish parliament, who staunchly defended Kuklinski.

I do not consider Kuklinski to be a traitor because what he [did] was not directed against the Polish state and the Polish Army. That army was not a sovereign army. At that time, it was a Polish-language-speaking unit of the army of the Soviet empire, acting on the latter's behalf and following the latter's orders. I do not deny patriotism of the Polish officers, entangled in that army, but the army as such did not act in a sovereign manner.

Szymanderski concluded, "I am convinced that Kuklinski is a Polish patriot."

But others on the program described Kuklinski as a traitor, such as Colonel Wieslaw Gornicki, a hard-line Communist journalist and former speechwriter for Jaruzelski.

The discussion about ex-Colonel Kuklinski is a little bit embarrassing. It indicates that there exists what I would call a revolving loyalty. If Kuklinski had worked for the Soviet military intelligence, he would have been considered a traitor, but because he had worked for the Americans there are attempts to make him a saint. I do not share this point of view. Not everybody could or should be a pilot, a train driver or a professional soldier. The latter professions require certain traits of character, such as loyalty and honesty beyond doubt.

Gornicki said that Kuklinski had "acted against the well-being of his fellow citizens," adding, "I do not see any reason to seriously think about absolving that man from his infamy.... If he returns, I would certainly not shake his hand."

Waldek read the news accounts with concern, and after the Polish weekly *Polityka* published a particularly negative article about his father, Waldek sent a letter to the editor, which was published.

Waldek cited Kuklinski's warning about Moscow's 1980 invasion plans and said it was time to recognize his contributions and those of like-minded Poles. "In my opinion, this is a matter of paying back a debt of honor to all those who fought for the independence of Poland, perhaps in an unconventional but effective manner," Waldek wrote in March 1992.

Brzezinski, in a speech to the Polish American Congress in October 1992, argued that the debate about Kuklinski showed Poles' continuing confusion about what their country stood for during Communist rule: "Was it an authentic Polish state or an imposed satellite? Was opposition to it therefore legitimate or illegitimate? The recently highly publicized case of Colonel Kuklinski I think reveals confusion and hesitation on this issue even by the best people," Brzezinski said.

He added, "The failure to recognize that opposition by Solidarity to the Communist and Soviet imposed regime, an opposition financially supported by America, was one form of resistance, and that the deliberate undermining of Soviet war plans and the forestalling of the Soviet military intervention in Poland by collaboration with America was another form of resistance, with both dedicated to the same goal: elimination of Poland's subordination to the Soviet Union."

Public opinion surveys in Poland suggested that the criticism of Kuklinski was having an effect. In one poll, 46 percent of those surveyed said they believed Kuklinski had "betrayed the interests of the Polish nation," whereas 16 percent responded that he had "behaved like a Polish patriot." The poll showed that 59 percent of the respondents felt Jaruzelski's martial-law crackdown had been a patriotic act; 15 percent saw it as betrayal of Poland's interests.

Some of Kuklinski's friends remained loyal. Roman Barszcz repeatedly defended Kuklinski. One November 11, on Polish Independence Day, he and a group of supporters visited the Tomb of the Unknown Solider in Warsaw and left a wreath bearing Kuklinski's name.

In 1992, I requested an interview with Kuklinski for an article I was writing for the *Washington Post*. Describing his new home in America, his garden, and his sailing on Chesapeake Bay, Kuklinski grew wistful. "I love this country, but I don't think I deserve to live in this comfort," he said. He recalled that he often stood on the shore of the Bay and looked east, toward Poland. "I deserve only what the Polish people have," he said. "If they have only bread, I want to share the bread. If they can also afford butter or sausage, I want to eat butter and sausage."

He added: "I struggled for what they have today, and I want to share their everyday burdens, their struggle for survival. Maybe, someday, my name will find its place."

I traveled to Warsaw to interview the generals Kuklinski had worked for. Florian Siwicki, the former chief of staff who became Poland's defense minister in the last days of Communist rule, told me bitterly: "We had full trust in Kuklinski.... He was also a man for whom loyalty, being loyal to his friends, to his duty, to his superiors above all, was a routine and daily issue. That is why his betrayal came as such a surprise to us."

General Czeslaw Kiszczak, the minister of interior during martial law, said he was still shocked at Kuklinski's betrayal and was convinced Kuklinski did not cooperate with the United States because of ideology. "He was a product of the Communist system, and everything valuable and positive that he possessed was derived from it," Kiszczak said. "This system had given him all of life's opportunities, education, and opened a career for him. Only this system could promote him and push him up in the sense of social promotion and status. He had no ideological motivation to oppose the system because he directly benefited from it."

Kiszczak remained unforgiving. "Kuklinski has betrayed the Polish state," he said. "It is not significant which adjective we attribute to Poland. If Poland is socialist, capitalist, social-democratic—it is always our Polish state, our country. We had no other land. We haven't and won't have in the future."

General Jaruzelski, who had retired, called Kuklinski's actions "a painful, personal disappointment." He suggested that Kuklinski was blackmailed into cooperating with the Americans, perhaps during his service in Vietnam. "We concluded that he must have found himself in some specific situation which made blackmail possible," Jaruzelski said.

He cited the case of a Polish sergeant who had been blackmailed into spying for a foreign government. "Some women were involved. History knows of many such cases."

Jaruzelski cited what he called the "moral issue." "If we shall say today that what Kuklinski did was right, we can simply then dissolve the Polish Army. All these officers were loyal and were carrying out orders and doing their military duty. And today, the same people are serving loyally in the army of the new, democratic Poland. And they are also Polish patriots."

He said he took personal affront at Kuklinski's actions: "He knew the secrets of the kitchen.... I had full confidence in him.... His lifestyle, behavior and manners gave no hint that he could be a spy. I even liked him. So what occurred was a double disappointment for me, first of all because of the military and political consequences, and secondly, because of my personal disappointment: Someone you trust is betraying you."

He concluded: "Agents and spies were, are, and always shall be—let's accept the fact—but don't make it more beautiful than it is. Don't spray it with perfume."

On Rajcow Street, where Kuklinski had once lived in the housing cooperative, there was a diversity of opinion. His former neighbor, General Hermaszewski, was critical: "If he would have been an American placed in this country as a resident of intelligence working for his country and organization, I would have respect for such a man, respect and credit for his courage and for his professionalism. I would accept such a game. But if someone says and affirms that he is a Pole serving in the Polish Army and wears a Polish uniform, and in the same time he serves some foreign master secretly, I see it negatively. This is unacceptable."

Another former neighbor, Colonel Kazimierz Oklesinski, was supportive. "I would welcome him as my friend," he said, recalling the paranoia of everyday life under Communist rule. "At home we were normal Poles. In the office, we were afraid of the shadows.... In this difficult and complex situation, he made the right choice—and a brave choice too."

Colonel Czeslaw Poltorak, who ran the Army Medical Corps, said, "From the point of view of the law, and principles of army morale and ethics, ... it was betrayal." But should Kuklinski be condemned? he asked. "Should he have acted *against* his conscience, obeying communist rules and principles? I was a member of the Communist Party too, but after bitter experience I sometimes regret that I so naively believed in communist ideology, and that I was active in its ranks.... At some historical moments, betrayal is heroism, a heroic act. In the case of Kuklinski, this is my personal view."

In September 1992, I first wrote about Kuklinski's activities in an article published in the *Washington Post*, which was followed by more debate in the Polish press, on radio call-in shows, and on street corners. *Trybuna*, the successor to Poland's Communist Party newspaper, declared, "In our opinion, a spy stays a spy. A traitor stays a traitor."

Another writer declared that Kuklinski had forced the Poles to confront a basic question: "In the face of total evil—that is Communism—could just about any activity directed against it be justified?"

In other words, having passed the secrets of the Polish communist state to American intelligence, did he in fact pass them to "us" or did he pass them to a foreign power, the power which we may like but which nevertheless remains foreign? Are "we" a community of nations and states that have fought against the evil of Communism for years, or are "we" a community of this society which has lived in our country and shared its history in the last fifty years? In other words, it is a question of identity: Who are we? Where are we?

Kuklinski is a deeply tragic figure, split internally in a way. He has been burdened with charges which are very difficult to repel. It may never be possible. Neither is it possible to give a short answer to a question—what was Poland during those 50 years?

Kuklinski refused to seek clemency or a pardon. He thought the Polish government should simply void his conviction and his sentence, along with all other political convictions from the Communist era.

The *Post* articles generated new political support for Kuklinski's case. In January 1993, a retired American diplomat, Richard Davies, who had served as ambassador to Poland from 1973 to 1978, began an energetic letter-writing campaign to persuade American officials to press for the clearing of Kuklinski's name. Davies found it incongruous that Poland, which wanted to join NATO, still considered Kuklinski a traitor. He wrote to members of Congress and other officials and received some sympathetic responses, but Kuklinski asked him to stop.

Writing to Davies on March 8, 1993, Kuklinski said his goal had been achieved: Poland was free. Although he saw no justification for the failure of Polish leaders to invalidate his sentence, he believed his rehabilitation had to result from initiatives of people and institutions in Poland. "It would be a great tragedy for me and a personal defeat," he wrote, "were the eventual postponement of my rehabilitation, even in the smallest degree, to complicate the efforts of Poland in its admission to NATO."

Davies ceased his campaign. But about a year later, on February 28, 1994, after a NATO summit in Brussels invited Poland and other former Soviet bloc countries to join a "Partnership for Peace" as a first step toward NATO membership, Davies sent a six-page letter to President Clinton.

"I hope you might call to the attention of President Walesa," he wrote "the grotesque irony of the fact that the one Pole who risked his life before 1989 to assist NATO remains officially a traitor and subject to incarceration, while the leaders of today's Poland pride themselves on their participation in NATO exercises and press for full membership in the organization."

On April 25, 1994, Davies received a form letter from the White House, which thanked him for "sharing your concern about human rights."

That same month, a legal adviser to Lech Walesa met privately with Kuklinski in Washington, telling him that he was still viewed as a traitor, and that only if he put forward a formal clemency request would the Polish president consider the issue. Kuklinski refused.

For Kuklinski, all issues related to his future became secondary when he and Hanka suffered a succession of devastating personal tragedies. In early January 1994, Bogdan, who had become an experienced sailor and professional diver, was lost at sea in a boating accident. Six months later, Waldek also died. Kuklinski and Hanka retreated in their grief.

In the spring of 1994, Jerzy Kozminski arrived in Washington as Poland's new ambassador to the United States. Kozminski, a slim man with brown hair, a short beard, and glasses, had served at high levels in the Polish government since 1989. An economist by training, he had been chief of staff of Deputy Prime Minister Leszek Balcerowicz, the architect of Poland's "shock therapy" economic reforms; then under-secretary of state under Prime Minister Hanna Suchocka; and finally first deputy foreign minister, confronting the question of Poland's entry into NATO. By the time President Walesa appointed him ambassador to the United States in May 1994, he had won the trust of many Polish leaders.

Kozminski knew that Poland had a number of obstacles to overcome before it could join NATO. Some, like democratic and economic reform, applied to all former Soviet bloc countries seeking to become members of the alliance. Others were specific to Poland, such as civilian control of the military, export controls on arms and technology, and Polish-Jewish relations. And there was the matter of the colonel.

Kozminski knew Poland had cleared two former ambassadors, one to the United States and the other to Japan, who had received death sentences for defecting after martial law. Kozminski concluded that if Poland truly wanted to be America's ally and strategic partner, Kuklinski's conviction and twenty-five-year sentence would be "a very strange dowry," as he put it.

The ambassador called Kuklinski, introduced himself, and said he wanted to open a line of communication. He also took up the matter with Brzezinski, who was by then based at the Center for Strategic and International Studies in Washington. Brzezinski made clear that in his view, Poland could hardly join NATO while Kuklinski still had a conviction on his record for his service to the United States. Indeed, Kuklinski had been the first Polish officer in NATO, Brzezinski pointed out. But Kozminski did not believe there was sufficient political will or imagination in Warsaw to act on the matter, particularly if Kuklinski refused to seek a pardon.

In December 1994, Kuklinski gave an interview to *Tygodnik Solidarnosc* (Solidarity Weekly), a newspaper in Poland that treated him unabashedly as a hero. Kuklinski spoke at length about his motivation. Near the conclusion, the interviewer asked, "You do not want to ask or appeal for anything. What do you expect from the Polish authorities?"

"I no longer expect anything," Kuklinski said, still consumed with grief over his sons' deaths.

Early in 1995, the acclaimed poet and moral voice of Poland, Zbigniew Herbert, called for Walesa to invalidate Kuklinski's conviction. "Kuklinski, risking his life, proved that Poland is an integral part of the West," Herbert wrote. "He cannot ask for parole because he is not guilty."

12

RETURN

THE DECADE-LONG DEBATE in Poland took a dramatic turn in March 1995 when the chairman of the Supreme Court of Poland called on the country's highest military court to conduct an extraordinary review of Kuklinski's case, saying he might "have acted out of higher necessity and for patriotic reasons."

There was speculation in the Polish news media that Kuklinski might travel to Poland later in the spring to attend a hearing in the matter. But in April, he released a statement to the Polish press saying he had no plans to seek a pardon or other review. "I am not guilty, and I do not feel any remorse," he said. "Everything I have done in my life I have done with Poland in mind."

The hearing was held May 25, 1995, in a white granite building on Nowowiejska Street. There was a sense of excitement as about seventy spectators and journalists crowded into a cramped courtroom on the second floor of the Court of Military Appeals in Warsaw. With its low ceiling and peeling paint, the courtroom was largely unchanged from Communist days, except for the new government's white eagle insignia that hung on the wall.

Krzysztof Piesiewicz, a prominent Polish lawyer, walked into the courtroom. Piesiewicz, who wore a flowing black robe, was also a well-known screenwriter (his movie credits included *Blue, White,* and *Red,* the trilogy directed by Krzysztof Kieslowski). But Piesiewicz, fifty, had made a name for himself defending Solidarity activists interned during martial law; he also represented the family of Father Jerzy Popieluszko, a popular Solidarity priest who was kidnapped and murdered in 1984 by the SB.

Piesiewicz was joined by two other lawyers working on Kuklinski's behalf—Jacek Taylor, who had defended Solidarity activists before Communist courts in the 1980s, and Piotr Dewinski, who had represented Kuklinski's interests in Poland for several years.

Piesiewicz had agreed to take on Kuklinski's case at the request of a friend, the editor-in-chief of *Solidarity Weekly.* He had never met or even talked to Kuklinski; he knew the case only from news accounts. He researched the military legal code under which Kuklinski had been charged and for two months studied the thick file of the government's investigation, which he was allowed to read on a confidential basis. When he finished his research, he pronounced the prosecution's case to be "rubbish." The file contained all sorts of papers that had no bearing on anything: lists of restaurants Kuklinski had gone to, furniture he bought, the make of his car.

As Piesiewicz saw it, Kuklinski had been convicted of violating the laws of the Polish People's Republic, as Poland was called in the Communist era. But the PPR had vanished along with Communist domination, and thus Kuklinski's case should logically also disappear.

As the hearing began, the five military judges took their seats. Each had served as an officer in the Communist era, and Piesiewicz suspected their loyalties still resided there. One judge, a navy commander, presented the charges and gave a short history of the case. He noted that Kuklinski's 1984 trial had never confirmed his cooperation with American intelligence.

The military prosecutor, Major Jaroslaw Cieplowski, suggested that the case against Kuklinski was strong, and that his betrayal had begun earlier than was previously known. The "charge of betrayal was undisputable," Cieplowski said.

Piesiewicz then rose. Calling the prosecutor's arguments "pure hypocrisy," he argued that Kuklinski's story did not begin with his decision to cooperate with the West but earlier. "Kuklinski's story starts back in 1944, when the new tragic history of Poland begins."

The lawyer addressed his client's motivations: "This courageous officer of the Polish Army understood that it is his duty to fight for the liberation and sovereignty of Poland," Piesiewicz said, adding that there was no indication Kuklinski had been motivated by money or had wanted to seek a better life elsewhere.

"Now, I ask—all those dachas, residences around Warsaw, what were they bought for? What money? Which intelligence service's money? Those who had and have them, which uniforms were they wearing?" Piesiewicz asked rhetorically, a clear reference to top Polish generals who had thrived in the days of communism and were still enjoying the fringe benefits.

"Please remember that his activity had a deeper sense," Piesiewicz said. "It was not just a delivery of documents and classified files. He operated conceptually—there was an idea behind his action. He was thinking about Poland, about [our] nation."

He noted that Kuklinski was charged under article 122 of the Polish Penal Code:

This code protected the People's Republic of Poland and its political interests. But today, we have a different Poland, the Republic. Back in the 1980s, Poland had a different constitution. And its political interests simply meant the lack of sovereignty. Poland after 1945 was not a sovereign country.

The crime, if we at all can call it a crime, simply does not exist today under the new amended constitution and Article 122 cannot be applied. We must then ask, in what kind of Poland are we living? ... Are we taking this change seriously? Or, is it another Polish illusion? Is our sovereignty today an illusion?

If Poland refused to accept its transformation, he said, then the Republic was merely "a pure continuation" of Communist Poland. Piesiewicz called for a complete vindication of Kuklinski.

After briefly recessing, the judges announced that they would lift Kuklinski's conviction and sentence, but ordered the case returned to military prosecutors for further investigation. The panel said the evidence presented before the military court in 1984 was "not convincing" and was insufficient to prove the crimes charged.

Outside the courthouse, Piesiewicz denounced the verdict. "I am not satisfied with the ruling." He asserted that the judges had abdicated their responsibility and ignored the central question. "What country are we living in?" he asked. "Do we have law or not?"

That night, Kuklinski called Piesiewicz and thanked him and the other lawyers. Piesiewicz said he was convinced the judges did not know what to do with the case.

In November 1995, Aleksander Kwasniewski, the presidential candidate of the Democratic Left Alliance, which had its roots in the former Communist Party, defeated Lech Walesa in an upset victory. With the unexpected result and other immediate controversies, Kuklinski's case receded temporarily, but in mid-1996, Ambassador Jerzy Kozminski raised the matter with Leszek Miller, a high-level official in the Polish government who was visiting the United States. The Kuklinski matter was an important issue on Poland's road to NATO, Kozminski said.

That summer, the military prosecutors in Warsaw announced they had dropped the arrest warrant for Kuklinski. But because he was still under investigation, the prosecutors said, he would be subject to arrest if he returned to Poland.

In January 1997, Leszek Miller, Poland's new minister of interior, called Ambassador Kozminski as he prepared to fly to Washington for his first official visit with the FBI and CIA. Miller told Kozminski that he expected the Kuklinski case might arise in his discussions. Miller had discussed the issue with President Kwasniewski in Poland, and they had agreed that a solution was necessary, but it would have to be fashioned within the Polish legal system.

A few weeks later, Miller visited Zbigniew Brzezinski in Washington and relayed Kwasniewski's position, saying there was no avoiding the fact that Kuklinski would have to submit himself to the Polish legal system. Miller and Brzezinski went back and forth on the subject, until Brzezinski said, "That's all well and good, but Kuklinski is not willing to submit himself to the Polish judicial process."

Brzezinski said he might be able to persuade Kuklinski to change his mind, but only under one condition. "I'd have to have some assurances from you," Brzezinski said.

Miller said he was confident in Poland's legal process, but no result could be guaranteed.

"That's not good enough," Brzezinski said. "We're talking about both a judicial process and political realities. I can deliver Kuklinski, but you have to deliver a constructive outcome, and you have to pledge yourself to it. If you do," Brzezinski added, "we have an agreement."

Miller finally gave Brzezinski the assurance he was looking for: He would obtain a complete vindication of Kuklinski. Brzezinski poured some cognac, and they shared a toast to a positive outcome.

Later, as Ambassador Kozminski drove with Miller to Dulles International Airport for his flight home, they agreed the matter should be resolved quickly. There was to be a NATO summit in Madrid that summer, where official invitations were to be issued to prospective candidates for NATO membership. The Kuklinski case should not become an impediment.

Brzezinski was aware that Kuklinski might balk at the deal, but later, when they spoke by phone, Kuklinski agreed to meet the prosecutors in Washington. He was sixty-six years old and felt it might be his only chance to have his name cleared during his lifetime. "I wanted to witness this moment," he said.

Over the next few weeks, Brzezinski, Miller, and Kozminski

worked out detailed arrangements for the meetings, which would take place in Brzezinski's office. Brzezinski insisted that the prosecutors treat Kuklinski with respect and address him as "Colonel."

Meanwhile, in late February 1997, unaware of the efforts being made on Kuklinski's behalf, former U.S. Ambassador Richard Davies published an essay in the *Washington Times* charging that the administration had relegated Kuklinski "to the memory hole." He wrote, "We owe it to Col. Kuklinski to help him get back his good name and enable him, without fear of arrest and imprisonment, to visit the homeland he served so valiantly."

Daniel Fried, a senior White House aide who had previously served in the embassy in Warsaw as a political officer, had given the Kuklinski issue much thought. Fried was special assistant to President Clinton and senior director on the National Security Council for central and eastern Europe. He was deeply involved in the effort to expand NATO and knew Brzezinski was pushing for a resolution of Kuklinski's case. Fried agreed Kuklinski should be exonerated, but felt that too much pressure by the U.S. government could be counterproductive and appear arrogant. The case raised the same question other honorable Poles had faced for hundreds of years as the country's borders had shifted: Does one serve the occupying power because it has a Polish flag and wait for a better time? Or does one resist? Fried understood why Polish officers had difficulty embracing Kuklinski's actions as patriotic, because of what that suggested about their decisions not to collaborate with the West. But Fried also believed honest Poles could differ about how to serve one's country, and the issue ultimately had to be worked out by the Poles. An ultimatum by the U.S. government would not help Kuklinski. Brzezinski's unofficial efforts seemed to be the best route, Fried felt, and he hoped the case might evolve from being a divisive issue in Poland to one of national reconciliation.

Over the next few weeks, Ambassador Kozminski stayed in touch with Miller in Warsaw and Brzezinski in Washington, working out the details of the interrogation of Kuklinski. Their efforts resembled a clandestine operation: Kozminski, fearing that a leak in Warsaw about their activities could doom their undertaking, put nothing in writing in the official cables he sent home. Instead, he spoke with Miller by phone, and the two men used code words such as "our friend" for Kuklinski, "the travelers" for the prosecutors, "head" for President Kwasniewski, and "the professor" for Brzezinski.

On March 10, 1997, Ambassador Kozminski gave a talk on Poland and NATO to a lunch meeting of the Association of Former Intelligence Officers in Fort Myer, Virginia. During a question-and-answer session, a retired CIA officer asked the ambassador when Poland would resolve Kuklinski's case.

Saying he was speaking only for himself, Kozminski offered cautious optimism. Afterward, the retired officer took Kozminski aside and asked more bluntly whether the Polish government had the resolve to confront the issue.

The questioner was David Forden. He introduced himself to Kozminski, and they discussed the case further. In their private conversation, Kozminski expressed more confidence about the likelihood of progress. Forden thanked him and said he would take Kozminski's statements as a pledge that the ambassador would continue to work on Kuklinski's behalf.

Forden, also then sixty-six years old, was no longer in the CIA. He and Aurelia had spent four years in Greece, after which Forden retired in 1988. He had been with the CIA for thirty-five years.

Within weeks of meeting Ambassador Kozminski, Forden learned from Kuklinski about the coming visit of the Polish prosecutors. He also learned that the CIA was not providing security. Forden was concerned, because it would be the first time since Kuklinski's exfiltration that Polish officials would know the colonel's precise location in the United States. Forden called another retired officer, Jack Platt, who had served with the agency in Europe and Asia. They decided to devise their own rudimentary security plan. They scouted the K Street building where Brzezinski's offices were located. They found a stocky six-foot retired FBI agent, whose forearms seemed as large as Platt's thighs, to serve as a bodyguard for Kuklinski. Forden and Aurelia (who had learned surveillance detection techniques during their four-year tour in Greece) and Platt's daughter Michelle, a private investigator, would remain on the street. They would drive Kuklinski to and from the meetings, ensure that he entered and left the building through a different door each day, and watch for suspicious activity, such as cars that might be parked with their engines running.

Ambassador Kozminski, following the plan, had kept the prosecutors' visit secret from even his Polish Embassy colleagues. On Sunday, April 20, he drove to Dulles Airport to pick up the prosecutors and took them for a drink at the Ritz-Carlton hotel in Washington's Embassy Row neighborhood. The prosecutors, Major Bogdan Wlodarczyk and Captain Jerzy Kwiecinski, were polite but reserved. Despite his anxiety, Kozminski was excited—he had never met the colonel.

Shortly before 4:00 P.M. on Monday, April 21, 1997, Kuklinski arrived at Brzezinski's office, accompanied by an elderly Polish-American lawyer and the retired FBI agent, who bustled around and maintained radio contact with the rest of the security team outside. Brzezinski escorted them straight to a sixth-floor seminar room and planted the retired FBI agent outside the door. Brzezinski then went to his office, where he met Ambassador Kozminski and the two prosecutors, Major Wlodarczyk and Captain Kwiecinski.

The prosecutors seemed nervous and stiff. As they shook hands with Brzezinski, Captain Kwiecinski clicked his heels. Before escorting them to the seminar room, Brzezinski discussed with them the significance of the proceedings. "They nodded their heads but they were not very communicative, each of them conveying a great deal of unease," Brzezinski wrote in notes he kept of the session.

The group convened in the seminar room, and introductions were made. Captain Kwiecinski shook Kuklinski's hand, clicked his heels again, and bowed his head. As promised, he and the other prosecutor addressed Kuklinski as "Colonel." Kozminski and Brzezinski, as the official witnesses to the proceeding, sat at opposite ends of a large table. Kuklinski and his lawyer sat on one side, facing the prosecutors on the other.

After a few words of introduction from Ambassador Kozminski, Major Wlodarczyk began to read the formal allegations—desertion and flight and transmitting classified information to NATO. Kuklinski sat impassively as the prosecutor reviewed the earlier 1984 trial, the conviction, the reduction of Kuklinski's death sentence to twenty-five years, and the 1995 military appeals court decision voiding the conviction and sending the case back for more investigation.

Major Wlodarczyk said that for the previous accusations to be invalidated permanently, Kuklinski would have to offer evidence and testimony that he had acted out of higher necessity. To Ambassador Kozminski, the notion of Kuklinski's acting out of "higher necessity," a concept in Polish law, seemed a reasonable way to allow him to be exonerated.

The two prosecutors stressed that they had been required to review the history of the case in order to make the proceedings formal. They continued, one interrupting the other, as they emphasized that the procedure was voluntary, that Kuklinski did not have to answer all their questions, and if he decided to remain silent, that would not be held against him. Then Captain Kwiecinski sighed loudly, as if he was embarrassed to have to explain this to Kuklinski.

They asked Kuklinski to sign a document acknowledging that he was willing to go forward with the interrogation. Kuklinski, feeling a surge of disgust, was hesitant at first, but went ahead and signed.

At that moment, Major Wlodarczyk, smiling broadly, handed Kuklinski a piece of paper that said the Ministry of Defense had restored his rank as colonel and considered him to be a colonel in retirement.

Kuklinski appeared surprised and then relaxed. He told the prosecutors that he assumed they would be objective, and that he wanted the issue resolved.

The prosecutors assured Kuklinski that neither of them had participated in the earlier trial or the investigation of him, nor were they
involved in the martial-law crackdown. Kuklinski said he would answer
any question, but he considered the allegations to be "repulsive."

At 5:00 P.M., the formal interrogation began with a series of questions. They asked for his current employment. Before Kuklinski could
respond, the major spoke up. "If you do not mind, we will simply say
that you are 'retired.'"

Brzezinski continued to take careful notes. At one point, he
observed, both prosecutors burst into laughter, as the questionnaire
asked whether Kuklinski was a Communist Party member. With some
embarrassment, the prosecutors explained they were using old ques-
tionnaires. Because of costs, the government had not printed new ones.
According to Brzezinski's notes:

Kuklinski was then asked formally whether he wishes to offer any
explanations. He responded by saying yes, and addressed first the
question of "desertion." He said that his departure was not made
by his free choice, but he was compelled by circumstances. He
wanted to deprive the regime of the opportunity to put him on
trial, and to use him in order also to embarrass the Solidarity
movement, which he felt would have been the case had he been
arrested and placed publicly on trial.

With respect to the more important accusation, he wishes to
stress that Poland was dominated by an imperial Soviet Union, the
Soviet Union subordinated the Polish armed forces to itself; the
world was divided and Poland was not given the opportunity to
choose freely its own place in a divided world. But the Polish
nation never abandoned its aspiration for freedom. Polish soldiers
always desired independence from Soviet command, and his
efforts involved an attempt to establish some connection between
the Polish Army and the U.S. Army.

Kuklinski then offered a detailed description of Moscow's war plans
for Europe and how they posed "a major threat to Poland's survival."

He described the role of the Second Strategic Echelon. "The Soviets were calculating that any nuclear counterattacks by the West against the second echelon of the Soviet forces would occur on Polish soil," Kuklinski explained. He said he was convinced that "Poland would perish" in such a sequence of events. He explained that other officers on the General Staff shared his view, but had no idea what to do. He mentioned his long-ago conversation with General Boleslaw Chocha, when he had suggested a "direct approach should be made to the American side regarding that danger and the Polish concerns over it."

The meetings resumed the next day at 8:10 A.M. Kuklinski recalled how he had first contacted the United States, sending his letter to the American military attaché in Bonn and asking to meet with a colonel of similar rank. In the first meetings, he had believed he was talking with American Army officers. He had told them he represented a group of about ten Polish officers who shared his views about the need to establish communication with the West in order to prevent the outbreak of war in Europe, although none was aware of his decision to reach out to the Americans. "These officers feel that Poland did not choose the Warsaw Pact, that Poland was not independent, and that they should do what can be done for Poland," Kuklinski said, according to Brzezinski's notes. "If the Warsaw Pact was attacked by the West, Poland would defend itself within the Warsaw Pact, but it was not in Poland's interest to participate in an aggression against the West."

Kuklinski criticized the West's reliance on nuclear deterrence, which had placed Poland in such jeopardy. He explained how he had hoped some form of cooperation could be secretly negotiated between the Poles and the American Army, perhaps to "exclude Poland's participation from the very beginning of the war, or to act jointly to disorganize and paralyze the Soviet strategic operation, particularly the Second Strategic Echelon and to disrupt its system of command, once war has broken out," Brzezinski wrote.

Kuklinski said that when he had proposed his "conspiracy," the Americans had not agreed to it, saying the "best Polish officers" would lose their lives. The Americans had wanted to work with him exclusively, Kuklinski said. He described how he had shown up at the first covert meeting in Warsaw in full uniform, appalling his American contact, who asked that he dress less conspicuously the next time.

He detailed the intelligence he had provided the Americans, from war plans to the Soviet command-and-control systems in the Warsaw Pact in a time of war to details of the secret Soviet command bunkers. He was upset at criticism that he had somehow subverted the Polish Army through his actions. He said he wanted the Polish Army "to be as strong as possible so that it could assert itself when the need arose." He said he did not view the U.S. Army as Poland's enemy. "He wanted Poland to be neutral or pro-USA," Brzezinski noted.

The meetings in Brzezinski's office continued through the week, with Kuklinski answering questions about the planned Soviet invasion in 1980 and the martial-law preparations in 1981. Brzezinski at one point spoke; he emphasized the geopolitical conditions of the 1970s, "stressing that the Soviet Union was seeking to attain strategic superiority, and how important the information that Kuklinski provided was in offsetting that."

Over the course of the meetings, the prosecutors grew more cordial, and Brzezinski sensed a growing affinity for Kuklinski. After the meetings ended, Ambassador Kozminski told Brzezinski that he had not fully grasped the heroic dimension of Kuklinski's actions. Brzezinski was also deeply moved, particularly by one of Kuklinski's final comments.

"Kuklinski told the Polish officers that even if he is fully rehabilitated, his life will not change in any significant degree, that he realizes that he has nothing to return to in Poland, and his life has been altered forever," Brzezinski noted. "He made no reference, but I think there was also an allusion here, to the fact that he lost his two sons—and he probably would not have lost them if he had not undertaken the task which he shouldered."

As for Kuklinski, he says he has asked himself many times about the price he and his family paid for his decision to reach out to the West.

★

The months passed without word from the Polish government, and Ambassador Kozminski grew concerned. He knew Miller was advocating on Kuklinski's behalf in Warsaw, and there had also been some important if isolated gestures of support for Kuklinski in Poland. In May, Kuklinski learned he had been named "Honorary Citizen of the Royal City of Krakow." The city council had invited him to return to Poland to accept his award. Gdansk followed with a similar invitation.

In June 1997, when Ambassador Kozminski returned to Poland for meetings in advance of the Madrid NATO summit, he went to see Miller to review the situation. He also met with President Kwasniewski and reiterated his view that the matter had to be resolved promptly.

On July 8 and 9, President Kwasniewski led a delegation of Polish officials to Madrid for the NATO summit, at which Poland, Hungary, and the Czech Republic were formally invited to join the alliance. On July 10, President Clinton flew from Madrid to Warsaw, where he received an enthusiastic welcome from more than ten thousand cheering Poles as he stood with President Kwasniewski in Castle Square.

Clinton also visited the Presidential Palace, where he and his aide, Daniel Fried, were led by President Kwasniewski and Ambassador Kozminski onto a flagstone terrace that overlooked a garden.

The two presidents and their aides sat at a table for about twenty minutes and discussed several issues too sensitive to include in any public agenda. One was Kuklinski. Clinton said he wanted to thank the Polish president for his involvement in resolving the matter. Clinton did not ask for anything; his expression of gratitude was intended to send its own message.

Later in the month, at the request of the White House, Brzezinski met separately with Miller and Kwasniewski in Poland, pressing them to move more forcefully in resolving the Kuklinski matter, which Brzezinski felt was stalling. Kwasniewski made clear there was still opposition at the highest levels of the Polish government, including the Justice Ministry and the chief military prosecutor's office. But he agreed to inject himself more actively in the case.

Around Labor Day, Ambassador Kozminski received a call from the Polish justice minister, who said Kuklinski would be exonerated on grounds that he had acted out of "higher necessity." The decision was read to Kuklinski in Brzezinski's office, and he was told he was free to return to Poland without fear of arrest. The Polish military prosecutor's office revealed the decision publicly on September 22.

The announcement drew scorn from Kuklinski's critics. In October, about thirty retired generals released a letter calling the justification of Kuklinski's actions "an accusation against us." That same month, Polish military prosecutor Piotr Daniluk said in an interview with *Gazeta Wyborcza*, the largest and most influential newspaper in Poland, that Kuklinski had not acted for a higher purpose but rather for money.

At a conference just outside of Warsaw in November, Marshal Victor Kulikov, the former Warsaw Pact commander, disparaged Kuklinski as a traitor "who gave all our military plans to the enemy," and suggested that his intelligence value to the United States had been exaggerated. Responding a few minutes later, Brzezinski told Kulikov that thanks in particular to Kuklinski's intelligence, the entire Soviet command, including Kulikov, would have been dead within three hours of a Soviet attack on NATO. "Kulikov was stunned, and simply gulped," Brzezinski recalled.

In December, the *Los Angeles Times* quoted Jaruzelski as citing the thousands of other officers who had served in the Polish Army. "If you come to the conclusion that Kuklinski's act was the act of a hero—that he was helping Poland—then it's logical to ask: Are all the others traitors?"

Shortly after the decision, Kuklinski issued a short statement in which he said he accepted the decision with some relief but that it had "symbolic rather than practical meaning for me. I thank God for letting me live to see this moment." In interviews in the United States and Poland, he has repeatedly denied being blackmailed or motivated by money when he reached out to the United States. Kuklinski has also since said that during his nine years of clandestine activity, he received only limited sums of money from the Americans for operational expenses, along with communications and technical equipment like transmitters, cameras, film, and concealment devices.

In an interview with Newsweek's Andrew Nagorski in October 1997, Kuklinski said that he hoped someday to return to Poland, in part to thank the people of Krakow for inviting him to accept honorary citizenship, but that he did not expect to remain in public view. "I'd like to retreat into the shadows," he said.

Forden was pleased at Kuklinski's news, but he was still bothered by the compromise of the Gull operation. It had been sixteen years since General Skalski cited "Rome sources" as the basis for the information about the leak that had forced Kuklinski to flee Poland. Forden knew the Gull operation had never involved Rome. After the exfiltration, CIA counterintelligence was asked to try to identify the meaning of "Rome sources" and to trace the leak. The FBI was also consulted. But no answers were found.

In 1992, Forden found some tantalizing clues: The popular Italian weekly magazine Panorama published an interview with Boris Solomatin, the KGB Rezident in Rome in the period 1976–1982. Asked about his sources, the Soviet spymaster said he had "four men of gold." He added, "We could get everything we wanted." One of those men, he claimed, was an important spy in the Vatican. That same year, Forden also read an article in Time magazine by Carl Bernstein that described a secret alliance between CIA director Casey and Pope John Paul II to support Solidarity, including trips to the Vatican and the sharing of intelligence.

Forden began to wonder whether Casey or other U.S. officials had revealed too much in their secret dealings with the Vatican. A 1996 book by Bernstein and Italian journalist Marco Politi seemed to confirm his fears about a Vatican connection. The book suggested that a short time after Kuklinski provided the Americans with Poland's martial-law plans in August 1981, the pope was told by Washington of Kuklinski's information.

Then Forden learned that his friend Jack Platt, who had helped with security during Kuklinski's meetings with the Polish prosecutors, had gotten to know Solomatin, who was now almost eighty, through his legitimate business dealings. (Platt's company worked with former KGB operatives to provide security for visiting American businessmen and to investigate Russian companies to screen out those with links to organized crime.)

Platt knew Solomatin as a chain-smoker with a full head of hair, bushy eyebrows, and often bloodshot eyes. Solomatin could be charming and clever as he rattled off his war stories, but Platt suspected the old KGB man was dismayed that he had given his life to a cause that no longer had meaning.

In fall of 1997, Platt was making another trip to Moscow for business. Forden asked him to visit Solomatin and gave him some background notes, citing the *Panorama* interview, the book on the Pope, and a list of questions for Solomatin about his sources in Rome. Was his "spy" in the Vatican the key to understanding the "Rome sources" mystery? Many years had passed, and Forden hoped Platt might be able to extract an answer.

In Moscow, Platt met Solomatin over drinks and caviar. Solomatin laughed when Platt asked about his comments to *Panorama*. "I was joking around with these journalists," Solomatin said, adding that it was ridiculous to think he would actually reveal his sources. Solomatin claimed that what he had meant in the interview was that all an intelligence officer needed to be successful were several well-placed sources. Solomatin said he had heard of Kuklinski, but knew nothing of how Moscow had learned of the leak of the martial-law plans.

Platt told Forden when he returned from Moscow that they were no closer to the truth than before.

"Do you believe him?" Forden asked Platt.

"I do," Platt replied. He knew Solomatin might have lied to him or might have lied to *Panorama*. But he also knew no good case officer ever betrayed a source. That was a vow they all made, and their word had to be good. The answer would probably die with Solomatin, Platt believed. Forden realized he would have to reconcile himself to living with the mystery.

On February 28, 1998, Kuklinski was invited to the Polish Embassy on Sixteenth Street in Washington for a celebration organized by the Polish-American Congress commemorating the 252nd anniversary of the birth of Kosciuszko, the Polish hero in America's Revolutionary War, who has long been a symbol of the friendship between America and Poland. Kuklinski, the guest of honor, was making his first visit to the embassy. He shared a poignant moment with Ambassador Kozminski, who offered him a new Polish passport. Kozminski then introduced him to the hundreds of admirers who were attending the festivities.

The next month, Kozminski received a letter from Forden, who recalled their conversation one year earlier at the luncheon in Virginia during which Kozminski had expressed optimism about resolving Kuklinski's case.

"I was skeptical," Forden admitted in his letter. "You were right!" He thanked Kozminski for his "wise and courageous effort."

On Monday, April 27, 1998, the week Congress was to approve Poland's membership in NATO, Kuklinski flew to Warsaw on a Polish airline for a visit that took him to six Polish cities over ten days. Kuklinski was overwhelmed with emotion. During the flight, a Polish television reporter interviewed him. "It's hard for me to breathe," Kuklinski told the reporter.

"If I could find a moment, I'd like to shave off my beard, change my appearance completely so as to be unrecognizable, and walk along Marszalkowska [Street], Nowy Swiat, Krakowskie Przedmiescie [in Warsaw city center], and to the Old Town—that would be fantastic. But it's probably impossible."

Asked what he hoped to see during his visit, he said he admired the rhododendrons and azaleas that bloomed in the United States in springtime. In Poland, he said, his favorite flower was the lilac. "I love this time of year," he said, "and I want to see lilacs, and carry some to the grave of my mother."

After the plane landed in Warsaw, a SWAT team of security officers sent by the Polish prime minister boarded the airplane, saluted, and told Kuklinski they were there to protect him. They whisked him through a private exit to avoid the press and drove him to the residence of the Polish prime minister, Jerzy Buzek. There, Kuklinski had lunch with Buzek, his wife, and closest aides, after which both men stepped before a crowd of more than 100 reporters. Buzek told the reporters Kuklinski had acted heroically in a time of great peril for Poland. "We can presume that these decisions saved our country from bloodshed," he said.

Kuklinski became emotional. "My 25-year journey to a free Poland is over," he said. "Today I feel that freedom. I am counting on your sensitivity, on your allowing me to see this country as I wanted."

Asked when he would return to Poland permanently, he replied, "I don't want to leave here at all."

Afterward, Kuklinski was driven to the cemetery in Rembertow, where his mother was buried and where, on her headstone, his father's name was also engraved. As the car pulled up, Kuklinski could see a crowd of well-wishers near the gate, some carrying small bunches of lilacs. He placed some of the flowers on his mother's stone.

On his first night in Warsaw, Kuklinski was invited for dinner to the apartment of Roman and Barbara Barszcz, where he and Hanka had spent their last evening in Warsaw in 1981. One guest, a representative from the coal-mining region of Katowice, gave Kuklinski a brick from a wall that a Polish tank had demolished in an attack in a Silesian coal mine on the first day of martial law.

The next day, Kuklinski flew to Krakow, where he spent the night in a VIP apartment in the Wawel Royal Castle. He awoke the next morning, April 29, to a glorious sunny day. At noon, a trumpet blared in the city council chamber to announce the beginning of a gala session. Guests were ushered through rigorous security. A choir sang hymns, and the audience broke into loud applause as the city's mayor bestowed honorary citizenship on Kuklinski.

He then delivered an address that was widely anticipated and broadcast live on national radio, saying in part:

> I never doubted that I would return to a free Poland, to the land of my ancestors, of my childhood, adult life, and action which was devoted to that Poland. I did not think, however, that the road to the homeland, so rough and long, would lead in the end through the Royal City, which ennobles truly outstanding people by its heritage. I never aimed, nor do I now aim, so high.
>
> I consider myself to be an ordinary soldier of the Republic, who did not do anything beyond the sacred duty of serving one's homeland in need. What perhaps differentiates me from the enormous number of people involved in the historic transformations of Poland and Europe is the specific nature of the mission I undertook and the [consequences it caused.] It is, therefore, still hard for me to believe that everything I am experiencing at the moment is really happening here in Krakow, and not in my dreams about Poland; that the Republic is today a sovereign state and Poles can unrestrainedly not only talk about their struggles against the evil empire, but honor so highly one of the participants in those struggles, which by some decree of fate, is me today.

There was enthusiastic applause as Kuklinski thanked his hosts, calling honorary citizenship not only "the highest distinction which I could receive in my lifetime," but an unequivocal statement to restore "the respect which was taken away from me and my good name." He thanked all who had supported him, a list he said was too long to recite. But there was an exception. "I cannot fail to thank," he said, "the greatest living Polish poet, Zbigniew Herbert, whose open letter to the former president of the Republic [Walesa] I took as an act of moral cleansing of my name."

Kuklinski said he hoped someday the Polish people would understand his "true goals, intentions, and motivation" and would be able
"to acquaint itself with the facts and documents prepared in those
years by the evil empire" for a "war of liberation" in Europe.

Kuklinski said the white and red banners of Solidarity had shaken
the Polish foundation of the Communist empire, but the Soviet "military challenges in Europe and the world could only be met by the
defensive alliance of the free world." NATO had to be made aware of
the threats and react appropriately.

"I cannot tell you how effective or even how helpful the [secret]
mission in which I—as a Pole and a soldier—had the honor and privilege to take part, was. I profoundly believe, however, that it was in the
deepest interests of a homeland that was enslaved and subordinated to
the imperial aims of the Soviet Union, and that it took the road leading Poland to freedom, and never against."

Kuklinski said his mission never would have succeeded without the
Americans, but it was not an American idea; it was an idea that crystal-
lized in Poland, in the General Staff, in the operations directorate,
where he and other officers pushed for a reversal of the military's "suicidal offensive concepts." But they had been ignored. Only later did he
start to consider whether there was any other way out, to develop a
plan that would protect Poland from the potential holocaust that
threatened it.

The 1968 Czech invasion made it clear, he continued, that reform of
the Soviet war machine would not happen. He said many Polish officers
recognized that the Soviet Union, "which attacked Poland in collusion
with Hitler and which divided up the Polish spoils in collusion with
Hitler, which was weighed down with the crimes of the mass deporta-
tion of the Polish population, Katyn, and the betrayal of the Warsaw
Uprising, was not an ally but an oppressor who had enslaved Poland,
[and] imposed a vassal government and a communist system on it."

The army's role in the crushing of the Czech revolution and in the
massacre of striking workers on the Polish coast in 1970 settled his
conversion, he said, "from enigmatic words and desires to deeds."

He described his "desperate attempt to enter into operational military cooperation with the United States." He explained how he had first contacted the Americans and how they rejected his proposal of a conspiracy between Poland and the West.

"In that way, I remained on the field of battle alone—in the minds of a certain part of Polish society still someone without honor—who acted to the detriment of Poland. I believe that history will correct this at some time."

Kuklinski noted he had worn the uniform of a Polish soldier for thirty-four years with pride, but he did not condemn officers who had made other choices. "I not only never placed the mission I had undertaken in opposition to the selfless service of my former comrades in arms," he said, "but I never placed it higher either.

"Collective opposition to Soviet hegemony in the army was impossible and pointless. There were among us people who saw in servility towards the Soviet Union their road to a career and to promotion. In the great majority, it was however a deeply patriotic army, and a cadre concerned about the security and the fate of our state."

Kuklinski recalled the motto—"Love demands sacrifice"—embroidered by the women of Vilnius on the banner that was sent through the underground during World War II to the Polish Airborne Division in Britain. He said that after he joined the army and his faith and beliefs "began to be taken away from me, I added one more word to that motto: Love demands sacrifice and loyalty—loyalty to one God, and to one, the only homeland, Poland." There was sustained applause.

"Today's beautiful ceremony," Kuklinski concluded, "the honorary citizenship of the Royal City of Krakow—[a city] which appeared to me since childhood as the heart and soul of Poland—confirms my belief that it was the right choice."

Thunderous applause and cheers erupted. In the evening, Kuklinski appeared before hundreds of students and professors at the historic Jagiellonian University, and the next day, he visited Market Square in Krakow, where he placed a flower at the site where Tadeusz Kosciuszko

---

took the oath as leader of the 1794 uprising against Russia. He also visited the Nowa Huta steel mill, site of an important Solidarity strike in 1981.

That evening, Kuklinski was among the audience of about 800 people that attended a concert in his honor at the philharmonic hall in Krakow. A young girl handed him a bouquet of red and white flowers, and the music of Chopin filled the auditorium. An actor in a black suit offered a reading of a poem by Zbigniew Herbert called "Report from the Besieged City," which was written after the 1981 martial-law crackdown.

> Too old to carry arms and fight like the others—
>
> they graciously gave me the inferior role of chronicler
> I record—I don't know for whom—the history of the siege
>
> I am supposed to be exact but I don't know when the invasion began
> two hundred years ago in December in September perhaps yesterday at dawn
> everyone here suffers from a loss of the sense of time . . .

The stirring words echoed through the hall as the actor concluded,

> cemeteries grow larger the number of defenders is smaller
> yet the defense continues it will continue to the end
> and if the City falls but a single man escapes
> he will carry the City within himself on the roads of exile
> he will be the city
> we look in the face of hunger the face of fire face of death
> worst of all—the face of betrayal
>
> and only our dreams have not been humiliated.

The next day, April 30, the U.S. Senate voted 80-19 to approve Poland's entry into NATO. Ambassador Kozminski, who watched the vote in the Senate chamber, later spoke by phone with Kuklinski, who offered his congratulations.

Over the following days, as Kuklinski traveled around Poland, he received plaques and medals, miner's hats, swords, postage stamps produced in the underground, and flowers. On Friday, May 1, the former Communist holiday in Poland, Kuklinski was taken by helicopter to a mountain near Zakopane. Accompanied by his bodyguards, he hiked down, greeting hundreds of tourists who asked for his autograph and posed with him for photographs.

On Saturday, Kuklinski flew to Katowice, a major industrial and mining center in Silesia in southern Poland where riot police had killed nine striking miners at the Wujek colliery in the early days of martial law. At the airport, an orchestra played folk melodies, and Kuklinski was given a tray of bread and salt, a traditional Polish welcome. On May 3 he received honorary citizenship from the Gdansk city council. A Home Army cross was pinned on his chest, and he was given a wooden armchair engraved with his name.

At noon he walked with many ceremony attendees to the huge St. Mary's Cathedral, where thousands were attending mass. To his surprise, the Catholic bishop, Tadeusz Goclowski, introduced him to the congregation. The crowd began to sing, "May he live 100 years," and "Stay with us."

Kuklinski's visit continued to spur a debate about patriotism and duty. On May 4 he told 500 students and professors at Gdansk University that he had decided he could not blindly obey Jaruzelski, and that loyalty to superiors did not rank higher than loyalty to his country. "Soldiers are not like the Mafia," he said. "They can refuse to obey commanding officers who are disloyal to their country."

Jaruzelski and other critics attacked Kuklinski on radio and television. Adam Michnik, editor of *Gazeta Wyborcza*, who had been imprisoned by Jaruzelski during martial law, wrote that Kuklinski should not be seen as a hero. "If this entire hullabaloo surrounding Kuklinski's visit is to signify that the attitude to Kuklinski and the American Special Services is to be a litmus test of patriotic Poles, then that will be the pitiful finale to the Polish dream of freedom."

On Wednesday, May 6, back in Warsaw, Kuklinski unveiled a monument to Polish officers massacred by the Soviets at Katyn. Thousands of people attended, including families of the murdered officers and an honor guard of firemen. That evening, Kuklinski paid a quiet visit to Zbigniew Herbert, who at age seventy-three was severely ill. (Herbert died three months later.)

The next day, after placing flowers at the Tomb of the Unknown Soldier, Kuklinski boarded a flight to Chicago. He would never forget the rousing welcome he had received in Poland, but he also remembered the last time he had made this flight westward seventeen years earlier. *The wind turned over only one page, and your city disappeared,* Waldek had written. Kuklinski understood what his son had meant, his feeling of loss and displacement. In deciding to cooperate with the West, Kuklinski at least knew he had made a choice freely, understanding the risks. *I have boundless faith in the rightness of what I am doing,* he once had written to Daniel. He did not regret his boldness. But his family had known nothing of his aspirations or his convictions, and when they did learn, they had accompanied him out of sheer faith. *I will follow you anywhere,* Bogdan had said. *We must try,* Hanka had insisted. Maybe now, Kuklinski thought, his name would find its place.

In recent years, Kuklinski has lived quietly in the United States, making infrequent public appearances, mostly to groups of Polish veterans. In November 1999, the George Bush School of Government and Public Service at Texas A&M University held a three-day conference on intelligence and the end of the Cold War. The session concluded with a memorial service, at which CIA Director George Tenet spoke of agency officers who had fallen in the line of duty. He noted that each was represented by a gold star on the granite wall in the agency's front lobby.

Tenet also cited another group of "Cold War heroes," the

men and women from behind the Iron Curtain who helped us.... They were like most of their countrymen, ordinary people who dearly loved their families and their native lands, and who wanted

to see a better future for them. But these courageous men and
women were extraordinary because they chose to act. They chose
to work for the West. Their honor and their convictions gave them
the fortitude to follow their conscience down a very lonely path
into mortal danger.

Many had not lived to see "that joyous day dawn."

Tenet then introduced Kuklinski and suggested that his mission
was emblematic of the kinds of clandestine operations that were pursued throughout the Cold War. Kuklinski, he said, was "a man who
risked great danger to work for us, and who by the grace of God survived." Tenet said it was because of "the bravery and sacrifice of patriots like Colonel Ryszard Kuklinski that his own native Poland and the
other once-captive nations of Central and Eastern Europe and the former Soviet Union are now free."

Kuklinski stepped forward. "I am deeply honored," he told the
crowd, "to represent my many anonymous comrades who served on
both sides of the front line. I am pleased that our long, hard struggle
has brought peace, freedom, and democracy, not only to my country,
but to many other people as well."

Kuklinski was later escorted to a waiting car, which took him to
the airport and the flight back to the neighborhood where he and
Hanka still live private lives under assumed identities.

POSTSCRIPT

Because of the strict compartmentalization of information in the CIA, until recent years a number of the CIA officers involved in the early stages of the Kuklinski operation had no idea how it had turned out.

John Dimmer, the chief of Bonn Station who had received Kuklinski's original letter and helped coordinate the first meetings, retired shortly afterward and did not know that the case became one of the most significant in CIA history. He now lives in retirement in rural Maine.

Colonel Henry, the avuncular officer who participated in the early meetings with Kuklinski, retired and never saw Kuklinski again. He died in the early 1990s.

Walter Lang, who accompanied Colonel Henry in the first meeting in 1972, has retired, and he occasionally returns to the CIA to discuss the case with young officers.

David Blee, the Soviet Division chief who first approved the Gull operation, retired in 1985 and died fifteen years later at his home in Bethesda, Maryland.

Tom Ryan, who made the drive with his wife Lucille from Berlin to Warsaw to help move Kuklinski out of Poland, has retired.

Sue Burggraf, who coordinated the exfiltration from Warsaw, has also retired and now works in charitable activities around Washington, D.C., such as library book sales and Meals on Wheels.

Stanley Patkowski, the original Gull operation translator, has died. Victor Kliss, his successor, retired and stayed in touch with Kuklinski until Kliss's death in late 2003.

Ted Gilbertson, who found Kuklinski's message in the snow in 1980, recently retired from the CIA. Aris Pappas, the martial-law analyst, retired in 2003 after twenty-eight years with the agency.

Jerzy Kozminski completed his tenure as ambassador in 2000 and is now president of the Polish-American Freedom Foundation. Leszek Miller became Poland's prime minister in 2001, a post he held until 2004.

Iza and Bogdan were married for about seven years, but the relationship ultimately failed, and they were divorced. Iza works today as a research scientist in New England. Bogdan began a new relationship with an American woman of Polish birth, which lasted until he died.

Ryszard and Hanka Kuklinski chose to remain in the United States, which they considered their home. After traveling to Poland in 1998, Kuklinski made several more visits, and he was greeted warmly each time. On one trip in the fall of 2003, he ventured into the streets of Warsaw for the first time without security, encountering smiles and shaking the hands of surprised passersby who recognized him.

David and Aurelia Forden were married for over nineteen years. In September 2003, five weeks after they moved into a new home outside Washington, Aurelia died of cancer. David still lives there, and he and Kuklinski remained close friends.

On February 11, 2004, several days after suffering a massive stroke, Ryszard Kuklinski died. He was seventy-three years old.

Kuklinski's ashes, and those of his son Waldek, were flown to Poland, and on June 19, they were buried in the historic Powazki military cemetery in Warsaw. The ceremony was attended by Kuklinski's widow, Hanka, and thousands of Poles, including war veterans, an Army honor guard, former prime ministers, and the U.S. ambassador, Christopher Hill. The Polish government sent no official representative.

In the months that followed, thousands of people visited the grave site, leaving candles and flowers.

AUTHOR'S NOTES

Bibliographical Note

This book does not attempt to offer a history of Poland or of the Solidarity period. But as I learned about the era, I benefited from a number of books and other works. These included: Tina Rosenberg's *The Haunted Land* (New York: Random House, 1995); Douglas J. MacEachin's *U.S. Intelligence and the Confrontation in Poland, 1980-1981* (University Park, Pa.: Penn State Press, 2002); Robert M. Gates' *From the Shadows* (New York: Simon and Schuster, 1996); Benjamin B. Fischer's "The Vilification and Vindication of Colonel Kuklinski" (*Studies in Intelligence*, Summer 2000, unclassified edition); Zbigniew Brzezinski's "A White House Diary" (*Orbis*, Winter 1988); Mark Kramer's "Colonel Kuklinski and the Polish Crisis, 1980-81" (*Cold War International History Project Bulletin 11*, Winter 1998) and the introduction by Malcolm Byrne; Bob Woodward's *Veil: The Secret Wars of the CIA 1981-1987* (New York: Simon and Schuster, 1987); and Ryszard Kuklinski's 1987 interview with *Kultura* (excerpts published in *Orbis*, "The Crushing of Solidarity," Winter 1988; and *Between East and West: Writings from Kultura*, edited by Robert Kostrzewa, Hill and Wang, N.Y. 1990.)

Several books on the CIA were also helpful: John Ranelagh's *The Agency: The Rise and Decline of the CIA* (New York: Simon and Schuster, 1986); David Wise's *Molehunt: The Secret Search for Traitors that Shattered the CIA* (New York: Random House, 1992); and *The Main Enemy: The Inside Story of the CIA's Final Showdown with the KGB*, by Milt Bearden and James Risen (New York: Random House, 2003). I also want to cite the writers Christine Spolar, Jane Perlez, Iwona Jurczenko, Carl Bernstein, and Michael Dobbs.

On Names

At the request of several of the officers cited in this book, their names have been replaced with pseudonyms. I have marked those names with an asterisk where they first appear.

On Cables

In the CIA archival material relied on for this book, cables were typically rendered in all capital letters, but for the sake of readability, I have avoided that style. Some cables are also written in "cable-ese," which is not always grammatical. I have rendered those as in the original text, except to add bracketed words in some cases to improve clarity.

On Translations

Kuklinski's recorded and written comments to the agency, usually made in Polish (and in the first year also in Russian), were typically translated quickly by the CIA, and not always grammatically. Kuklinski is an eloquent writer and speaker of Polish; I have corrected obvious errors in the translations of his words, and in some cases, I have added bracketed words for clarity.

On Code Names

During the operation, Kuklinski's name was generally replaced in cables or memos with a code name such as CKGULL or QTGULL (the CK and QT are "digraphs," which typically are used to identify the country of origin of an operation or a source). In the archival material released to me, these code names were removed. To keep the text clear, I have reinserted "Gull" wherever his name was deleted. Place-names, such as Warsaw or Moscow, were also deleted from the archival material. Where it is obvious which location is being discussed, I have reinserted the place-name in brackets.

On Dialogue

In most cases where dialogue is quoted in the text, it comes from transcripts of recordings or notes taken shortly after the conversation in question. In some cases, I have reconstructed quoted conversations where one participant, who is usually identified in the text or in the notes, recalled the discussion. Some sections of this text that are not otherwise footnoted are based on extensive interviews with Kuklinski over the years.

The Archive

My use of the phrase "archival note" below refers to summaries or observations made by Peter Earnest, the retired case officer who researched the archive, of materials that are not otherwise sourced to a specific document.

In the notes below, an asterisk (*) represents a pseudonym in the text. "HQ" stands for CIA headquarters at Langley, Virginia. "Field" is sometimes used for Warsaw Station. "RK" stands for Kuklinski. I have not footnoted an interview with Kuklinski each time one of his documents is cited, but he was interviewed about each, and the text often reflects his thinking at the time they were prepared or received.

Prologue

Key interview: Kuklinski.

Chapter 1   Crossing the Line

Key interviews: RK, John P. Dimmer Jr., Walter Lang*, David Blee, Katharine Hart, Richard Stolz, Clair George, Richard Helms, Bill Donnelly, David Forden, Peter Earnest, Ed Schooley*.

6   **"Bonn Station was led ..."** Interview Dimmer; excerpts of Dimmer cable to HQ and HQ response.

6   **"I'm sorry for my English ..."** Text of RK letter to the Army August 11, 1972.

7   **"Fifty-five years old ..."** Interviews Blee, Donnelly, Stolz, Helms, Hart, George.

8   **"thanks to the excessive ..."** Robert M. Gates, *From the Shadows* (New York: Simon and Schuster, 1996), p. 34.

9   **"Blee surrounded himself ..."** Blee's predecessor, Rolfe Kingsley, who served as Soviet Division chief 1968–1971, has been given credit for some of the changes that refocused the division and fended off Angleton from further interference with the division's officers. In some ways, one former officer said, Kingsley thus made it possible for Blee to arrive when he did and maintain the aggressive approach to developing new sources.

9   **"There's nothing he can tell us ..."** Interview Blee. Once Hart learned who P.V. really was, and the access he had, she was enthusiastically on board; interview Hart.

10–18   **"In Bonn, Dimmer summoned ..."** The account of setting up the first meeting with RK, and the meeting itself, is based on interviews with RK,

Blee, Lang, Dimmer, Forden, Earnest; also excerpts of Lang's and Henry's cable to HQ August 18, 1972; cable and detailed contact report pouched to HQ from Henry and Lang August 19; HQ cables to team August 18, 19; archival notes.

18 **"What does P.V. mean?..."** Interviews Lang, RK.

21–24 **"I live in Warsaw ..."** Account of meeting is based on interviews with RK and Lang and excerpt of meeting transcript.

22 **"Warsaw Pact commanders ..."** Besides the Soviet Union and Poland, the Warsaw Pact included East Germany, Hungary, Czechoslovakia, Bulgaria, and Romania.

23 **"They said the Americans would begin ..."** The CIA anticipated that if Kuklinski had to be exfiltrated, he and his family would leave Poland with nothing and would need support to rebuild their lives. The CIA's policy in such cases is to put aside funds regularly, over a period of time, and create an escrow account for such emergencies.

25 **"It was not unusual for Schooley to go driving ..."** Interview Schooley.

27–28 **"Please forgive me ..."** Transcript of RK.

28 **"they walked to the harbor ..."** Interview Lang.

Chapter 2 *"The Soil of Nobody"*

Key interviews: RK, Roman Barszcz, Florian Siwicki.

29–55 **"Kuklinski had always loved the sea ..."** The biographical material on RK comes primarily from many hours of interviews with him.

30 **"They breathed the air of patriotism ..."** Interview Barszcz.

43–44 **"Only the young ..."** Joseph Conrad, *The Shadow-Line* (New York: Oxford University Press, 1985), p. 3. Adam Gillon, professor emeritus, State University of New York at New Paltz, offered insights into Conrad. Gillon was the founder and longtime president of the Conrad Society of America and founding editor of the newsletter *Joseph Conrad Today*.

48–49 **"The symposium participants ..."** RK's interview in *Kultura*, April 1987. Translated excerpts published in *Orbis*, "The Crushing of Solidarity," Winter 1988; and *Between East and West: Writings from Kultura*, ed. Robert Kostrzewa (New York: Hill and Wang, 1990).

Chapter 3 *A Double Life*

Key interviews: RK, Carl and Nancy Gebhardt, Blee, Hart, Donnelly, Forden, Peter Falk, Alan Goldfarb, Ron Estes, Haviland Smith, Stolz, John Horton.

56 **"After Lang returned ..."** Interview Lang.

56–57 **"Blee sent a cable ..."** Excerpt of cable to field August 31, 1972.

57 **"At the time, the station consisted ..."** Interview Gebhardt.

58–61 **"Kuklinski had been just as impatient ..."** Interview RK.

61 **"Gebhardt and his wife Nancy began ..."** Interview Gebhardts.

61 **"waving energetically at them ..."** Kuklinski was later asked by the

Americans to dress in civilian clothing, so that he would not be recognizable. He ultimately rotated several changes of dark clothing to accomplish this. He also took care not to wear his own shoes, particularly those he wore to work. He did not want to leave a footprint that matched his own.

62 **"Gull looked like a first-rate person . . ."** Excerpt of undated memo by Gebhardt with impressions of first meeting with Gull.

62–63 **"On behalf of our representatives . . ."** Excerpt of letter written for delivery to RK. There is some imprecision in the archival notes I received as to precisely when RK received the "Eagle" letter, and whether it was in the envelope in his car, delivered to him in the cemetery, or slightly later. But it was very early in the operation.

63 **"The letter was signed Eagle. . . ."** Interview RK; archive.

63 **"This source has made excellent choices . . ."** Excerpt of commentary by senior CIA reports officer on RK's initial reporting, January 8, 1973.

63 **"a large quantity of very valuable . . ."** Excerpt of January 15, 1973, memo sent to CIA's Deputy Director for Plans.

63–64 **"the best placed source . . ."** Excerpt of paper, undated but likely January 1973, prepared "for use in high-level briefing."

64 **"Although full impact . . ."** Excerpt of HQ cable written for certain agency field officers who participated in initial stages of operation. In addition to Henry and Lang, these likely included the officers in Bonn and Warsaw.

64 **"Blee, in fact, was concerned . . ."** Interviews Blee, Hart, and Donnelly.

64 **"KC"** Hart, as she was known (she had the initials on her license plate), had risen to become the second-highest ranking woman in the CIA. A graduate of Bryn Mawr College with a degree in psychology, she joined the agency in 1949, shortly after its creation. Working first as a German translator at headquarters, she was later assigned to Frankfurt to oversee the reports of debriefings of Soviet-bloc defectors. In 1957 she returned to headquarters and was eventually made chief of the Reports and Requirements Staff for the Soviet Division. Hart worked in a corner office on the fourth floor and oversaw three dozen officers who were divided by intelligence specialty—political, economic, military, scientific, and technical—as well as two translation units, one Russian and one Polish. An administrative assistant with special clearances prepared the reports on an IBM Selectric typewriter.

64 **"Meanwhile, Kuklinski's Russian materials . . ."** Blee recalled that the Soviet source was a GRU general named Dimitri Fedorovich Polyakov (whose CIA code name was BOURBON, and whose FBI code name was TOPHAT). Polyakov had been recruited by the FBI in the early 1960s, and had remained a valuable CIA source for two decades, in Moscow and other locations. He was eventually betrayed by FBI mole Robert P. Hanssen and later by CIA mole Aldrich Ames, and was arrested by Moscow and eventually executed.

Hart and a third officer, now retired, recalled that Gull's Russian material may have been attributed to a different Soviet source. But the goal was the same, the third officer added: "to make fuzzier the appearance of a new flow of intelligence."

64   **"As Blee later described ..."** To Blee, attributing Kuklinski's materials to different sources was a "way of deceiving people without saying anything that wasn't true, just letting them deceive themselves—if they wanted to believe what I wanted them to believe—that this was the same old Polish source and same old Soviet source. And we got away with it, and I think protected Kuklinski."

65   **"Stan immersed himself ..."** Stan was born in Poland, the son of a farmer. At the time of the 1939 Nazi invasion, he had become an officer in the Polish Army and helped in an operation to smuggle Poland's gold reserves to Britain. There he joined with a group of Polish aviators and fought as a member of the free Polish forces. After the war he moved to the United States before returning to Europe in the early 1950s. He was hired by the CIA while living in Paris. With his ethnic background and proficiency in languages—he knew Polish, English, French, and some German—he was a valued contributor in the field and at headquarters. (Description of Stan from several colleagues.)

67   **"Still on edge ..."** Excerpt of January 1973 message by RK to Warsaw Station.

67   **"rendered in clear block print ..."** Archival note.

67-68   **"Blee considered Gull's request ..."** Interviews Blee, Donnelly.

69-82   **"Born in Buffalo ..."** Interviews Forden, Donnelly, Falk, Estes, Smith, Stolz, Horton, Goldfarb.

72   **"asked if he would replace ..."** Forden got the Warsaw post only after several other officers with Polish-language training were unable to, a retired officer said. One officer could not take the post because of an illness in his family. A second was ruled out after an embassy employee accidentally identified him at home in Warsaw, where he might have been overheard by Polish eavesdropping. A third officer could not go after his identity was compromised by the redefection of a minor East bloc agent he had once handled.

74-78   **"Learning from each tragic mistake ..."** The history of the brush pass and working the gap comes from interviews with Smith, Forden, Donnelly, Estes, Stolz.

78-80   **"Forden flew to Vienna ..."** Interviews Forden, Donnelly.

81   **"Forden pondered the possibilities for Warsaw ..."** The history of the moving car exchange is from interviews with Forden.

82-86   **"Colonel Henry walked around the harbor ..."** and the meeting with RK on June 23, 1973: Excerpt of field report to HQ.

Chapter 4 "Stabbing Back"

Key interviews: RK, Forden, Gebhardt.

87   **"On a quiet Sunday morning ..."** Forden's "Memorandum for the Record: Trip Report on Meetings with Gull in Germany 23 June to 2 July 1973" (memo).

88   **"When Daniel arrived ..."** Daniel's quotes as recalled by him.

88–96 **"He explained that ..."** and meetings of Daniel, RK, and Henry: Interviews RK, Forden, Gebhardt, and excerpts of meeting transcripts; Daniel's memo; Gebhardt's written account; Henry's contact report of June 23, 1973, meeting.

97–99 **"For now, I hope you understand ..."** Daniel's first letter to RK, undated but written shortly after the meetings.

99 "**offering 'hearty greetings' ...**" RK message November 6, 1973.

101–1020 **"Dear friends ..."** RK message January 3, 1974.

102–103 **"He began a second letter...."** RK letter to Daniel January 2, 1974.

103 **"operational sabbatical ..."** Excerpt of agency message to field early 1974.

104 **"The CIA ultimately gave ..."** Interview RK.

105 **"In a message to the agency ..."** Excerpts of RK letter to agency March 5.

106 **"Kuklinski looked up ..."** The account of the close call is based on interviews with RK and the archival notes.

108–109 **"On July 4 ..."** Archival notes and excerpts of meeting transcripts.

109–110 **"continue to be of primary ..."** Excerpts of HQ cable to field after July meetings.

110 **"Daniel also wrote ..."** Excerpt from Daniel letter cabled by HQ to field after July meetings.

110 **"The CIA also had questions ..."** Kuklinski had already reported on the Strela, and the full question posed by the CIA was typical in its precision and detail: "Please sketch Strela-1 missile if it is not identical in appearance to Strela-2. What is weight of one Strela-1? What is weight of pod when loaded with four missiles? You stated that two or four missiles are carried in each pod. Under what circumstances would the vehicle carry only two missiles per pod, i.e. only half of its load? Can one or three missiles be carried in a pod? If not, why not? How are the four missiles loaded in the pod? Can you sketch a rear view of the pod with four missiles? On July 22, during the military parade in Warsaw, a Strela-1 was displayed. Visible in each pod was only one missile, giving this vehicle a total of four missiles.

"1) Are there two versions of the Strela-1?

"2) Is there a training version? Could the one on display have been one? Can you obtain the dimensions of the training version missile?

"3) Are there two different missile pods? What are the dimensions of the pods?"

111(fn.) **"Kuklinski had been told that Eagle ..."** Interview RK.

113–115 **"The Mustang accelerated ..."** Interview RK; excerpt RK letter to CIA November 5, 1974.

115–116 **"Unaware of ..."** Excerpt of CIA message to RK prepared in October 1974.

119–120 **"After receiving ..."** Excerpt of cable from station to HQ November 20; HQ reply (undated).

120   **"By February 1975 ..."** Archival notes.

120   **"You must know ..."** Daniel letter cabled by HQ to Warsaw February 25 for delivery to RK.

Chapter 5   Near Miss

Key interviews: RK, Forden, Czeslaw Kiszczak.

121–124   **"Kuklinski had been sent ..."** Interviews RK, Kiszczak; RK letters to CIA and Daniel June 12, 1975.

124–126   **"The first summer meeting ..."** Henry cable to HQ July 16, 1975; team's cable to HQ July 7.

127   **"We have received ..."** October 1975 dispatch from HQ to field.

127–128   **"You know ..."** Daniel letter included in October 1975 to field for delivery to RK.

130–131   **"Dear Daniel ..."** Excerpt RK letter to Daniel December 21, 1975.

132–133   **"It is with great ..."** Excerpt RK letter to CIA February 5, 1976.

134   **"He conceded there had been ..."** Excerpt of transcripts of June meetings.

134–135   **"Consensus here ..."** Excerpt of Daniel cable June 8, 1976, to HQ; **"an atmosphere of peace ..."** excerpt of RK letter to CIA delivered August 22; **"smiling and relaxed ..."** excerpt of notes of field observation on August 22; **"may be a shade ..."** excerpt of field communication to HQ August 24; **"Daniel wrote ..."** excerpt of Daniel letter to RK delivered August 22.

135   **"The recognition ..."** Excerpt of message from RK to CIA October 31, 1976.

135   **"We, too ..."** Excerpt November 3, 1976, Soviet Division Chief memo to CIA Director.

135–136   **"match the public honors ..."** Excerpt Daniel letter delivered to RK October 31.

136–137   **"collided with a massive ..."** encounter with pillar: Interview RK; excerpt of message passed by RK to CIA December 12, 1976; archival notes of field reaction; excerpt of field response for February 1977 delivery.

138–139   **"Dear P.V. ..."** Excerpt Daniel's letter to PV; **"For a long time ..."** excerpt RK letter to Daniel, both delivered February 13.

Chapter 6   "Standing on Ice"

Key interviews: RK, Forden, Ruth Brerewood*, Harold Larsen, Robert Lubbehusen, Victor Kliss.

140   **"We share many things ..."** Excerpt letter Daniel to RK, delivery in April 1977.

141   **"For the past five years ..."** Excerpt of memo to DDO April 18, 1977, from Chief of Soviet Division.

142 **"The events of the past . . ."** Excerpt of RK April 17 message to the CIA.

142–143 **"Chances of . . ."** Excerpt of field cable to HQ May 10, 1977.

143 **"Comrade Colonel . . ."** Excerpt of RK message to CIA June 12, 1977.

144 **"gives me much joy . . ."** Excerpt of RK message to CIA July 24, 1977.

144 **"modest efforts on behalf . . ."** Excerpt of RK message to CIA on October 14, 1977.

145 **"Colonel, what are you doing?"** Interview RK.

146–147 **"irrefutable proofs . . ."** Excerpts of RK letter to the CIA delivered January 22, 1978.

147 **"As you will recall . . ."** Excerpts of CIA message delivered to RK in January 1978.

147–148 **"Even had we . . ."** Excerpt of Daniel message delivered to RK in January 1978.

148 **"passed the tests . . ."** Excerpts of RK message delivered to CIA June 25, 1978.

149–151 **"I recommend that two documents . . ."** Excerpts of RK messages to CIA and Daniel delivered in exchange April 16, 1978.

152 **"Robert Kennedy . . ."** Excerpt Daniel message delivered to RK in June 1978.

152–154 **"I await . . ."** Excerpts of RK messages to CIA delivered in June 1978.

154 **"But the Soviet Division . . ."** The CIA, meanwhile, was describing his latest documents as extraordinary. One 363-page Russian document detailed the tactical and technical specifications of Soviet weaponry to be introduced into the Warsaw Pact through 1985. There was also a fifty-two-page "Secret" account of a speech by Gribkov, Chief of Staff of the Warsaw Pact command in Moscow, on cooperation among the General Staffs of the Warsaw Pact countries.

154–155 **"should be told to destroy . . ."** HQ cable to field June 28, 1978; **"We want to tell . . ."** text of HQ letter to field for delivery to RK.

155–156 **"Your letter—as always . . ."** Excerpt of RK letter to Daniel passed in July 3, 1978, exchange. The field officers noticed a lessening of SB surveillance activity in the days before the exchange, which they attributed to a visit to Warsaw by Libyan President Muammar Gadhafi.

156–157 **"This time, when asked . . ."** Interview RK.

158–160 **"Eyes Only . . ."** Excerpts July 14, 1978, CIA counterintelligence investigation.

162 **"at a prodigious rate . . ."** Archival note of summary prepared in October 1978; **"20 rolls . . ."** excerpts from list of January 21, 1979, delivery.

162–163 **"I will not attempt . . ."** Excerpts RK message delivered to CIA in December 1978 or early January 1979.

163–165 **"The Russian-language document . . ."** Excerpt HQ message to RK, as later cabled to field in late January along with Daniel letter.

165 **"soon be a significant change . . ."** Interviews Forden, Brerewood, Lubbehusen, Larsen, Kliss.

Chapter 7 Tremors of Change

Key interviews: RK, Brerewood*, Sue Burggraf, Dave Forden, Michael Dwyer*, Ted Gilbertson*, Earnest.

166-167 **"A former high school ..."** Interview Brerewood.

167-169 **"In early March ..."** Interviews Burggraf, Earnest.

170 **"In a delivery ..."** Ten-page excerpt of RK delivery list for May 6, 1979.

170-172 **"I continue to belong ..."** Excerpt RK letters to CIA and Daniel delivered May 6.

172 **"One CIA memo ..."** Excerpt of HQ memo that says decision reached on May 23 to restrict access to fourteen-page letter from Jaruzelski to Kulikov.

172 **"I feel as if I were ..."** Excerpt of RK message to CIA July 8, 1979.

173 **"In the exchange ..."** Excerpt of text of "Daniel" letter cabled to field for delivery to RK in July 1979.

173-175 **"In August 1979 ..."** Interviews Gilbertson, Dwyer.

175-178 **"In early September ..."** Interview RK; excerpts of RK letters delivered to CIA and Daniel September 24, 1979.

178 **"He delivered the pen ..."** He also said that he was including photographs of a 1977 Russian manual titled "Offensive Operations of the Front," published by the Academy of the General Staff of the Soviet Armed Forces. Siwicki had requested the manual, and the Soviets had delivered it on the condition it would not be shared with other officers. "The document has no traces that it originates from Polish sources," Kuklinski wrote.

178-180 **"Over the next few weeks ..."** Excerpts of RK message to CIA December 16 and 18, 1979; interview RK.

181 **"to speed up communications ..."** Field cable to HQ dated September 5, 1979.

182-183 **"Dwyer had spent most of ..."** Interview Dwyer.

183-184 **"On December 16, Kuklinski wrote ..."** RK letter to agency December 16, 1979.

184 **"Kuklinski responded to ..."** Kuklinski wrote of the T-72: "The initial velocity of the sub-caliber [projectile] equals 1,800 meters per second. The [projectile] has an additional propelling charge weighing 4.5 kg. Fins which fall away during flight give the [projectile] a rotational movement of 800 rpm." He noted that the T-72's [projectile] could penetrate armor plate "500 mm. thick if it is located at a right angle to the path of the flight of [projectile]; 200 mm. thick if it is located at an angle of 60 degrees to the path of flight of the [projectile]."

185 **"His films contained ..."** Excerpt of list of films delivered December 18, 1979.

185 **"The CIA's package ..."** CIA letter to RK delivered December 18, 1979; includes note from translator Patkowski.

185 **"employment of front rocket troops ..."** The CIA also provided in this delivery a list of materials it was seeking, including "Details on Soviet or Warsaw

Pact alert systems, doctrine and practices (including deception) regarding reaction to U.S. reconnaissance satellites." The agency also had questions about a document Kuklinski had turned over in June 1977 that contained tables comparing combat capabilities of Soviet and NATO armaments and equipment, rating each side's weaponry on firepower, armor, and survivability.

That document "is still causing great interest among our military analysts," the CIA said, and his answers "would materially affect our intelligence exploitation of these documents." How were the ratings derived? "Are these documents used by Soviet military planners in evaluating the quality and quantity of military equipment, organization, and force structure of the Warsaw Pact and NATO forces? Are these documents used only in exercise scenarios, or in actual war planning?"

Chapter 8   "Out of the Shadows of Darkness"

Key interviews: RK, Larsen, Lubbehusen, Hart, Burggraf, Gilbertson, Forden, Zbigniew Brzezinski, General Jerzy Skalski, Donnelly, Tom and Lucille Ryan.

186–187   "In a well-lit..." Interviews Larsen, Lubbehusen, Hart.

187–188   "this deplorable act..." RK letter to CIA February 10, 1980; "received a black Volga..." RK letter of February 17, 1980.

188–189   "of immense value to our common cause..." CIA to RK delivered February 17, 1980.

189–190   "Before leaving, she prepared a memo..." Memo commenting on Gull case March 4, 1980.

190–194   "By April 1980..." Interviews Burggraf, Gilbertson, Donnelly.

194   "seventeen new rolls of film..." April 13, 1980, list on RK's latest delivery.

195   "safer and surer..." Excerpts RK letter to CIA April 13, 1980.

195   "all in all..." Excerpt field comment after April 13 exchange.

195   "It's probably very little consolation..." Excerpt of "Daniel" letter for delivery to RK April 13.

196   "sent a memo to the CIA's..." Excerpts of March 26, 1980, memo from Soviet Division Chief to awards panel; excerpts of undated signed memo by Director Turner to DDO McMahon.

196   "most dangerous aspect..." Archival note of HQ-field dialogue on RK's security.

196   "Wish to inform you..." Excerpt of HQ cable to Forden April 22, 1980; "Deeply grateful..." excerpt Forden response April 23.

197–199   "one of the few shows on TV..." Excerpt RK letter to Daniel June 7, 1980.

199   "critique of a Warsaw Pact..." List of RK documents delivered June 8, 1980.

200 **"was asked by Skalski ..."** Interview RK; RK letter to CIA September 13, 1980.

201 **"During the turbulent summer ..."** Interview Ryans.

201–203 **"with utmost apprehension ..."** Excerpt RK letter to CIA September 13.

203 **"which included a forty-one-page ..."** Excerpt RK document delivery list September 14, 1980.

203–205 **"Our greatest hope ..."** Excerpt of HQ and "Daniel" letters delivered to RK September 14.

205 **"sent an 'Alert' memorandum ..."** Gates, *From the Shadows*, p. 163.

205–207 **"Before going out ..."** Excerpts of RK letter to Daniel September 22, 1980.

207 **"top White House national security officials ..."** Gates, *From the Shadows*, pp. 163–164.

208 **"Kuklinski, who was already ..."** Interview RK; excerpt of RK letter to CIA October 26, 1980.

208–209 **"Skalski had been ..."** Interview RK; interview Skalski by Marek Skrzydelski.

210 **"In Washington the next day ..."** Zbigniew Brzezinski, "A White House Diary," *Orbis*, Winter 1988, pp. 32–48.

210–212 **"a reliable prognosis ..."** Excerpt of RK letter to CIA October 26, 1980.

212–213 **"psychological conditioning ..."** Excerpt of RK letter to CIA October 30, 1980.

213(fn.) **"These documents included ..."** Additional martial-law documents provided by RK in delivery of October 30, 1980:

1. Effects of Introducing a State of Martial Law Within the Scope of Universal Duty to Defend the PPR [Polish People's Republic]. Secret. Polish. 4 pages.

2. Initial Draft. Resolution of the State Council Pertaining to Introduction of a State of Martial Law. Secret. Polish. 2 pages.

3. Public Notice on the Introduction of a State of Martial Law. Secret. Polish. 3 pages.

4. Official Note Pertaining to a State of Martial Law. Secret. Polish. 15 pages with attachments.

213 **"I am becoming increasingly concerned ..."** Brzezinski, "A White House Diary," p. 34.

215 **"On November 25, the CIA sent President Carter ..."** Gates, *From the Shadows*, p. 165.

215 **"Three days later ..."** Gates, *From the Shadows*, p. 165.

215 **"project known as Discus ..."** Excerpt archive note from HQ to field December 1, 1980.

215 **"was of outstanding intelligence significance ..."** Excerpt HQ comments to field December 1, 1980.

215–217 **"as Kuklinski was preparing ..."** Interview RK; RK message to CIA December 14, 1980.

217 **"I believe the Soviets ..."** Gates, *From the Shadows,* p. 166.

217 **"urged Carter to send Brezhnev ..."** Brzezinski, "A White House Diary," pp. 36–37; also Gates, *From the Shadows,* p. 167.

217–218 **"foreign military intervention ..."** Text of "U.S. Statement on Poland," *New York Times,* December 4, 1980, p. 10.

218 **"departed airports in the order ..."** Interview RK.

219 **"The night of the exchange ..."** Interview RK; excerpt of field cable to HQ describing RK message.

219–221 **"Dear friends ..."** RK message to CIA delivered December 4, 1980.

222–223 **"felt something crinkle ..."** Excerpt of archival note from field; interview Gilbertson.

223 **"Report is of critical importance ..."** Excerpt of HQ cable to field after receiving RK message of December 4.

223–224 **"At Langley, a summary ..."** Excerpt of HQ message to field relaying text of memo hand-carried to president.

224–225 **"At 9:10 a.m. on Friday ..."** Brzezinski, "A White House Diary," pp. 38–43; interview Brzezinski.

225–226 **"Skalski gave a briefing ..."** Excerpt of RK message to CIA December 8, 1980.

226 **"weekend's high meetings ..."** Excerpt HQ message to field December 8, 1980.

227 **"In the final analysis ..."** RK message to CIA December 14, 1980.

227 **"preparations for pushing ..."** RK message to CIA delivered December 23.

228 **"Your information ..."** Excerpt of HQ message to field for delivery to RK.

Chapter 9 Preparing to Crush Solidarity

Key interviews: RK, Forden, Donnelly, Burggraf, Tom Ryan, Aris Pappas, James Simon, Iza.

229 **"a play on the title of ..."** Lenin's journal, published in Germany in 1900, was called "Iskra" and said on its masthead, "Out of this spark will come a conflagration." Adam Ulam, *The Bolsheviks* (Cambridge: Harvard University Press, 1965), p. 159.

229 **"information of extraordinary ..."** Excerpt HQ cable to station December 1, 1981.

230 **"Not long after, he learned ..."** As General Hermaszewski had described the conspiracy to Kuklinski, the candidate to assume Siwicki's post as chief of staff was General Tadeusz Hupalowski, who was "in daily contact with the Russians," Hermaszewski said. Although aspects of the plot made it seem

unlikely to Kuklinski, he considered Hermaszewski, the commander of the First Air Defense Corps, to be a credible source because he was close to officials in the Russian Embassy in Warsaw. Kuklinski told the CIA that his "information on the preparation for the *coup d'etat*" should be treated "with utmost care."

230 **"he learned from a neighbor ..."** Excerpts of RK message to the CIA January 2, 1981.

230 **"The indicators ..."** Excerpt of RK message January 2.

231 **"Then, without Bogdan's knowledge ..."** Interview RK.

231 **"Bogdan had also fallen in love ..."** Interviews Iza, RK.

232 **"Kuklinski successfully used it ..."** Excerpts of message from field to HQ; **"highest party-government circles ..."** excerpt of first Iskra message January 21, 10:00 P.M; **"I hope this is the first ..."** excerpt of SE Division Chief's cable to field and HQ cable to field January 23.

232 **"Gull obviously likes ..."** Excerpt of HQ cable to field, January 29, 1981.

233 **"Hurried preparations are ..."** Excerpt of RK message about the Iskra February 9, 1981.

234 **"There exists a serious uneasiness ..."** Excerpt of RK letter to CIA February 22, 1981.

234 **"I must add that ..."** Kuklinski also included three pages on Moscow's position in the strategic arms limitation talks and diagrams of the organizational structure of the Warsaw Pact armies for 1981–1985, including command elements, personnel strengths, military equipment, and reserves.

234 **"They are of outstanding ..."** Excerpt of HQ cable to field March 5, 1981.

234 **"That day, the Reagan ..."** "Warsaw Pact Games Arouse U.S. Concern; a Warning Is Issued." *New York Times*, March 6, 1981.

235 **"Kuklinski included films ..."** Kuklinski's films also included these items (excerpt of RK delivery list of March 13, 1981):

Memorandum from Soviet Army General Gribkov to the Polish Defense Ministry listing all employees of the Warsaw Pact staff who enjoy privileges and immunities for 1981. 5 pages. Secret. Russian.

Report on the State of Scientific Research and Experimental-Design Programs of Warsaw Pact Armies/Countries for 1980. 15 pages. Top Secret. Russian.

Summary of the Soyuz 81 Operational-Strategic Command-Staff Exercise to be delivered by the Deputy Manager. 22 pages. Secret. Russian.

List of participants in the decision-making game of February 16, 1981. 3 pages. Confidential. Polish.

Information on the state of preparations of the State in the event of introducing martial law and on the proposals from the decision-making game. 10 pages. Top Secret. Polish.

236 **"Introduction of the state of martial law ..."** Excerpt of RK message about the Iskra April 1, 1981.

237 **"Jaruzelski visited ..."** This translation from RK interview with *Kultura*;

also similar wording in RK message about the Iskra written April 12, recovered from the defective Iskra when the device was given back during the April 26, 1981, exchange.

238   **"On three occasions ..."** Responding to his difficulties, the agency wrote back that the CIA's designers and engineers were "equally disappointed," were laboring to solve the problem, and were confident they would succeed. "It is a complex piece of sophisticated equipment not previously used by anyone, and unfortunately we are finding that it is not infallible," one "Daniel" letter said.

238   **"so I can give you a timely alert ..."** Excerpt of RK letters to CIA April 26, 1981.

238   **"Under Moscow's pressure ..."** One document turned over in this exchange, a briefing paper summarizing Soyuz 81, was described in a CIA note to Kuklinski as "of unique value," because it was the first indication of the formation of a mobile army group. The Soviets had a new operational concept to develop fast-moving air and land forces that could break through front lines and penetrate far into NATO territory. The CIA said it would "have an impact on our assessment of the future doctrine and tactics of Soviet and Warsaw Pact forces."

239   **"We Poles are deeply aware ..."** Excerpt of RK letter to Daniel April 26, 1981.

239   **"We must face stark reality ..."** Excerpts of cable from HQ to field April 9, 1981.

239–240   **"the best view ..."** Excerpt of field response to HQ; interview Ryan.

240–241   **"On June 17 ..."** and account of safe incident: Interview RK; excerpt of RK letter delivered to CIA June 22, 1981. Around this time, after the close call with the safe, the CIA proposed outfitting Kuklinski with a briefcase containing a false bottom and a combination lock that would allow him to carry documents from the General Staff more securely. His own briefcase had no such lock. Kuklinski rejected the idea, writing on July 10, 1981: "Because of the recent incident, I do not wish to make any new changes in my normal and routine equipment." Maybe in the future, he added.

242–245   **"It is likely that few people appreciated ..."** Interviews Pappas, Simon.

245–247   **"Burggraf had completed ..."** Interviews Burggraf, Ryan.

247–248   **"As the July party congress ..."** RK letter July 10, 1981, delivered July 14.

248   **"if there is one ..."** RK letter July 14, 1981.

249   **"Absolutely not ..."** Excerpt of HQ message for RK.

249–250   **"As you gentlemen know ..."** Excerpts of RK letter to CIA September 6, 1981. Kuklinski's letter also included an intelligence report on NATO forces covering mid-June to mid-July prepared by the Soviet General Staff. As it was meant for a small circle in Moscow, Kuklinski had taken special precautions, covering up certain Russian identification numbers before he photographed the documents to make them harder to trace.

250–251 **"I am indeed fortunate ..."** Excerpts of RK letter to Daniel September 6, 1981.

251–252 **"Daniel had served ..."** Interview Forden.

252 **"Gull has regularly produced ..."** Excerpts of CIA summary of Gull operation. It notes that his material had produced "disseminations" to the intelligence community averaging about sixty-six per quarter.

252–253 **"Jaruzelski interrupted ..."** Excerpt of RK message September 10, 1981.

253 **"Kuklinski included film of ninety ..."** RK list of film delivered with letter:

1. List of legal documents pertaining to the state of martial law in consideration of national security. Secret. 10 pages.

2. Resolution of the State Council (space left for date) pertaining to introduction of the state of martial law in consideration of national security (for signature of the chairman of the State Council). Secret "S." 2 pages.

3. Decree on the state of martial law (space left for date) (for signature of the chairman of the National Council). Secret. 29 pages.

4. Decree on special proceedings pertaining to crimes and violations while martial law is in force (space for date). Secret. 12 pages.

5. Order of the chairman of the Council of Ministers pertaining to suspension of the activities of trade unions and certain other social organizations while the state of martial law is in force. Secret "S." 5 pages.

6. Order of the Council of Ministers (undated) pertaining to implementation of regulations of the decree of martial law with regard to communications. Secret "S." 12 pages.

7. Order of the Council of Ministers (undated) pertaining to principles of proceedings in matters of internment of Polish citizens. Secret. 5 pages.

8. Order of the chairman of the Council of Ministers (undated) pertaining to principles and procedures for issuing permission to propagate publications and spectacles and utilization of printing shops and equipment while the state of martial law is in force. Secret. 3 pages.

9. Order of the Minister of Internal Affairs (undated) pertaining to permission to change residence while the state of martial law is in force. Secret. 6 pages.

10. Order of the Minister of Internal Affairs (undated) pertaining to the exclusion of certain public meetings and gatherings from the obligation to obtain permission while the state of martial law is in force. Secret. 2 pages.

11. Order of the Minister of Internal Affairs (undated) pertaining to limiting freedom to move while the state of martial law is in force. Secret "S." 2 pages.

12. Order no. – of the Minister of Justice (undated) pertaining to establishment of isolation centers. Secret "S." 1 page.

13. Order of the Minister of Justice (undated) pertaining to temporary rules for detention of internees in isolation centers. Secret "S." 1 page.

254–255 **"Intensive preparations ..."** Excerpt RK letter to CIA September 13, 1981.

255 **"The Soviet maneuvers ..."** "SS-20 launchers were presented.... Aircraft carriers with the vertical takeoff aircraft Yak-23. Large landing ships—tenders carrying 56 tanks and floating means to lift those tanks to shore; new models of 152 MM Howitzers; battle vehicles (BMP-2), armed with 37 MM standard guns for engaging land and air targets; UAZ landing vehicles with mounted AT weapons and other modern weapons....

"There was a demonstration of a battle (two-sided exercises) of two armored divisions in which over 600 T-72 tanks participated in infantry and hundreds of WBP-2 transporters. The T-80 tanks were not shown. The sea landing of an entire mechanized division and a brigade of marines was demonstrated. Also observed was a drop of an airborne division ... and also a new type unit, air-assault brigade."

256 **"No one is to blame ..."** Excerpt of cable from Soviet Division Chief to field September 14, 1981.

257 **"That is when factories will not operate ..."** Interview RK; excerpt of RK message intended for CIA September 15, 1981.

258 **"Burggraf reported to Ryan ..."** October 11 Iskra message from RK to field; interview Burggraf.

259 **"In mid-September ..."** UPI, "Moscow Orders Poles to Control 'Anti-Sovietism,'" New York Times, September 18, 1981; **"The U.S. State Department ..."** Associated Press, "U.S. Says Kremlin Trying to 'Intimidate the Polish People,'" September 18, 1981.

259 **"Kuklinski, feeling the strain ..."** Interview RK.

259–261 **"Daniel was soon faced ..."** Interview Forden; **"We want to alert you ..."** excerpt HQ message October 8, 1981, to field for delivery to RK; interview RK.

261–262 **"With our officer ..."** Daniel message for RK cabled to field October 7, 1981.

262–263 **"Today I have proof ..."** Excerpt RK letter to CIA October 9, 1981.

263 **"Kuklinski smiled broadly ..."** Field cable to HQ October 10, 1981.

263 **"in the 'President's Daily Brief' ..."** Archival mention of HQ message to field.

264 **"I did something wrong ..."** Interview RK.

264 **"It was my fault ..."** RK Iskra message of October 10, 1981, to CIA, received October 11.

264–265 **"The military are on alert status ..."** Cable from field to HQ reporting RK Iskra message of October 18, 1981.

265 **"penetrate all fields ..."** October 25, 1981, Iskra message from RK to CIA.

265 **"only when necessary ..."** Iskra message for RK October 21, 1981, received October 25.

Chapter 10 *"Everything Is Pointing to the End of My Mission"*

Key interviews: Kuklinski, Forden, Burggraf, Iza, Tom and Lucille Ryan, Francis Meehan, Wladyslaw Hermaszewski, Jerzy Skalski, Stanislaw Radaj, Roman and Barbara Barszcz, Brerewood, Brzezinski, Pappas.

266–268 **"the latest version of the martial-law plans ..."** Interview RK; **"Today [Skalski] declared ..."** RK's Iskra message to CIA November 2, 1981.

268 **"The Americans might ..."** Interview RK; Memorandum for the Record, account of exfiltration (hereafter Memo).

269 **"As Bogdan provided cover from a distance ..."** Memo; RK interview.

270 **"Field [officers] in process ..."** Excerpt of field cable to HQ November 3, 1981.

270 **"Langley initially instructed ..."** Interviews Forden, Burggraf, Tom Ryan.

270 **"We appreciate ..."** Excerpt cable from Casey to Ambassador Francis Meehan in Warsaw.

271 **"Your message received ..."** Excerpt HQ cable to field November 3 for delivery via Iskra to RK.

271 **"Were you present ..."** Excerpt HQ cable to field with questions for Burggraf to discuss with RK.

272 **"We desperately need ..."** Interview Forden.

273 **"He found blank sheets of paper ..."** Memo; interview RK.

273–274 **"Everything is pointing ..."** Excerpt RK note given to Burggraf on night of November 3, 1981.

274–276 **"he entered a path that led into ..."** Memo; interviews RK, Burggraf.

277 **"Bogdan had wanted to see Iza ..."** Interview Iza; Memo. The Memo says Bogdan gave Iza the news in her apartment on Tuesday night, November 3; Iza recalls that Bogdan picked her up at her mother's house, perhaps Tuesday or Wednesday, and gave her the news as they drove. Either way, it is unlikely Bogdan told her later than Wednesday, since he knew he might be leaving Poland as early as Wednesday night. I have placed the incident on Tuesday, the earlier date, as the Memo states, but have used Iza's account of how she was told.

277 **"We are prepared ..."** Excerpt HQ cable to field after receipt of RK note.

278 **"for his beloved dog, Zula ..."** Interview RK. He does not recall the precise date he visited Czeslaw Jakubowski, except that it was probably early in the week, again because his departure was imminent. Jakubowski gave a similar account in a 1992 article by Iwona Jurczenko, in which he said RK's visit occurred

Wednesday or Thursday. I have used the earlier date. (Iwona Jurczenko, "The Ideal Agent," *Prawo I Zycie* [Warsaw], no. 33, 1992.)

279 **"Burggraf was anguished..."** Interview Burggraf.

279 **"Share frustration..."** Excerpt HQ cable to field November 5, 1981.

279 **"Kuklinski was summoned to see Skalski..."** Memo; interview RK.

280 **"If they were unsuccessful..."** Interview Burggraf.

280 **"The continuing presence..."** Excerpt of cable from field to HQ November 6, 1981.

280–281 **"Copies of the cables..."** Interviews Tom and Lucille Ryan.

281 **"So you also have..."** RK interview.

281 **"You don't look well..."** Radaj interview.

282 **"Security situation unchanged..."** RK Iskra message to station November 6, 1981.

282–283 **"Our officers had..."** Excerpt CIA Iskra message to RK delivered November 6, 1981.

283 **"Kuklinski felt enormous relief..."** Interview RK; Memo.

283 **"both teams heavily..."** Excerpt of Warsaw Station cable to HQ November 7, 1981.

283 **"confusion about where Kuklinski would turn up..."** Memo; interviews RK, Burggraf, Forden.

283 **"we wonder if the heavy surveillance..."** HQ to field November 8, 1981.

283–284 **"Tom and Lucille had trained together..."** Interview Ryans. Tom and Lucille Ryan were so moved by the deprivation of the Poles that they had stopped shopping for food in Polish grocery stories. Lucille had felt as though she was taking food from the Poles. Instead, they shopped at the commissary in the embassy and at a store for diplomats, where food was abundant and more expensive.

284–285 **"Hermaszewski, was standing in..."** Interview Hermaszewski by Marek Skrzydelski.

285 **"Today, we do not have to hurry..."** Interview RK. He also gave an account of this last drive home in the *Kultura* interview.

286 **"sensed some tension..."** Interview Barbara Barszcz.

286 **"it would not matter to you..."** The text of Bogdan's fake letter first appeared in print in Iwona Jurczenko's "The Ideal Agent," *Prawo I Zycie* (Warsaw), no. 33, 1992. Iza told me that she recalled the text of the letter to be essentially the same. The letter also appears to have been introduced as evidence in RK's trial-in-absentia in 1984.

286 **"He then wrote a second letter..."** Interview Iza.

287 **"It was mid morning..."** Memo; interviews Ryans, RK.

288 **"the van pulled out of the lot..."** Interviews RK, Ryans, Forden, Burggraf.

288   **"Don't tell me who you are ..."** Interview RK.

288–289   **"After the plane ..."** Interviews RK, Forden.

289   **"Well done, Warsaw ..."** Excerpt of "Flash" cable from reception team in Berlin to HQ.

289   **"Skalski asked ..."** Interview Skalski by Skrzydelski.

289   **"Zula, meanwhile ..."** Jurczenko, "The Ideal Agent."

290   **"solemnly addressed him ..."** Interview Brzezinski.

290   **"Pappas was not told ..."** Interview Pappas.

Chapter 11   Patriot or Traitor?

Key interviews: Kuklinski, Forden, Tom and Lucille Ryan, Les Griggs, Pappas, Simon, Kliss, Al Gray, Richard Stolz, Hubert Romanowski, Jacek Szymanderski, Zbigniew Brzezinski, Jerzy Kozminski, Siwicki, Kiszczak, Roman Barszcz, Wojciech Jaruzelski, Wladyslaw Hermaszewski, Kazimierz Oklesinski, Czeslaw Poltorak, Richard Davies.

292–293   **"One Monday evening ..."** Interviews RK, Forden.

294   **"One day shortly ..."** Interviews RK, Forden, Kliss.

294   **"While facing great personal danger ..."** Translation of citation.

295   **"debriefed Kuklinski for six months ..."** Interviews Griggs, Pappas, RK.

295–296   **"*Newsweek* magazine reported ..."** David C. Martin, "A Polish Agent in Place," *Newsweek*, December 20, 1982, p. 49.

296   **"A few days later ..."** Letter to RK from William J. Casey December 15, 1982.

297–298   **"In early September ..."** Interviews RK, Forden, Iza, Dwyer.

298   **"In November 1983 ..."** Interview RK.

299   **"Waldek ended his story ..."** Waldemar Kuklinski, "Fulfillment," 1983 manuscript (provided by RK; translated by Kliss).

299–300   **"On May 23, 1984 ..."** Translation of RK sentence, May 23, 1984, archive.

300–301   **"During Kuklinski's first three years ..."** Interviews Forden, RK.

301–302   **"In early June 1986 ..."** Interviews Pappas, Simon, Gray.

302–303   **"*Post* had published ..."** Bob Woodward and Michael Dobbs, "CIA Had Secret Agent on Polish General Staff," *Washington Post*, June 4, 1986.

303   **"The U.S. administration could have ..."** Urban press conference, "USA Accused of Advance Knowledge of Martial Law in Poland," BBC, June 9, 1986 (Warsaw home service 2005 and Polish Press Agency in English).

303–304   **"Kuklinski sailed ..."** Interview RK.

304   **"There is no question that ..."** RK interview in *Kultura*, April 1987.

305   **"In mid-November, 1990 ..."** Interview Stolz.

306   **"Kuklinski decided not to risk ..."** Interview RK. RK says he returned the next day and met with Hubert Romanowski, the newly appointed consul

general, who had not been available the previous day. Romanowski later told me that he and Kuklinski had a good meeting, which lasted about an hour, during which Kuklinski asked about his citizenship status. "It is possible that Col. Kuklinski felt comfortable in meeting with me because I was not only the first noncommunist consul general in Chicago since WWII, but was a former political refugee to the United States," Romanowski wrote to the *Washington Post* in December 1992 after the *Post* articles appeared. Romanowski died five months later in a car crash near Waverly, Tennessee, where he was on embassy business.

306 **"I am deeply concerned ..."** Translation of Walesa letter to Brzezinski, January 12, 1991.

306–307 **"In July 1991, Polish television ..."** Excerpts from Polish television broadcast July 21, 1991.

307 **"In my opinion ..."** Waldek's letter to *Politika* March 1992.

307–308 **"Was it an authentic Polish state ..."** Brzezinski speech at Polish American Congress Heritage Dinner October 15, 1992, Washington, D.C.

308 **"Some of Kuklinski's friends ..."** Interview Roman Barszcz.

309–310 **"We had full trust in Kuklinski ..."** Interviews Siwicki, Kiszczak, Jaruzelski.

310 **"If he would ..."** Interview Hermaszewski by Marek Skrzydelski.

310 **"I would welcome ..."** Interview Oklesinski by Skrzydelski.

310–311 **"From the point of view ..."** Interview Poltorak by Skrzydelski.

311 **"In September 1992, I first wrote ..."** Benjamin Weiser, "Polish Officer Was U.S.'s Window on Soviet War Plans" and "Traitor or Patriot: Puzzle for Polish Military," September 27, 1992, *Washington Post*; "A Question of Loyalty," *Washington Post Magazine*, December 13, 1992; on reaction, Blaine Harden, "Poles Debate Who's a Real Patriot; Defector's Claims, Jaruzelski's Testimony Ignite Controversy," *Washington Post*, October 9, 1992.

311 **"In our opinion ..."** *Trybuna*, quoted in UPI, "Traitor or Hero: Controversy Rages," Warsaw, September 30, 1992.

311 **"In the face of total evil ..."** Damian Kalbarczyk in *Zycie Warszawy*, as quoted by Dariusz Fikus, "Wallenrodism," *Rzeczpospolita* (*Zawsze w Sobote supplement*), Warsaw, October 24–25, 1992, p. 1.

311–312 **"began an energetic letter-writing campaign ..."** Interview Davies, who provided me with copies of his many letters and responses.

312 **"It would be a great tragedy ..."** RK to Davies March 8, 1993.

312 **"I hope you ..."** Davies letter to Clinton February 28, 1994.

312 **"sharing your concern ..."** White House letter to Davies April 25, 1994.

313 **"In the spring of 1994 ..."** Interview Kozminski.

314 **"I no longer expect anything ..."** RK interview with *Tygodnik Solidarnosc* (Solidarity Weekly), December 9, 1994.

314 **"Kuklinski, risking his life ..."** Herbert letter to Walesa, quoted by UPI, January 9, 1995.

Chapter 12   Return

Key interviews: RK, Forden, Krzysztof Piesiewicz, Brzezinski, Kozminski, Jack Platt, Davies.

315–318   **"in a white granite building ..."** Marek Skrzydelski covered the court hearing on May 25, 1995; I later interviewed Piesiewicz in New York.

318   **"Ambassador Jerzy Kozminski ..."** Interviews Kozminski, Brzezinski.

320   **"to the memory hole ..."** R. T. Davies, "The Hero Anthony Lake Has Forgotten," *Washington Times*, Op-Ed, February 24, 1997.

321   **"Kozminski gave a talk ..."** Interviews Kozminski, Forden.

321   **"Forden learned ..."** Interviews Forden, Platt.

322–326   **"The prosecutors seemed nervous and stiff ..."** The detailed account of RK's sessions with the Polish prosecutors is based on interviews with Brzezinski, Kozminski, RK, and seven pages of "informal notes for the record" kept by Brzezinski. All direct quotes from the meetings quoted in the text, as well many other observations, are from these notes.

328   **"an accusation against us ..."** BBC, "Generals Demand Explanation of Spy Case Decision by Prosecutor," October 8, 1997.

328   **"conference just outside of Warsaw ..."** The conference was jointly organized by the Institute for Political Studies of the Polish Academy of Sciences in Warsaw and the National Security Archive at George Washington University, with the Cold War International History Project at the Woodrow Wilson International Center for Scholars. Kulikov's quote is from Jane Perlez, "Iron Curtain Chills: A Cold War Spy Doesn't Dare Go Home," *New York Times*, November 16, 1997. Thanks also to Malcolm Byrne.

328   **"If you come ..."** Mary Williams Walsh, "Poland's Spy Who's Still Out in the Cold," *Los Angeles Times*, December 17, 1997.

328–329   **"Kuklinski has also since said ..."** Interview RK.

329   **"I'd like to retreat ..."** Andrew Nagorski, "In from the Cold," *Newsweek*, October 27, 1997.

329   **"The popular Italian weekly ..."** Solomatin interview with *Panorama*, March 22, 1992, according to Forden's notes and translation.

329   **"That same year ..."** Carl Bernstein, "The Holy Alliance," *Time*, February 24, 1992.

329   **"Forden began to wonder ..."** Interviews Forden, Platt.

329   **"A 1996 book ..."** Carl Bernstein and Marco Politi, *His Holiness: John Paul II and the Hidden History of Our Time* (New York: Doubleday, 1996).

331   **"I was skeptical ..."** Forden letter to Kozminski March 15, 1998.

331   **"It's hard for me to breathe ..."** "Former Spy Has Emotional Return After 17 Years," from TV Polonia satellite service, Warsaw, in Polish 1730 gmt, April 27, 1998/BBC Monitoring, April 29, 1998.

332   **"I love this time of year ..."** Interview RK.

332 **"My 25-year journey ..."** "Former Spy Has Emotional Return," TV Polonia April 27, 1998/BBC Monitoring.

333–335 **"I never doubted ..."** RK speech; interview RK. Speech excerpts, Source: Polish Radio 1, Warsaw, in Polish 1034 gmt 29 April 98/BBC Monitoring.

336 **"Too old to carry ..."** Selected lines from Zbigniew Herbert, "Report from the Besieged City and Other Poems," trans. with an introduction and notes by John Carpenter and Bogdana Carpenter (New York: Ecco Press, 1985). Copyright © 1985 Zbigniew Herbert. Reprinted by permission of HarperCollins Publishers Inc.

337 **"To his surprise ..."** Interview RK.

337 **"Soldiers are not like the mafia ..."** BBC, "Former Spy Explains His Silence on Martial Law to Solidarity Presidium," May 5, 1998 (source PAP news agency, Warsaw, May 4, 1998).

337 **"If this entire hullabaloo ..."** Adam Michnik, "The Trap of Political Beatification," *Gazeta Wyborcza*, May 1998, pp. 10–11. (I have used the translation that appears in Benjamin B. Fischer, "The Vilification and Vindication of Colonel Kuklinski," *Studies in Intelligence*, Summer 2000, no. 9, unclassified edition.)

338–339 **"In November 1999 ..."** Transcript "U.S. Intelligence and the End of the Cold War," Texas A&M University Memorial Ceremony, November 20, 1999; CIA Public Affairs.

339 **"Kuklinski was later ..."** Interview RK.

ACKNOWLEDGEMENTS

This book could not have been written without the extraordinary assistance of Colonel Ryszard Kuklinski, who opened up his life and memories to me over the years and endured my endless questions with patience and good humor. I also thank Hanka Kuklinski, who welcomed me when I arrived for interviews. The contribution of Peter Earnest, a retired CIA case officer, was also invaluable. He was a strong advocate for the project from the start, spent hours painstakingly researching the agency archive for me, and offered many thoughts about the history of the period as I pursued my interviews and writing. Peter has since gone on to become executive director of the International Spy Museum in Washington. I am grateful for his assistance.

Marek Skrzydelski acted as a skilled interpreter and guide in Poland, conducted several interviews for me on his own, and covered an important court hearing which appears in the book. Halina Potocka and Jola Ciborowska were helpful in setting up and translating interviews in Warsaw.

Several friends gave me critical readings of the manuscript, discussed it conceptually, and offered valuable insights at the end. They include Evan Thomas, Andrew Nagorski, Steve Engelberg, David Remnick, Bob Woodward, and Phillip Blumberg. I thank them all. Dr. Zbigniew Brzezinski, who always understood the importance of the case, answered questions, offered context, and provided notes he took during an important meeting in 1997 that figures prominently in one chapter. Thanks also to Jerzy Kozminski, the former Polish ambassador to the United States, for his observations about Poland and the Kuklinski case.

I first wrote about the case in 1992 for the *Washington Post* and *Post Magazine*. Former *Post* colleagues who gave me good counsel about the CIA and Poland as I proceeded include Bob Woodward, Steve Luxenberg, David Maraniss, Blaine Harden, Jackson Diehl, Mary Battiata, David Ignatius, Rick Atkinson, Chuck Babcock, Michael Getler, Lucy Shackelford, and the staff then at the magazine, including Linton Weeks, Bob Thompson, John Cotter, and Deborah Needleman. Thanks also to Olwen Price. A number of editors at the *New York Times* were supportive, particularly in the months I brought this project to completion. They include Jon Landman, Susan Edgerley, Joe Sexton, Richard Berke, Joyce Purnick, Matt Purdy, Gerry Mullany, Tony Marcano, Christine Kay, Bill Goss, Anne Cronin, and Wendell Jamieson.

I was lucky at various stages to receive encouragement and advice from Stephen Sestanovich, Delia Marshall, John Orefice, Nick Lemann, Elsa Walsh, Chris Drew, David McCraw, Maggie Drucker, Dale Russakoff, Jay Mathews, Adam Liptak, Jim Risen, John Darnton, Jeff Frank, Linda Healey, Sara Forden, Megan Barnett, Joanna and Ren Weschler, Simon Schama, Vint Lawrence, Anne Garrels, Luke Menand, Jonathan Karp, Rick Hertzberg, Kris Dahl, Malcolm Byrne, and the late Robert Jones, Charles Rembar, and Michael Dorris. Thanks to Caroline Backlund, Jamie Baylis, David Wickenden and Cindy Snyder, Joy and Murray Zinoman, Whitney Pinger and Roger Pollak, and Ellen Dennis and Rudi Pribitzer for listening and welcoming me on reporting trips in the U.S. and abroad. A special thanks to Judy Dennis for always being there, and, of course, to Norma Weiser and Hermione Wickenden.

During my negotiations with the CIA, two officials—Molly J. Tasker, then chair of the Publications Review Board, and Carolyn M. Ekedahl, then Director of Media Relations—were strong supporters of allowing me access to the archival material. I thank them, and John Hedley, who succeeded Molly at the PRB, and other CIA personnel who are not known to me, for their efforts. I also thank Mark Mansfield, Tom Crispell, Midge Holmes, and their colleagues in the CIA's public affairs office.

Dozens of current and former CIA officers and officials, some of whom I can't identify, granted me extensive interviews. Most had never talked to a reporter before. David Forden's unfailing judgment and good sense shaped our discussions, and will be evident to anyone who reads this book. I also thank him and his late wife Aurelia for their graciousness on my visits. I appreciate the help of Tom and Lucille Ryan, Sue Burggraf, Aris Pappas, Bill Donnelly, Katharine Hart, Richard Stolz, Ron Estes, Haviland Smith, Carl and Nancy Gebhardt, James M. Simon Jr., the late David Blee, John Dimmer, Bobby Ray Inman, Clair George, John Horton, the late Victor Kliss, Bob Lubbehusen, Jack Platt, Hal Larsen, the late Richard Helms, Douglas J. MacEachin, Kurt Taylor, Mary Gormley, and several people who are identified in this book only by pseudonyms: Ted Gilbertson, Michael Dwyer, Ed Schooley, Ruth Brerewood, and Walter Lang. Several people portrayed in the book were kind enough to read the manuscript, or parts of it, and to point out inaccuracies or to make other suggestions.

Many thanks to Michael Pollak, Bill Vourvoulias, and Ida May Norton for their careful checking of the manuscript; to Victor Kliss for translating the poetry of Waldemar Kuklinski; to Thaddeus Mirecki for his guidance and to Adam Gillon for his insight into Joseph Conrad. Others who spoke to me over the years about the Kuklinski case include: the late Richard Davies, Jan Nowak, Francis Meehan, Richard Pipes, William Odom, Les Griggs, Krzysztof Piesiewicz, Al Gray, Edmund Thompson, the late Roy Jonkers, Peter Falk, Alan Goldfarb, Roman and Barbara Barszcz, Stanislaw Radaj, Jacek Szymanderski,

Stanislaw Przyjemski, Wojciech Jaruzelski, Florian Siwicki, Czeslaw Kiszczak, and Janusz Onyszkiewicz.

My agent, Amanda Urban, was an early and enthusiastic advocate of this project, and offered expert guidance along the way. Peter Osnos and his editors at PublicAffairs have been unflagging proponents of the book. In particular, I thank my editor Kate Darnton, whose enthusiasm was infectious, and who deftly guided me through the editing process. Much appreciation also goes to Robert Kimzey, Melanie Peirson Johnstone, Nina D'Amario, Kasey Pfaff, Gene Taft, Matthew Goldberg, and Lindsay Jones.

In the end, no one deserves more thanks than my daughters, Sarah and Rebecca, and my wife, Dorothy, whose discernment and wisdom informed this book at every turn.

INDEX

The abbreviation RK is used in this index for Ryszard J. Kuklinski.

Afghanistan, Soviet invasion, 188
Andropov, Yuri (Soviet KGB chief), 236
Angleton, James J. (CIA Director of coun-
    terintelligence), 8

Balcerowicz, Leszek (Deputy Prime Minis-
    ter), 313
Barszcz, Barbara (wife of Roman Barszcz),
    285–286, 332
Barszcz, Leon (brother of Roman
    Barszcz), 157, 162
Barszcz, Roman (friend of RK), 30–31, 101,
    102, 157, 231, 285–286, 308, 332
Bernstein, Carl (reporter), 329
Blee, David (Soviet Division Chief)
    profile of, 8, 103
    RK communication plans, 56–57
    RK motivation for collaboration, 57
    RK suicide pill request, 67–68
    Soviet operations, 7–9, 64
Boggs, Sally (pseudonym)
    Gull operation counterintelligence
        review, 158–161
    Gull operation security issues review,
        189
    retirement, 189
Bonn Station
    CIA staff in, 5–6, 56

initial contact from Polish officer (P.V.),
    6–7
Brerewood, Ruth (pseudonym)
    Gull operation, 166–167
    safe house for Kuklinski family, 289–290
Brezhnev, Leonid (Soviet Leader)
    appointment as Warsaw Pact Supreme
        Commander, 194
    martial law plans, 250, 262
Brown, Harold (Defense Secretary), 210,
    217, 224
brush-pass technique and development of,
    74–78, 81
Brzezinski, Zbigniew (National Security
    Adviser)
    honors Kuklinski, 290
    Kuklinski case negotiations, 306,
        307–308, 319
    Soviet intervention in Poland, 201, 205,
        207, 210, 217, 224, 225
Burggraf, Sue (CIA operations officer)
    Kuklinski family exfiltration, 269–272,
        274–275, 277, 279–283
    meeting with RK, 274–275
    Warsaw Station assignment, 167–168,
        190–194, 245–247, 258
Bush, George (CIA Director), 135
Buzek, Jerzy (Polish Prime Minister), Kuk-
    linski visit, 332

cameras for filming secret documents
  CIA supplies for RK, 63
  darkroom of RK, 59–60, 92
  Tubka (CIA miniaturized camera), 63,
    106, 110
  Zorka (Soviet camera), 59
car pass/moving car delivery (MVD) technique and development of, 81, 82,
  229
cars and exchanges
  black Volga as official car for RK, 188
  car parts for RK as cover for meetings,
    88, 89, 92
  RK's in repair shop, 199
  vehicles driven by CIA officers in War-
    saw, 188
Carson, Sally. See Forden, Sally (Carson)
Carter, Jimmy (U.S. president)
  CIA Director appointment, 137
  foreign military intervention in Poland,
    message to Moscow, 217–218
  foreign military intervention in Poland,
    public statement opposing, 224–225
  inaugural address, 138–139, 144
  martial law in Poland, CIA "Alert," 215,
    217
  trip to Warsaw, 145–146, 148
Casey, William (CIA Director)
  Distinguished Intelligence Medal
    awarded to RK, 294
  Kuklinski family exfiltration approved
    by, 270
  leak to Vatican, 329
  Newsweek article on Kuklinski, 296
Chocha, Boleslaw, Gen.
  chief of the General Staff appointment,
    47
  Kuklinski introduced at General Staff
    Academy, 44
  Kuklinski as staff officer under, 45–47,
    50–53
  profile of, 45–46
  surveillance missions of the Legia,
    approval for, 54
Church, Frank (Senator), CIA investigative
  hearings, 131–132

CIA (Central Intelligence Agency)
  Congressional investigative hearings,
    131–133
  Deputy Director of Operations (DDO),
    132
  founding of, 8
  safe houses, 87–88
  secret document priorities, 57, 90,
    109–110, 111–112
  secret writing or scorch technique, 23
  source identity, masking of, 64–65
  SOVA (Office of Soviet Analysis), 242
  Soviet agent betrayal, 8
  Soviet agent recruitment, 9
  training of spouses in denied areas, 61
  translators (Russian and Polish) for Gull
    operation, 186–187
  See also Bonn Station; Soviet Division;
    Vienna Station; Warsaw Station
Cieplowski, Jaroslaw, Maj. (military prosecutor), Kuklinski case, 316–317
clandestine communications
  brush-pass technique and development
    of, 74–78, 81
  car pass/moving car delivery (MVD)
    technique and development of, 81,
    82, 229
  "dead drop," 73, 81, 229
  Discus/Iskra (electronic transmitting
    device), 181, 215, 229–230, 232, 235,
    236, 238, 253, 276
  list of options for communicating with
    RK, 117–118
  mailings, 73–74, 78
  signaling/chalk marks for messaging,
    121, 123, 124, 229
  tradecraft of CIA, 88
classified documents. See secret documents; security issues
Clinton, Bill (U.S. president), Kuklinski
  case, 312, 320, 327
Colby, William (CIA Director), 132
Colonel Henry
  health of, 148
  meetings in Copenhagen (1974), 108–109
  meetings in Copenhagen (1976), 133–134

meetings in Europe (1973), 82–86, 87–89, 92, 94, 97
meetings in Kiel (1975), 124–126
mistaken identity of "twin" by RK, 104
profile of "Wally," 10–11
P.V. operation (1972), 11–18, 64
retirement, 148, 150
shopping for Kuklinski (1973), 87–89, 92, 94
communications in denied areas, 73–78
concentration camps, 36–37
Conrad, Joseph, 41, 43–44
Czechoslovakia, Prague Spring/Operation Danube invasion of, 47–49, 57, 119, 198, 210, 334

Daniel (code name for David Forden)
description of RK, 96–97
exfiltration of Kuklinski family, 270, 277–278, 289
first meeting with RK in Hamburg (1973), 87–89
gift of pen to RK, 95–96
Gull case operation, 82, 103–104, 252
letters from P.V., 102–103, 118–119, 130, 138–139, 150–151, 155–156, 171–172, 176–177, 205–207
letters to P.V., 97–99, 110–112, 120, 127–128, 131, 138, 147–148, 152, 164–165, 261–262
meeting at Andrews Air Force Base, 289
meetings in Copenhagen (1974), 108–109
meetings in Copenhagen (1976), 133–135
meetings in Europe (1977), 140
meetings in Hamburg (1973), 87–99
meetings in Kiel (1975), 125–126
RK's American citizenship celebration, 293
Soviet Division Chief appointment, 252
Soviet Division chief of operations appointment, 137
Vienna Station appointment, 151–152, 161
See also Forden, David W. (CIA officer)
Daniluk, Piotr (Polish military prosecutor), 328

Davies, Richard (U.S. Ambassador to Poland), Kuklinski case, 311–312, 320
Davis, Evan (pseudonym), at Warsaw Station, 246, 270, 271
debriefings of Kuklinski in U.S., 290, 295, 301
Defense Ministers Committee Meetings, 142, 146, 177
Bucharest (1980), martial law in Poland, 215–217
Budapest (1977), Warsaw Pact forces, 144–145
meeting in Poland (1979), 183
depression. See psychological toll of double life
Dewinski, Piotr (Polish lawyer), 316
Dimmer, John P., Jr.
profile of, 6
P.V. operation (1972), 6–8, 10
Discus/Iskra (electronic transmitting device), 181, 215, 229–230, 232, 235, 236, 238, 253, 268, 276
Distinguished Intelligence Medal, 140–141, 196, 199, 203–204, 205, 294
Dobbs, Michael (reporter), 302
dogs
as cover in "denied areas," 58
RK's family pet Zula, 60–61, 169, 278, 289, 299
Donnelly, Bill (Warsaw Station Chief), 68, 72, 78–80
Dulles, Allen (CIA Director), and CIA operations, 10
Dwyer, Michael (pseudonym)
arrested during exchange, 181–183
Warsaw Station assignment, 174–175

Eagle (CIA officer)
identified as Richard Helms, 111
letter of welcome for Kuklinski, 62–63, 67
Earnest, Peter (CIA case officer), 168
economy in Poland
crisis situation, 150
food price increases, 136
Soviet war plans and, 90

Eighteenth Anti-Landing Battalion in
Kolobrzeg, 41
Eleventh Mechanized Regiment in
Biedrusko, 39
Estes, Ron (CIA officer), training for
denied areas, 72, 75, 77–78
exfiltration of Kuklinski
CIA evaluation, 154, 161
contingency plans for, 57, 92–93, 104, 111,
120, 125–126, 151, 252
emergency escape plans, 66, 155, 180–181
failed pickup attempts, 278–283
family response to exfiltration, 250,
267–269, 290
for Kuklinski family, 273–274, 277,
286–289
travel documents for RK's family, 99,
108, 111, 112, 115–116, 124
use of sidearm during escape, 112–113,
116
Warsaw Station procedures, 271–272
See also suicide pill

Falk, Peter (TV detective Columbo), 70–71
Fifteenth Anti-Landing Battalion in Kolo-
brzeg, 40
Fifth Mechanized Regiment in Szczecin, 42
First Mechanized Division, 46
Forden, Aurelia (wife of David Forden),
301, 321–322
Forden, David W. (CIA officer, code name
Daniel)
Athens Station Chief appointment, 301
case officer for Kuklinski, 68
CIA assignments, 72, 82
CIA interview and junior officer training
(JOTS), 70–71, 75
courtship and marriage to Sally Carson,
69–70, 72
divorce from Sally Carson, 251
friendship with Kuklinski in U.S.,
296–297, 300–301
friendship with Peter Falk, 70
Kuklinski case, 321, 321–322
leak to "Rome sources" investigation,
329–331

marriage to Aurelia, 301
profile of, 69–70
Soviet Division Chief appointment, 252
tutoring in Polish, 68–69, 72
Vienna Station Chief assignment,
151–152, 161, 251–252
Warsaw Station Chief assignment, 78,
80–82
See also Daniel (code name for David
Forden)
Forden, Sally (Carson), wife of David For-
den, 69–70, 72, 80, 81, 161, 251
Franke, Egon (Olympic fencing star), 21
Fried, Daniel (White House aide), Kuklin-
ski case, 320, 327

Gates, Robert M.
as CIA Director, on Angleton and counterintelligence, 8
as national intelligence officer, on mar-
tial law in Poland, 215
Gazeta Wyborcza, 328, 337
Gebhardt, Carl E. (Warsaw Station Chief)
first contact with RK (1972), 61–63
safe-house meeting in Hamburg (1973),
95
Warsaw Station operations, 57–58
George, Clair, 9, 270
Gierek, Edward (party chief)
Brezhnev resolution, 194
Carter state visit, 145
dismissal from office, 201, 202
legalized the union, 202
Moscow trip approval, 196
RK introduction, 108
wartime statute, 175–176
Gilbertson, Ted (pseudonym)
Gull operation exchange, 221–223
Warsaw Station assignment, 173
Warsaw Station operations, 190–194, 246
Goldfarb, Alan, friendship with David For-
den, 71
Gomulka, Wladyslaw (party secretary), 41,
42, 48
Gornicki, Wieslaw, Col., views Kuklinski
as traitor, 307

Gray, Al, Gen., meeting with Kuklinski, 302
Great Synagogue, Warsaw, 30, 32, 33
Gribkov, Anatoly, Gen., 147, 178, 187, 237
Griggs, Les, Col., debriefings with RK, 295
Gull operation
Blee assigns code name Gull for RK, 56
counterintelligence review, 158–161
RK's personal security, 190
security issues, 189
translation of materials, 186–187
See also Daniel (code name for David Forden)

Haig, Alexander M., Jr. (Secretary of State), 256, 270
Hart, Katharine Colvin (chief of Reports and Requirements Staff, Soviet Division), 9, 64, 186
Helms, Richard (CIA Director)
appointment of Blee to Soviet Division, 7, 8
identified as Eagle, 111
Penkovsky case influence on, 77
Herbert, Zbigniew (poet), Kuklinski case, 314, 333, 336, 338
Hermaszewski, Wladyslaw, Gen.
friendship with Kuklinski family, 101, 131, 143, 230, 263, 276–277
Kuklinski case interview, 310
last farewell, 284–285
Home Army. *See* Polish Home Army
Honecker, Erich (East German leader), 194
Horton, John
Mexico City Chief, 82
Soviet Division Chief, appointment, 103
human and emotional interchanges, importance of, 88–89, 98
Hupalowski, Tadeusz, Gen., martial law in Poland, 216, 219, 240

identity of sources
CIA protecting RK's identity, 64–65
Washington Post article revealing Kuklinski identity, 302–303

Inman, Bobby Ray (National Security Agency Director), 172, 270
International Control Commission (ICC, Vietnam), 17, 20, 46
Iran, American hostages, 183–184, 189, 268
Iskra. *See* Discus/Iskra (electronic transmitting device)

Jakubowska, Barbara (friend of RK), death of, 169, 171, 176–177, 189
Jakubowski, Czeslaw (friend of RK), 169, 278, 299
Jaroszewicz, Piotr (Prime Minister), 170, 175
Jaruzelski, Wojciech, Gen.
anti-Soviet actions in Poland, 259
defense minister appointment, 47
at defense ministers committee meeting, 183
Defense Ministry five year plan, 279, 281
Fifth Mechanized Regiment in Szczecin division, 42
Gierek's dismissal, 202
Kuklinski as staff officer under, 2, 22, 45, 47, 124, 134–135, 145, 153
Kuklinski trial, 302–303
Kuklinski viewed as traitor, 309–310, 328, 337
martial law in Poland, 208, 216, 218–220, 224, 225, 237–238, 241, 247–250, 255, 262–263
NATO nuclear attack response, 122
party ambitions, 202
party chief election, 265
party congress elections, 248
Prague Spring "exercise," 48–49
Prime Minister inaugural speech, 233
secret war game (martial law implementation), 233–234
Siberian labor camp experiences, 42
Soviet plot to remove, 230
talks with Ustinov in U.S.S.R., 199
Warsaw Pact training exercises, 22, 45, 48–49
wartime statute (Soviet control in wartime), 172, 175–176, 178–180

Jasinski, Antoni, Gen., 240
Jewish ghetto in Warsaw, 31–34
John Paul II (Pope)
    Soviet intervention in Poland briefing,
        225
    support for Solidarity, 329
    visit to Warsaw, 174
Joseph Conrad Yacht Club, 41, 43

Kalaris, George (Soviet Division Chief),
    157–158, 161, 173, 196
Kania, Stanislaw (party chief)
    anti-Soviet actions in Poland, 259
    appointment, 201
    Gierek's dismissal, 202
    martial law in Poland, opposition to,
        224, 225, 237, 250, 254, 255, 262
    ousted from party, 265
    party congress election, 248, 249
    Soviet plot to remove, 230
Karamessines, Thomas H., 77–78
Kiszczak, Czeslaw, Gen., Solidarity and,
    121–122, 255, 257, 305, 309
Kliss, Victor (CIA translator)
    debriefing with RK, 290
    Distinguished Intelligence Medal award
        ceremony, 294
    interpreter for RK, 294, 295
KOK (National Defense Committee of
    Poland)
    martial law in Poland briefings, 214,
        240–241, 248, 253–254, 256
    Poland's national preparedness, 253
KOR (dissident organization), 200
Kosciuszko, Tadeusz (Polish hero in Revo-
    lutionary War), 259, 331, 335–336
Kozminski, Jerzy (Polish ambassador to
    U.S.), 313, 318–328, 331
Krakow (Poland), Hanka and RK's visit to,
    259
Kufel, Teodor (chief of military counterin-
    telligence), 148, 153
Kuklinski, Anna (mother of RK), 30–31, 34,
    36
Kuklinski, Boguslaw "Bogdan" (son of RK)
    assisting RK with exchanges, 264, 276

car accident with pedestrian, 146, 170
courtship with Grazyna, 101, 102, 129
cruise to Europe on Legia (1972), 13,
    20–21, 54–55, 101
dead drop assistance to retrieve glove,
    264
depression in U.S., 297
exfiltration with family, 269, 286–289
farm in the country, 231–232, 258
marriage to Iza, 298
medical studies, 129, 130
relationship with Iza, 231–232, 258, 277,
    293–294, 297–298
Kuklinski, Hanka (wife of RK)
    exfiltration to U.S., 286–289
    health of, 131, 148–149, 169–170, 281
    marriage to RK, 40, 59
    mother of, 285
    relationship with RK, 21, 129–130, 131,
        188
    vacations with RK, 195, 259
    yacht trip to Europe (1974), 102, 108–109
Kuklinski, Ryszard J., Col. (Polish General
    Staff officer)
    American citizenship celebration,
        292–293
    on birthday wishes, 88–89
    birth of, 13
    childhood years, 30–34
    commendations from General Staff, 135
    consultant to U.S. government, 294–295
    daily life in Warsaw, 21–22, 23
    on death and dying, 176
    disappearance from Poland, 289, 299
    Distinguished Intelligence Medal,
        140–141, 196, 199, 203–204, 205, 294
    family life, 129–131
    forced laborer in German Silesia, 35
    health of, 139, 148, 204, 207
    housing cooperative on Rajcow Street,
        100–101, 131, 143–144, 150
    identity of protected, 64–65
    interview with Kultura, 304
    land for summer homes, 230–231
    letter drops from Warsaw Station, 58, 61
    letters from the Americans (CIA), 127,
        147, 163–164, 228

letters from Daniel, 97–99, 110–112, 120, 127–128, 131, 138, 147–148, 152, 164–165
letters to the Americans (CIA), 23, 62, 102, 123–124, 132–133, 152–154, 162–163, 183–185, 197–199, 219–221, 240–242
letters to Daniel (P.V.), 102–103, 118–119, 130, 138–139, 150–151, 155–156, 171–172, 176–177, 205–207, 239
letters under Daniel's name, 165, 189, 195–196, 199, 203–205
life in U.S., 293–297, 338–339
marriage to Hanka, 40, 59
military service: Eighteenth Anti-Landing Battalion in Kolobrzeg, 41; Eleventh Mechanized Regiment in Biedrusko, 39; Fifteenth Anti-Landing Battalion in Kolobrzeg, 40; Fifth Mechanized Regiment in Szczecin, 42; First Dept. for Strategic Defense Planning, 141; General Staff Academy in Warsaw, 44; General Staff appointment, 44; International Control Commission in Vietnam, 22; Ninth Mechanized Regiment in Pila, 40
military trial, 299–300, 303, 306
motivations for collaboration, 57, 95, 96, 118–119, 126, 197–198, 209
officers training school experiences, 37–39
psychological toll of double life, 125, 126, 127, 130, 143
relationship with wife Hanka, 21, 58–59, 92, 129–130, 131, 188, 264
sailing on Chesapeake Bay, 303–304, 308
sailing and Joseph Conrad Yacht Club, 41, 43, 195
vacations and yacht trips with Hanka, 102, 108–109, 195, 259
visit to Poland after exoneration (1998), 331–338
and Voroshilov Academy (Moscow), 100–105, 121–122, 123
voting rights in Poland suspended, 305–306
See also Kuklinski case; P.V. operation; Warsaw Pact training exercises

Kuklinski, Stanislaw (father of RK), 30–32, 34, 36–37
Kuklinski, Waldemar "Waldek" (son of RK)
birth of, 40
book collector and writer, 129, 130, 298–299, 338
defense of his father, 307
exfiltration to U.S., 286–289
moral character of, 129, 130
response to exfiltration to U.S., 268
Kuklinski case
Brzezinski negotiations, 306, 307–308, 313, 319–328
conviction controversy, 306–314
conviction and sentence lifted, 318
Davies support for RK, 311–312, 320
death sentence, 303, 306
exoneration of RK, 328
Forden's efforts, 321–322
Gornicki views RK as traitor, 307
Herbert support for RK, 314, 333, 338
Jaruzelski interview, 309–310
Kiszczak interview, 309
Kozminski's negotiations, 313–314, 318–328
Kuklinski testimony before Polish prosecutors, 324–326
military court review, 315–318
military trial for desertion and treason, 299–300
Miller negotiations, 318–320, 321, 327
Newsweek article, 295–296
Oklesinski interview, 310
Polish television documentary, 306
Poltorak interview, 310–311
public opinion in Poland, 308, 311
Siwicki interview, 309
supporters in Poland, 308
Szymanderski defense of RK, 306–307
Tygodnik Solidarnosc interview with RK, 314
Waldek's defense of his father, 307
Washington Post article, 302–303
Washington Post interview with RK, 308, 311

Kulikov, Viktor, Soviet Marshal
    Brezhnev appointment as supreme com-
        mander of Warsaw Pact, 194
    Kuklinski case, 328
    martial law implementation, 237, 241,
        247, 249
    "Project Albatross" inspection, 106
    "Soyuz 81" (Soviet intervention in
        Poland), 235
    Warsaw Pact commander appointment,
        141
    wartime statute (Soviet control in
        wartime), 146–147, 151, 153, 170–171,
        172, 176, 178–180, 183, 187
Kwasniewski, Aleksander
    Kuklinski case, 319, 327
    Polish presidential election, 318
Kwiecinski, Jerzy, Capt. (Polish prosecu-
    tor), 322

Lang, Walter (U.S. Army officer)
    profile of, 10
    P.V. operation, 10–18, 56, 64
Larsen, Hal, (CIA Reports and Require-
    ments Staff), 186–187
letters from "Daniel". See under Daniel
    (code name for David Forden)
Lubbehusen, Robert (CIA Reports and
    Requirements Staff), 186

McMahon, John N. (DDO), Distinguished
    Intelligence Medal for RK, 196
martial law in Poland
    Carter's message to Moscow, 217–218
    Carter's public statement, 224–225
    CIA analysis, 242–245
    command-and-control group led by
        Puchala, 254
    Defense Ministers Committee Meeting,
        215–217
    Gull's description of invasion plans,
        223–228
    implementation of, 290–291
    planning group led by Kuklinski, 254
    plans for, 208, 211–215, 218–228

    secret documents pertaining to, 213, 253
    "Soyuz 81" exercise and, 236–237
Mazowiecki, Tadeusz (Solidarity activist),
    305
Meehan, Francis (Ambassador in Warsaw),
    223, 269, 270
Michnik, Adam, 337
Mickiewicz, Adam, 259
Milewski, Miroslaw (Interior Minister),
    martial law and crushing of activists,
        214
Military Council of the Warsaw Pact, 142,
    146
Miller, Leszek (Polish Interior Minister),
    Kuklinski case, 318–320, 321, 327
Molczyk, Eugeniusz, Gen.
    martial law in Poland, 216, 220, 238
    "Soyuz 81" exercise, 235
Morton, Henry P., Lt. Col. (cover name for
    "Wally"). See Colonel Henry
    motivations for RK's collaboration, 57, 95,
        96, 118–119, 126, 197–198, 209
Muskie, Edmund S. (secretary of state),
    210, 217, 224
MV (Czech secret police), 74

Nagorski, Andrew, Newsweek interview
    with RK, 329
NATO membership for Poland, 311–313,
    318–321, 327, 331, 336
NATO nuclear attack, Warsaw Pact
    response, 44–45, 51–53, 121–122
Nazi brutality, 31–34
Ninth Mechanized Regiment in Pila,
    40
nuclear weapons, 44–45, 51–53, 90, 122

Office of Strategic Services (OSS), 8, 10
Ogarkov, Nikolai (chief of the Soviet Gen-
    eral Staff), 219
Oklesinski, Kazimierz, Col., 310
Operation Danube, 47–49
    symposium on Poland's role, 48–49
"Operation Spring" (martial-law plan), 237,
    256

Ostaszewicz, Wlodzimierz, Col., defection of, 259–261, 263, 271, 277

Pacepa, Ion, Lt. Gen., 164
Pappas, Aris (CIA analyst)
  debriefings with RK, 290, 295, 301
  martial law in Poland, 242–245, 290–291
Patkowski, Stanislaw Longin (Soviet Division translator), 65
  gift of pen from RK, 177–178, 185
  gift of Polish flask to RK, 188
  letters from "Daniel" written by, 165, 166, 173
  retirement, 173, 177
Pawlowski, Jerzy, Lt. Col.
  conviction and sentencing of, 134
  espionage case, 123, 125, 127, 131, 133
Penkovsky, Oleg (Soviet GRU colonel)
  arrest and execution of, 7, 77, 125
  secret files of, 243
Piesiewicz, Krzysztof (Polish lawyer), 316–318
Pilsudski, Jozef, 259
Pinkowski, Jozef (Prime Minister), martial law in Poland, 214
Platt, Jack
  interview with Solomatin, 330–331
  security in U.S. for RK, 321
Polish American Congress, 307, 331
Polish Home Army, 34, 37, 174
Polish resistance, 33–35
Polish Viking (P.V. code name for RK). See P.V. operation
Political Consultative Committee (PCC), 142
Politi, Marco, 329
Poltorak, Czeslaw, Col, Kuklinski case interview, 310–311
Popieluszko, Jerzy, Fr., murder of, 316
Po Prostu (reformist newspaper), 41, 42
Powstancow Warszawskich cemetery, 26, 147
Prague Spring "exercise," 47–49, 119
  symposium on Poland's role (Warsaw), 48–49
prisoners of war (POWs), 35

"Project Albatross" installations, 105–108, 242
psychological toll of double life, 125–127, 130, 143, 198–199, 250–251
  CIA evaluation of RK, 199
  morale boosting, 197, 199
  stress and pressure and, 189, 196
  See also suicide pill
Puchala, Franciszek, Col.
  martial law plan leak, 265, 266
  martial law in Poland, 216–219, 254
Putek, Jozef, Lt. Col. (counterintelligence officer)
  transfer to Egypt, 172
  visits to RK, 143, 151, 153
P.V. operation
  first contact from P.V., 6–7
  first meeting in The Hague, with Lang and Henry, 9–18
  first meeting in The Hague, team observations on, 18–20
  second meeting in Rotterdam, 20–24
  surveillance detection run in Warsaw, 24–26
  third and fourth meetings in Ostend, 22, 24, 26
  final meeting in Kiel, Germany, 27
  shredding of Lang files, 56

Radaj, Stanislaw, RK's classmate from military school, 38, 83, 281
Radio Free Europe, RK's attempt to contact, 47
Reagan, Ronald (U.S. president), 251, 252, 302, 303
recruitment operations
  CIA junior officer training in, 71
  of Soviet agents, 9
Rogers, Bernard W., Gen. (Supreme Allied Commander, Europe), 256
Rokossowski, Konstanty (Polish defense minister), 37, 41
Romania, wartime statute opposed by, 178, 183, 184, 187
Rural Solidarity, police brutality and, 235
Rutherford, Ben (Theater Forces Division Chief), 242, 291

Ryan, Lucille (wife of Tom Ryan), 201, 269, 281

Ryan, Tom (Warsaw Station Chief)
appointment, 201
exfiltration pickup of Kuklinski family, 284, 287
Gull operation security concerns, 239–240
surveillance detection runs, 283–284
vacation in Berlin with wife and daughter, 269, 270, 280–281

safe houses
description of, 87–88
for Kuklinski family, 289–290
SB. *See* Sluzba Bezpieczenstwa (SB; Polish secret police)
Schooley, Ed (pseudonym for CIA officer), surveillance detection run, 24–26
Second Strategic Echelon, 15, 16, 45, 52, 54
secret documents
"blue border" series for CIA reports, 65
CIA priority "wish lists," 57, 90, 109–110, 111–112
classified note-taking by RK, 122
photographing of, 58–60, 92
"Series K" documents, 60, 109
Soviet journals on military exercises, 112
Voyennaya Mysl (Military Thought), 66
See also cameras for filming secret documents
secret writing ("SW"), 23, 61
secure communications. *See* clandestine communications
security issues
accident while carrying briefcase with classified documents, 136–137
CIA evaluation of RK's risk, 157–161, 253
dead drop of glove location error, 258–264
French diplomat's arrest, 99–100, 101
handling of intelligence reports, 189–190
for Kuklinski in U.S., 321–322
leaks of martial-law plans, 256, 257, 265, 266, 270, 271, 274

leak to "Rome sources," 329–331
lost rolls of film, 151, 154, 162, 188, 195
missing secret document, 99–100, 101, 105
risks of filming in office, 106, 108
RK's personal safety, 96, 190, 239–240
SB surveillance of RK incident, 113–120
suspension of activity, 125, 154–157
See also exfiltration of Kuklinski
The Shadow Line (Conrad), 43–44
Shtemenko, S. M., Gen., 50
Sikorski, Wladyslaw, Gen., 259
Simon, James M., Jr., 301
Siwicki, Florian, Gen. (chief of General Staff)
counterintelligence investigations, 162
Kuklinski case interview, 309
martial law in Poland, 218, 220, 225, 233, 237–238, 247, 255, 262–263, 285
martial law in Poland briefings for KOK, 240–241, 253–254
Operation Danube/Prague Spring, 48
Polish troop strength and Vienna arms talks, 196–197
"Project Albatross," 105–108
relationship with RK, 117, 134–135, 141, 230
wartime statute, 175–176, 179–180
weapons development speech, 151
Skalski, Jerzy, Gen. (deputy chief of General Staff)
Defense Ministry's five-year plan, 279–280
General Staff promotions for RK, 99, 100
martial-law plan leak, 265–267, 329
martial law in Poland, 208, 214, 225, 238, 240, 254–255
monitoring strikes, 200
profile of, 208–209
relationship with RK, 105, 108, 139, 141, 153, 248
Sliwinski, Gen., 51
Sluzba Bezpieczenstwa (SB; Polish secret police), 2, 113–115, 230
Smith, Haviland (Prague Station Chief),

"brush contact" method innovator,
74–78
Solidarity (Polish trade union)
creation of, 1, 2
detention operations, 257, 291
first national convention (Gdansk), 249
internment of activists, 214, 238
marital law proposal and, 209, 214
national strikes, 200, 207
Newsweek magazine article, 295–296
plans to crush, 225–226, 229–265
police brutality and, 235, 237–238
Polish Army resistance to crushing, 227
as a resistance movement, 308
Russian officers opposition to, 212, 233
SB infiltration of, 255, 295–296
"Soyuz 81" training exercise and, 231–235
talks with government, 305
Washington Post article, 302–303, 304
See also marital law in Poland
Solidarity Weekly, Kuklinski case, 314, 316
Solomatin, Boris (KGB *Rezident* in Rome),
329–331
source identity, masking of, 64–65
Soviet Division (CIA)
Discus/Iskra development, 229–230
Forden appointment as Chief, 252
Horton appointment as Chief, 103
operations, 7–9, 63–64
See also Blee, David; Kalaris, George
Soviet troops
Afghanistan invasion, 188
brutality in Germany, 36
communications sites in Poland, 239
martial law in Poland plans, 208, 211–215
Soviet intervention in Poland assessment, 201–202, 205, 210–211, 217–221
wartime statute, 146–147, 151, 153, 156,
170–172, 176–184, 187–188, 195
Soviet weapons
chemical warfare training, 170
comprehensive weapons development
(1981–1985), 154
Russian document detailing tactical and
technical specifications of Soviet
weaponry to be introduced into

Warsaw Pact (through 1985), 163, 351
Strela (surface-to-air missile), 110
T–72 battle tank, 149, 172, 184, 188, 245
weapons systems, 172
See also nuclear weapons
Stalin, Svetlana, political asylum for, 8
Staniszewski, Konstanty, classmate and
friend of RK, 38, 40
Stein, John (DDO), 270, 297
Stolz, Richard (DDO), 305
Strong, Jack (pseudonym for Kuklinski)
Burggraf meeting with, 274–275
emergency escape plans, 180–181
letters to the Americans, 23, 62, 102,
132–133
Suchocka, Hanna (Prime Minister), 313
suicide pill, 67–68, 85–86, 92, 102, 104, 267,
282
surveillance detection run (SDR), 24–25
officers using routine patterns, 74–75
attempts to contact RK, 61
break-off and recovery points, 193
in CIA junior officer training, 71
patterns by the SB, 95
Ryan (Tom and Lucille) training runs,
283–284
Warsaw Station operations, 173, 192–193
water bottle for destroying incriminating material, 192
surveillance missions on the *Legia*
(1972), 13–14, 54–55
(1973), 67, 82–86
(1974), 102, 108
(1975), 124
(1976), 131, 133
(1977) cancelled, 140, 142
See also P.V. operation
surveillance traps in Warsaw, strategic war
games, 148, 153
Svoboda, Ludvik (Czech president), 48
Sword and Plow, 34
Szklarski, Waclaw, Gen.
martial-law plan leak, 266
Soviet invasion of Poland, 218, 225, 240
Szymanderski, Jacek (Polish parliament
member), Kuklinski case, 306–307

Taylor, Jacek (Polish lawyer), 316
Tenet, George (CIA Director), memorial
  for fallen agency officers, 338–339
termination measures. *See* suicide pill
Thompson, Edmund R., Maj. Gen., 172
Tighe, Eugene F., Jr., Lt. Gen. (Defense
  Intelligence Agency Chief), 172
travel documents, for Kuklinski family, 99,
  108, 111, 112, 115–116, 124
Turner, Stansfield J. (CIA Director), 137,
  148, 161, 196
  martial law "Alert" memos, 215, 217
  Soviet intervention in Poland, 201, 205,
    210, 215, 224
  Soviet troop movements briefing, 207
Tweedy, Bronson (East Europe Division
  Chief), 77, 78
Tygodnik Solidarnosc (Solidarity Weekly),
  interview with RK, 314

Urban, Jerzy, 302, 303
Urbanowicz, Jozef, Gen. (deputy defense
  minister), 84–85
Ustinov, Dmitri F. (Soviet Defense Minis-
  ter)
  at Warsaw Pact defense ministers com-
    mittee meeting, 183
  Jaruzelski's talks with, 199
  Soviet intervention in Poland, 263
  Soviet vs. U.S. armaments, 255
  "West 77" exercise, 142

Vienna arms talks, 112, 162, 163, 196–197,
  259
Vienna Station
  Forden appointment, 161
  Forden assignment, 151–152, 161, 251–252
Voroshilov Academy (Moscow), RK's
  nomination and attendance, 100–105,
  121–122, 123
Voyennaya Mysl (Military Thought), 66

Walesa, Lech (Solidarity activist)
  gift of flask from Kuklinski, 305

Kozminski appointment, 313
Kuklinski case, 306
presidential elections, 305–306, 318
Solidarity movement, 1, 2, 200–201, 209,
  249, 291, 305
"Wally" (CIA operative from Estonia), profile of, 10–11
Warsaw Pact committees, 142. *See also*
  Defense Ministers Committee Meetings
Warsaw Pact forces, 14–16
  comprehensive weapons development
    plans (1981–1985), 154
  conventional force strength, 122
  defensive vs. offensive war plan in
    Poland, 91
  detailed report 1981–1985, 194
  early-warning capability, 56
  "Project Albatross" installations,
    105–108, 242
  Soviet troops in Poland, 150
  wartime statute, 146–147, 151, 153, 156,
    170–172, 176–184
  wartime statute ratification, 183, 184,
    187–188, 195
Warsaw Pact Supreme Command
  (Moscow), 2, 121
Warsaw Pact training exercises
  NATO nuclear attack response, 44–45,
    51–53
  Operation Danube/Prague Spring,
    47–49, 119
  role as chief author of exercises ("Sum-
    mer 70", "Summer 71", "Spring 69"),
    22
  Second Strategic Echelon, 15, 16, 45, 52, 54
  "Spring 69" (Western Theater of Mili-
    tary Operations), 49–53
  "Spring 80," 199
  "Summer 74" (wartime field communi-
    cations testing), 100, 101
  wartime command-and-control proce-
    dures, 149
  "West 77" (Moscow centralized com-
    mand), 142, 143
Warsaw Station
  communication plans, 56

contact attempts to Kuklinski, 57–58, 61
Donnelly as Warsaw Station Chief, 78–80
Forden appointment as Station Chief, 78
Gull operation, 167–185
SB monitoring of compound, 230
staffing, 57, 173–174, 246
wartime statute. *See under* Soviet troops; Warsaw Pact forces
weapons
  Marisat (U.S. communications satellite system), 170
  See also nuclear weapons; Soviet weapons
Webster, William (CIA Director), 305
Welch, Richard (Athens Station Chief), assassination of, 251–252
Wilcox, Jason (pseudonym), at Warsaw Station, 246, 270, 271
Wilhelmshaven, history of, 54–55
Witt, Czeslaw
  martial-law plan leak, 265, 266–267, 274
  martial-plan preparations, 273

Wlodarczyk, Bogdan, Maj. (Polish prosecutor), 322–324
Wojskowe Sluzby Wewnetrzne (WSW), military counterintelligence, 143, 162
Woodward, Bob (reporter), 302
workers movement
  creation of Solidarity, 1–2
  factory workers strikes, 1, 200–201
  food price protests, 136, 200
  national strike for Solidarity, 207
  reform agreements, 201
  shipyard workers demonstrations (1970), 53, 200, 209
  See also Solidarity
Wyszynski, Stefan (Cardinal), 136, 175

Yakubovsky, Ivan (Warsaw Pact forces commander), 47, 50

Zarek, Jan, Col., 123, 139, 141
Zula (dog, RK's family pet), 60–61, 169, 278, 279, 299

PublicAffairs is a publishing house founded in 1997. It is a tribute to the standards, values, and flair of three persons who have served as mentors to countless reporters, writers, editors, and book people of all kinds, including me.

I.F. STONE, proprietor of *I. F. Stone's Weekly*, combined a commitment to the First Amendment with entrepreneurial zeal and reporting skill and became one of the great independent journalists in American history. At the age of eighty, Izzy published *The Trial of Socrates*, which was a national bestseller. He wrote the book after he taught himself ancient Greek.

BENJAMIN C. BRADLEE was for nearly thirty years the charismatic editorial leader of *The Washington Post*. It was Ben who gave the *Post* the range and courage to pursue such historic issues as Watergate. He supported his reporters with a tenacity that made them fearless and it is no accident that so many became authors of influential, best-selling books.

ROBERT L. BERNSTEIN, the chief executive of Random House for more than a quarter century, guided one of the nation's premier publishing houses. Bob was personally responsible for many books of political dissent and argument that challenged tyranny around the globe. He is also the founder and longtime chair of Human Rights Watch, one of the most respected human rights organizations in the world.

For fifty years, the banner of Public Affairs Press was carried by its owner Morris B. Schnapper, who published Gandhi, Nasser, Toynbee, Truman, and about 1,500 other authors. In 1983, Schnapper was described by *The Washington Post* as "a redoubtable gadfly." His legacy will endure in the books to come.

Peter Osnos, *Publisher*